Object Data Management

Revised Edition

Object-Oriented and Extended Relational Database Systems

R.G.G. Cattell

Sun Microsystems, Inc.

Addison-Wesley Publishing Company

Reading, Massachusetts • Menlo Park, California • New York • Don Mills, Ontario
Wokingham, England • Amsterdam • Bonn • Sydney • Singapore
Tokyo • Madrid • San Juan • Milan • Paris

The programs and applications presented in this book have been included for their instructional value. They are not guaranteed for any particular purpose. The publisher does not offer any warranties or representations nor does it accept any liabilities with respect to the programs or applications.

Many of the designations used by manufacturers and sellers to distinguish their products are claimed as trademarks. Where those designations appear in this book, and Addison-Wesley was aware of a trademark claim, the designations have been printed in caps or initial caps.

Library of Congress Cataloging-in-Publication Data

Cattell, R. G. G. (Roderic Geoffrey Galton)
    Object data management : object-oriented and extended relational
database systems / R. G. G. Cattell.
        Rev. ed.
        p.   cm.
    Includes bibliographical references and index.
    ISBN 0-201-54748-1
    1. Data base management. 2. Object-oriented data bases.
3. Relational data bases.   I. Title.
QA76.9.D3C3834   1994
005.75--dc20   93-39690
                                                                    CIP

Reprinted with corrections August, 1994

2 3 4 5 6 7 8 9 10-MA-969594

PREFACE

This is a book about database management systems (DBMSs) that manipulate *objects*. These systems have been developed to support new kinds of applications—applications whose needs are quite different from those of traditional business database applications. These applications include computer-aided design (CAD), computer-aided software engineering (CASE), computer-aided manufacturing (CAM), office automation, scientific applications, telecommunications, expert systems, and other applications with complex and interrelated objects and procedural data. The new database systems also open new possibilities for traditional business applications.

In this book, we study a wide variety of DBMSs advanced since the development of relational systems in the early 1980s. We examine new applications and the characteristics of their data, in order to understand the shortcomings of current DBMSs and the need for object data management systems (ODMSs) for these more sophisticated uses. The ODMSs we study include object-oriented DBMSs, extended relational DBMSs, functional-semantic DBMSs, DBMS generators, and simple object managers. We examine specific commercial products and research prototypes for object data management, and compare the merits of different approaches.

Some readers might call this a book about object-oriented database systems, inasmuch as "object-oriented" has been used by one author or another to characterize nearly all the approaches we cover. However, in order to avoid confusion among divergent approaches, we use the term "object data management." Object-oriented database programming languages [Bancilhon and Buneman 1990] are the DBMSs most precisely called "object-oriented." The primary focus of the book is on these systems and on extended relational database systems, because these approaches have been the two most widely accepted in the database research and development communities.

This book is aimed at an engineer, programmer, technical manager, or student interested in recent advances in database systems. In addition to introducing basic concepts and approaches to object data management, it covers important factors that the reader might overlook when comparing and using the new database systems. The area of object data management is new and is not well understood; this book sorts through conflicting claims for these new DBMSs. There are substantial differences in the performance and functionality among existing products and approaches.

The book is also appropriate for the reader involved in designing and implementing a DBMS. It provides a review of new object data management technology, with references to more detailed coverage of specific implementation issues. In contrast to most other sources currently available, the book provides a comparison of different object approaches from a unified, balanced perspective, and a study of database architecture requirements on the basis of application requirements, rather than most popular research areas.

This book complements, and may be supplemented by, existing collections of articles [Zdonik and Maier 1989, Kim and Lochovsky 1988, Cardenas and McLeod 1990, Bancilhon and Buneman 1990].

We assume that the reader has a basic familiarity with computing and programming concepts. Background in traditional DBMSs, particularly in relational systems, will also be important; however, we review conventional DBMSs, and references are provided for more background. This book would be a good text for a second course in database systems, to follow an introductory text such as [Date 1990, Ullman 1989, Elmasri and Navathe 1990]. Alternatively, the book could be used for a first course by instructors wanting to put special emphasis on next-generation database systems.

The reader needs no background in applications such as CAD, CASE, and office automation. In fact, we begin by covering these, because it is important to understand applications *before* proceeding honestly with a study of DBMSs to satisfy the application's needs—a fact often forgotten. A study of any one of these applications could fill entire volumes in itself [McClure 1989, Rubin 1987, Groover and Zimmers 1984], however, relatively simple examples will illustrate the needs for new database functionality.

The need for object data management sprang from advances in software technology for the applications we study in this book, particularly CASE and

CAD, enabled by the widespread introduction of engineering workstations and networking in the past decade. These applications have become more powerful and better integrated. Application designers and users naturally are seeking the next step: a DBMS that can provide a higher level of integration, acting as a common repository for objects shared by many applications and users.

Many engineering and office systems are already built around custom "database systems," with data structures that can be written out to disk files for interchange with other software. These custom database systems are not true DBMSs, however: true DBMSs are application-independent and provide many more features. Unfortunately, traditional DBMS products have not provided the performance and features these applications need. ODMSs were developed to meet those needs.

The business applications market has undergone a major revolution, moving from application-specific index-based file storage to general DBMSs, and more recently to relational DBMSs [Codd 1970, Date 1990]. However, it is difficult to modify traditional DBMSs, including relational DBMSs, to satisfy the performance and functionality requirements of the applications we study in the book. As we shall see, quite different architectural tradeoffs are necessary to support their needs.

This book addresses a new DBMS revolution, as CASE, CAD, office automation, and other applications move to the more powerful and flexible platform of object data management. ODMSs are also likely to be used in traditional business applications, as many of the new capabilities are important there as well.

ENHANCEMENTS IN REVISED EDITION

A number of corrections and improvements have been made to this book since it was published in 1991. This revised edition represents a substantial update to bring the book up-to-date with the latest technology and events in this fast-moving field, and to improve the presentation based on feedback from readers and instructors using the book over the last few years.

A new chapter (Chapter 6) has been added to cover standards work in OMG, ODMG, and the ANSI SQL committee. As noted in the first edition, standards were an important missing link in the future of object data management. The recent completion of the ODMG-93 standard as well as progress on a SQL3 standard are very important to new database technology.

The Appendix covering products and prototypes has been expanded and updated. The original edition covered fewer systems in detail. Since many readers are using this book to make a decision between alternative products, or are using a particular product or publicly-available research system for hands-on experience in conjunction with this book in an advanced database course, a more extensive coverage of the major systems has been added to the Appendix. The existing sections of the Appendix have been updated, and expanded in some cases.

Corrections and improvements have been made throughout the book. The notation used in the data schema figures has been improved. New figures and examples have been added. The bibliography has been expanded. Corrections and clarifications have been made in all of the chapters. Material has been added to cover new work in a number of areas.

In contrast to when this book first appeared, there are now many textbooks available on the topic of object-oriented databases; however, this book generally represents a more thorough and balanced coverage of new database technology. It discusses a much wider range of approaches, giving attention to extended relational as well as object-oriented DBMSs. It also provides deeper insight into the implementation and architecture of these systems; because the new systems differ more in architecture and performance than in features and data models, this insight is essential to both the student and industrial user of these systems.

READING INSTRUCTIONS

This book is divided into three main parts. The first three chapters comprise background material that provides an overview of object data management, examines applications that motivate this new technology, and reviews traditional database systems. Chapters 4 and 5 provide a core study of object data management. Chapters 6, 7, and 8 provide analysis and comparison of approaches and standards for object data management, with predictions for the future. The seven chapters are organized as follows:

- Chapter 1, *Introduction*, covers basic data-modeling concepts that will be important throughout the book, and explains the history and motivation for object data management.

- Chapter 2, *Advanced Database Applications*, covers new database applications in detail; these applications will serve as examples for the remainder of the book. The examples will be useful to illustrate specific database concepts; more important, they will help us to understand the database functionality and performance we need for object data management. At the end of Chapter 2, we summarize the database needs of the new applications.

- Chapter 3, *Traditional Database Systems*, reviews data management, with a particular focus on relational systems. This chapter is included not simply for historical perspective; much of object data management is based on extensions to the traditional technology. Readers with a background in database systems may skip this chapter, or may use it as a review; for other readers, this chapter provides an overview, with pointers to reading in specific topics.

- Chapters 4 and 5 cover object data management. Chapter 4, *Object Data Management Concepts*, covers functional issues, such as complex objects, type hierarchies, procedures, and version management. Chapter 5, *Implementation Issues*, covers physical implementation tradeoffs, the programming-language interface, query processing, remote and distributed access, and overall system performance,

- Chapter 6, *Future Database Standards*, covers work in a number of groups that are likely to shape future standards for object data management.

- Chapter 7, *Goals for Object Data Management*, provides a basis to compare ODMSs, deriving a set of basic properties that new database systems should satisfy.

- Chapter 8, *Conclusions*, evaluates the different approaches to object data management. It also covers future directions for research on ODMSs, and reviews what we have learned in the book.

In the Appendix, *Products and Prototypes*, we study specific commercial products and research prototypes to illustrate further the approaches to object data management discussed in the book: extensions to relational DBMSs, object-oriented DBMSs, functional and semantic model DBMSs, database generators for building tailored systems, and simple object managers based on file system extensions.

In addition to an Index, the book includes an Annotated Bibliography of reference materials covering seminal papers in object data management, new object data management systems, and important background material in programming languages and traditional database technology. A smaller System Bibliography indexed by system name is included at the end of the Appendix, for convenience in finding documentation for each system. The System Bibliography also serves as a glossary of terms used to categorize ODMSs, with a categorization of all the major ODMS products and prototypes.

For use in a course on advanced database systems, the book can be covered in approximately four equal portions taking about 8 instructional hours each: (1) introduction and motivation in Chapters 1 and 2, (2) object data management concepts in Chapter 4, (3) object data management implementation in Chapter 5, and (4) future work in object data management in Chapters 6 through 8. Chapter 3, on traditional database systems, and the Appendix, detailing specific systems, are optional depending on course background and goals.

For the reader using this book to evaluate object data management systems for use in a specific application, Chapters 1, 4, 7, and 8 are essential reading. Chapters 2 and 3 are optional, depending on background in applications and traditional database technology; Chapters 5 and 6 should be useful as a reference. The Appendix should be useful for readers examining specific products and approaches.

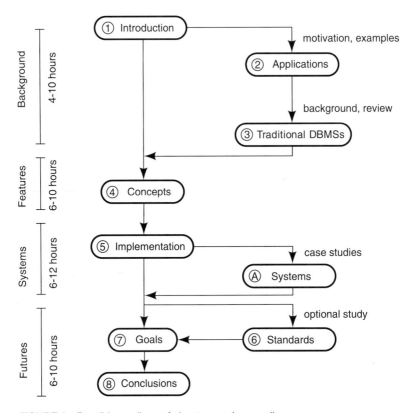

FIGURE 0 Possible readings of chapters and appendix

OBTAINING PRODUCT INFORMATION

Readers planning to purchase one of the ODMSs describe in this book will probably want to consult additional sources before making a large investment. Best efforts have been made to assure that the systems described in the text and in the Appendix are accurate and up-to-date, and this book probably covers more systems in more detail than any other; however, it is not feasible to do detailed comparisons of these systems in a book, nor is it possible to update the information as quickly as the products change.

To assist readers with this problem an independent consulting firm, Barry and Associates, has prepared a quite comprehensive, regularly-revised report on ODMS products. This report is the best source to my knowledge for making a product selection, and it was prepared with my consultation. See the bibliography [Barry and Associates 1994] for information on obtaining this report.

CORRECTIONS AND SUGGESTIONS

Compiling a book categorizing and analyzing half a dozen different approaches to database systems, and referencing hundreds of technical papers that have never been brought together in a single discussion of future directions in database systems, has been a substantial task. Many of the areas covered are not well understood, or are subject to substantial disagreement in the database research community. Despite these problems, I have attempted to provide an understanding of the issues and to take a position on most of them. I hope I have elucidated more often than I have confused in so doing. My apologies to any authors whose work or positions I have represented poorly. Since the study of this subject is so vulnerable to errors, disagreements, omissions, and confusion, your input is solicited for future editions; the area is changing rapidly, so it is likely that a new edition will be needed soon. Comments, corrections, and constructive suggestions should be sent to Addison-Wesley, Reading, Massachusetts, 01867, or by electronic mail to

`odmbook@eng.sun.com.`

ACKNOWLEDGMENTS

My wife, Susan, deserves special recognition for her substantial and flexible support of this book and of my career. I also thank my parents for their encouragement in my academic endeavors, and my sons, Eric, Aaron, and Elliott, for sharing me with the work I bring home.

Leon Guzenda, David Jordan, Mohammed Ketabchi, Fred Lochovsky, Bill Paseman, and Mike Robson deserve special thanks for the substantial effort they invested in reading and commenting on the manuscript. Dirk Bartels, François Bancilhon, Chris Keene, Johnny Martin, Sergiu Simmel, Michael Stonebraker, Craig Thompson, and Drew Wade donated system descriptions that were adapted for use in the Appendix. I also received helpful feedback from Doug Barry, Michael Davis, Lyn Dupré, Ira Greenberg, Toni Guttman, Donovan Hsieh, Bill Kent, Dan Koren, Krishna Kulkarni, Geoff Lewis, David Maier, Jos Marlowe, Hakan Mattson, Dennis McLeod, Eliot Moss, Silvia Osborn, Niki Pissinou, Gudrun Pollack, Tom Rogers, Bruce Spatz, Jacob Stein, Richard Steiger, Dave Stryker, Fred Tou, Khanh Vu, Dan Weinreb, Darrel Woelk, and other people on ideas presented in the book. Finally, I am grateful to the staff at Addison-Wesley; in particular Peter Gordon, Helen Goldstein, and Mary Beth Mooney who have been very flexible in working with me.

CONTENTS

Chapter   5
Implementation Issues   149

Chapter   7
Goals for Object Data Management   253

Chapter 8
Conclusions   273

Appendix
Products and Prototypes   283

1

Introduction

1.1 NEED FOR OBJECT DATA MANAGEMENT

The past decade has seen major changes in the computing industry. There has been a widespread move from centralized computing to networked workstations on every desk. We have seen an entirely new generation of software aimed at exploiting workstation technology, particularly in engineering, scientific, and office applications.

In database systems, there have been major changes in products for business applications, including the widespread acceptance of relational DBMSs. However, existing commercial DBMSs, both small-scale and large-scale, have proven inadequate for applications such as computer-aided design, software engineering, and office automation; new research and development in database systems has been necessary.

This new research has generated excitement in both the application and database communities. Over a dozen companies, research laboratories, and universities have completed major projects to construct a new kind of DBMS for these applications. This book is about these new DBMSs—*object data management systems (ODMSs)*.

1.1.1   Defining Object Data Management

On cursory examination, the only factor common to the new ODMSs is that they all profess to store "objects." Indeed, many are called "object-oriented" DBMSs. However, the term "object-oriented" has been used to mean many different things by different writers. We avoid controversy by defining our goal operationally: An ODMS is a DBMS aimed at satisfying the needs of computer-aided design, software engineering, office systems, and the other new applications we cover in the next chapter. In subsequent chapters, we shall refine this definition further, with a list of features required in an ODMS. We shall see that ODMSs include DBMSs based on object-oriented, semantic, functional, and extended relational models of data, and even systems that traditionally would be considered extended file systems or programming languages, rather than DBMSs. There is wide disparity in the degree to which the ODMSs actually satisfy our application needs, as will become apparent when we compare the approaches.

There is no general agreement about the future of ODMSs. Some people think that ODMSs will replace relational database systems. Other people think that ODMSs will fall by the wayside as relational database systems are enhanced with most of the same features. Perhaps the most likely scenario for the rest of the 1990s is that the market will be split: enhanced relational DBMSs will address primarily business applications, and ODMSs will find a market primarily in the new applications covered in this book.

1.1.2   Evolution of Database Systems

[Ullman 1989] defines three kinds of database needs:

- *Data management* is concerned with simple data structures and operations, such as those required by traditional business applications. Relational DBMSs, with tabular data structures of integers, strings, and other simple data, address the needs of data management.

- *Object management* is concerned with more complex data structures, such as those required to represent the parts of a document, program, or design. ODMSs, the topic of this book, were designed to address these needs.

- *Knowledge management* is concerned with maintaining complex rule bases, used to derive information about a domain through an inference system. These logic databases are descended from theorem-proving systems developed with research on artificial intelligence (AI).

These three kinds of database capabilities can be regarded as a progressive evolution of database systems to support more complex applications. Data management systems have existed as commercial products for some time. Products with object management capabilities are just beginning to appear, either as extensions of data management systems or as completely new products. Knowledge management is the least understood and most complex function to integrate into a database system. However, rules have been added to many systems.

In this book, we focus primarily on object management. However, most of the systems that we discuss provide object management capabilities without sacrificing data management features, and some provide primitive knowledge management. In the long run, there is a need for single database systems that satisfy all three kinds of database requirements. Few applications fit neatly into just one category, and some applications have requirements for two or more, especially when we consider the entire environment in which the application will operate.

For example, consider a database of documents. The authors of the documents require object management capabilities to represent parts and versions of documents. A librarian dealing with the documents requires more traditional data management capabilities, executing transactions to check out documents or querying the database to find documents overdue for return to the library. An expert system used by attorneys might augment the document database with rules about the structure for components of legal documents, or about the logical dependencies between documents. A company might have all three kinds of users, and thus would require a database system that could provide all the capabilities.

For most of the 1990s, however, it is likely we shall see database systems primarily focused on any one of data, object, or (possibly) knowledge management. It is difficult to build a single DBMS that satisfies all three requirements— especially one with satisfactory performance characteristics; the entire architecture of the DBMS often must be changed for the DBMS to be used for a different application domain. A DBMS that has object or knowledge management capabilities is typically too complex to satisfy ease-of-use requirements in data management. Also, in the DBMS marketplace, customers will not be willing to wait for one DBMS that does everything—their engineering department may buy an object management system, while their business department buys a data management system. Gateways can be built to exchange information between the two.

The focus of this book is object management, because that is where most of the new work is being done in database systems research and development, and no other book covers the range of work in the area. We use the term *object data management* to indicate that these systems typically include both object and data management capabilities. We study applications requiring object management capabilities, briefly summarize the state of data management systems, and then concentrate on object management for the remainder of the book, providing limited coverage of knowledge management where such capabilities have been integrated into data and object management systems.

1.1.3   New Database Applications

What are the characteristics of the applications in which we are interested? Object data management is a useful area to study only because there is a group of applications with new and similar DBMS requirements—large and complex data structures, multiple data versions, nested and heavily interrelated data. These applications demand a new kind of DBMS.

The following are examples of applications addressed by ODMSs:

- *Computer-aided software engineering (CASE)*: Design, specification, implementation, analysis, debugging, maintenance, and evolution of programs and documentation

- *Mechanical computer-aided design (MCAD)*: Design of everything from aerospace vehicles to buildings, including structural components as well as interdependent designs for electrical or mechanical interconnections

- *Electronics computer-aided design (ECAD)*: The logical and physical design of integrated circuit chips, circuit boards, and entire systems; as is CASE, ECAD and MCAD are needed for the entire design lifecycle, including specification, simulation, version maintenance, and synthesis

- *Computer-aided manufacturing (CAM)*: Discrete production (such as cars on an assembly line) and continuous production (such as chemical synthesis)

- *Office automation*: Computer control of information in a business, including electronic mail, documents, and work orders

- *Computer-aided publishing (CAP) and hypertext*: Tools to store, manipulate, and search parts of complex documents, including documents with dynamic behavior and multiple versions

- *Graphics*: Software packages and end-user tools to store and manipulate graphical representations of complex objects, possibly as a component of one of the preceding applications (CAD, CAP)

- *Scientific and medical applications*: Manipulating and analyzing complex chemical, biological, or physical representations, such as complex organic molecules

- *System services*: Operating system or file system additions to provide information to client programs; for example, for an application-integration framework, network routing, user authorization, and name lookup

- *Manufacturing and real-time control*: Computer control of processes, for everything from a laboratory experiment to a nuclear reactor

- *Knowledge bases*: Artificial intelligence (AI) applications with a rule base or information base too large to store efficiently in programming language data structures

Nearly all these applications evolved on computer workstations in the 1980s. They all store complex objects, and they exhibit use characteristics different from those of traditional business applications; for example, highly concurrent update of the same data by different users is rare. These applications thus represent new opportunities and problems in data management, and drive the new research and development discussed in this book.

1.2   DATA MODELS AND DATABASE ARCHITECTURES

Readers who have a background in traditional databases know that there are two kinds of information in a database: *data* and *schema*. The schema is metadata describing the structure of the data. It is analogous to the data-type declarations in a programming language. The data themselves make up the bulk of the database, and may consist of simple data such as integers and strings, as well as more complex data, such as records, or even procedural data. Different types of database systems have different constraints on what kinds of data and schema are allowed, just as different programming languages have different capabilities in their type declarations. These DBMS type system constraints are called the *data model*—the type system for specifying data and operations on data. In this section, we look at the most important data models we shall encounter in this book.

1.2.1   Relational Model

The relational data model is of great importance, because of its popularity in the research community and in commercial business data processing, where the relational model is supplanting systems based on earlier models [Date 1990, Codd 1970]. Thus, the relational data model is a good place for us to start, serving as a useful benchmark for comparison to more advanced systems.

The popularity of the relational model has stemmed primarily from this model's simplicity. There is only one data structure: a table with rows and columns containing data of specified types, such as integers or strings. The query language is based on a few simple operations on tables, and the more complex features (such as integrity constraints on data and view definitions to hide or restructure data) do not need to be understood by the end user.

The simplicity of the relational model is a benefit in ease of use and mathematical tractability, but is also a limitation. As we shall see in the next chapter, many applications' data are too complex to represent using relational tables and queries. The ODMSs we discuss are designed to remedy this shortcoming, albeit at the expense of a more complex data model.

1.2.2   Extended Relational Models

The most obvious way to remedy the shortcomings of the relational model is to extend the model. *Extended relational data models* are used in systems based on enhancements of the relational data model to incorporate procedures, objects, versions, and other new capabilities. Since relational database systems are simple, are well understood, and are popular in both the research and product worlds, extended relational systems benefit from this research and popularity.

There is no single extended relational model; rather, there is a variety of these models, whose characteristics depend on the way, and on the degree to which, extensions were made. All the models do share the basic relational tables and query language, all incorporate some concept of "object," and all have the ability to store procedures as well as data in the database.

1.2.3 Object-Oriented Models

Systems based on object-oriented data models originated with the object-oriented programming paradigm. The programming languages most frequently cited as originating and popularizing the object-oriented programming paradigm are Simula [Dahl and Nygaard 1966] and Smalltalk [Goldberg and Robson 1983]. More recent examples are C++ [Ellis and Stroustrup 1990], CLOS [Bobrow et al 1988], and CLU [Liskov et al 1977].

The object-oriented programming paradigm subsumes the concept of abstract data types in programming languages [Micallef 1988, Stroustrup 1988, Stefik and Bobrow 1986]. Abstract data-type declarations explicitly define a public and private portion of a data structure, or *object*. Abstract data types in object-oriented languages, called *classes*, are said to *encapsulate* private data portions of the object with public procedures, called *methods*. The argument for encapsulation is one of simplifying the construction and maintenance of programs through modularization. An object is a black box that can be constructed and modified independently of the rest of a system, as long as its public interface (method) definitions are not changed.

There is no single object-oriented paradigm, and therefore there are a variety of object-oriented data models. Generally, object-oriented programming languages share common concepts in addition to encapsulation, in particular the use of a hierarchy of types of objects with inheritance of type attributes and methods. However, the specific features vary, and even the strict definition of encapsulation provided by abstract data types—that procedures are public, whereas data are private—is often too restrictive for object-oriented DBMSs. [Atkinson et al 1989] distinguish a different kind of encapsulation, in which either data or procedures may be in the public and private portions of an object. Some authors use the term "object-oriented" for database systems without the requirement for encapsulation at all, based simply on the grouping of data with objects. We shall consider these variations on the object-oriented approach in more detail in Chapter 4.

1.2.4 Functional and Semantic Models

Functional data models are a particularly elegant way to represent databases. They use a data-access language based on mathematical function notation, with a declarative functional query language, analogous to relational query languages, to define the function values. If the query language is extended to allow procedural specification of functions as well, we call the DBMS an *extended functional* database system.

The basis of a functional model is *objects* and *functions*. Functions map objects onto other objects and data values. Relationships between objects, attributes of objects, and procedures associated with objects are all represented by functions, as we shall see. The functional model is worth studying because of the advantages it offers, among them simplicity of notation and ability to define virtual data.

Various other data models were proposed in the 1980s, notably *semantic* data models [Hammer and McLeod 1981, King 1988]. These models contributed a number of new concepts, many of which have been incorporated into other data models.

1.2.5   Data Models and Database Architectures

The new data models—extended relational, functional, semantic, and object-oriented—generally provide similar functionality. In fact, the term "semantic data models" has sometimes been used generically to include all these models, because they all incorporate more semantics of data than the relational approach. The term "object-oriented" also has been used to refer to systems based on all these models, because recent versions of all these data models incorporate concepts from the object-oriented paradigm.

The important observation to make from this confusion of data-model terminology is that the many data models are slowly converging on a single data model that has a combination of features. It is the convergence of these models that makes the current organization of this book possible, with a single presentation of data modeling accompanied by side comments on minor differences in syntax and semantics of various approaches.

Because of the convergence of approaches, the categorization of systems according to data model should not be taken too literally. The data model is most useful as a way to distinguish the *genealogy* of a system; that is, as an indication of from which previous systems and philosophies an ODMS evolved. Most of the current prototypes and systems evolved from object-oriented programming languages or from extension of relational DBMS ideas, so the book focuses primarily on the object-oriented and extended relational models.

It is also important to note that data models are not the only important distinction between systems. In fact, some systems have no data model, or allow the users to choose their own. Systems may differ according to *database architecture*, which is the way in which the ODMS is implemented and combined with application programming languages. In Chapter 4, we introduce a variety of approaches to object data management that differ in data model, database architecture, and other aspects.

1.3   OBJECT DATA MANAGEMENT CONCEPTS

So, what *is* an object? Objects are real-world or abstract entities that we model in a database. They might be documents, airplane parts, transistors, people, scientific hypotheses, or chemical formulae. All database applications deal with objects in some sense. In the case of our applications, however, the objects are more complex and take a more central role in the application. Objects may have relationships to other objects, and may exist in multiple versions.

Objects may have behavior as well as data. Some authors distinguish between *structural* and *behavioral* object-orientation [Dittrich and Dayal 1986, Zdonik and Maier 1989]. Structural object-orientation means treating data in an object-centric fashion; for now, that will be our focus. Later, we shall return to behavioral object-orientation, which is concerned with methods and encapsulation of object data using the object-oriented paradigm from programming languages.

The structural properties of complex objects alone necessitate the new ODMS technology. These properties may be useful in new database applications, as well as in traditional business applications. The object-oriented, extended relational, functional, and semantic data models all incorporate structural object-orientation. In this section, we introduce some basic concepts from these models. We also introduce important database terminology and a graphical notation that we shall use throughout the book to describe database applications and systems.

1.3.1   Data Schemas

Before embarking on a study of applications and database systems, we need a notation for understanding the structure of application data. This structure is the data schema. To describe data schemas we shall use a derivative of *entity–relationship diagrams* developed by [Chen 1976].* Although we defer discussion of data schemas for different DBMSs to Chapters 3 and 4, we introduce the data-schema notation here, because we shall use it throughout the book to describe applications and data-schema representations.

It is important that you understand the concepts and figures, as we shall use this notation in all our examples. We shall also use the example presented here, a hypothetical database of documents and associated information, to understand database concepts in Chapters 3, 4, and 5, and to contrast the data models used by different DBMSs. Readers who want more background in data modeling and notation are referred to [Teory 1990, Tsichritzis and Lochovsky 1982]. Database textbooks such as [Date 1990, Ullman 1989] also provide a basic background in the

---

* For those familiar with Chen's notation, we differ in using ovals instead of diamonds for relationships, using arrowheads instead of numbers to indicate multiplicity of relationships, and showing attributes inside the entity boxes to reduce the complexity of the diagram. The notation has been extended to define subtypes and procedures.

FIGURE 1.1 Two types of objects, documents and chapters, with a one-to-many relationship between them.

area. [Kent 1981] focuses on fundamental issues in data modeling, such as, "What is an object?"

Our notation for data schemas is intended to be independent of the data model used by specific database systems. In fact, we shall use our notation to compare relational, functional, semantic, and object-oriented systems. Our notation captures a superset of the semantics covered by most of the DBMSs we discuss. However, the notation is *not* designed to describe entire applications—it describes only database structure. Behavioral object-orientation is also important in the design and modularization of application programs, as we shall see in the next chapter.

1.3.2   Example Database

We use a data schema notation that is graphical, using boxes, ovals, and arrows. Each box represents a type of object used by application programs. The ovals and associated arrows represent a type of relationship between objects. In Figure 1.1, we have drawn boxes for the two types of objects in our example database, **Document** and **Chapter**, with type names at the top of the boxes. The figure shows a relationship between documents and chapters, named **contains**, indicating which chapters belong to each document. The relationship is represented by a line connecting the two boxes, with the name of the relationship in an oval in the center.

Figure 1.1 also illustrates several other features of our notation:

1. Inside the boxes, we have drawn other boxes, showing what information is associated with an object. Each piece of information, which we will call an *attribute* of the object, has a name and a type.* For example, documents have a title, which is a character string, and a revision, which is a date. Chapters also have titles, plus a chapter number, which is an integer.

2. The **contains** relationship between **Document** and **Chapter** is one-to-many. That is, each chapter belongs to exactly one document, but each

---

* Note that, in the figure, the object names are capitalized. To help you distinguish objects throughout this book, we have capitalized object type names; attributes and relationships are not capitalized. Built-in types, such as STRING and INT, are set in all capital letters.

document may have many chapters in it. This one-to-many relationship is indicated by an arrowhead on the "one" side (documents) and a double arrowhead on the "many" side (chapters). The object types connected by a relationship—in this case, chapters and documents—are generally called the *roles* of the relationship. We examine relationships, roles, and their graphical representation in more detail in the next section.

Do not confuse this graphical representation of a data *schema* with object *instances* that the schema describes. As an example of object instances, consider this book, which would be represented by one object of type `Document` and eight objects of type `Chapter`, with the appropriate `title` and other attribute values. In addition, eight `contains` relationships would be required to connect the chapters with the book. We could draw a graphical diagram of these object instances similar to the one in Figure 1.1; however, we generally will not use these diagrams to show data—we will use them for only the data schema.

1.3.3   Objects and Relationships

Relationships may be one-to-one or many-to-many, instead of one-to-many. Examples of these kinds of relationships are shown in Figure 1.2, adding a `doc-index` relationship between a `Document` and `Index` object (each document has one index, each index is for one document), and an `author` relationship between `Document` and `Person` objects (each document may have multiple authors, each person may author multiple documents).

Thus, each role of a relationship may be "many" or "one." We call the number of objects that may participate in a role the *multiplicity* of the role. For example, the roles of the `author` relationship have multiplicity "many" and "many;" the roles of the `doc-index` relationship have multiplicity "one" and "one;" and the roles

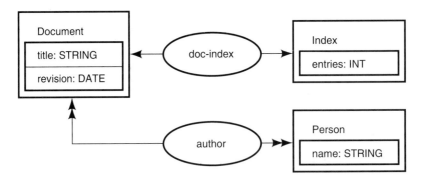

FIGURE 1.2 An illustration of relationships with multiplicity different from that in Figure 1.1: One-to-one and many-to-many relationships. Each document has one index, each index is for one document. Each document may have multiple people as authors, and each person may be the author of multiple documents.

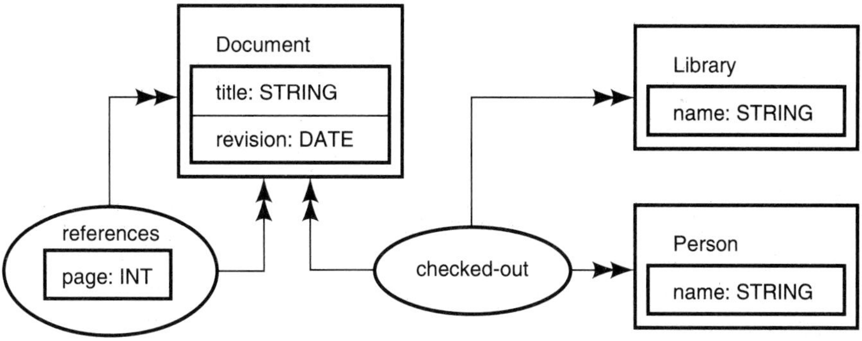

FIGURE 1.3 An illustration of more complex relationships, both of them ternary. The `references` relationship is an association between two objects of the same type. This relationship has an attribute of its own: a page number indicating where the reference occurs in the text of the document. The `checked-out` relationship associates three objects: a document, a person, and a library from which the person has checked out the document.

of the **contains** relationship have multiplicity "one" and "many." We draw a double arrow from the oval to the box for the "many" role(s) of relationships, and a single arrow for the "one" role(s).

Multiplicity constraints may be more complex than just "many" or "one." For example, a database may be constrained to require exactly two parents for every person, to require two or more chapters for a document, or to require every employee to have either zero or one boss. DBMSs generally demand that these more complex multiplicity constraints be maintained by procedures written by the programmer—they are not built in to the semantics of the schema. Our schema notation could be modified to place integer multiplicity ranges on each arm of a relationship, instead of arrowheads; however, it will not be necessary to show more complex multiplicity constraints for the databases with which we shall deal.

Relationships may involve more than two types of object. All the relationships in Figures 1.1 and 1.2 are binary relationships: **contains, doc-index, author**. Relationships involving more objects are represented by several arrows emanating from the oval containing the association name—one for each object participating in the association.

As an example of a ternary relationship, consider the **checked-out** relationship shown in Figure 1.3, an association between a person, a document, and a library from which the person has borrowed the document. This relationship is ternary because three objects are involved, and there is no way to decompose it into binary relationships without inventing an artificial object to represent the relationship itself, or to represent individual copies of documents.

Relationships may also have simple attributes, just as objects can. For example, the **references** relationship of Figure 1.3 has an integer attribute indicating the page number where a document references another document. We illustrate this graphically in Figure 1.3. Note that this relationship is ternary, technically speaking, because it relates three items: a document, a page number, and a referenced document. However, only two of these (the documents) are user-defined object types; the page number is simply an integer. In some object-oriented systems, this integer is treated as an object just like user-defined object types, so the distinction may be subtle.

The number of objects participating in a relationship is generally called the *degree* of the relationship. The binary relationships, in Figures 1.1 and 1.2, have degree two. The ternary relationships, in Figure 1.3, have degree three.

Relationships of degree two are most common. Degrees of three or greater do not occur as much in practice, and a degree of one is not very useful—it simply produces a set of objects for which the relationship exists. Perhaps because of these facts, many object-oriented systems do not support nonbinary relationships, and even those that do may not support attributes of relationships—they often require the introduction of an artificial "relationship object" to which binary associations are attached.*

Note that relationships of degree greater than two result in many more alternatives for multiplicity. The multiplicity of a ternary relationship may be many-many-many, many-many-one, many-one-many, and so on: There are eight different possibilities. However, the situation is no more complex if we view each participant role (or "attribute") of a relationship separately: each can permit either "many" or "one" relationship instance for each object instance.

To refer to relationships in an application, we may need to name the roles of the relationship. For example, the references relationship might be referred to as the `reference` or `referenced-by` attributes for a document, depending on the direction to which we are referring. We could place these labels on the lines, but we have not done so, in order to reduce clutter.

1.3.4 Procedures

Applications of ODMSs require the ability to describe procedures as well as data in the database. In fact, in a true behaviorally object-oriented system, these procedures are the only externally visible features of an object. Incorporating procedures into the application schema allows ODMSs to support encapsulation, and more generally to support the entire application design, not just the data.

We show procedures associated with an object type as a second group of boxes inside the box, with rounded corners to distinguish them from the attribute boxes above. In Figure 1.4 we show an example of this convention with a new object type, `SourceProgram`, which has an attribute `language`, an enumerated type indicating the programming language in which the source program is

---

* Some may disagree with calling this relationship object "artificial." In fact, some systems merge the concepts of relationship and object, since both are simply records with attributes. We separate the two to distinguish data that can be referenced elsewhere in the database (objects) from data that are used solely to connect other data (relationships).

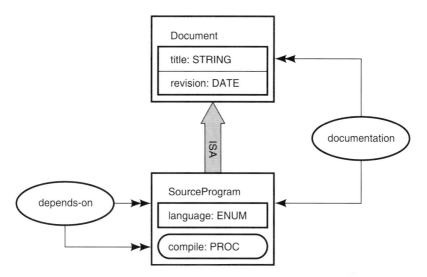

FIGURE 1.4 Subtypes are indicated by the wide "ISA" arrow. For example, a source program is a subtype of document. It may depend on other source programs and reference a document that explains what it does. Note that source-program objects also have a procedure field, executed to compile them.

Note: for brevity, object attribute names are shown without their types (for example, STRING, DATE) in most of the subsequent figures of the book.

written, and a procedure **compile**, which contains the commands to compile and link the program for execution.

1.3.5 Type Hierarchy

Figure 1.4 also illustrates another feature that will be important to the applications we discuss in the next chapter: a type hierarchy. Object types may have *supertypes* and *subtypes*.

Documents that have additional attributes or associated procedures, such as a source program, a technical report, or a book, may be declared to be subtypes of document. Such objects are said to *inherit* the attributes, relationships, and procedures associated with documents, and may have their own attributes, relationships, or procedures as well. We show a wide arrow labeled **ISA** from a subtype to its supertype, as shown in Figure 1.4 from **SourceProgram** to **Document**, to indicate that a source program "is a" kind of document. Subtypes are usually called *subclasses* in object-oriented languages [Goldberg and Robson 1983]. Subtyping is usually called *generalization* in the database literature [Smith and Smith 1980]. The **ISA** label comes from the AI literature, where the subtype concept originated.

A type hierarchy is a useful feature for almost any non-trivial database application, because it greatly simplifies the data schema description and it allows the same queries or procedures to operate without change on a variety of subtypes of data. Without this feature, the combinatorial explosion of unrelated types complicates application programming.

1.3.6   Other Concepts

To set the stage for our study of applications and databases, we have covered many concepts: object types, instances, attributes, relationships, multiplicity, degree, procedural attributes, and type hierarchies.

There are other features of objects that are not apparent in our data schema notation:

- Objects may have names that are not human-meaningful (such as transistors, pipes, wires), or names that frequently change, in contrast to objects most frequently stored in business databases (employees, departments, customers), yet the objects must be referenced by many other related objects in the database (for example, to show wire connections). Thus, a unique machine-generated identifier must be used for the objects.

- Objects may be composed of other objects. For example, an airplane may be divided into major components such as wings and fuselage, the wing divided into major air surfaces and internal components, and so on down to the level of individual nuts and bolts.

- Objects or their attributes may be very large, even when they do not explicitly contain other objects. For example, a bitmap image or voiceprint may be represented as a single object with encoded data.

- There may be multiple versions of objects to be maintained. For example, versions of documents, engineering drawings, or software modules must be kept for maintenance of existing products, or to support two parallel development projects until they can be merged.

Our notation also does not encompass the operational aspects of object data management, such as programming or query languages to manipulate objects, encapsulation of object data with procedures, or concurrency control and recovery. However, this basic understanding of objects and database terminology is adequate to let us proceed at this point; we shall investigate other features of object data management as we study systems and applications in more detail in the remainder of the book.

2

Advanced Database Applications

2.1 INTRODUCTION

In this chapter, we look at new applications that motivate object data management technology. The reader who is not interested in application descriptions, or who wants to understand database technology more fully before studying applications, may safely skip to the following chapters and return to Chapter 2 at a later time.

2.1.1 Design Applications

The applications most commonly cited in the context of object data management are in three areas:

- *Software Engineering:* Programming both small and large software systems.
- *Mechanical and Electrical Engineering:* Design and production of physical and electronic products.
- *Documents:* Text documents, hypertext, graphics, and office automation.

We will find that these application areas have many similarities in their requirements for data manipulation. This may be surprising at first glance, since the applications manipulate very different kinds of data. However, they are identical in principle: all use computers to help people in design—the creative construction of artifacts. In the case of software engineering, these artifacts are programs; for mechanical and electrical engineering, they are engineering designs; and for documents, they are a combination of text, graphics, and hypertext.

Sections 2.2, 2.3, and 2.4 cover these three applications, respectively.

2.1.2   Other Applications

In Section 2.5, we discuss other applications that might particularly benefit from object data management:

- *Science and medicine:* Representation and manipulation of complex data, such as molecular models for organic compounds, spectral analyses, or genetic encoding

- *Manufacturing and real-time control:* Use of computers to monitor and control processes such as chemical processing

- *System services:* Simple information management, such as object-oriented window systems, mail routing, application intercommunication, and user authorization on a network of workstations

- *Expert systems:* Representation of knowledge and rule bases for AI applications

- *Business applications:* Extensions of traditional applications that require new database features

We shall focus on applications that stand to benefit most from recent advances in object data management, but you should keep in mind that the preceding list is not exhaustive, and note that traditional business applications will benefit as well.

Space does not permit us to discuss the database requirements of each of these applications in detail; this discussion would be repetitive, in any case, since the applications have similar needs. However, simplified schemas are illustrated for many of the applications. The schema diagrams will be used as examples throughout the book.

In the final section of this chapter, Section 2.6, we examine the database requirements that the applications have in common, including needs for traditional database features as well as new ones, and the requirements that differ across the applications. Our summarization of database requirements will set the stage for our presentation of object data management in the rest of this book.

2.2   SOFTWARE ENGINEERING

Computer-aided software engineering (CASE) is the application of computers to assist in developing and maintaining software. CASE has been one of the most common uses of engineering workstations in the past decade. In this section, we study the software-engineering process and the CASE tools designed to assist in that process.

2.2.1   CASE History

In a limited sense, CASE was one of the first applications of computers, in the early 1960s. High-level language compilers, debuggers, and flow-charting tools all assisted in the development of software, before programming was even called "software engineering."

In the late 1970s, software-engineering tools were divided into two broad categories, for *programming-in-the-large* and *programming-in-the-small* [DeRemer and Kron 1976]. Programming-in-the-large deals with coordination of software projects—for example, handling multiple versions of software, avoiding simultaneous update of software modules by two or more programmers, maintaining multiple system versions, and scheduling interdependent software-development subprojects. Programming-in-the-small deals with tools used by an individual programmer—for example, program-design tools, symbolic debuggers, syntax-directed program editors, and tools to manage compilation dependencies.

Nowadays, the term "CASE" refers to tools for the entire software lifecycle, including specification, design, development, and maintenance. Let's look at the lifecycle and CASE tools in more detail.

2.2.2   CASE Tools

CASE tools might be classified into four broad categories according to the CASE problems on which they focus [MacDonald 1990]:

1. *Front-end CASE tools,* or *upper-CASE tools,*   deal with the high-level design, specification, and analysis of software and requirements. These tools include computer-aided diagramming tools oriented toward a particular programming design methodology [DeMarco 1978, Yourdon & Constantine 1978], more recently including object-oriented design.

2. *Back-end CASE tools,* or *lower-CASE tools,*   deal with the detailed design, coding, assembly, and testing of software. These tools may aid the programmer [Raeder 1985] directly; for example, they include graphical debugging aids and query and browsing facilities to find quickly a particular procedure or uses of a variable.

3. *Maintenance tools*   deal with software after initial release. These tools may assist in tracking bug fixes and enhancement requests, porting to new platforms, or performing new releases.

4. *Support software and frameworks*   provide basic functionality required in tools of type 1, 2, and 3. Support software includes basic operating-system functionality as well as higher-level support such as project management and scheduling software, and database support to track different versions and configurations of software releases [Ellison 1986, Riddle and Williams 1986]. Various projects have been directed toward standardizing frameworks to support and integrate CASE applications; these include PCTE, CAIS-A, and IRDS [Lewis 1990].

In addition to CASE methodology based on traditional programming languages and tools, there are two quite different approaches to CASE, particularly for back-end tools:

1. *Higher-level languages and packages:*   Some commercial products have focused on specific applications. For example, there are dozens of fourth-generation languages (4GLs), forms packages, and database design tools oriented toward the large market for business database applications on character terminals. Some more recent products are targeted at simplifying development of user interfaces in window systems. It is possible to make large gains in application programming productivity by focusing on a single application area.

2. *Expert systems:*   The application of artificial intelligence to programming, to select designs and produce code automatically in limited domains is another approach [Balzer 1985]. So far, this approach has seen limited application— sufficiently general automatic programming is very difficult to do.

2.2.3   Software-Engineering Lifecycle

The full lifecycle of a software project goes through many stages; a simplified view of the steps in the process is shown in Figure 2.1:

- *Requirements:*   Determine the need and requirements for software, often producing a requirements document.

- *Decomposition:*   Decompose the software project among programmers and across major functional boundaries.

- *Specification:*   Decide which functions each programmer's subcomponents must perform, and what the interfaces between them must be.

- *Coding:*   Implement each subcomponent. Before coding can begin, it may be necessary to perform recursive decomposition and specification steps on each programmer's subcomponent.

- *Testing and integration:*   Verify that each subcomponent performs as specified (unit test) and that the entire system performs as specified (system test).

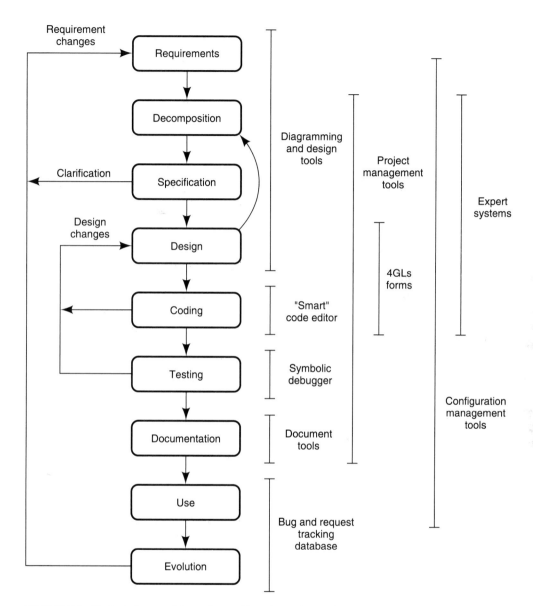

FIGURE 2.1 Typical phases of the software lifecycle, and associated development tools. The order in which these steps are followed may vary.

- *Documentation:* Provide user documentation for the program(s). This step may proceed in parallel with some of the preceding steps. (Indeed, errors in requirements and specification are often discovered in the documentation process, before the system is coded.)

- *Use:* Have users operate the resulting program(s), providing feedback on performance and functionality. During this process, problem reports and usage statistics are typically collected for evaluation.

- *Evolution:* Repeat some or all of the preceding steps. The largest effort in most software projects goes into bug fixes and improvements to the programs dictated by user feedback.

Figure 2.1 also shows some of the tools used in these steps of the software lifecycle, as discussed in the previous subsection. Note that the requirements, decomposition, and specification steps roughly correspond to front-end tools; the coding, testing, and documentation steps correspond to back-end tools; and the use and evolution steps correspond to maintenance tools.

Software development does not always follow the steps in the order shown in Figure 2.1; it may be necessary to return to earlier steps in many cases, or some steps may be skipped. In fact, almost any ordering is possible, and any one may be best for a particular software problem. The key aspect to note is that the software lifecycle is complex, particularly as software evolves. For this reason, modularization, reusability, and other aspects of the object-oriented paradigm are very important in CASE.

2.2.4   Program Symbol Management

To understand CASE database needs, we shall look at a few examples of the kinds of information needed to support CASE tools. Our first example, described in this subsection, is programming-in-the-small data that might be used in back-end tools.

Although a lot can be done to increase overall productivity in a programming project by the right specifications and by good coordination among programmers, the productivity of individual programmers in the edit–compile–debug loop will always be an important factor in CASE. The edit–compile–debug loop can be improved in a variety of ways. Some recent work in this area has focused on getting more information to the programmer in the debugging process:

- *Graphics:* Use of the mouse and graphics in the debugging process—for example, setting breakpoints by pointing at code, displaying data structures or procedure call hierarchies graphically, or continuously updating status information in parallel windows.

- *Query and browsing:* Programmer tools to find references to a particular procedure or variable, to find the definition of a particular procedure or variable, or otherwise to query program information

These tools require symbolic information about programs, typically produced by a compiler and then read by debuggers and display tools. This information is typically stored in an extension of the symbol-table file associated with each object module.

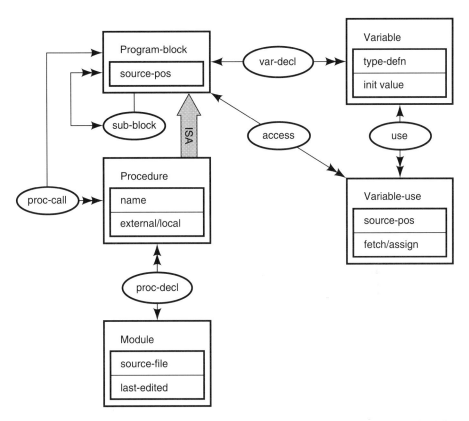

FIGURE 2.2 Schema for representing software at a fine grain, as would be required for debugging or for querying information about program symbols.

Figure 2.2 shows an example of information that might be stored in a symbol-table file. **Program-blocks** (statements or groups of statements) are represented individually with information about the variables and procedures they use. A **Procedure** is a special kind of program block (a subtype, marked with **ISA**) with additional attributes—a name and an indicator of external or local scope. A **Procedure** also has relationships to indicate the **Module** in which the procedure is defined, and the **Program-blocks** in which the procedure is used. The schema defines each **Variable** used in a program, with a **var-decl** relationship to indicate the **Program-block** where the variable declaration occurs. Each use of a variable is represented by a **Variable-use** object, linked to the **Program-block** where the use occurs by an **access** relationship.

Note that the data schema in Figure 2.2, and the other application data schemas presented in this chapter's figures, are oversimplified due to space constraints. However, the schemas give an overview of the information that actual application tools would require. For example, the Figure 2.2 schema would be adequate to find which procedures and variables could be affected by recompilation of a module, or to query which procedures could change the value of a variable. For more complete data schemas, see [Hauser et al 1983, Powell and Linton 1983].

2.2.5   Project and Configuration Management

There are two important kinds of tools for coordination between programmers:

*   *Configuration management:*   Management of concurrent access to code among multiple programmers, tracking of different versions of code in use by programmers, and recording of dependency information (which compilations depend on which others).
*   *Project management:* Specifications, dependencies, and scheduling of the subprojects of a software project; project-management software can assist in tracking progress, as well as in estimating and assigning time

[Lacroix 1989] reviews some of the work in configuration management. Figure 2.3 shows a simplified example of a schema that might be used for a

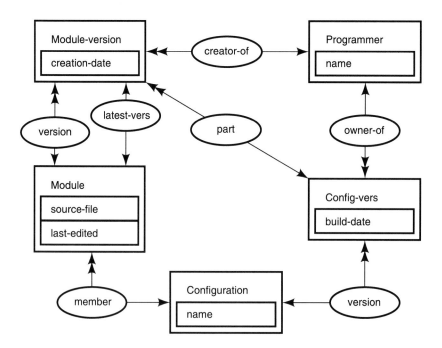

FIGURE 2.3   Partial schema for configuration-version management.

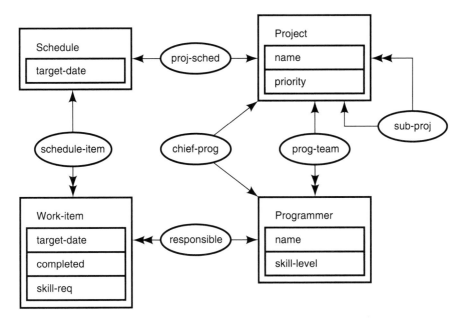

FIGURE 2.4   Partial schema for project management.

configuration-management database. The "objects" in this database are at a granularity of entire software **Modules**, and for each there may be multiple **Module-versions**. The information for the different versions—in our example, the **creation-date**—is stored as an attribute of the **Module-version**, and the information all versions have in common is stored as attributes of the **Module** representative. Each **Module** is a member of a **Configuration** of modules that represent a complete system or subsystem. Configurations are also versioned; each **Module-version** is part of a **Config-vers**. A **Programmer** may be the **owner-of** zero, one, or more **Config-vers**, and similarly for **Module-versions**.

Figure 2.4 illustrates kinds of information that might be needed for project management. Again, this schema is only a partial one, presented to give you a feel for the kinds of objects in a project-management database; a more complete schema can be found in [Brown 1989] or in [Hitchcock 1988].

In the figure, project **Schedules** are decomposed into individual **Work-items**. **Work-items** are assigned to a responsible **Programmer** with a **target-date** for completion, and the overall progress of the project is tracked by recording of actual **completed** dates for the work items. Each programming **Project** has a **name** and **priority**, and is linked by a **proj-sched** relationship to its schedule, by **prog-team** and **chief-prog** to the **Programmers** on the project, and by **sub-proj** to subprojects with their own schedules.

2.3   MECHANICAL AND ELECTRICAL DESIGN

Designing complex systems is one of the most difficult tasks people undertake. It is difficult for many reasons:

- The design itself may be very large. In an integrated circuit, there may be millions of transistors; in a Boeing 747, there are millions of individual parts.

- There are often many interdependent subsystem designs. For example, for a building, there might be a structural design, an electrical wiring plan, a layout for heating and cooling systems, a design for the plumbing, and perhaps even interior designs. These designs interact in terms of physical space, cooling requirements, and so on.

- The design evolves with time. When a design change occurs, its implications must be propagated through all design representations. Often, many design alternatives are being considered for each component, and the correct version for each part must be tracked.

- There may be hundreds or thousands of engineers, managers, technicians, and other workers involved. They must work in parallel on multiple versions of a large design, yet the end-product must be consistent and coordinated.

People have always used tools to help them design large systems. However, computers—particularly engineering workstations—have enabled a new generation of design tools for this purpose.

2.3.1   Computer-Aided Design

Computer-aided design (CAD) is the use of computer-based tools in the design process. We distinguish between two broad categories of CAD:

- *Mechanical CAD (MCAD)*   is concerned with physical artifacts that may range from individual cogs or bolts to entire chemical plants and airplanes.

- *Electrical CAD (ECAD)*   is concerned with electronic components on a very small scale (that is, integrated circuit chips) as well as with board layout and complete systems.

2.3.2   Design Process

ECAD and MCAD tools must deal with the entire lifecycle of a design. The lifecycle of a mechanical or electrical design is similar at a high level to that for software, which we examined in the previous section (in fact, CASE has been referred to as "software CAD" [Rowe and Wensel 1989]). The CAD steps are these:

- *Requirements:*   Determine the constraints that a system must satisfy, or the relative weights of design parameters. Examples might be the speed, fuel consumption, and passenger capacity of an aircraft.

- *Partitioning:*   Define the major components of a system to satisfy the requirements. This is the gross-level architecture of the system. Often, there are well-known ways to partition the solution: for example, a computer might consist of a processor, memory, buses, I/O subsystems, and peripherals. The decomposed subcomponents may be assigned to different engineers or groups at this point.

- *Specification:*   Decide what functions subcomponents must perform, and the interfaces between them. This process decomposes the requirements for the whole system into the requirements for the subcomponents. When multiple engineers are involved, the specification is particularly important, because it defines the boundaries and mutual agreements among design groups. Mechanical subcomponents are developed with 2-D or 3-D models, and electronic ones with a hardware language such as VHDL.

- *Design:*   Choose a detailed implementation of each subcomponent. This step involves mapping the subcomponent models into a specific technology. For example, different tools allow decomposing an electronic design into different levels of abstraction: behavioral, register transfer level, structural (gates), and transistors. Engineers may construct and evaluate multiple alternative designs in parallel at this point.

- *Analysis and verification:*   Examine the design, at multiple levels, for consistency and adherence to specification. The goal is to answer the question: "Will this design work?" Examples of analysis are simulation to determine whether a circuit functions properly, and finite element analysis (FEA) to determine the stress on a mechanical design under load.

- *Implementation:*   Build a physical realization of the system and integrate the components into a final system. This step is sometimes called "prototyping," in cases where mass production is intended later. Computers may assist in the implementation phase in a variety of ways. For example, in a mechanical design, computer-controlled machine tools may be used to fabricate a part from the CAD system data.

- *Testing:*   Verify that the prototype satisfies the original requirements. Ideally, a test methodology has been developed during the design process.

- *Documentation:*   Provide user documentation for operation and maintenance of the system. As in the software lifecycle, this step may proceed in parallel with other steps.

- *Manufacturing:*   If the system is not one of a kind, then take many additional steps at this point, some requiring redesign of the prototype for manufacturability, or design of the manufacturing process. We shall deal with this area later, when we discuss computer-aided manufacturing (CAM).

- *Use:*   Have customers of the design operate the resulting system, providing feedback on its performance and functionality. During this process, problem reports and usage statistics may be collected for evaluation.

- *Evolution:*   Repeat parts of the preceding steps during the lifetime of the product, to fix or improve the system. For example, automobiles may be recalled to replace parts that have been found to fail. It is necessary to track usage of components through configuration control, to make such changes possible in the field.

Figure 2.5 shows the steps graphically as boxes, with arrows to represent the most common sequencing of the steps.

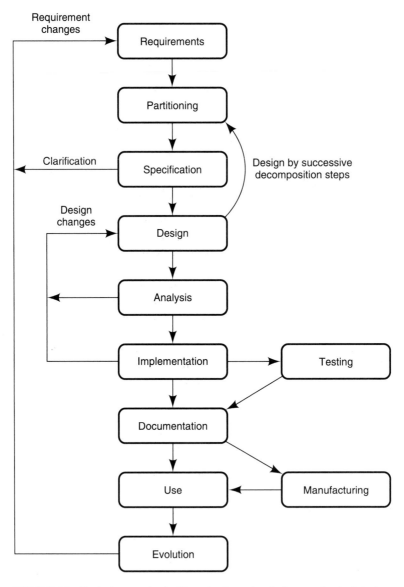

FIGURE 2.5 Typical stages in the lifecycle of an electrical or mechanical design. Note the similarity to the software-design lifecycle shown in Figure 2.1.

As with software engineering, the design process often defies definition—it is more of an art than a science. Almost no design follows the steps in strict sequence. It may even be necessary to return to the first step to modify requirements, if they are found to be impossible or ambiguous. To avoid starting over when returning to an earlier step, designers must propagate changes selectively through the later steps. DBMS facilities to track this change propagation would greatly simplify design applications, and the object-oriented paradigm is again important.

2.3.3   Design Tools

For both electrical and mechanical design, there are three general kinds of design tools:

1. *Design synthesis:*   There are tools to derive part of a design automatically from a higher-level description of the requirements or specifications. In the extreme case—for example, a "silicon compiler" that could derive an integrated-circuit mask from a procedural description of the chip behavior—design-automation tools could completely eliminate most of the steps listed in the previous section. The technology has not yet reached this point, and may never do so, but much of the design (for example, partial placement and routing of components in ECAD), can be performed automatically.

2. *Design entry:*   There are tools to edit or create a design—for example, a circuit layout or a drawing of a building. These tools are also used for browsing or searching through a design. These drawing and viewing tools are the ones people often mean when they refer to CAD.

3. *Design analysis:*   There are CAE analysis tools used to evaluate a design. ECAD examples are a circuit simulator and a design-rule checker. MCAD examples are a structural-stress analysis and weight estimation.

All these tools have a database system embedded inside them, typically a vendor-written data manager that is not accessible to the user. The end user must often deal with design tools from a variety of different vendors, all with incompatible data representations. This is a major problem today, although standardization projects are underway [PDES 1990, CFI 1990, EDIF 1990]. A common database interface is needed, with much more powerful capabilities than those offered by the simpler database facilities used in the past.

So that we can gain a deeper understanding of the design applications, let us examine ECAD and MCAD tools in more detail.

2.3.4   Electronic Design Applications

Electronic design tools are concerned with the development of integrated circuits, printed circuit boards, or complete electronic systems. As our example, we shall look at integrated circuit design, which is probably the most complex of the three.

There are many levels of design representation used in electronic circuit design:

1. *High-level–language description of circuit behavior.* Examples are register-transfer-level description languages, data-flow diagrams, and algebraic circuit-description languages.

2. *Block-level diagram.* This diagram shows an overall breakdown of the major components of a design. The components might be the memory, processor, arithmetic, and I/O subsystems. This block diagram will typically be carried all the way down to individual functions, such as instruction decoder, memory-addressing logic, and adders. Figure 2.6a shows an example of a block-level diagram. The block diagram is a logical rather than physical description of the circuit, although the designer may already have a rough physical breakdown of the surface areas to be apportioned to each subsystem at this point.

3. *Logic diagram.* This diagram shows the logical gates, inverters, and memory flip-flops that implement the block diagram functions. Figure 2.6b shows an example logic diagram.

4. *Circuit diagram.* Figure 2.6c is such a diagram, showing transistors, resistors, and capacitors, but no physical layout.

5. *Specialized sublevels.* These are used for electrical (capacitance, impedance) models, timing analysis, and a semiphysical "stick diagram" representation showing general circuit layout without exact dimensions.

6. *Integrated circuit mask.* This mask is processed to use in the actual production of the chip, as shown in Figure 2.7.

The integrated-circuit designers typically use all these representations of a design before reaching the physical circuit. Sometimes, additional intermediate notations may be important.

As we noted earlier, there may be multiple designers involved on different parts of the chip, and they all will go through several iterations of their designs, requiring propagation of changes through the other representations.

Altogether, there is a significant database component to the design problem, which involves tracking the many different representations and knowing "what, when, why, how, which, and who" for each design component.

The size of an ECAD database may be relatively large, perhaps including millions of transistors and logical gates. However, there is typically a much smaller library of unique components from which the database is built. At the stick-diagram level, for example, every NAND gate may have been chosen from just three different physical NAND gate layouts. Also, there is significant repetition natural in most circuits; for example, 32 1-bit adder cells might be connected together, or thousands of 1-bit memory cells might be identical except for addressing logic.

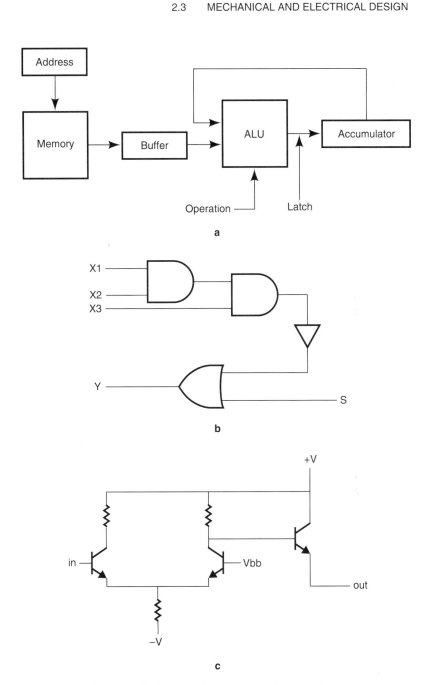

FIGURE 2.6   An electronic design is viewed at many levels of abstraction. **(a)** High-level block diagram. **(b)** Logic diagram, representing a small part of the block diagram. **(c)** Bipolar circuit diagram for inverter gate used in logic diagram.

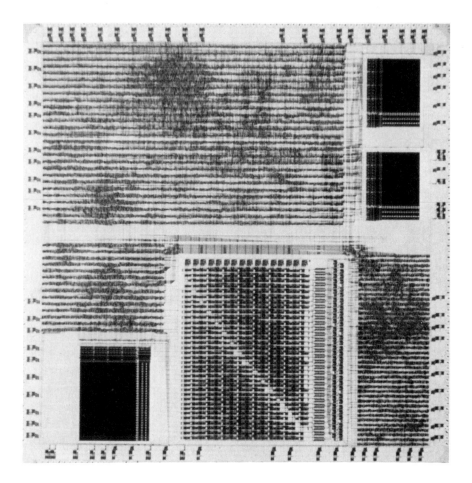

FIGURE 2.7   An integrated circuit with about 200,000 transistors. Courtesy of LSI Logic Corporation.

Parts of the design process may be automated. In some cases, the design automation may translate automatically between the representation levels. Examples of design automation are these:

- Automatic derivation of a circuit logic diagram from a higher-level register-transfer description (generating level 3 from level 1 or 2 in the preceding list)
- Automatic layout generation from the circuit diagram (generating level 6 from level 4)
- Automatic optimization of a circuit layout (generating a new diagram at level 3 or 4)

Substantial energy has gone into design automation, as illustrated by the number of papers on the topic in the *Design Automation Conference Proceedings* and other sources (see bibliography). Despite these efforts, there will still be a significant manual component to ECAD design for the foreseeable future; we still have work to do before we can automate the entire design process. Indeed, the most important ECAD tools are currently those for editing and analyzing designs.

Graphical editors for logical and physical circuit layout (levels 3 through 5) are among the most widely used ECAD tools. In addition to simple drawing capabilities, these editors may have built-in "smarts" about circuits for the convenience of the designer, such as design-rule checks.

There is also an array of analysis and synthesis tools for ECAD:

- Simulation tools—for example, for the circuit-diagram level 4—to check for proper behavior
- Electrical noise and thermal analysis at level 5
- Design-rule checking at level 6, to find errors made in circuit mask layout
- Programs to produce an improved physical layout at level 5 or 6 by rearranging components

The most stringent ECAD database performance constraints arise from these analysis and synthesis tools. For example, circuit simulation must be extremely fast to produce useful results: Software is orders of magnitude slower than are the actual circuits, even in the best of circumstances. Even with the fastest conceivable database to store circuit layouts, it may be necessary to download and compile the portion of the circuit being simulated into specialized data structures and procedures for the circuit.

Figure 2.8 shows a schema for an electronic circuit diagram, including its graphical layout. Simple electrical components are grouped together as `Cells`, the circuit building blocks, and `Net-lists` are used to electrically connect the cell terminals, called `Ports`. The abilities to nest subcells to create more complex cells, and to include a cell as a subcell by reference rather than by copying, are important features. Subtyping is also important. For example, we see that the simplest cell type, a `Simple-component`, might be a `Transistor`, a `Resistor`, or a `Capacitor`; depending on its type, it may require different attributes to describe it.

In a complete ECAD design database, the schema would have to include all levels of the design, not just circuits, and to show correspondences between the levels (for example, which portions of the circuit level correspond to a particular logic-level gate). See [McLeod et al 1983, Stonebraker and Guttman 1982, Harrison et al 1990, Ketabchi and Berzins 1987] for more detail.

2.3.5   Mechanical Design Applications

Mechanical CAD and CAE are concerned with the design of physical parts and structures, machined and constructed from a variety of materials. Mechanical design is performed by architects, civil engineers, the automobile industry, the aerospace industry, even interior designers. Figure 2.9 shows an example of a mechanical design.

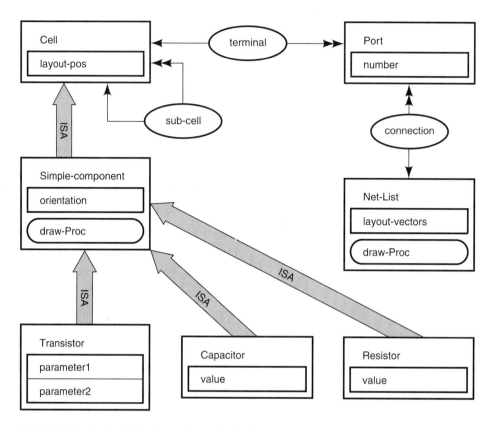

FIGURE 2.8 A simplified schema for a circuit diagram consisting of cells that may be Simple-component cells (transistors, capacitors, resistors) or compound cells built from simpler cells or components. Cell terminals (Ports) that are electrically connected are indicated by their being associated with a Net-list. Layout information to draw components and connections is stored, as is electrical information.

Figure 2.10 illustrates the tools and phases for mechanical design. Drafting tools are used to draw the design. A solids-modeling notation may also be needed, if the drafting tools do not generate such a description automatically. CAE analysis tools are then used to check the consistency of the design—structurally, whether the design will stand up to the vibration or stresses to which it will be exposed; thermally, whether the design dissipates heat properly; hydrodynamically, whether the design satisfies the specifications for fluid flow; and electromagnetically, whether the design will operate properly with internal or external interference. Finally, the design must be fabricated. For this, there are a variety of automated tools available, using numerically controlled (NC) machining equipment, or industrial robots. Or, the design drafts may be used directly, in the case of a contractor or prototype.

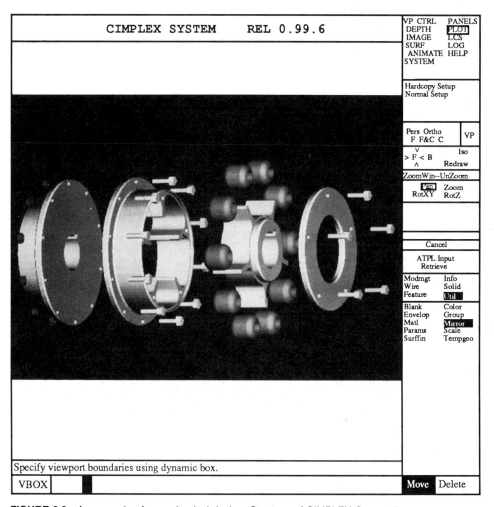

FIGURE 2.9   An example of a mechanical design. Courtesy of CIMPLEX Corporation.

Mechanical CAD tools have become widely available in the form of graphical design editing programs, such as AutoCAD [Merikel 1987].

Some important features to make large designs manageable in CAD drawing tools are the ability to "layer" designs to deal with one portion at a time, and to zoom and pan features to get around quickly in a design. The better available CAD drawing tools do provide these capabilities to some extent. However, they do not deal with the rest of the design process as described in Figure 2.10. Even the more powerful mechanical design tools on computer workstations go only part way in this process.

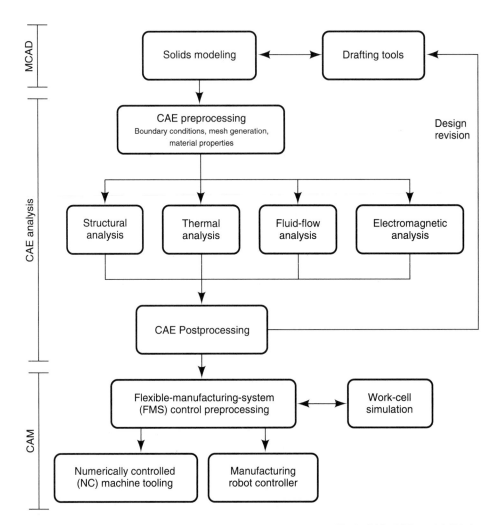

FIGURE 2.10   Three stages of computer-integrated manufacturing (CIM): CAD, CAE, and CAM. An interface to the materials planning (MRP) process is also needed.

Two other important features of CAD tools are:

1. *True three-dimensional solids modeling.*   Many drawing tools and representations provide only two or 2.5 dimensions (multiple two-dimensional layers). A three-dimensional representation is necessary to communicate the design unambiguously between engineers, and to run CAE tools to examine and evaluate a design.

2. *Data interchange between tools.*   The same standards projects we mentioned in our discussion of ECAD promise to solve data interchange through a common design representation. Today, drafting tools may not be three-dimensional, or

may not provide a freely translatable notation to other tools, so we must redundantly define the design in a solids-modeling notation. The mechanical-analysis tools typically require yet another notation—one that must be recreated every time the design is changed. The NC machine input or robot-control language also must be recreated.

2.4 DOCUMENTS AND OFFICE APPLICATIONS

Our third major application area is the design, use, and manipulation of *documents*, principally in office-automation applications. We define "document" loosely, to include traditional text documents, hypertext, graphics, office forms, memos, electronic mail, and any other computer-representable aggregate of data used for communication between people.

There are two fundamentally different kinds of document databases:

- *Intradocument databases:* Applications where a document itself is decomposed in the database; examples are editors and browsers of various kinds, such as a text editor, graphics editor, or hypertext system

- *Interdocument databases:* Applications where the bodies of documents are stored as single units, and a database is used to store information about the documents; examples are electronic mail and bulletin boards, and office automation, such as automatic routing of forms

We cover intradocument databases in Section 2.4.1; we cover interdocument databases in Section 2.4.2.

2.4.1 Document Browsers and Editors

Consider some ways in which document technology has become more sophisticated and complex in the past decade through the use of computers:

- Documents may be shared among many users. Shared documents such as electronic bulletin boards, electronic mail, and shared notes [Stefik et al 1987, Grief 1988] provide a medium for communication among members of a project or computer community.

- Graphics documents (that is, documents that are drawings) incorporate many complex relationships among, and attributes of, objects in the drawing.

- Documents may incorporate hypertext [Conklin 1986], allowing a user to jump around in a multidimensional text space. Hypertext links allow a phrase in a document to be selected to locate a cross-reference instantaneously, or to be expanded as a subdocument.

- Documents may include "hot links" for dynamic data interconnection to other documents or applications. Changes in one document (for example, a spreadsheet) may be propagated automatically to another (for example, a graph).

Two or more of these capabilities may be combined; for example, a shared hypertext document may also include graphics. As the data structures for documents become more complex, and particularly when they may be shared by multiple users on a network, object data management becomes more important. As we shall discuss in the next section, DBMSs have already been used for storing and indexing the entire documents—for example, in office and library automation. As the granularity of storage and access becomes smaller, it makes sense to store parts of the documents themselves in a database.

The data schema in Figure 2.11 illustrates objects that might be stored in a document database containing a mixture of graphics, text, and hypertext. The

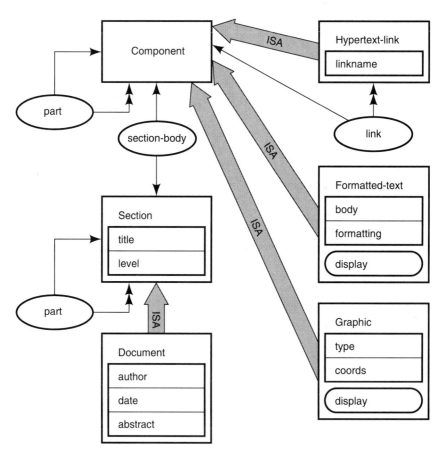

FIGURE 2.11 Simple schema for a text-management system with hypertext, regular formatted text, and graphics, and a hierarchy of document sections (chapters, sections, subsections).

basic `Component` of a document may be a `Hypertext-link`, plain `Format-ted-text`, or a `Graphic` element. Hypertext connects a `Component` to another component using the `link` relationship, and the formatted text and graphic components contain the necessary attributes to display themselves. A `Component` may also be used simply to group together simpler components using the `part` relationship, or may be the `section-body` of a `Section`, which may in turn be nested as subsections, sections, chapters, and other levels using a `part` relationship. A `Document` in this schema is simply a topmost-level `Section`, with additional attributes (`author`, `date`, and `abstract`).

2.4.2   Office Automation

Interdocument applications generally fall under the label of office automation or library systems. These applications are concerned with routing, processing, and finding documents. [Bracchi and Pernici 1983, Tsichritzis et al 1985, Ahlsen et al 1984, Ellis and Bernal 1982, Dayal et al 1990] discuss some of these applications and the associated data.

As an example, consider the handling of electronic mail, where mail messages are the objects in the database. In addition to the body of a message, these objects have a number of attributes: a sender, recipient, subject, date, and so on. The operations we can perform on a message might include sending, deleting, and categorizing with keywords. For an example of a schema and operations for such a database, see [Kent et al 1988].

Similar examples are an electronic bulletin board, or electronic forms routed between offices for action. All these applications involve data objects that are routed between users as a form of communication, and are filed for later reference. The objects may be archived, deleted, routed, categorized, or searched. It may be necessary to associate special procedures with objects—for example, to validate an electronic signature on a form.

In some cases, using a database for office-automation applications can obviate the need for explicit communication mechanisms. For example, if an electronic-mail database is located on a server, a message can be sent from one user to another, at least at the local site, by simply updating the database to associate a new owner with the message. The message need not be copied to be sent to multiple recipients; they can all be given references to the same copy of the message, as long as deletion simply severs a user's link to the message, rather than removing the message from the database.

A somewhat different example would be a library information-retrieval system, with a large database of abstracts of documents indexed by keyword. Traditionally, this type of database has been handled not by DBMSs, but rather by specialized text-retrieval systems. However, object data management technology can be applied to such a database with some benefit, particularly if it is desirable to custom-tailor the database or to associate procedures with the data.

2.5   OTHER APPLICATIONS

In addition to the design applications we have considered in the previous three sections, there is a variety of other applications that are poorly satisfied by traditional database systems. These applications are also potential clients of an ODMS:

- *Scientific and medical:*   Many disciplines (chemistry, physics, biology, medicine) encounter data sufficiently complex to benefit from object data management.

- *Expert systems:*   The rules and data in AI applications can become numerous enough to require the facilities of a database system.

- *System services:*   Operating systems, window systems, and network managers are being extended to incorporate successively more complex data services.

- *Manufacturing and real-time:*   Applications that monitor and control processes must access shared status and process information to do so, and may benefit from the higher performance of new ODMSs.

- *More complex business applications:*   Many new and existing business applications can benefit from object data management capabilities to deal with text, hierarchies of types, and other functionality.

In this section, we consider these applications in more detail.

2.5.1   Scientific and Medical Applications

A variety of scientific, medical, and closely related applications could benefit from object data management:

- *Chemistry:*   Particularly in organic chemistry, object data management could be useful in the representation and manipulation of complex molecules.

- *Genetics:*   The same is true of the representation of DNA: the information, particularly when there is a need to query and maintain multiple alternatives, is too complex to store in traditional databases.

- *Chromatography:*   Databases of chromatography patterns can be very large and require efficient indexing to match to samples.

- *Cartography:*   Maps contain data with complex structure, requiring flexible data structures.

These applications all have the property that they are not satisfied by traditional database systems, but have data sufficiently complex that significant effort is required to implement a data repository from basic programming-language data structures. Programming-language structures are inadequate because many megabytes of data must be managed, with indexes and query-processing facilities. Relational database systems are inadequate because the applications store ordered data in addition to sets, require new access methods for spatial data, and have high performance demands for single-user access.

2.5.2   Expert Systems

Many of the features that have recently been incorporated into database systems originated in AI for knowledge representation: objects, type hierarchies, procedures, and so on. However, knowledge-representation systems generally have not provided database capabilities to store a large quantity of data, to perform fast associative queries, and to allow concurrent access under multiple processes.

There may be uses for object data management in AI, for expert-systems databases (rule bases, world descriptions, and natural-language syntax and semantics) that are persistent and become too large to store in main memory, that require concurrent access to shared "blackboards" for interaction, or that require efficient query processing to find rules or objects that satisfy given conditions. In such cases, the capabilities of an object data management system to deal efficiently with a large store of persistent data, without all of the overhead of traditional DBMSs for database access, may be very useful.

2.5.3   System Service Applications

Consider some examples of system service applications:

- *Application management:*   Object-oriented window systems, office information systems, and operating systems have been extended to serve as information repositories and coordinators between integrated applications. [Tsichritzis 1985, OMG 1990] provide examples of use of the object-oriented paradigm to coordinate applications in this way. Object data management can be useful in such systems to provide basic properties such as object persistence, methods, and concurrency control.

- *Electronic mail:*   Given a recipient name on a network, it is necessary to determine the destination computer for data packets or electronic mail, and the best path to get there through various alternative means. Also, a database with the right properties could be used to store rather than copy electronic mail to its destination.

- *Network management:*   On a network of heterogeneous computers, authentication and authorization of users to access particular data and programs is more complex than are traditional password lookups in a file. Also, to tailor application parameters, some operating systems provide a database of values that can be queried at run time.

System services are typically not satisfied by traditional DBMS technology because use of DBMSs is "overkill" for the problem. The memory requirements and performance for these applications are critical. There is both space and time overhead for DBMS features that are *not* required for system service applications such as transaction processing and forms and schema management tools.

Without database systems, system service applications must provide their own implementations of persistent data, crash recovery, indexing, locking, simple queries, and other database facilities. Remote data access and distributed database capability are also needed in some of these applications.

2.5.4   Manufacturing and Real-Time Applications

Consider some examples of manufacturing and real-time applications:

- *Assembly-line control:*   A single computer or network of computers may be dedicated to monitoring and controlling a manufacturing floor. The system must keep information about the location and status of assemblies on the floor, control automatic test equipment, and upload and download information from traditional commercial databases maintaining customer orders.

- *Chemical-process control:*   A computer may control a chemical plant or experiment, monitoring sensors such as pressure and temperature, and controlling valves and heating and cooling elements. Such a system requires a database to maintain current status and historical values for pertinent measurements, and actions to take under specified circumstances.

Although outwardly quite different from the system service applications we discussed in the previous section, real-time control applications have similar database requirements—performance constraints are not satisfied by traditional DBMSs, and simple data management capabilities are required.

Computer-aided manufacturing (CAM) has real-time aspects in the assembly-line control just mentioned, complex data structures transferred from CAD systems we discussed in Section 2.3, and traditional business application requirements in conjunction with corporate database systems. CAM is thus difficult to categorize as well as to implement. However, it is also a potential application of object data management.

2.5.5   New Business Applications

Object data management will find use in business applications, even though traditional database systems have captured this market up to now.

Note that "business applications" encompasses a wide variety of databases. There are on-line transaction-processing applications, such as airline reservation systems or automatic-teller machines, and decision-support applications, such as customer accounts queries or marketing analyses. The need for object data management increases as a wider variety of business applications are addressed.

For example, an application database of students and employees would be simplified by the introduction of a "person" supertype to store information common to both. Airline reservation systems might benefit from the ability to store and modify spatial data, such as seat-assignment diagrams. A customer order-entry application could benefit by the introduction of procedures or rules in the database to enforce integrity constraints or to trigger further processing automatically.

2.6   CONCLUSIONS

In this chapter, we have studied a number of applications not adequately addressed by traditional DBMSs. To avoid repetition, we have deferred most of the discussion of database requirements to this last section, where we summarize needs for object data management.

We shall also examine application requirements that *are* satisfied by traditional DBMSs. This examination will point out features we must not give up in the move to ODMSs. We complete the section with suggestions for determining your own application needs, and a summary of what we have learned in the chapter.

Readers with little background in database systems may have difficulty understanding this section, because we refer forward to database features described in the next two chapters. Use the index to find sections describing terms with which you are not familiar.

2.6.1   Object Data Management Needs

We can identify a number of requirements for ODMSs in the applications we have covered:

- *Unique object identifiers:*   The ability to generate automatically identifiers for objects represented in the database is important in essentially all the engineering and design applications, because they represent objects that have no human-meaningful identifiers, or objects whose identifiers (part numbers, module names) may change. Object identifiers may also be useful in business applications.

- *Composite objects:*   Most design applications require the ability to define objects that contain other objects, such that all the subcomponents and their subcomponents act as a single object for the purposes of database operations. Composite objects may also be useful in other applications.

- *References and integrity:*   It is universally important to be able to reference one object from another (relationships), and to have the DBMS automatically maintain the integrity of these references. Referential integrity is represented by the small arrows between boxes in our schema notation. We shall discuss further the requirements of referential integrity in Chapters 3 and 4. Although referential integrity can be useful in a variety of applications, references are generally more important in our applications than in business applications, and have not been implemented efficiently in traditional database systems.

- *Object-type hierarchy:*   The ability to define new object types that have all of the attributes of an existing type, plus some additional data or behavior, is useful in almost any application with a complex schema. In our schema notation, these subtype relationships are represented by the wide ISA arrows.

- *Associated procedures:*   The ability to store procedures as well as data in a database is important in most of our applications. In current business applications, procedural information is encoded in application programs and database language statements.

- *Object encapsulation:*   Because of the importance of reusability, interoperability, and modularization in most applications, the ability to use procedures associated with object types to encapsulate data structure is very important. Although an object-oriented application programming language may provide encapsulation, the DBMS must provide support for this capability as well.

- *Ordered sets and references:*   Nearly all the applications we have discussed require the ability to place an ordering on relationships for an object, and to have object attributes that are lists rather than simple sets. It is difficult to represent ordered sets in relational databases.

- *Large data blocks:*   Large data items, such as images or text stored as attributes of an object, are now recognized as useful in almost all application areas; some traditional database systems have already been augmented to include this feature.

- *Efficient remote database access:*   Transparent access to databases stored on other machines on the network is the rule rather than the exception in most engineering and design applications built on workstations, and is becoming more common in business applications. Although traditional DBMSs generally provide remote access, this feature usually is not efficient for design applications that "check out" data for a long period, as we shall see in Chapter 5.

- *Ease of schema changes:*   In nearly all applications, it is important to be able to modify a schema with minimum impact on existing applications. This can be even more important in design applications, because the user as well as the application programmer may modify the schema (for example, to define new types of design components or design constraints). Current DBMSs do not provide good facilities to migrate data to new schemas.

- *Programming language interface:*   The integration of the DBMS data manipulation language with the user's programming language is useful in most of our applications. Traditional DBMSs use a different language for the database and for programming, and the former must be interleaved and compiled into a program to transfer data between program variables and the database.

- *Multiple database versions:*   The ability to maintain more than one version of individual objects or an entire database is very important in design applications, because earlier versions must be kept to maintain previous releases or to coordinate and merge parallel subprojects. It is generally less important in business applications, although a user–time audit trail of updates might find wide use.

- *Long-term lock and checkout:*   The ability to lock a large group of data, such as a composite object or an entire design, is important in many of our applications. For example, existing data may be made read-only, creating new versions whenever updates are performed.

- *Single-user performance:*   The speed of a DBMS when one user has locked out all other writes on the portion of the database being used is generally most important in our design and engineering applications, because there is little concurrent access at a fine grain. In contrast, business applications with on-line transaction processing require high multiuser throughput with fine-grain locks.

2.6.2   Traditional Database Needs

Most of the applications we examined also have some requirements for traditional database features:

- *Large, persistent record storage:*   The ability to store a large volume of structured data that persists between program executions is important to all of the applications we have discussed.

- *Query language:*   A simple query language that allows the user to phrase on-the-spot queries to examine the database is of less importance in some of our applications, but is still useful—for example, to inquire about a database of documents or programs. Compatibility with the standard relational query language, SQL [X3H2 1984], may be less important than in business applications, but is still a factor, especially for access to existing databases.

- *Application forms package:*   Most commercial DBMSs provide facilities for designing screen layouts and defining the layouts' correspondence to database fields. These facilities are generally of less importance to our applications, particularly those with graphical displays too complex to be described in simple forms languages. However, new, more flexible application user-interface systems are being developed that may find greater demand.

- *Distributed databases:*   Distributed capability, in which multiple databases on one or more machines appear as a single database, is useful in a wide variety of applications. Even in document databases, where each document could easily be a separate database, there may be references (hypertext or otherwise) between documents on different machines.

- *Trigger execution:* Many applications require procedures to be executed when a defined condition becomes true of the data. For example, a special procedure might be executed in a real-time application to open a valve when pressure reaches a certain level. Triggers are important in real-time, office-automation, and some design applications.

- *Concurrency at fine grain:* Traditional business applications have required the ability to lock small units of the database to limit access by other users. In design applications, users typically check out a large portion of data for a long period, and cannot afford the performance overhead of locking individual components for every read or write operation. However, frequently accessed data ("hot spots"), such as shared component libraries in a design application, may still require fine-grain locking for update.

- *Crash recovery:* The ability to bring a database back to a consistent state automatically when software or hardware errors cause a system to crash is obviously desirable in any application. In a few cases, the overhead may not be worth the benefit. In some cases—for example, in design applications—it may be possible to revert to an earlier version or database instead (current design tools do this).

- *Data independence:* In essentially all our applications, it is desirable to be able to change the data stored in a database without modifying existing applica-tion programs. In relational databases, this data independence is provided to some extent by views. In object-oriented databases, this capability is provided by procedures that are the only externally visible attributes of objects. We shall discuss these mechanisms later in Chapter 4.

We see that most of the features of traditional DBMSs are important, although some to a lesser extent, in applications of ODMSs. Thus, it is important that ODMSs not drop these capabilities at the expense of the new features. Only a few features of traditional DBMSs are much less important to our applications (protection, and transaction throughput for large numbers of users).

2.6.3 Evaluation of Application Needs

In this chapter, we have discussed a number of applications, many of them relatively new ones that appeared with the advent of computer workstations and networking. Our purpose in this chapter has been twofold:

1. To review applications that may not be satisfied by traditional DBMS technology, to see potential requirements for object data management

2. To help you recognize your own application requirements, to determine which DBMS alternatives are best, as we cover different approaches in the remainder of the book

A number of requirements are common to the majority of applications in the chapter: object identifiers, object references, ordered sets, closer integration with the programming language, and longer-term version and concurrency-control mechanisms. These needs and others distinguish the applications we have discussed from traditional database applications.

Other DBMS features differ widely in importance: query languages, fine-grain concurrency, crash recovery, distributed databases, and application forms. Performance requirements may range from a speed satisfied by relational DBMSs to many times faster. Thus, you should study the needs of your own applications carefully before choosing a DBMS.

If you have in mind a particular application, you will find it useful to classify your needs according to the categories just discussed. However, you will need a deeper understanding of database technology to understand your tradeoffs and choices. In examining database technology in the next three chapters, we shall cover the database system features in more detail, and shall study different approaches to grouping these features in database systems.

Since the applications we have covered differ somewhat in their DBMS requirements, some are more likely to be first to convert to ODMS technology. Those applications most likely to benefit from new object data management technology can be identified by three properties:

1. They are not satisfied by traditional DBMS technology features or performance, and these shortcomings cannot be remedied easily in a layer on top of the DBMS.

2. Their database is large or complex enough to benefit from using a DBMS rather than files and programming languages.

3. Their performance constraints are not so stringent that the applications can be satisfied only by specially tailored code.

The most important examples of such applications we have presented are probably CAD databases used to coordinate design versions and subcomponents among multiple engineers on a project, CASE databases for configuration management and coordination among programmers, office-automation databases used to communicate among users in a company, and complex scientific and system service applications. On the other hand, there are certainly many prime applications of object data management that we have not even considered in this chapter; our list has not been exhaustive.

3

Traditional Database Systems

3.1 INTRODUCTION

This chapter is a review of traditional DBMS technology, covering both concepts and implementation. It is important that you be familiar with this technology, particularly with relational databases, to understand the DBMS advances that we discuss in the remainder of the book.

A full treatment of traditional database technology is beyond the scope of this book. However, the reader with some database background will find this chapter suitable as a review of concepts important to the more advanced DBMS work. The reader with no database background at all can use this chapter as an overview of database systems adequate for understanding the rest of this book, or can use it as a starting point to understand concepts in more detail through reading the supplemental materials referenced here. A good general reference would be an introductory database systems textbook such as [Date 1990, Elmasri and Navathe 1989, Frank 1988, Ullman 1987].

3.1.1   Chapter Overview

In the first few sections of this chapter, we focus on database concepts. This section introduces DBMS history and basic approaches. Section 3.2 covers database architecture and terminology. Sections 3.3 and 3.4 focus on the relational data model and query language. In the following four sections, we cover DBMS implementation: Sections 3.5 and 3.6 cover storing and indexing records, Section 3.7 covers query processing, and Section 3.8 covers concurrency and recovery issues. In the final sections, we cover miscellaneous topics and summarize progress on relational database technology.

3.1.2   Need for Database Systems

It is important to remember that database systems are designed for one purpose: to simplify the development of data-intensive applications. In the best cases, DBMSs can eliminate development altogether, by providing enough functionality that the end user can use the tools immediately to enter, examine, and process application data.

Generally speaking, the more functionality implemented in a DBMS, the less code needed to implement applications. This generalization is not universal, of course: Functionality that is not needed by an application can reduce system performance unnecessarily, and also can make the DBMS more difficult to understand. It is thus important to consider what functionality is needed by the target class of applications, and how best to implement and present the functionality to the application programmer.

3.1.3   Historical Perspective

Database technology evolved in products for business applications, probably because these applications have large development investment and deal with a large quantity of data.

The earliest development was indexed files. These files provided a simple way to store records on disk with fast lookup according to the values stored in them. The advanced indexed file systems provided the most basic features of modern DBMSs:

1. Fixed-length records with data fields of various types
2. The ability to store the records in a disk file, to deal with more data than fit in memory, and to provide a persistent storage medium for them.
3. Indexes, including hash indexes and more recently B-trees, to locate quickly records satisfying constraints on field values
4. File and record locking, to control concurrent access

In the 1970s, the first complete DBMSs evolved, using the *hierarchical* and *network* models of data, providing the preceding features plus several more capabilities:

5. Record identifiers or addresses, and link fields used to connect records together for fast direct access, the links being used to create hierarchical or network structures of records

6. Multiple indexed files that could be open simultaneously, treated as a single database with the link interconnections

7. Protection constraints, to limit record access to authorized people or programs

8. Transactions, to provide automatic crash recovery, deadlock detection, and database consistency with multiple users

In the 1980s, relational DBMSs were developed and achieved commercial product status, providing additional features:

9. A high-level query language with operations to define as well as manipulate data, along with high-level tools for forms and application generation

10. Data independence, which is the ability to change the way that data are physically or logically stored without changing application programs

The greatest contribution of the relational model was that it was much simpler to understand than were earlier systems of equal or less power. This simplicity was primarily a result of just a few concepts: relations, query languages, and transactions. These capabilities freed the user from dealing with low-level details of physical data organization, recovery, and coordination among users. The relational model also provided a greater degree of data independence, and standardization of query language.

The 10 features we listed are the basic capabilities of all DBMSs. Some DBMSs provide more advanced capabilities, such as triggers and integrity constraints. Relational DBMSs have been applied successfully to a range of business and commercial applications, ranging from small-scale mailing lists on personal computers to large-scale on-line transaction-processing (OLTP) applications on mainframes. Relational technology continues to evolve to address more semantics of these applications.

3.1.4 Data Models

In this chapter, we shall focus on relational DBMSs, because they represent the state of the art in traditional DBMSs and they are most widely studied in the database literature. As we discussed, the relational model is based on *relations*—tables of rows and columns. A relational database consists of a set of tables, each table consists of a set of columns, and each column contains a particular type of data, such as integers or strings. The data schema is simply a set of table names, a set of column names for each table, and a data type for each column. The data in a particular relational database are simply the rows of the tables.

The preceding description oversimplifies relational DBMSs for illustrative purposes. Nevertheless, it illustrates the point that the relational model, schema, and data are quite straightforward—the relational model's best features are that it is simple and is consistent across many implementations. The advanced database systems discussed in subsequent chapters, including those based on extensions of the relational model, have a more complex data model, and are less consistent across implementations. Thus, the relational data model is a good place for us to start, and serves as a useful benchmark for comparison.

The nonrelational data models in common use today—namely, the *network* and *hierarchical* models—are not covered in this book; for a discussion of them, see [Date 1990, Tsichritzis & Lochovsky 1980]. To put the relational model in context, however, we shall consider these two other models briefly.

The *network* data model encodes the objects (boxes) in our schema notation as records stored on disk, like the relational model, but uses pointer structures to encode the relationships instead of data values. Numerous variations of a network model are possible—for example, in how many-to-many relationships are represented and used—but most systems use the standard CODASYL model [DBTG 1971].

The *hierarchical* data model is based on using a tree structure of records to represent the relationships in our schema diagram. IMS and System 2000 [Tsichritzis and Lochovsky 1976] were designed as hierarchical systems. The hierarchical model is generally more limited than is the network model because a particular relationship must be chosen as *the* parent–child link for each box in our diagram. For example, `Chapter` records may be nested inside `Document` records to show the `contains` relationship of Figure 1.1 in Chapter 1, but other independent relationships on the same objects, or many-to-many relationships such as `author` in Figure 1.2, must be encoded separately from the hierarchy.

3.2 DATABASE CONCEPTS

We start with definitions of basic database concepts, such as physical and logical data independence.

3.2.1 Three-Level Architecture

The data in a DBMS are traditionally viewed at three levels:

1. *Internal:* The organization of data on the physical storage medium, including the ordering and encoding of field values, the ordering and size of records, and available access methods (links, indexes)

2. *Conceptual:* The data-modeling level, including the types of records and fields and their interrelationships

3. *External:* The data interpretation imparted by an application, or by a group of application programs; this may include additional constraints on data and their meaning

These three levels are commonly referred to as the *three-level architecture* for database systems [Tsichritzis and Klug 1978]. We shall refer to internal, conceptual, and external levels and schemas throughout the book. In some of the literature, the term "physical" may be used to refer to the internal level, and "logical" may be used to refer to both the conceptual and external levels.

Database design—the process of planning and creating schemas for databases—ideally goes top-down through these levels; that is, it goes from external to conceptual, and then to internal designs [Ullman 1987]. A variety of design tools, both research prototypes and products, has been produced to assist in this process. We shall cover relational database design further in Section 3.3.

3.2.2   Data Independence

An important property of relational DBMSs is data independence, allowing changes in data organization without modifying application programs. Data independence is important at both the internal and conceptual levels:

- *Physical data independence* is the ability to change the internal organization of data, such as indexes or record layout, without changing applications. In the three-level architecture just mentioned, physical data independence is independence of the internal and conceptual levels.

- *Logical data independence* is the ability to change data schema—for example, adding relations or attributes—without modifying applications. In the three-level architecture, it is independence of the conceptual and external levels.

The internal or conceptual database schema may be modified for many reasons. New information may be necessary as a result of a change in policy, or a new application. Information may be restructured or removed, to make it simpler to deal with or more efficient to store. When many programmers are involved, schema changes may be made somewhere in a database every week, or every day. Frequent schema changes pose significant overhead if all database applications must be modified every time a change is made. As we shall see, data independence is an important advantage of relational DBMSs.

3.2.3   Database Administrator, Programmer, and End User

Commercial business-database shops usually face an organizational problem in administering the internal and conceptual, and sometimes the external, levels of a shared database, because application programmers must coordinate schema changes that affect others.

This problem is typically solved by the assignment of a *database administrator,* a person responsible for maintaining the internal and conceptual database schemas. The database administrator must coordinate updates to the conceptual data schema that affect users and programmers, and must try to strike the best compromise in the physical data organization to produce the best performance for the overall set of applications used.

Thus, there are really three kinds of users of a DBMS:

- *Administrator:* The database system administrator is responsible for the conceptual and internal levels of the architecture. This administrator defines the conceptual and internal data schema for all the applications that use a database.

- *Programmer:* The database application programmer is responsible for the external level of the architecture, defining the external schema and data-manipulation commands for specific applications. The programmer is the client of the administrator.

- *End-User:* The end users are the people who actually do something useful with the database, running application programs. They are the clients of the programmer, and they generally do not have programming or database expertise. However, more sophisticated end users may perform ad hoc operations on the database directly, using a high-level query language.

People often use the term "user" without specifying which of these categories they mean. It is important to distinguish these three kinds of users to understand the context of statements in this book. Except when referring to all users, therefore, we shall qualify the type of user with one of these three terms: DBMS administrator, programmer, or end user. In later chapters, we shall define a fourth category of user, the database *implementor* who defines the data model and access methods themselves. For now, we require only the three classifications.

For more coverage of the topics in this section, including the three-level architecture, data independence, data models, and database administration, see [Date 1990, Frank 1988, Tsichritzis & Lochovsky 1980, Ullman 1988, Wiederhold 1977].

3.3 RELATIONAL DATABASES

In this section, we study the relational model in more detail.

3.3.1 Tables

To understand the relational model, we shall represent the document application we examined in Figure 1.1 as relational tables. We shall use the document example again in examining other data models, so our exercise will be useful for comparison purposes.

We will need two tables (relations) for our relational data schema, one for each kind of object in our application — documents and chapters. Figure 3.1 illustrates these tables.

DOCUMENT TABLE

DocID	Title	Revision
5345	Relational Databases	1984
6099	Data Models	1972
2533	Object Data Management	1990
...	...	...

CHAPTER TABLE

Number	Title	DocID
1	Introduction	2533
2	Applications	2533
...	...	...
1	Introduction	5345
2	Relations	5345
3	Query Language	5345
...	...	...
1	Overview	6099
...	...	...

FIGURE 3.1 Part of a relational database for our example schema in Chapter 1 (Figure 1.1).

The figure shows some rows in the tables, representing individual documents and chapters. The rows of tables are usually called *tuples* or *records* in a relational database.

The columns of the tables (also called attributes, or fields) are exactly the attributes from our schema diagram in Figure 1.1, except that there is an additional attribute in each table:

- We have added a **DocID** attribute for documents. This attribute must be assigned a unique value by the application program for each document

- We have added a `DocID` attribute to the chapters, to encode the **contains** relationship. This attribute indicates the document to which a chapter belongs.

Note that, instead of introducing `DocID`s, we could simply assume that the title of each document is unique in the database. Then, we could store the document title as an attribute of chapters, and check that document titles are unique when they are entered. Titles also would be more meaningful than document numbers to a person examining the database. However, this database design would not be good unless the application programmer wanted to constrain all document titles ever entered to be different. Also, this design requires more storage space, because titles are usually longer than numeric identifiers, and a title will be repeated in every **Chapter** for a **Document**. So, for our example, we use numeric `DocID`s generated by the application program.

3.3.2   Primary and Foreign Keys

The attributes that we added for documents and chapters serve an important purpose, central to all relational database systems.

The `DocID` attribute of the **Document** table is called a *primary key*. A primary key is an attribute or group of attributes whose value must be unique in every row of a table. Think of a primary key as a unique identifier for the real-world objects that the rows represent.

The `DocID` attribute of the **Chapter** table is a called a *foreign key*. A foreign key is an attribute or group of attributes in a table that take on values of the primary key of another table. That is, a foreign key is a reference to objects (the rows of another table).

The relational model does not permit duplicate rows in a relation; that is, no two tuples may be identical in every attribute. Therefore, *every* relation has a primary key by the strict definition: all the attributes of the relation. However, this degenerate form of primary key is generally not very useful; for the purposes of this book, we shall deal with only *simple primary keys,* which are primary keys that are human-meaningful identifiers, typically only one attribute or the concatenation of two.

Now, let's look at how simple primary keys are used to represent objects (that is, the boxes in our schema notation) and how foreign keys are used to represent relationships (that is, the ovals and arrows).

3.3.3   Entity and Relationship Tables

In most modern uses of the relational model, users distinguish between two kinds of tables. Tables with simple primary keys are called *entity tables*. Entity tables represent object types (boxes), each row represents one object of that type. The other tables are called *relationship tables*. Relationship tables are used to represent relationships between objects (the ovals and arrows), using foreign keys.

Not all relationships require relationship tables. Binary relationships that are one-to-one or many-to-one from an object may be represented by adding a foreign key attribute directly to an entity table, as we just did in the **Chapter** table to represent the many-to-one relationship to **Documents**. Even relationships of higher degree can be represented by adding attribute(s) to the entity table for the "many" attribute of the relationship, as long as there is only one many-valued role (attribute) of the relationship. For example, additional attributes could be added to the **Chapter** table even if the **contains** relationship had additional roles.

Relationship tables are necessary when a relationship has more than one "many" attribute. For example, the many-to-many **author** relationship between documents would be represented as shown in Figure 3.2. This relationship table has two attributes, both of them foreign keys: The first references a person, the second references a document. Documents are represented, using **DocIDs** as keys, in the **Document** table of Figure 3.1. People are represented, using names as keys (for simplicity, we assume that names are unique), in the **Person** table of Figure 3.2.

We need one row in the **author** relationship table for each unique author–document pair. For example, "John Doe" appears in two rows, since he is the

AUTHOR TABLE

Person	Document
John Doe	5345
Gregory Smith	6099
John Doe	6099
Susan Fraenkel	2533

PERSON TABLE

Name
John Doe
Humbert Engle
Susan Fraenkel
Karen Schuettler
Gregory Smith

REFERENCES TABLE

from	to	page
2533	6099	17
5345	6099	43
2533	5345	205
2533	5345	144

FIGURE 3.2   Unary, binary, and ternary relational database tables for Person objects, author relationships, and references relationships from the schema design in Figures 1.2 and 1.3.

author of two documents. Document ID 6099 (the book on Data Models) appears in two rows, since it has two authors.

The **author** table does *not* require a primary key, since individual "authorships" are not themselves referenced elsewhere in the database. That is, for our purposes they are not objects—they just connect objects.

Figure 3.2 also illustrates how we would represent the ternary **references** relationship in the relational model. Note that two of the attributes are foreign keys (**DocIDs**), and the other is a simple integer.

3.3.4   Domains and Referential Integrity

Referential integrity is a set of constraints on the foreign keys used in a database. A good relational DBMS checks for validity of these constraints: When a value is stored in a foreign key attribute, the DBMS makes sure that a record exists with that primary key in the referenced table. For example, a document must exist with the correct **DocID** when a chapter record is created for it. When a record is deleted in a table, records that still reference its primary key must be flagged as errors, or, in some systems, may be deleted or invalidated automatically (by assignment of null foreign keys).

As an example, suppose a document is deleted. So that referential integrity is preserved, we want the DBMS to delete all the document's chapters, and all references to the document from other documents. Note that this deletion process may cascade, deleting sections of chapters, paragraphs of sections, and so on.

In addition to primary and foreign keys, the relational model defines the concept of a *domain*. A domain is an attribute type—that is, a range of values that an attribute can take on. Simple primary and foreign keys have attribute types taken from an *entity* domain. The **DocID** attributes we invented would be defined on a **document-id** domain. Only valid document ids appear in these attributes. Other attributes have built-in types. The creation date for a document is defined on the built-in **DATE** domain.

Domains can be useful to check that operations on attributes make sense. For example, it does not make sense to compare document ids and revision dates, or dates and chapter numbers. However, most relational implementations do not implement domains, and a flexible implementation of domains can be very difficult, since domains may overlap. For more information on domains, see [Ullman 1987, Date 1990]; we do not discuss them further here.

3.3.5   Normalization

Much database research work, particular in the early 1980s, was performed on relational *normalization*. Normalization is concerned with the best conceptual representation of application data as relational tables; it can become quite complex with large schemas. The essence of normalization of relational database schemas is to break up larger tables into smaller tables when too much information is being represented in one table.

What does it mean for there to be "too much" information in a table? Essentially, it means that the representation can lead to confusion in database applications, because the same information is represented in more than one place, or the wrong information is associated together. For example, we could avoid the need for a **Document** table in our example by storing information about documents (titles and revision dates) in the chapters for the document. However, to change the title or revision date for a document, we would then need to change this datum in every single chapter record for the document. Moreover, if the document had no chapters yet, there would be no place to put the information. The redundant storage of document information would also result in a waste of space; however, normalization is generally performed to produce a logically more manageable schema, not to reduce space usage (in many cases, it will demand more).

A series of *normal forms* has been defined in the database literature to eliminate successively more sophisticated anomalies in relational database representation. First normal form, for example, requires "flat" tables; that is, only one value may be stored in each attribute. Our database schema would not be in first normal form if the list of chapters were stored as an attribute of a document; this would require a list-valued attribute. Second, third, and other normal forms are concerned with semantic dependencies between the actual data in tables. These normal forms may be useful for a database administrator designing a relational schema; for the purposes of this book, however, you will not need to understand these formalisms—a little common sense will do for the examples we shall use. Chapter 7 of [Ullman 1989] provides a good overview of database design and normalization.

3.3.6   Properties of Tables

The relational model derives much of its simplicity from three properties of relational tables:

- Tables are mathematical sets: duplicate rows are not allowed, and there is no ordering defined on the rows.

- Attributes have no order; they are always referenced by name, and attribute names must be unique within a table.

- Values stored in the rows and columns are atomic; that is, they are *not* sets or lists (if the tables are in first normal form, as required by essentially all relational products).

These properties are also limitations, as we shall see in Chapter 4. For example, it is difficult to represent efficiently objects that are naturally ordered in an array or list—such as chapters in a book or terminals on an integrated circuit—in relational tables. However, the three properties make it possible to define a simple query language on rows and columns of tables, as we shall see next.

3.4   QUERY LANGUAGES

The term "query language," as it is currently used, is actually a misnomer. A query language in a relational database is indeed used to query the database, but it is also used to modify data, and to examine and modify the data schema. To be more precise, some authors use the terms "data manipulation language" (DML) and "data definition language" (DDL). We shall also use these terms, but we shall stick with the more common term, "query language," to refer to the combination of DML and DDL capabilities.

3.4.1   Data Manipulation Language

Essentially all relational database systems provide some variant of the de facto industry standard query language, SQL [Date 1987, X3H2 1984]. Some provide another query language as well. Some include substantial nonstandard extensions to common SQL.

There are two most important features of a query language:

1. The language provides an English-like syntax that simplifies database access, so that end users and programmers have minimal new language to assimilate.

2. The language provides data independence, because high-level statements may be compiled automatically into low-level operations according to the structure of the data and indexes available. The user specifies what data are desired, but the DBMS can determine how to get them.

As an example, consider an SQL query to fetch recent documents from our example database:

```
SELECT TITLE, REVISION FROM DOCUMENT
WHERE REVISION>1985
```

To print titles of chapters of the book "War and Peace," a user might enter this query:

```
SELECT CHAPTER.TITLE FROM CHAPTER, DOCUMENT
WHERE CHAPTER.DOCID=DOCUMENT.DOCID
AND DOCUMENT.TITLE="WAR AND PEACE"
ORDER BY CHAPTER.NUMBER
```

A query language is not called *relational* unless it provides at least three basic operations: selection, projection, and join. *Selection* produces a subset of the rows of a table; the preceding queries do this by specifying constraints on dates and on document titles after the **WHERE** keyword. *Projection* produces a subset of the columns of a table; the preceding queries do this by specifying attribute names after the **SELECT** keyword. The *join* operation matches up records in two different tables that have equal or related values in specified attributes.* The preceding

---

* More precisely, an *equijoin* requires equal values in the joined attributes, and a *join* may specify any relationship between them, such as greater-or-equal.

query performs a simple join on the document identifier in the chapter and document tables. Note that the query language is *closed* under the operations of selection, projection, and join: The result of any one of these operations is another relation. This property is an important source of power and simplicity in the relational model.

A query language provides many advantages over programming-language calls made to access databases in indexed file systems or older DBMSs. End users may phrase ad hoc queries with relatively little training. When programming is necessary, query-language statements may be compiled interleaved with pro-gramming-language statements, to retrieve and operate on database records. This approach not only is easier for the users but also provides physical data independence. The query-language compiler automatically chooses the best way to execute a query; the presence or absence of an index or other access method is invisible to the user.

SQL is not without limitations, however. Although set-oriented selection, project, and join operations are relatively easy to understand for simple queries, end-users and programmers alike can find SQL clumsy and difficult to use for more complex operations involving several steps. In the next chapter, we shall discuss more powerful query languages, and alternatives to allow either program-ming-language or query-language access to data.

3.4.2   Data Definition Language

The query language also contains a data definition language (DDL) syntax used for defining the data schema. This is an example of a DDL statement:

```
CREATE TABLE DOCUMENT (
    DOCID INTEGER,
    TITLE CHAR(40),
    REVISION DATE )
```

The DDL is used to define other aspects of the internal and conceptual data schema: It specifies what indexes to create on table attributes (Section 3.6), relational views (Section 3.4.3) and so on. For the purposes of this book, however, it will not be necessary to study the syntax and semantics of the DDL further.

3.4.3   Relational Views

An important feature of relational query languages that deserves mention is relational *views*. A view is a relational table that is not stored directly; instead, it is defined in terms of a query language. For example, our first query in Section 3.4.1 could be used to define a view of the document table in which only recent titles and dates are "visible."

Relational views provide logical data independence. If the representation of a table or tables is changed, an application programmer can often define a view of the new table that matches the old table, so that existing programs will continue to work.

Relational views can be used for other purposes, as well. They can be used to define a subset of a table that particular users are authorized to read or update. The external (application) level of the three-level architecture can be defined entirely in terms of views. The concept of a view is powerful, especially in combination with a sophisticated query language.

The power of relational views, however, does not come for free. It is not always possible to perform updates on views as if they were ordinary tables, since the intent of the update may be incomplete or may be inconsistent with the view definition [Ullman 1989].

3.5   STORING RELATIONS

Up to now, we have discussed the conceptual level of the DBMS. In the next few sections, we shall examine the relational database implementation. This implementation technology will be important to our discussions in later chapters, because most of it is applicable to more advanced DBMSs with some extensions.

Figure 3.3 shows the levels of a relational DBMS implementation. The file-system level is concerned with managing blocks of storage on disk; this function-ality is often provided by the operating system. The storage-management level, which we cover in this section, is concerned with how records are stored in pages of disk files provided by the file system. Access methods, covered in Section 3.6, are concerned with index and link structures used to look up records. The uppermost level, query processing, is concerned with mapping user requests in the query language efficiently into calls to access methods. Query processing is covered in Section 3.7.

3.5.1   Records

The placement of records on the disk pages is very important to the performance of a DBMS because disk-access speed is often (almost invariably, for business applications) the limiting factor in DBMS performance, and pages are the unit of access to the disk.

Records in a relational table are typically stored sequentially on the disk, with fixed-sized fields (attributes) of each record stored one after another. Indeed, if all the fields are of fixed size (integers, reals, strings with a maximum length, and so on), then records can simply be stored using one disk file per table, at a location given by record number times record size. Early relational systems did just that.

Nowadays, fixed-size records and attributes are generally considered inad-equate; it is necessary to deal with records that can vary in size. Let's look at how that is done.

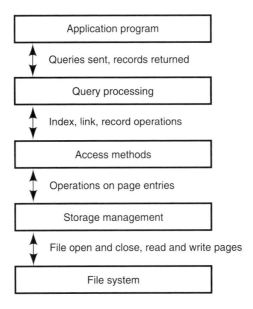

FIGURE 3.3 Levels of a DBMS implementation.
Not shown are type (schema) management and
transaction and lock management, which are part
of the level labeled "storage management" in this
diagram.

3.5.2   Pages and Record IDs

Most modern relational DBMSs store records on pages as done in System R
[Astrahan et al 1978], one of the first and most widely known relational implementations. In that implementation, shown in Figure 3.4, records are assigned
identifiers (IDs) that are neither purely physical addresses nor a purely logical
numbering. Instead, record IDs contain two parts:

1. The high-order bits of the record ID are the file segment and page number
    where the record is stored. Segments (contiguous pages of physical files) can
    be assigned to different portions of one or more files by a segment mapping
    table, but these high order bits provide a physical address, practically
    speaking, since the page containing a record can be fetched in a single disk
    access.

2. The low-order 4 to 8 bits of the record ID indicate the number of the record on
    the page. This record number is used to index into a *slot* array stored at the
    beginning of the page (or in any fixed location), where the actual address of
    the record on the page can be found.

This record ID technique has a number of advantages over other approaches:

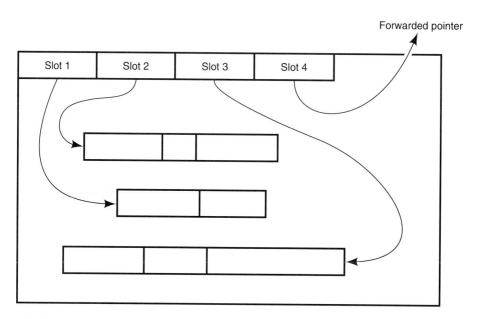

FIGURE 3.4 Representation of records of file pages. Records can be resized and moved on the page, because record identifiers consist of (page, slot) and the slot table can be updated to point to the new location, or can even be forwarded to another page if there is no more room.

- It is typically just as fast, in terms of disk accesses, to fetch a record as it is to use the full address (page and byte) of the record, but the former approach allows the record to change in size and to be moved, even to another page, because the slot entry can be modified to point to the new location. If it is necessary to move the record to another page, we do incur one extra page access until all references to the old record ID are fixed, but we never pay more than one extra access (because the original slot entry can always be reforwarded).

- It is usually faster than using a purely logical record ID, sometimes called a "surrogate," because surrogate identifiers require the overhead of an extra level of indirection. At best, a hash table can be created to map the surrogate IDs to physical locations, and the lookup may require one or more extra disk accesses.

3.5.3   Variable-Sized Attributes

Large variable-sized attributes (those that can exceed any reasonable maximum fixed-sized area allocated in a record) are difficult to handle efficiently, so relational DBMS implementations generally treat them as an exception. Perhaps the most common solution is as follows:

1. Allocate a fixed amount of space for the attribute in the record. Store the value in-line if it fits.

2. If the allocated space overflows, set a flag bit in the record with a pointer to a special kind of record where the value is stored.

3. Make cases 1 and 2 transparent to the user.

Many DBMSs currently require that large variable-sized attributes be declared of a type different from types for fixed-size attributes to give the DBMS the hint to use the technique described. (Thus, they lack physical data independence on this point).

3.6   ACCESS METHODS

Access methods are concerned with file organization techniques to allow quick lookup of records given desired attribute values or relationships with other records. We shall cover three main kinds of access methods: hash indexes, indexed sequential (B-tree) indexes, and links.

3.6.1   Hash Indexes

Hash indexes are used to find a record or records with a particular value for an attribute or group of attributes. They are most commonly used to find records by primary key.

Hash indexes are based on the idea of a hash *function*, a mathematical procedure to compute a value uniformly distributed in a range $[0...N]$ used to assign a disk address where the record is stored. The value is computed using simple arithmetic operations on the attribute value(s) that will be used to look up the record (for example, the primary key).

For example, a simple hash function on an integer attribute might use the low-order bits of the integer. For a small table, we might use 10 bits, giving $N=1023$. We would attempt to store each record at a location given by the record size times the hash-function value. If two or more records must be stored at the same location, the extras can be stored in successive available locations, or a list of records with the given hash value can be constructed.

There are numerous problems with hashing: it is difficult to create hash functions with uniform distribution in the range $[1...N]$ without prior knowledge of expected input values, the value of N may have to be increased (and therefore all the records rearranged) if the file becomes larger, and many disk accesses may be necessary to find a record in the worst case (when many records hash to the same location).

We eliminate most of the problems with hashing by using more sophisticated hash indexing techniques, in particular *extensible hashing*. Extensible hashing, and most other improvements on hash indexing, utilize an intermediate table in memory to redirect the hashing function dynamically when it becomes unbalanced or too dense. [Kjellberg and Zahle 1984] survey these hashing techniques.

With all access methods, the number of disk accesses required to retrieve a record is typically more important than are other factors (for example, the CPU time required), because disk seek speed is the limiting factor. With modern hashing techniques, it is possible to find a record with a given primary-key value in at most two disk accesses, and usually in one.

3.6.2   B-Tree Indexes

Hash indexes are *not* generally useful when a lookup must be done based on a range of values for attributes (rather than a single value), or when we wish to sort records and to retrieve them by sequentially increasing values. In this case, B-trees are normally used. B-trees also may be used for exact matches with performance nearly as good as hash indexes. As a result, some relational DBMSs support some variation of B-trees as their *only* access method.

B-trees are tree-structured indexes; the nodes of the tree are disk pages. Each node contains a sorted list of key values with associated pointers; the pointers may reference a record with a given key value, or another node in the B-tree to search for records in the range between successive key values. Search is initiated at the root, and completed when a leaf node of the B-tree is found that references the record(s) with the given key value or range of values.

There are many variations on B-trees. Some keep the entire tree better balanced for best performance, or compress key values to fit more on a page. Other variations store the actual records in the leaf pages of B-trees, or cluster together the records associated with leaf pages. Space does not permit more detailed discussion of B-trees; they are covered adequately elsewhere [Comer 1978, Wiederhold 1977].

3.6.3   Parent–Child Links

We also cover a third access method, physical link structures, which is used more frequently in nonrelational than in relational DBMSs. Links are pointers used to chain together related records. The pointers usually are not physical addresses, but rather are the record IDs discussed in Section 3.5.2.

Parent–child links are most frequently used to chain together records in a table that have the *same foreign key* values, and to connect these records with the record that they reference (with the corresponding primary key). In terms of our schema notation, the parent–child links are created for the "arrows" (relationships), forming a *prejoin* of tables according to key values. The links typically can be traversed in both directions (in the direction the arrow points, and back) by the DBMS.

In our example database (Figure 1.1), chapters reference documents: Each document, or parent record, has multiple chapters, or child records, associated with it. (Joins of tables connected by arrows in our schema notation are sometimes called *entity joins,* because these joins connect entities in an entity-relationship model [Chen 1978]. Other joins are called *value joins.*)

There are two main ways to represent parent–child links in a DBMS. Figure 3.5a shows the "array" method; Figure 3.5b shows the "chain" method.

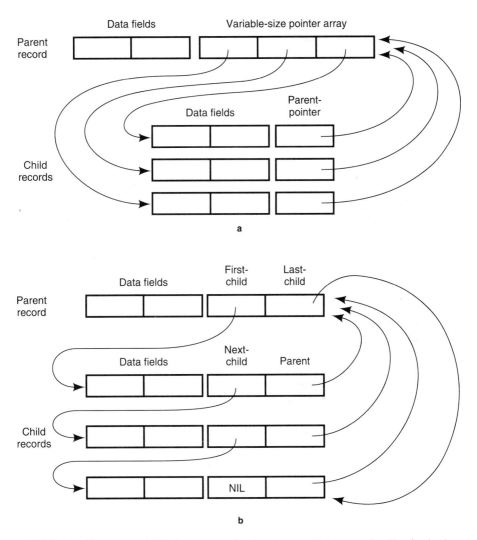

FIGURE 3.5   The parent–child link access method can be used to join records with a foreign key (children) to those with the primary key (parent). For example, documents would be parent records, and chapters children. The links are created for matching DodID attributes in the parent and child records. **(a)**   One implementation of parent–child links uses a variable-sized array for back-pointers from parent to child records. **(b)**   A variation of parent–child links uses a chain through the children so that a variable size is not necessary.

In both methods, the child record contains a field with a pointer to the parent record. This pointer allows us to find the parent record quickly; for example, we can find the **Document** when we have one **Chapter** of it. The difference between Figures 3.5a and 3.5b is in the method used to store the reverse pointers. In the array method, the parent record contains an array of pointers to all its children. In the chain method, space is set aside in each child for a singly or doubly linked list through all of the child records. The parent record may be the head of the list, or NIL may be stored in the first and last children. There are other variations on the chain method—for example, using a doubly linked list to allow fast insertion or deletion of children anywhere in the list.

Parent–child links allow a related record to be located in a single disk access when relational joins are performed, instead of two or more disk accesses typically required by indexes. For example, we could find the **Document** for a **Chapter** in our example database by following a parent link directly to the correct disk page, whereas an index lookup by **DocID** would require intermediary index page fetches.

The existence of links, like that of B-trees and hash indexes, is invisible to the relational DBMS user—the appropriate access method is selected by the query processor discussed in the next section. However, links have been implemented in only a few relational DBMSs to date; they are more prevalent in earlier network and hierarchical DBMSs. In Chapter 5, we shall see that there is renewed interest in parent–child links in object data management.

3.7   QUERY PROCESSING

A significant portion of the effort in implementing a relational DBMS is invested in processing the DML and DDL. We call this *query processing*: parsing, optimizing, and executing query-language statements.

3.7.1   Query Optimization

Query processing translates the user's commands into calls to the access-method and storage-management levels. Optimization is performed to select the most efficient query execution plan for the given query.

For example, a simple selection query such as the example we used earlier,

```
SELECT TITLE, REVISION FROM DOCUMENT
WHERE REVISION>1985
```

may be processed by calls to a B-tree access method using an index on the date field, followed by calls to the storage manager to fetch the appropriate fields to print. If no B-tree was created on dates when the database was defined, the query execution plan would instead search all documents sequentially, rejecting those with a date before 1986.

To compute joins, a number of techniques can be used, involving any of the three access methods we discussed in Section 3.6, depending on the structure of the database and of the query. If no indexes or links are available on the joined attributes, an index may be created, or the records may be sorted to make the join efficient.

A complete discussion of query processing and optimization is beyond the scope of this book; see [Date 1990, Wiederhold 1977]. There are two important facts for our purposes:

- The user specifies the results desired in the DML, and the query processor is free to select any execution plan that achieves those results, based on the data-schema information and available access methods. This physical data independence (the ability to change the database structure transparently to users) is an important feature of relational DBMSs.

- The data schema is typically defined by a database administrator and programmer, not by the user. The definition of the internal data schema (what B-trees and other access methods should be maintained on tables) and the conceptual and external data schemas (table, attribute, and view definitions) is performed in the DDL. This process can be more complex than using the DML, which is designed for ease of use, and is important because it affects both the performance and the content of a database.

We shall not discuss processing the DDL portion of the query language here; the DDL is translated in a relatively straightforward manner into calls to the storage manager to modify record layouts and indexes.

3.7.2 Embedded and Compiled Queries

Query-language commands may be interpreted or compiled. Interpreted queries are executed "on the fly"; that is, access method calls are selected and results are produced immediately. Compiled queries are parsed and optimized, then are translated into code or pseudocode that may be executed repeatedly to produce results without invocation of this overhead.

The query language may be utilized directly by an end user for ad hoc queries and updates, or it may be used in application programs. Indeed, the real value of compilation is in the latter case, called *embedded queries*. Embedded queries are queries that are interleaved with programming-language statements in C, FORTRAN, COBOL, or other compiled languages. A preprocessor is used to strip out the query-language statements, replacing them with calls to a run time DBMS library linked with the program. The record attribute values resulting from the queries at run time are transferred into programming-language variables specified in the embedded query syntax (or transferred from programming-language variables, in the case of an update).

3.7.3   Views, Security, and Integrity

The query processor is often responsible for other functionality of the DBMS, including views, authorization, and integrity constraints.

At the query-processor level, relational views are typically translated like "macros" into operations on the underlying stored tables. No other portion of the DBMS needs to be aware of views; this greatly simplifies the implementation.

Security—the control of data access based on user class, table attributes, and arbitrary run-time conditions—is typically handled by the query processor. An easy way to deal with security, in fact, is to define relational views that each user class may access. This reduces security to controlling access to views.

Integrity constraints are specifications that database updates must satisfy to maintain a valid database. Current DBMS products have relatively little in the way of integrity constraints, beyond the specifications that the data schema already provides on domains and keys. More sophisticated constraints—for example, to check the proper form for a social-security number or to ensure that salaries do not violate job-grade maximums—typically must be performed in application code. However, many DBMSs provide a sufficiently powerful query language (or fourth-generation language) that such constraints can be performed within views or high-level procedures.

Two other DBMS features that are important to maintain database integrity are concurrency control and data recovery. We discuss these features in the next section.

3.8   CONCURRENCY AND RECOVERY

Database concurrency control and recovery mechanisms are important features of a DBMS—they help to maintain the logical and physical integrity of a database, respectively. The implementations of concurrency and recovery mechanisms are often intertwined in a DBMS, so we cover both in this section.

3.8.1 Recovery

Recovery mechanisms allow a consistent state of the DBMS to be reinstated after a system crash. Because data in a database are long-lived—they may last many years, in contrast to the seconds over which programming data structures persist—it is essential to avoid corrupted data that will cause problems later. For example, creating a parent–child link or hash-index entry without creating the record that it references could have unpredictable results when the DBMS attempts to operate on the "record" it finds later.

Backups are the oldest and simplest solution to recovery. Backup copies of the database are made at regular intervals—for example, at midnight every night—so that no more than 1 day's work is lost if the database is irreparably damaged. It may be possible to do incremental backups, backing up only those portions of the database that have changed since the last backup, if the DBMS keeps records of modified data segments at a reasonable granularity.

With midnight backups, all application programs must be rerun if there is a major crash during the day. This can obviously be expensive, especially when updates were made by on-line entry. Today, most DBMSs provide recovery through transactions, as we discuss shortly. However, backups are still important in the use of transactions, and provide a simpler alternative to transactions in some cases.

3.8.2   Concurrency

Concurrency control limits simultaneous reads and updates by different users, so that all users see a consistent view of data. Although there is more than one definition of "consistent," with different levels of consistency [Date 1990], all concurrency-control mechanisms are basically aimed at isolating other users' database updates until a logical operation is completed.

In our example database, if two different users attempt to remove the first **Chapter** of a **Document**, then only one of them should succeed. On the other hand, it is acceptable for different users to modify *different* **Chapters**.

Data locking is the traditional solution to database concurrency control, and is still a component of nearly all concurrency-control mechanisms, so let's start with it.

3.8.3   Locks and Deadlocks

The simplest use of locking is for a user explicitly to place exclusive locks on every record important to the work being performed. For example, if a transfer is being made from one account to another in a banking application, records for both customer accounts must be locked. Data that are read, as well as data that are written, must be locked if the updates performed depend on the values read. Otherwise, another user may modify the data concurrently, causing the wrong results.

There are two kinds of locks: physical and logical. Logical locking is based on an expression in the query language defining a set of data to be locked. Physical locking is associated with specific data, and can be performed at more than one level: record locking, page locking, or table locking. Page locking is most common in modern DBMSs, and probably is the best overall choice, because it is efficient to lock the same physical units that are read and written from the disk. However, somewhat less concurrency is possible than with record locking. Table locking is useful when many records will be read or modified—it saves the overhead of acquiring many locks, at the cost of disallowing any other user updates in the table in the meantime.

When a user attempts to acquire a lock on data that are already locked by another user, the lock call fails. The user (an end user or a program) may wait and reattempt to acquire the lock, or may give up and release all locks.

If users repeatedly attempt to reacquire locks, a *deadlock* condition can occur. User A may be waiting for user B to release a lock, and user B may be waiting for user A to release a lock. This brings us to transactions and deadlock detection.

3.8.4 Transactions

Most modern DBMSs implement *transactions,* which provide both recovery and concurrency control.

Transactions are logical units of work in an application. The example in the previous section, transferring money from one bank account to another, is a transaction. The database is in a logically consistent state at the beginning and end of a transaction, although it may pass through [invisible] inconsistent states during its execution—for example, when one account has been debited and the other not yet credited.

A DBMS transaction mechanism guarantees that every transaction a user initiates will run to completion (that is, the updates will be made permanently on disk), or that the entire transaction will be backed out, as if the updates the transaction made never occurred. Transactions provide a useful recovery mechanism, because they are based on maintaining consistency of the database.

Transactions initiated by different users are guaranteed to have the same effect *as if they were executed serially.* For example, if transactions A and B involve reads and writes of completely different data, they may be executed in parallel without violating logical serialization. Transactions that touch the same data can be interleaved only in ways that achieve the same result as would occur were they executed sequentially in some order.

A transaction is begun when an end user or application programmer executes a *begin transaction* command in the query language. The user explicitly indicates the end of transactions through a *commit* command. Both the begin and commit transaction commands may be implicit in some systems; for example, a transaction may be started automatically when a program begins or when a previous transaction is ended. In such systems, transactions are entirely transparent to the user unless an exception occurs and the transaction is backed out.

Transactions may be aborted explicitly by a *rollback* command, in which case all updates made by the transaction are backed out. A transaction may also be aborted by the DBMS—for example, in the event of conflicts or system crash. In either case, all the database updates performed by the transactions are undone, or *rolled back.*

Under most transaction implementations, users do not (or cannot) make explicit commands to lock or unlock data; locks are implicitly placed on all records read and written by the end user or program.

The problem of deadlocks is handled automatically by a transaction implementation. Deadlocks may be detected automatically through analysis of dependencies between locks requests, or the system can simply give up on transactions when they have waited a specified time-out period for a lock. However a deadlock is avoided, the offending transaction is aborted automatically by the DBMS. Thus, a transaction may be aborted as a result of deadlock, system crash, or explicit user rollback request.

Transactions provide a much better solution to concurrency control and recovery than do manual locks and backups. The user does not need to deal with locks, deadlocks, backups, or system failures. Transactions do have some drawbacks: for example, current implementations do not deal well with long-lived transactions required in engineering applications where records may be locked for days at a time. We discuss other concurrency-control alternatives in Chapter 4.

3.8.5   Implementation

A variety of approaches has been taken to the implementation of transactions; most use locks, deadlock detection, and a log of updates on disk. Space does not permit us to discuss these implementations here; see [Gray 1981, Date 1990] for background reading.

3.9   DISTRIBUTED DATABASES

The term *distributed databases* has been used with many meanings in the research and product domains. For our purposes, two primary capabilities are important. The first capability is remote access to databases—databases stored on a machine different from the one where the user or application is executing. The second capability is splitting data between two databases—databases that may be on different machines, or be administered separately on the same machine.

3.9.1   Remote Access

Most relational DBMS products now support remote access to databases. The fact that the database is located remotely is typically transparent to the user or application program.

Remote access is almost universally implemented in the same way. A small part of the DBMS resides with the application program on the *client* machine. This portion is responsible for encoding queries, sending them over a network to the *server* machine where the remainder of the DBMS resides, and receiving any records returned over the network to decode and pass to the client application program.

Remote access is not particularly difficult to implement. However, additional complexity is introduced by a *heterogeneous network* of machines, where the encoding of data types is different on the client and server machine architectures. In this case, a machine-independent representation of records must be used on the network, or the server must translate to the client machine representation.

Using this client–server architecture, with remote access to databases, may provide higher performance than can be achieved by a single processor for many applications: There is no overhead on the server machine from application execution. There is relatively little network traffic if the query language is sufficiently powerful to express the application's operations as single calls to the DBMS.

In other cases, performance can be much less efficient. If a large quantity of data must be retrieved (for example, for a complex user display), or if many query language calls must be made to achieve the application's result, then it may be better to use a single processor, or to find some way to cache data on the client machine (current implementations of remote database access cannot do this).

3.9.2   Distribution

We define a *distributed database* to be multiple databases that appear as a single database to the user. In the simplest cases, distributed databases may not even be "distributed" on the network; that is, the databases may reside on the same machine.

Distributed databases are useful for a variety of purposes. Because a database is typically the smallest unit controlled by a database administrator, distributed databases allow two or more departments to design and maintain their data independently, yet to express queries that span all data—a very important feature in a large organization with different needs. Distributed databases can also be used to improve performance, by distributing the load of processing queries across multiple machines, when there exists a logical *partitioning* of databases across machines that requires relatively little intermachine communication for typical queries.

Data may be partitioned in a variety of ways. Different tables may reside in different databases. Individual tables may be split across databases as well, *horizontally partitioned* with some rows in one database and the rest in another, or *vertically partitioned* with some columns in one database and the rest in another. However the data are distributed across databases, it must be possible to perform selections, joins, and other operations on tables as if the multiple databases were a single one. Except for some initial setup, the fact that there are multiple databases must be transparent to the user.

Distributed implementations differ in how the data schema is distributed. Some allow the schema of each participating database to be independent, requiring a mapping between tables in different schemas be defined by the database administrator. Other implementations define a global database schema that spans multiple machines. This alternative simplifies distributed access, but may require that the global schema be maintained separately, and the machine where it resides be accessible at all times.

Additional background on the implementation of distributed databases, and additional variations such as federations of DBMSs from different vendors, can be found in a database systems textbook [Elmasri and Navathe 1989].

3.10   APPLICATION TOOLS

The point should not be lost, in our discussion of relational DBMSs, that the most important reason that relational database products are selected for an application is often the application tools that the DBMS provides for the end user or the application developer. Application tools are where the greatest productivity gains of using a DBMS are to be found, since significant effort goes into application development and modification over time.

3.10.1   Forms and 4GLs

Most relational DBMS implementations provide forms packages or 4GLs (fourth-generation languages tailored to database application development, normally an extension of the query language) to simplify the development of applications. Forms packages and 4GLs simplify the definition of screen layout by mapping screen forms to and from database record attributes, sequencing forms and user operations, validating the correctness of user input, and automating many other routine but tedious application tasks.

Programming productivity using a 4GL rather than a 3GL (a programming language such as C, FORTRAN, or COBOL) can make a big difference in the usefulness of a DBMS. Applications can require an order of magnitude less code using 4GLs, since much of the support for windows, forms, menus, and error checking are built in to the language. Of course, this savings is realized only if the application fits the constraints of the 4GL's user-interaction model, but new more powerful 4GLs are being developed every year.

3.10.2   End-User Tools

With appropriate end-user tools, some applications do not require programming. A common example is on-line access to data, for ad hoc queries and report generation. This capability is necessary for marketing analyses, reports for management, and other simple information-retrieval applications.

In addition to a 4GL, most relational DBMSs provide query-by-example and report-definition tools. These tools automatically generate commands to the underlying query language and report generator to produce results a user specifies by filling in forms on the screen and by selecting report layouts.

More recently, end-user tools and application-development tools have been enhanced to exploit bitmap graphic displays and mice, rather than simple character-oriented terminals, further simplifying the user interface.

End-user tools for graphical data schema design have recently received attention. These tools allow graphical notations (such as the one we defined in Chapter 1 figures) to be used in schema design. Designing a data schema for an application and maintaining a data schema for many applications are difficult tasks. The data schema must include all the necessary information for applications, but must not violate relational normalization rules. The sheer number of tables and record attributes can make the database schema difficult to maintain and difficult to communicate between application programmers.

3.11 PERFORMANCE

Performance is often the most important factor in selecting a DBMS, so overall performance issues deserve mention before we move on to advanced database systems. Unfortunately, a complete treatment of traditional database performance issues is beyond the scope of this book. This section simply touches on issues that will be important in contrasting ODMSs to traditional DBMSs in the next two chapters.

3.11.1 Queries

With a sufficiently good query processor to compile application commands, the limiting factor in good relational DBMS implementations for most commercial business applications is disk I/O speed. The implementation of the query compiler can be complex, and current products do not generally use the latest techniques, but we now have good experience with query optimization. The Wisconsin Benchmarks [Gray 1991] are a good measure of query optimizers. Most products compile, rather than interpret, queries, achieving a factor of 10 or more in execution speed by parsing and optimizing queries at the time a program is compiled.

An awkward data representation can be a problem for some queries. For example, it can be time consuming to produce a "bill of materials" with many nested components in query-language implementations without parent–child links. Hundreds of index lookups may be required to find subcomponents, and the SQL standard provides no syntax to perform a "transitive closure" to find them all. ODMSs address some of these issues.

3.11.2 Architecture

Most of the recent industry activity on relational DBMS performance has focused on simple transaction processing where query optimization is of little importance. The TPC benchmarks [Gray 1991] are gaining attention as a standard for transaction-processing performance. As we shall see, performance for engineering applications may require a very different kind of optimization and database architecture.

Relational DBMS products generally have been implemented using a two-process architecture: application programs make interprocess calls to one or more database server processes that execute the queries. The separation of processes provides some advantages; for example, it helps to protect database integrity because application programs cannot directly address database pages or data structures. However, in most operating systems, there is a significant penalty for the interprocess call—as many as 10,000 machine instructions—so performance can be adversely affected in programs that make frequent database calls.

Concurrency control can be a performance bottleneck where there are concurrency conflicts between applications, or when only record-level locking is provided by the DBMS. Transaction-commit overhead may predominate, since updates must be flushed to disk.

The process architecture and concurrency-control implementations in ODMSs differ in important ways, as we shall see in the next two chapters.

3.12   SUMMARY

This chapter provided an overview of traditional database systems, focusing primarily on the relational model and its implementation. Let's review what we learned, and examine directions for future work.

3.12.1   Relational Model

The relational data model is simple. This simplicity makes it attractive because it is easy for users to understand and utilize. In addition, the model results in mathematically simple structures, making possible a concise and powerful query language that can perform perhaps 90 percent of data retrieval and manipulation that typical business applications require. Thus, little conventional programming is required.

Many relational DBMS products do not implement the full relational model; particularly, they often omit foreign keys, referential integrity, domains, integrity constraints, and views. Indeed, some shortcomings of relational DBMSs for the applications we consider are merely a result of these incomplete implementations. However, even the ideal relational implementation falls short in other ways. We discuss these shortcomings in the next chapter.

3.12.2   Relational Implementation

Relational database products and research prototypes are surprisingly similar in implementation. Nearly all implementation architectures have the following components:

1. *A storage manager*, built on the operating-system files or with its own direct access to raw disk; this level implements records and record identifiers

2. *Access methods*, including B-trees, hash indexes, and links used to locate records associatively

3. *Query processing*, translating the high-level query language into calls to the storage manager and access methods

4. *Remote and distributed databases*, built as an extension of the query processing

5. *End-user tools and 4GLs* to provide productive use of the underlying DBMS

Considerable experience has now been amassed on relational implementation. Because it is well defined in terms of both the concepts and the implementation, the relational model provides a good basis for comparison with other DBMS alternatives.

3.12.3   New Database Directions

Recalling the DBMS requirements from Chapter 2, we recognize some capabilities that relational systems do *not* provide: unique IDs, long-term checkout of data, versions, procedures, subtypes, and subparts. Relational query languages typically do not provide the capabilities of a programming language; they provide only table operations—select, project, and join.

Relational DBMS implementations are optimized for business applications, rather than for the engineering and scientific applications of Chapter 2. Distributed relational implementations are based on DBMS servers, and do not provide the capability to cache locally data that are checked out of a database.

In the next two chapters, we discuss database advances and implementations aimed at alleviating these and other shortcomings of relational DBMSs.

CHAPTER

4

Object Data Management Concepts

4.1 INTRODUCTION

In the remainder of the book, we examine advances in database technology beyond the relational model: ODMSs aimed at supporting engineering, scientific, and office applications, and more sophisticated generations of traditional business applications. In this chapter, we focus on the functionality provided by ODMSs, and the approaches that have been taken to building these functions.

The work on object data management is still in its infancy. There is no single data model as there is for relational systems, and there are many open research issues. As we noted in the first chapter, ODMSs have been built with a variety of data models and implementation architectures. Because so many approaches have been taken, it is impossible to provide a single, simple description of object data management, and at least half a dozen different chapters would be necessary for self-contained descriptions of all the approaches. Instead, the basic approaches to object data management are introduced in the remainder of this section, and the rest of the chapter covers each of the basic features of ODMSs, and describes how features are presented in each approach.

4.1.1   Chapter Overview

Taking this bottom-up approach, the seven major sections (4.2 through 4.8) of this chapter cover, respectively:

- General features of objects, including object identifiers and attributes
- Relationships, reference attributes, and sets
- Procedures (methods) and encapsulation
- Composite objects (aggregates) and their semantics
- Object types (classes), type hierarchies, and type (schema) evolution
- Query-language and programming-language interfaces
- Concurrency control, versions, and recovery

Generally speaking, a sophisticated ODMS will have most of these features, whereas a simple one will have only a few. In practice, it is not important that a system have as many features as possible; it is important that it have the features that the desired applications require.

After understanding these features, we shall examine their implementation in Chapter 5. For convenience, Sections 5.1 through 5.8 of Chapter 5, covering the implementation of the features enumerated here, correspond in subject matter to Sections 4.1 through 4.8 in this chapter. Thus, to examine implementation issues associated with any of the concepts covered here, simply refer to the identically numbered top-level section of the next chapter. This organization allows us to isolate implementation details from basic concepts without losing easy reference between the two.

Before proceeding to cover features of object data management, let us categorize the important approaches.

4.1.2   Database Architecture

In Chapter 1, we defined the extended relational, functional, and object-oriented data models. Data models are one dimension in which ODMSs may differ. Another difference is in *database architecture,* the way in which an ODMS is implemented and integrated with other system components.* Since the different data models have converged to provide almost the same capabilities, the differences in database architectures are even more important than are genealogical differences in data models.

There are four important database architectures for our purposes:

1. *Extended database systems:* This architecture represents database systems that provide new functionality through new or extended database query lan-

---

* The term "database/programming system architecture" would be more accurate; we use "database architecture" for brevity.

guages that incorporate procedures and other ODMS features. Extended database systems present the programmer with two separate environments: the application programming language and the extended database query language. Either language can invoke the other, but the two have different type systems and run-time execution environments. The database language may have its own procedural constructs, or allow application procedures to be stored and invoked. Extended database systems have been built with a variety of data models.

2. *Database programming languages:* The second architecture represents database systems that extend existing programming languages, such as C++, to provide persistence, concurrency control, and other database capabilities. The result is called a *database programming language* [Bancilhon and Buneman 1990]. These ODMSs typically provide a query language, but both the query language and the programming language execute in the application program environment, sharing the same type system and data workspace. At present, the only ODMSs that have been built with a database programming language architecture are based on an object-oriented programming language and data model. This architecture provides a single environment for data—database objects appear semitransparently as programming-language objects.

3. *Object managers:* This architecture represents packages that may be regarded as extensions of file systems. An object manager generally has a limited data model, at a physical level: It provides a repository for persistent objects. Object managers do not have all the features we cover in this chapter, and do not include a query or programming language, but they are important for simple applications where more sophisticated features are not needed.

4. *Database system generators:* The final architecture represents systems allowing a database implementor to construct a DBMS tailored to particular needs. Database system generators generally do not have their own data model; they allow a DBMS designer to "tailor" the data model and implementation to a particular group of applications.

Figure 4.1 is a graphical representation of the relationships among these four architectures, which are nested according to their respective capabilities. An object manager provides the most basic functionality: storage of persistent objects. An extended database system adds new capabilities, including a query language and more sophisticated concurrency control, on top of an object manager. A database programming language adds integration with a persistent programming language on top of an extended database system. A database system generator can be used to construct all these system levels.

The definitions of the architectures will be refined as we proceed through the chapter; Figure 4.1 should not be taken too literally. For example, a database

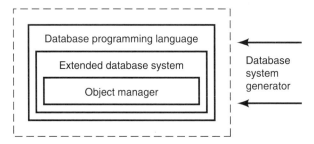

FIGURE 4.1   A simplified view of the relationship between the database system architectures introduced here, by nesting of functionality. A database system generator can be used to construct all of these levels of functionality.

programming language may not be *implemented* on top of a query language, and an extended database system may not actually *contain* a separable object manager. Also, we shall see that the distinction between the architectures can sometimes be subtle.*

Having introduced these four architectures, we are now ready to define the approaches to object data management we shall use as a basis for ODMS comparison in the remainder of the book. The approaches correspond exactly to the four architectures, except for the extended database system architecture, for which we distinguish systems based on extended relational models from those based on extended functional and semantic data models.

Altogether, then, there are five approaches. These approaches are described in the next five sections, with examples of products and prototypes for each. The approaches are not equally important for the purposes of this book; we shall focus on the two based on object-oriented and extended relational models, because these have been most popular in research and development communities. However, the other approaches are important in some applications, and also provide context to understand the alternative future directions.

The Appendix to this book covers examples of the approaches in more detail. References to full descriptions of products and prototypes can be found in the System Bibliography, at the end of the Appendix.

---

* For example, if an entire application program can be written in the database query language provided by an extended database system, and programmers are willing to switch to that language for their work, then the result will be equivalent to a database programming language; see Section 4.7.

4.1.3   Object-Oriented Database Programming Languages

Essentially all ODMSs based on the object-oriented data model are what we call *object-oriented database programming languages*. We will therefore use the more popular term "object-oriented DBMS" interchangeably, where there is no ambiguity. These systems are based on the database programming language architecture: Applications are written in an extension of an existing programming language, and the language and its implementation (compiler, preprocessor, execution environment) have been extended to incorporate database functionality. Examples include O$_2$ [Bancilhon et al 1988], ObjectStore [Object Design 1990], Objectivity/DB [Objectivity 1990], ONTOS [Ontologic 1989], POET [Poet 1993], VERSANT [Versant 1990], GemStone [Bretl et al 1988], STATICE [Weinreb 1988], ZEITGEIST [Ford et al 1988], MCC ORION [Kim et al 1988], and ITASCA [Itasca 1990].[*]

Most of these object-oriented DBMSs have been integrated with C++ [Ellis and Stroustrup 1990] or a derivative, probably because of the wide popularity of this language. A few have focused on Smalltalk or an object-oriented LISP derivative. Most of them provide a procedure-call interface for C as well, but generally would not be considered "integrated" with C in the sense that C data structures can transparently be made persistent. More recently, some systems have been integrated with more than one language: GemStone and VERSANT with both C++ and Smalltalk, and O$_2$ with both LISP and C++. It is the intent in most of these ODMSs to integrate with multiple programming languages, but, as we will see, the multilanguage access problem can be challenging in database programming languages because of the close association this approach requires between the database and programming-language type systems.

Some of the earlier ODMSs based on an object-oriented model (for example, VBase [Ontologic 1986] and VISION [Innovative Systems 1988]) more closely resemble an extended database system than they do a database programming language architecture, since they defined their own languages (for example, COP in VBase), rather than integrating with existing languages. The distinction between a database programming language and an extended database system is actually more a continuum than a two-way categorization, since there are degrees of integration between the programming language and database system. COP may be regarded as an object-oriented database extension of the programming language C, or as a new language. However, the evolution in object-oriented DBMSs has been toward database programming languages, and almost any of the object-oriented DBMSs can be transformed into an object-oriented database programming language relatively easily, since the object-oriented programming-language data models are so similar. So, we focus on object-oriented database programming languages in this book.

---

[*]   ITASCA is a product follow on to the ORION research prototype at MCC. All comments about ORION in this book also apply to ITASCA, unless otherwise noted.

Persistent programming languages [Atkinson 1987], such as PS-Algol [Atkinson et al 1983] and Trellis [Schaeffert et al 1986], are closely related predecessors of database programming languages. However, persistent programming languages were intended to provide neither full database functionality, nor access to persistent data from multiple languages, so we do not cover them.

Programming languages with extensions for database records, such as Pascal/R [Schmidt 1977] and Rigel [Rowe 1979], are also related to database programming languages. However, these languages simply provide a convenient link between programming-language records and database records; they do not combine the programming-language and database type systems.

4.1.4   Extended Relational Database Systems

The second approach, *extended relational database systems*, provides a relational data model and query language that have been extended to include procedures, object identity, a type hierarchy, and some or all of the other features we shall study in more detail in this chapter. The extended database system architecture is used; that is, the query language has been extended with programming capability, and the application communicates with the DBMS through embedding query-language calls in the application program. The query language may provide control constructs with all of the capability of a programming language, and these constructs may be used in defining actions to be taken when a field is fetched or modified, or the query language may allow calls to procedures written in a conventional programming language.

Examples of extended relational database systems include POSTGRES [Stonebraker and Rowe 1986], Starburst [Schwarz et al 1986], UniSQL [UniSQL 1993], Montage [Montage 1993], and ALGRES [Ceri et al 1990]. Some products could be considered extended relational databases, although with more modest extensions than these systems. INGRES [Ingres 1990], SYBASE [Sybase 1990], and Xidak Orion [Xidak 1990] are being marketed as such. A variety of other research has been done to extend the relational model, including R^2D^2 [Kemper and Walrath 1988], RM/T [Codd 1989], and others [Dadam et al 1986]. Not all of the extended relational research meets the needs of the applications we covered in Chapter 2, however, and some of the proposals have not yet been implemented. We shall primarily use POSTGRES, UniSQL, and Starburst as examples in this chapter, since they represent the most advanced implementations aimed at object data management applications. These systems are covered in more detail, along with examples of the other approaches, in the Appendix.

There is no single "extended relational approach," in the sense of DBMSs built on the relational model with a common query language and model; indeed, there may be less standardization and consistency than in some other ODMS approaches. However, the extended relational approach is popular because this work can benefit from much of what has been learned about relational systems, and, more important, it may be possible to migrate users from existing relational database products to ODMSs using this approach.

Some recent research and development has been done to bring extended relational database systems closer to database programming languages [UniSQL 1993, Persistence 1993, Keller 1993, Rowe 1990, Wiederhold et al 1990]. In this approach, a mapping is defined between programming language objects and relational types to allow semi-transparent retrieval and update of relations through programming language operations.

4.1.5 Extended Functional and Semantic Database Systems

We call extended database systems based on a functional data model *extended functional database systems*. Examples of ODMSs taking the extended functional database system approach are IRIS [Fishman et al 1987], OpenODB [Hewlett Packard 1993], PROBE [Dayal and Smith 1986] and ADAPLEX [Smith 1983]. Semantic and functional data models are historically closely related [Hull and King 1987], so are considered together in this book. CACTIS [Hudson and King 1988] and SIM [Fritchman et al 1990] are primarily based on semantic models.

Recall from Chapter 1 that the bases for functional models are *objects* and *functions*. Functions map objects onto other objects, including both entities and literal values. Functions may be defined procedurally, or may be defined as *stored*. The values of a stored function are represented by the ODMS in any fashion desired; for example, the values may be stored in groups with one or more of the objects that are arguments of the function. Attributes, relationships, and procedures are all represented as functions in this model. Relationships between two or more types of objects are represented as multiple-argument functions defined in terms of each other. Most functional model systems allow functions to be multivalued; for example, the function `chaps(Document)` might return a set of chapters in a document in the database we introduced in Chapter 1.

4.1.6 Database System Generators

All of the approaches to object data management we have discussed have been designed to provide extensibility in the implementation and definition of types and operations provided by the ODMS. *Database system generators* such as EXODUS [Carey et al 1986], the Open OODB toolkit [Wells, Blakeley, Thompson 1992], and GENESIS [Batory et al 1986] go further in this regard, allowing the data model itself to be custom-defined.

The data model is defined by a special user called the *database implementor*. Both the conceptual data model and the internal data model must be described. The conceptual data model specifies the query and representation capabilities of the system, such as tables, keys, relationships, and query syntax. The internal data model specifies the access methods and the ways in which conceptual data schemas can be mapped to them.

A database system generator can be used to produce ODMSs, relational DBMSs, or even file-management systems providing only access methods. However, database system generators are included in this book because they represent another option for object data management: constructing a custom ODMS for a particular set of applications.

4.1.7   Object Managers

The last ODMS approach we consider is an *object manager*. Object managers, sometimes called *persistent object stores,* have less functionality than other ODMSs we have covered. In some cases they are used as the storage management level of one of the more complete systems. Examples of object managers include POMS [Cockshot et al 1984], Mneme [Moss and Sinofsky 1988], ObServer [Zdonik 1987], Kala [Simmel, Godard 1993], Cypress [Cattell 1983], the iMAX-432 file system [Pollack et al 1986], Camelot [Spector et al 1988], and LOOM [Krasner 1986].

Object managers provide the ability to persistently store simple objects, and generally provide multi-user concurrency control, but lack a query language or programming language. These systems might be thought of as an extension of a file system, as opposed to an extension of a programming language or database system as in the other approaches we discussed.

4.1.8   Conclusions

We have defined five different approaches to object data management. We shall reference these approaches throughout the book, and also refer to the different data models and database architectures on which the approaches are based. The terminology we have introduced is important to understanding the book, because names for ODMS approaches are not used consistently elsewhere in the literature. The System Bibliography provides a glossary of this terminology and a categorization of all the ODMSs discussed in this book.

There is some basis for the terminology confusion in the literature: the actual features of, say, an extended relational database system, such as object identity and a type hierarchy, can be identical to those in an object-oriented database programming language, or those in the other approaches we discuss. In many cases, the ODMS implementations differ primarily in language syntax.

Our distinctions among the approaches should simply be regarded as convenient ways to distinguish among systems on the basis of their architecture and genealogy. Perhaps someday, there will be general agreement on the best approach to next-generation database systems, and the functionality and implementation distinctions among the approaches will blur to the point of becoming indistinguishable.

As we discussed earlier, the close similarity between the approaches lends the systems well to a unified study in the remainder of the chapter. We therefore proceed with a feature-by-feature discussion of object data management at this point, starting with the most basic properties of objects. As we discuss the features—for example, attributes and relationships—we contrast how they are handled in the different approaches.

4.2   OBJECTS

The term "object" has many meanings in database systems. However, essentially all ODMSs incorporate the two most basic features of objects:

1. *Object grouping:* Objects can serve to group data that pertain to one real-world entity—a transistor, a document, a person. A weak form of object grouping is incorporated in implementations of the relational model that have primary and foreign keys. [Chen 1976], in a discussion of the *entity-relationship* data model, provided an early discussion of object grouping as *entities*, including relationships between objects in relational databases. For the purposes of object grouping, objects are simply records or sets of records in traditional database systems.

2. *Object identity:* Objects can have a unique identity independent of the values that they contain. The relational model is *value-based:* an entity or object is identified via its primary key. A system that is *identity-based* allows an object to be referenced via a unique internally generated number, an *object identifier,* independent of the value of its primary key, if any. The concept of object identity (but not primary key) already existed in the network model.

We define an ODMS that provides object grouping and identity to be *structurally* object-oriented [Dittrich and Dayal 1986, Zdonik and Maier 1989]. In this section, we study structural object-orientation. More sophisticated semantics of objects are covered later; specifically, we shall discuss *behavioral* object-orientation, in which objects serve as abstract data types to encapsulate implementation details and to invoke procedures.

4.2.1   Object Identifiers

The idea of unique system-generated identifiers for objects appears in many data models put forward after the introduction of relational systems [Codd 1979, Hall et al 1976, Kent 1981, Shipman 1981, Hammer & McLeod 1981]. The earliest reference to object identifiers may be [Abrial 1974], who called them *surrogates.*

All this work in data models recognized the shortcomings of primary keys and value-based models, and introduced object identifiers, also known as OIDs, to remedy these difficulties. Primary keys demand that application programmers either generate their own unique identifiers, or use human-meaningful names as identifiers. Neither of these is an attractive solution in general:

- It is more efficient and convenient for artificially generated identifiers to be created by the DBMS. The application programmer is thereby relieved from a cumbersome task, particularly in a distributed multiuser environment. More important, performance can be significantly improved if the DBMS can generate OIDs in a fashion to speed object lookup (as in record or tuple IDs in relational databases; see Section 3.4.2).

- Human-meaningful names have merit, but they suffer from the dilemma that the short, efficient ones (part numbers, social-security numbers, customer numbers) tend to be least meaningful to users, and the longer ones (book titles, employee names) tend to be both inefficient to store as foreign keys and more likely to be nonunique.

The importance of OIDs is in referencing an object elsewhere in a database; for example, in an association with another object, or in an application program. From a functional point of view, there is little difference in the ways that various ODMSs deal with OIDs. The only *visible* difference is that some systems allow the user direct access to the identifiers—for example, the identifiers can be printed out, and then reused months later to look up the same object—whereas others allow the use of identifiers only in special "handles" that cannot be examined further or stored anywhere outside the database. Restrictions on the use of OIDs are made for implementation reasons—as we shall see in the next chapter, the representation of OIDs can be an important factor in the performance of an ODMS.

Record IDs in most relational implementations are analogous to OIDs, but they are generally hidden from the end user, or their use is strongly discouraged. Record IDs do not work well as user-visible identifiers because they become invalid if a tuple is moved or deleted, and they are not available if a tuple is part of a relational view or of a distributed database. ODMSs must also deal with these implementation issues for OIDs—indeed these issues are often the basis for restrictions on use of OIDs—but these systems are specifically designed to address these problems through controlled use of OIDs.

4.2.2   Object Keys

Some ODMSs allow objects to have human-meaningful names as well as object identifiers. For example, in our document database, we might use titles to refer to documents and chapters. These names are equivalent to primary keys in the relational model; we call them *object keys* here. Indeed, database systems that provide unique object identifiers but *give up* object keys in the process have lost some of the functionality of the relational model. [Stein, Anderson, and Maier 1989] discuss this point.

Of course, any object attribute could be used as a key as long as the DBMS allows associative lookup of objects. What is the benefit of having keys? Primarily, it is a convenience: a simplified syntax may be used to refer to objects by key, and the DBMS may automatically verify the integrity constraint that keys be unique.

Constraints on the uniqueness of keys currently differ between implementations. Some may require that the key be unique over a single object type, roughly analogous to relational primary keys. In ODMSs allowing a hierarchy of types, this uniqueness may be extended to demand uniqueness over all subtypes as well. Other implementations base key uniqueness on arbitrary collections, unrelated to the object type structure.

Do not confuse object keys with names given to objects through variable names in programs. For example, GemStone allows a persistent variable **foo** to be stored in a database (using a symbol dictionary). The value of **foo** can refer to a particular object in the database, such as a **Document**. The variable name **foo** is unique in the scope it is defined, and might always refer to the same object, but it is entirely independent of the key used for that object (say, the **title**, which might be "Object Data Management").

4.2.3 Simple Attributes

Recall the distinction between *literals* and *objects* from Chapter 1. Literals are integers, floating-point numbers, character strings, and other simple values. Objects are user-defined representatives of real-world or abstract entities, such as a **Document** or **Person**. In the relational model, objects are represented as records, and literal values are stored as attributes of records.

Objects may have attributes whether represented in a relational DBMS or in an ODMS.* ODMSs typically allow more flexibility than does the relational model in the types of attribute values permitted, however:

1. Object attributes may have *complex* values, such as sets or references to other objects. We shall discuss complex values shortly.

2. Users may define their own literal value types to augment the built-in literal types such as integers and strings, by specifying the representation and common operations on the type [Stonebraker 1986].

In some object-oriented systems, literal values are called "objects" as well, and can be treated syntactically and semantically just like other objects. For efficiency, however, the implementation usually treats literal types differently; to avoid confusion in this book, we continue to use the term "object" to refer to entities, not to literal values treated as objects.

---

* Object attributes are called "instance variables" in some object-oriented programming languages.

Like attributes of relational records, attributes of ODMS objects have names, and they are generally referenced by a "dot" notation. For example, the **revision** attribute of a document **d** may be referenced as*

```
d.revision
```

If the ODMS is integrated with a programming language, this syntax may be used on either the left or right side of an assignment statement; that is, the value may be fetched or assigned just like programming-language records.

Very large variable-sized attributes (generally called binary large objects, or BLOBs) may be treated specially, since copying the entire value into memory when it is accessed is not desirable. BLOBs are still literal values, although they are large, and may be used to store multi-media data such as images, text, and audio. Regardless of their type and size, we refer to all these data, including BLOBs and user-defined types, as literal values. Attributes that contain literal values we call *simple* attributes.

4.2.4   Reference Attributes

We have seen how *simple* attributes are those that take on literal values of various kinds. There are three kinds of *complex* attributes: references, collections, and procedures. We start with reference attributes, and define collection and procedure attributes shortly.

Reference attributes, or associations, are used to represent relationships between objects. They take on values that are objects—that is, references to entities. Reference attributes are analogous to pointers in a programming language, or to foreign keys in a relational system. However, they have important differences:

1. Reference attributes cannot be corrupted, whereas pointers can be. Reference values are invalidated automatically when the referenced object is deleted, as we shall see in Section 4.3.

2. Reference attributes are not associated with a user-visible value, whereas foreign keys are. All the values in the referenced object may be changed, and the reference attribute will still point to the same object.

Instead of using a foreign key as in the relational model, we could define a **Document** reference attribute of **Chapter** in our document database to indicate

---

* C++ programmers may be more familiar with the notation **d->revision** for this example, since C++ does not use a "dot" when **d** is a *pointer* to the object. However, the "dot" notation is used in this book, and in most of the database research literature.

to which document a chapter belongs:*

```
Chapter: {
     title: STRING;
     number: INTEGER;
     doc: Document }
```

We discuss the important features of reference attributes in Section 4.3.

4.2.5 Collection Attributes

The second kind of complex attribute, *collections,* is used for lists, sets, or arrays of values. In the case of a list or array, an explicit ordering on the values is maintained by the DBMS. The collections may include simple attribute values and also references.

As an example, we can define two collection-valued attributes of the **Document** object type in our example database:

```
Document: {
     title: STRING;
     revision: DATE;
     keywords: SET[STRING];
     chaps: LIST[Chapter] }
```

The first collection, **keywords,** is a set of keyword strings associated with the document, perhaps used to look up documents associatively by subject matter. The second collection, **chaps,** is a list of **Chapter** objects for this document.

Note that we chose to make the keywords a set, since there is no particular reason to order them, but we chose to make the chapters a list, rather than sorting by a chapter number when retrieving them.

Recall that relational first normal form does not permit collection-valued attributes; in contrast, most of the ODMSs we discuss do allow collections. Thus, we diverge in an important way from the relational model on this point, making sets and lists of objects first-class citizens in the data model.

The **SET[STRING]** and **LIST[Chapter]** attributes types are examples of *parameterized types.* "Parameterized" means that the constructs **SET** and **LIST** take types as parameters, and define new types depending on the parameter values.

Parameterized types are a familiar construct from programming languages. Nearly all languages have the built-in parameterized type **ARRAY**, taking an array size and element type as parameters. Some languages have built-in **SET** and **LIST** constructors, as well. A few languages allow the user to define his own parameterized types.

Collections (sets, lists, and arrays) are the most common example of parameterized types in ODMSs. They are the only parameterized types we use in this

---

* A simple programming-language syntax will be used from here on to describe object types; the syntax should be self-explanatory with the help of the accompanying text.

book. Collections are useful in every application schema we considered in Chapter 2.

Currently, ODMSs based on object-oriented models generally provide sets, lists, and arrays, whereas those based on extended relational and functional models generally provide only sets. However, this difference is primarily a byproduct of the evolution of relational and functional models from declarative set-oriented languages; this shortcoming can be remedied.

4.2.6 Derived Attributes

Attribute values can be defined procedurally rather than stored explicitly, if a procedure is specified to be executed when the value is retrieved or assigned [Gilbert 1990, Bloom and Zdonik 1987].

For example, suppose we adopted a new mechanism for keeping track of revisions of documents in our example database, defining a **Document** attribute called **creation** that is an integer used for file-creation dates by the operating system (such as seconds since midnight on January 1, 1950). We could then redefine our old **revision** attribute procedurally in terms of **creation**, so that application programs would not have to be rewritten. We might define **creation** and **revision** using a syntax like this:

```
Document: {
    ...
    creation: INTEGER; /* seconds since 1950 */
    revision: DATE PROC () =
        secsToDate(creation + secsTo1950 );
}
```

Now, old programs that fetch the value

```
d.revision
```

from a document **d** will continue to work properly, calling the new **revision** procedure instead of retrieving the old **revision** attribute. Derived attributes thus provide logical data independence, as we discussed in conjunction with relational views in the previous chapter. When it is transparent to the programmer whether attributes are derived or are stored explicitly, we call the attributes *virtual attributes*. POSTGRES and O_2 provide virtual attributes.

Virtual attributes cannot be used in languages where the syntax used for fetching an attribute is different from that used for invoking a procedure, method, or function. In C++ [Ellis and Stroustrup 1990], the most popular language for integration with an object-oriented data model, the syntax for access to a method associated with an object is different from the syntax for access to attributes:

```
d.revision()
```

Thus, in C++, an attribute cannot be redefined as a method, or vice versa, without existing programs being modified (addition or removal of parentheses).

Many of the ODMSs we discuss use C++ as the primary access language, and would require a C++ preprocessor in order to implement derived attributes. O_2 provides virtual attributes by using a derivative of C++.

Note that we can obtain virtual attributes in C++ by *programming convention*—by defining a method for retrieving every attribute, and always using the method rather than explicit retrieval to fetch attributes. For example, if existing programs all use `d.revision()` rather than `d.revision` in our example, then we have the benefits of virtual attributes when we must redefine this attribute.

There are many issues with respect to derived and virtual attributes in an ODMS. An ODMS may permit derived attributes to be defined in a query language, a programming language, or a mixture of the two. The issue of *update* of derived attributes introduces special problems. As we noted in the discussion of relational views in the previous chapter, it is sometimes possible to do updates automatically when derived data are defined in a query language, although there are cases where the programmer must specify update semantics explicitly. When derived data are defined in a programming language, the update problem is even more complex. In our example, `d.revision` cannot be used on the left side of an assignment statement.

The only practical way to allow updates in the programming-language case may be to define two separate procedures, to specify both the retrieval and update semantics for derived attributes. In our example, we could define both `d.getrevision()` and `d.setrevision()` methods. Again, it would be more convenient, and more amenable to the use of query languages, if the language itself provided complete virtual-attribute capability, permitting procedural definition of both retrieval and assignment operations on derived attributes. This capability is provided as "syntactic sugar" in some programming languages, such as CLU [Liskov et al 1977].

No current ODMS implementations allow update of derived attributes, even in extended relational database systems. In object-oriented database programming languages, the designers may not think it necessary, because of the degree of data independence already provided by encapsulation. We return to the problem of implementing derived-attribute updates in the next chapter.

In discussing programming and query languages in Section 4.7, we explain the use of derived attributes to provide logical data independence, and examine the relationship between derived attributes and encapsulation. In Section 4.5, we cover procedures associated with objects in more detail; derived attributes are just a special case of this.

4.2.7   Attributes in Functional Data Models

In a functional data model, *all* attributes appear to the user as procedures—or, more precisely, as functions. If we wish to store explicitly, rather than to compute, functions mapping objects to simple values, we can define these functions to be *stored*. The ODMS then allows the stored functions, and other functions for which both retrieval and update procedures have been defined, to appear on either side of an assignment statement. Using our document database as an example, we might write expressions such as

```
revision(d)
```

in a functional model as opposed to **d.revision** in an object-oriented or relational model, and assign a new title to a document **d** by writing

```
title(d) = "Object Data Management".
```

Procedurally defined functions may appear on both sides of an assignment statement only if the user has defined both the retrieval and update actions for the function. Again, this is the same issue as for derived attributes in the relational and object-oriented models. In fact, some people may regard the use of a functional data model as a difference in syntax and presentation, not as a difference in the underlying "model" or semantics of data structures, since the representation of objects in the different data models is very similar.

Note that our earlier comments about BLOBs, references, and parameterized types as values of attributes in the object-oriented model also apply to the values of functions in the functional data model; a rich type system is important in an ODMS for integrity and documentation of data.

4.3   RELATIONSHIPS

Recall the definition of relationships from Chapter 1, and the representation of relationships in the relational model in Chapter 3. Now let's look at the way that relationships are represented in ODMSs. The representation of relationships is one of the most fundamental ways in which data models differ.

We start by examining how relationships are represented in an object-oriented data model; we look at binary and nonbinary relationships and referential integrity in the following subsections. The representation of relationships in a functional model is similar but with a different syntax; we examine this next. Finally, we contrast these representations to relationships in the relational and extended relational models.

4.3.1   Binary Relationships

Relationships are represented in an object-oriented data model using the complex attributes described in the previous section: references and collections of references. The representation used depends on both the multiplicity and the degree of the relationship.

Binary relationships can be represented as follows:

- We represent a one-to-one relationship between two object types A and B by adding a reference attribute to each type.

Declarations   Instance examples

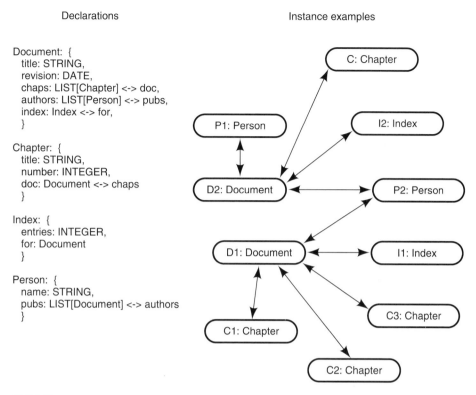

```
Document: {
    title: STRING,
    revision: DATE,
    chaps: LIST[Chapter] <-> doc,
    authors: LIST[Person] <-> pubs,
    index: Index <-> for,
}

Chapter: {
    title: STRING,
    number: INTEGER,
    doc: Document <-> chaps
}

Index: {
    entries: INTEGER,
    for: Document
}

Person: {
    name: STRING,
    pubs: LIST[Document] <-> authors
}
```

FIGURE 4.2   Binary relationship representation in an object-oriented data model. The figure on the right represents *instances* of the declarations on the left, not the schema diagram, which is shown in Figure 1.1 and 1.2.

- We represent a many-to-one relationship between two object types A and B by adding a reference attribute to A and a reference-set attribute to B.
- We represent a many-to-many relationship between two object types A and B by adding a reference-set attribute to each type.

Figure 4.2 provides examples of these three cases of binary relationship, taken from our document database example. The left side of the figure shows the declarations for object types using the same syntax as that in earlier examples. In all these cases, the relationship is manifested as a new attribute of an object that references the associated object, and a new attribute of the associated object that provides a "back reference;" we shall explain this back reference and the "<->" syntax used in the figure momentarily.

The right side of the figure shows graphical examples of object instances and references that might result from the declarations. The document **D1**, for example, has index **I1**; three chapters **C1**, **C2**, and **C3**; and a single author **P2**. Document **D2** has two authors, **P1** and **P2**, with only a single chapter **C** and index **I2** entered in the database.* Do not confuse the right side of Figure 4.2 with the *schema* diagram for the document database, which is shown in Figures 1.1 and 1.2. The diagram in Figure 4.2 represents *instances* of actual documents, chapters, and people stored in the database. We have used instances to better illustrate that the relationships may be many-to-many, many-to-one, or one-to-one.

4.3.2   Inverse Attributes

Names must be given to the new attributes used to represent relationships, analogous to the names given attributes representing relationships in the relational model. For example, in Figure 4.2, the relationship between documents and chapters is represented by the **chaps** attribute of the document objects, and by the **doc** attribute of the chapter objects.

Note that the figure does not simply define the **doc** attribute of a chapter; for example,

```
doc: Document;
```

Instead the syntax on the left side of the figure specifies both the **doc** attribute and the inverse attribute (the **chaps** attribute of document objects), using a double arrow:

```
doc: Document <-> chaps;
```

Conversely, the inverse attribute is defined with a similar syntax in the **Document** declaration:

```
chaps: LIST[Chapter] <-> doc;
```

We call the two attributes *inverses*. They represent exactly the same information, the underlying **contains** relationship.

There are two other pairs of inverse attributes in the figure. The one-to-one relationship between documents and their indexes is represented by the **for** and **index** attributes, and the many-to-many relationship between documents and their authors is represented by the **pubs** and **authors** attributes.

Note that the inverse attribute pairs must be kept in sync with each other. For example, if we add another chapter to a document by setting the chapter's **doc** attribute, the ODMS must add the chapter to the document's **chaps** list. If a chapter is moved to another document, then both attributes must likewise be updated. [Rumbaugh 1987] discusses in more detail the problem of representing relationships as attributes.

You may recognize the problem of synchronizing inverse attributes as a form of *referential integrity*—maintaining the correctness of references when an object is

---

* In a complete representation of object instances, it would be necessary to label the arrows between objects to show the attributes and directionality they represent. These labels are omitted for simplicity here.

deleted or a relationship is changed. DBMSs differ significantly in their treatment of referential integrity; let's look at the problem more closely.

4.3.3   Referential Integrity

If we wish to provide referential integrity in an object-identity-based representation comparable to that provided by keys in the relational model, we cannot simply verify that attributes refer to valid objects of the appropriate types. On close examination, we see that there are several *levels* of referential integrity:

1. *No integrity checks.* A system may provide no checks on references. In this case, a reference could be to an object of the wrong type, or even to a nonexistent object, unless the application properly maintains references. If an object (for example, a document) is deleted, the user must ensure that all references to the document are removed or are set to NIL. The identifier used for the reference could be reassigned by the system to a new object, so this approach is dangerous: The application program can modify the wrong object, or one that does not exist. Despite these drawbacks, many compiled programming languages, such as C, do not guarantee the integrity of pointers.

2. *Reference validation.* The system may ensure that references are to objects that exist and are of the correct type. This may be achieved in either of two ways:

    a. The system may delete objects automatically when they are no longer accessible by the user, as GemStone does [Servio 1990]. The system generally does this by disallowing explicit deletion by the user and performing reference counting or other garbage-collection algorithms to determine when objects should be deleted automatically. Smalltalk and LISP, which were originally interpreted programming languages, have provided this kind of facility for many years. In database applications where it is desirable for *all* objects to be accessible associatively by attribute values, even if they are no longer referenced by other objects, the garbage-collection approach requires users to disable the automatic deletion of objects, usually by putting objects in a special collection at the time they are created. For example, the user can maintain a collection of all **Documents**. In this case, a **Document** must be removed manually from the collection by the user when it is no longer used.

    b. The system may require that objects be deleted explicitly when they are no longer used, but may detect invalid references automatically. This approach can be achieved in a variety of ways. If OIDs are not reused, references to deleted objects can be detected later. If an efficient mechanism is implemented to find all references to an object (such a mechanism is essential in the remaining alternatives), then references to the deleted object can be set to NIL or the deletion can be disallowed as in IRIS [Fishman et al 1987]. VERSANT 1.0 [Versant 1990] provides reference validation. Note that, in most programming-language representations, memory addresses are used for references and there is no back-reference mechanism—for example, to find every **Chapter** that references a **Document**—so reference validation cannot be provided.

3. *Relationship integrity.* The system may allow explicit deletion and modification of objects and relationships, and may maintain automatically the correctness of relationships as seen through all objects. The inverse attributes we discussed in the previous section provide relationship integrity, as does the relational model, but alternatives 1 and 2 do not, since they demand that real-world relationships between objects be represented by multiple user-defined attributes that are not maintained or synchronized by the DBMS. For example, relationship integrity would allow the user to retrieve all **Chapters** for a **Document**, as well as the **Document** for a **Chapter**; and deletion of a **Chapter**, or modification of a **Chapter** to be associated with a different **Document**, would cause the corresponding **Document** object(s) to be updated to reflect the change. The majority of ODMSs provide relationship integrity; Objectivity/DB [Objectivity 1990], ObjectStore [Object Design 1990], ONTOS [Andrews et al 1989], Cypress [Cattell 1983], and PROBE [Dayal and Smith 1986] are just a few examples. Some, such as Objectivity/DB and ONTOS, give this level of integrity as an option, allowing users to choose application-maintained integrity at their own risk to avoid the overhead.

4. *Custom reference semantics.* The most sophisticated systems allow the database designer to specify custom-tailored referential integrity semantics for each type of object or relationship [Rumbaugh 1987, 1988]. For example, a user may wish to delete dependent **Chapter** objects when a **Document** is deleted, whereas only the relationships connecting them would be deleted to maintain relationship integrity under alternative 3, setting the **doc** attributes to NIL. Or, a user may wish to disallow deletion of a **Document** object altogether if that object is still in use for purposes of which the user is not aware. ODMS products and prototypes currently do not provide custom reference semantics except for limited existence dependency constraints, such as the one just mentioned between documents and their components.

Custom reference semantics could be encoded in methods associated with objects, as we shall see in the next section. As long as these procedures are written correctly, and all updates to the related objects go through them, referential integrity can be guaranteed and any sort of reference semantics can be supported. However, it is much better for referential integrity to be handled by the ODMS, as that makes the semantics explicit in the data schema, where it is visible to programs and users, and is less vulnerable to errors in coding.

Referential integrity constraints arise in the context of maintaining multiple versions of objects, as well as in simple operations such as changing relationships and deleting related objects. We return to references to object versions in Section 4.8.

Declarations   Instance examples

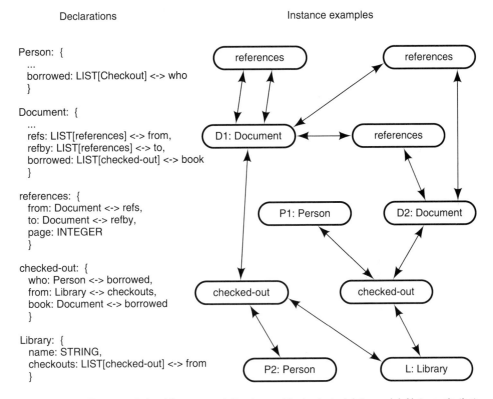

Person: {
   ...
   borrowed: LIST[Checkout] <-> who
   }

Document: {
   ...
   refs: LIST[references] <-> from,
   refby: LIST[references] <-> to,
   borrowed: LIST[checked-out] <-> book
   }

references: {
   from: Document <-> refs,
   to: Document <-> refby,
   page: INTEGER
   }

checked-out: {
   who: Person <-> borrowed,
   from: Library <-> checkouts,
   book: Document <-> borrowed
   }

Library: {
   name: STRING,
   checkouts: LIST[checked-out] <-> from
   }

FIGURE 4.3 Ternary relationship representation in an object-oriented data model. Note again that the diagram on the right represents instances, not schema. The schema representation for the declarations is shown in Figure 1.3.

Remember that an ODMS may implement relationships in a variety of ways, including the ways we discussed for the relational model in Chapter 3. For example, we could create a B-tree on the **doc** attribute of chapters, or use parent–child links as in Figure 3.4. We are concerned with the user's conceptual view of relationships here; their implementation is covered in the next chapter.

4.3.4   Nonbinary Relationships

Now consider relationships of higher degree: object-oriented representations of ternary relationships are illustrated in Figure 4.3. The layout of the figure is similar to that of Figure 4.2: type declarations are shown on the left side of the figure; pictorial examples of instances of objects and relationships are shown on the right. The pictorial representation of the *schema* (the **checked-out** and **references** relationships) is given in Figure 1.3.

Note that it is necessary to create new object types to represent these ternary relationships. We have given the new object types the same names as the relationships they represent in Figure 1.3: `checked-out` and `references`. In an object-oriented model, it is necessary to create new object types for ternary relationships even if the third attribute of the relationship is a literal value such as the page number for `references`. By contrast, the binary relationships in Figure 4.2 can be represented using only inverse-attribute pairs.

From the user's point of view, the introduction of an intermediate object for ternary relationships might make the schema seem more complex. However, the relational representation of the same schema (Figure 3.2) requires an additional relation. Furthermore, if the ODMS allows the "dot" notation to be applied to a collection of objects (to yield another collection), then the introduction of an intermediate object is not an inconvenience; we can still follow the many-to-many relationships between objects with expressions such as

`D1.borrowed.who`

that will reveal who has borrowed document `D1` from any library (person `P2` in the figure), or

`D1.refby.to`

that will reveal the documents that `D1` references (itself, plus the two references to document `D2`). The use of dot notation to navigate connections between objects is convenient. Dot notation can be used in this way in an extended relational model as well, and is analogous to composition of functions in the functional model.

Note that all of the inverse-attribute pairs in Figures 4.1 and 4.2 are defined as lists rather than sets, so the ODMS is instructed to maintain an ordering specified on the relationships. The ordering on document `authors` might have meaning in the real world, for example, and the library `check-outs` may be ordered according to the order of the actual library client transactions.

In the applications we discussed in Chapter 2, ordering is important in some cases and not in others. For example, the order in which `Procedures` are defined in a program `Module` in a CASE application may be irrelevant, but the order in which `Sections` appear in a `Document` in a text-processing application is crucial. An ODMS programming and query language must therefore provide both set- and list-manipulation operations.

4.3.5   Derived Relationships

Relationships, like attributes, may be defined procedurally rather than explicitly. In an object-oriented DBMS with derived attributes, derived relationships can also be defined, since relationships are defined in terms of attributes. Unlike attributes, of course, relationships require more than one retrieval method—they need one for each of the inverse attributes involved in the relationship.

For example, we could define methods for the **doc** and **chaps** attributes we discussed in Section 4.3.2. These methods could associate documents with chapters by an arbitrary algorithm, even by using a foreign key as in the relational model.

We return to both derived attributes and derived relationships later. Now, we turn to the representation of relationships in the functional and relational data models.

4.3.6   Relationships in Functional Models

Relationships in a functional data model differ in syntax and terminology from those in an object-oriented model, but have the same underlying properties.

As with the representation of relationships as object attributes in an object-oriented model, relationships require more than one function in a functional model. For example, the binary relationship between documents and chapters requires both a function and its inverse. We might call these functions **chap** and **doc**, as we did in the object-oriented model. The relationship and attribute functions can be composed: for example, to refer to the title of the document to which a chapter **C1** belongs, we can write

```
title(doc(C1))
```

If the relationship functions are defined to be *stored* rather than computed, then either the function or its inverse may appear on the left side of an assignment statement, thereby modifying and creating relationships:

```
doc(C1) = D1
```

A functional data model implementation must deal with the same issue as object-oriented ones in maintaining inverse representations of a relationship. Instead of using inverse attributes of objects to represent relationships, the functional model uses inverse functions. If a relationship is updated by changing the value of one function (for example, **doc(C1)**) then any subsequent access through the corresponding inverse function (**chaps(D1)**, in this case) must reflect the new relationship(s). The inverse-function maintenance can be performed automatically by both functions being defined in terms of a single underlying stored representation of the relationship; IRIS does this using relational tables as the underlying representation, for example.

Unlike other data models, functional data models do not required introduction of objects to represent ternary relationships; the relationships can be represented directly by functions. For example, **checked-out** in our example database could be represented by functions such as

```
borrower(D1, L1)
```

which would return the person(s) who checked out document **D1** from library **L1**. Note that a family of multiple-argument functions is required to represent ternary and higher-degree relationships, but again, like inverse attributes, all of the functions are defined in terms of one stored function representation. For example, the functions

```
docborrowed(Person, Library) -> Document
libsource(Document, Person) -> Library
```

could be defined in terms of the **borrower** function.

If preferred, of course, intermediate objects may be introduced to represent ternary relationships as in other models. Our earlier **D1.borrowed.who** example would become

```
who(borrowed(D1))
```

in a functional model.

4.3.7   Comparison to Relationships in the Relational Model

The representation of relationships in the object-oriented and functional data models is more powerful and convenient than is the relational representation, in the sense that these models provide a superset of relational semantics (ordering, navigation). Consider the most obvious differences in the relational representation of relationships:

1. References are represented using primary keys instead of OIDs in the relational model, although all the models use references as the basis to represent relationships.

2. Relationship tables (defined in Section 3.3.3) are approximately equivalent to the intermediate objects we found it necessary to introduce for relationships in an object-oriented model, but they are needed in more cases (for many-to-many binary), to satisfy relational normalization.

3. The object-oriented and functional models "package" all the relationships in which an object type participates as attributes or functions associated with the object. For example, we see all the relationships for a **Document** in the schema definition in Figure 4.2. In the relational model, it is necessary to examine the entire schema to determine which tables have foreign keys involving an entity table such as the **Document** table.

4. Object-oriented models allow manual ordering of relationships using lists.

5. The access syntax and semantics are quite different.

TABLE 4.1 A guide to comparing the representation of relationships of different degree and multiplicity, using the figures in Chapters 1, 3, and 4.

Relationship characteristics		Illustrative figures		
Degree	Multiplicity	E-R definition	Relational	Object-oriented
binary	one-one	1.2 doc-index	typically merge	4.1 doc+index
binary	one-many	1.1 contained-in	3.1 doc+chapter	4.1 chapter+doc
binary	many-many	1.2 author	3.2 author	4.2 doc+person
ternary	many-many-literal	1.3 references	3.2 references	4.2 references
ternary	many-many-many	1.3 checked-out	same as above	4.2 checked-out

To facilitate a comparison of object-oriented and relational representations, Table 4.1 lists the figures from Chapters 1, 3, and 4 illustrating the definition of relationships of different degree and multiplicity, their representation as relational tables, and their representation in an object-oriented model.

In the relational model, binary one-to-one relations are generally represented by merging of two entity tables into a single table. For example, the attributes of documents and indexes could be placed in a single table. If we wish to have views of documents and indexes as single tables, then we can define views on the relation to give that effect. In an object-oriented model, the two objects could similarly be merged into one, but this has not been done in Figure 4.2 because object-oriented models generally do not provide an analogous object view mechanism.

Binary one-to-many relationships are represented similarly in both models, if we view entity relations as similar to object types.

Binary many-to-many relationships can be represented directly in the object-oriented model through two list-valued attributes, but they demand the introduction of a relationship table in the relational model (if the database is to be in first normal form).

Ternary relationships require the introduction of an intermediate structure (relationship tables or additional objects) in all of the data models. It is necessary to introduce an intermediate structure even if the third attribute of a relationship is a literal value. For example, the `linkname` of a `Hypertext-link` between two document `Components` in the text-management application (Figure 2.11) necessitates representing the hypertext links using intermediate objects or relationship tables.

As we noted earlier, some object-oriented DBMs do not provide inverse-attribute pairs; that is, they do not provide relationship integrity. Other object-oriented DBMs do provide inverse-attribute pairs but also allow the user to define attributes *without* inverses. These more limited object-oriented models do not guarantee the same level of referential integrity as that provided by the relational model. For example, if **Chapters** reference **Documents**, but not vice versa, it may not be practical or even possible to find the **Chapters** for a **Document** in these implementations. Or, if inverse attributes reference each other but the DBMS does not keep the references in sync, anomalies could arise from updates that do not modify both the **Document** and **Chapter** attributes when making a change.

4.3.8 Relationships in Extended Relational Models

Implementations of relationships in current extended relational models are the same as those in the standard relational model, with one exception: OIDs may be used instead of keys to reference objects (entity tables).

OIDs in an extended relational model are generally treated as system-defined attributes of tuples. The OID field is treated as a primary key, and is not updatable. It is thus straightforward to define a reference to objects using the OID as a foreign key: The syntax is the same as if the primary key were a string or any other type of value.

Systems based on extended relational models may stray from the relational algebra in other ways as well—for example, incorporating ordering or allowing nonnormalized tables [Scheck and Scholl 1986].

4.4 COMPOSITE OBJECTS

Aggregation is the grouping of parts into a whole. In database systems, the term has been used to refer to two kinds of grouping:

- *Attributes* may be aggregated to form *objects*. For example, a **Document** in Figure 2.11 consists of an **author, date**, and **abstract**.

- *Objects* may be aggregated to form *composite objects*. For example, a **Section** in the same figure is composed of some number of **Components** or other **Sections**.

In this book, the term "aggregation" is used to denote only the latter form of grouping. Aggregation of attributes into objects is handled by object type definitions; we return to these in Section 4.6. Aggregation of objects into composite objects is the topic of this section.

Generally speaking, the relationships a user defines in a database are all the same to a database system. However, *aggregation* relationships are singled out as special by ODMSs that provide composite objects. The `part` relationships in Figure 2.11 are examples of aggregation relationships. Chapters may be grouped together to form a document. Mechanical parts may be grouped together to form an assembly. People may be grouped together to form organizations. Almost any kind of object can be grouped together into collections that have meaning in the real world. These aggregations are all composite objects.

Aggregation may be nested many levels. For example, paragraphs are parts of sections, sections are parts of chapters, and chapters are parts of documents.

Do not confuse aggregation of objects into hierarchies of composite objects with *generalization* of object types into hierarchies of types. We discuss generalization and type hierarchies in Section 4.6. [Smith and Smith 1977] provide one of the earliest explanations of both generalization and aggregation.

4.4.1   Aggregation Semantics

Why single out aggregation relationships and composite objects as built-in constructs in an ODMS? How are objects that are grouped as composite objects different from any other set of objects grouped or connected by relationships? There are at least two answers.

First, the ODMS can provide conveniences automatically on the basis of the composite-object abstraction. For example, when a composite object is deleted, the ODMS can automatically delete component objects (and their component objects, if the aggregation is nested). When a composite object is copied, the DBMS can automatically copy all nested objects [Objectivity 1993].

Second, composite objects can be used as a basis for physical clustering of objects [Kim et al 1987]. We defer discussion of clustering to Chapter 5.

The convenience of composite objects for deletion, copying, clustering, and other uses can be substantial, if the user is able to specify which operations should be applied to composite objects. For example, in MCAD applications, it is generally desirable to apply clustering and copy operations to all the elements of an assembly of parts, but not to apply deletion in this way—when an assembly is deleted, the individual parts are generally retained. In our document application, in contrast, it is appropriate for deletion of a document to remove that document's chapters, index, and any other dependent data.

4.4.2   Aggregation Relationships

ODMSs differ in their definition of aggregation relationships. Traditionally, probably descended from knowledge representations in AI, a system-defined `PART-OF` relationship was used.

More recently, researchers have recognized that it is more useful to allow users to define and name their own aggregation relationships according to the type of objects being grouped. For example, in the CASE application in Figure 2.4, we may aggregate **Work-items** using the **schedule-item** relationship, **Programmers** using the **prog-team** relationship, and program **Modules** using the **member** relationship.

Thus, most ODMSs provide a declaration mechanism (for example, a keyword) to specify that a user-defined relationship is the aggregation relationship for a particular type of object. We might define the **doc** attribute of a chapter as follows:

```
doc: PARENT Document <-> chaps;
```

Additional semantics (such as delete, copy, and cluster semantics) may be specified by additional keywords on the declaration. Alternatively, the user may specify at the time an operation is performed whether it should be applied to all the subcomponents of the composite object. [Rumbaugh 1988] studies the problem of custom-tailoring the propagation of delete, copy, and other operations according to the type of relationship between objects.

Nested subcomponents could be represented in an extended relational model by nested (non–first-normal-form) relations stored as an attribute of a composite object. Note, however, that this approach is not as powerful as is the previous one, unless operation propagation semantics can be controlled by the user. The existence of a subcomponent may or may not depend on the existence of the composite object, for example.

A single composite object might participate in more than one aggregation hierarchy. For example, a representation of a building could have separate aggregations for mechanical, plumbing, and electrical hierarchies. Most of the ODMSs that provide an aggregation abstraction do allow an object to be part of more than one composite object. However, even when this feature is not supported, multiple aggregation hierarchies can be stored separately in the database, using parallel representations of the composite object where the hierarchies meet. For example, the user could define and connect three separate **Building** objects, one for each composite object dimension (electrical, and so on), each with its own aggregation hierarchies.

4.5   PROCEDURES

Up to now, this book has dealt with *structural* object-orientation—that is, with objects as data structures [Dittrich 1986]. In this section, we deal with procedures that operate on the objects.

In contrast to traditional DBMSs, ODMSs provide a language for database access that is *computationally complete*; that is, the database language can perform the same operations as a programming language can. In addition, ODMSs may provide the capability to associate procedures with database objects, and store procedures in a database.

A variety of approaches has been taken to support procedures in databases; in this section, we look at the alternatives. We begin by examining *behaviorally* object-oriented systems, in which procedures are used to encapsulate the semantics of an object. In the remainder of the section, we examine other data models and their treatment of procedural data.

We shall not concern ourselves with the language in which the procedures are written, or with a comparison of the merits of programming-language features such as encapsulation with query-language features such as views. These issues we defer to Section 4.7, on programming and query languages.

4.5.1   Procedures and Encapsulation

Recall the object-oriented paradigm we defined in Chapter 1: It is the basis of behaviorally object-oriented systems. The object-oriented paradigm is derived from the concept of abstract data types. Abstract data-type declarations explicitly define a public and a private portion of a data object.

Methods are procedures used in behaviorally object-oriented systems to encapsulate or "hide" the attributes of an object [Goldberg and Robson 1983, Moss 1988, Stroustrup 1986]. The attributes associated with an object are private, and only an object's methods may examine or update these data; the methods are public. Many authors (for example, [Zdonik and Maier 1989]), do not consider a DBMS object-oriented unless it encapsulates object semantics. We avoid this terminology controversy by referring explicitly to structural and behavioral object-orientation. We use the term "method" exclusively to refer to procedures used to encapsulate objects in a behaviorally object-oriented system; some ODMSs may permit procedures in other contexts.

You may recognize the argument for encapsulation as similar to the argument for *data independence* in the relational model: It allows an implementation to be changed without affecting programs using a data type. In the relational model, the data type is a table; in an object-oriented model, it is a class (an object type). Despite the similarities in goals, the ways in which these two models achieve data independence are quite different, and, in some ways, they conflict. We shall contrast these mechanisms for data independence in Section 4.7.

4.5.2   Variations on Encapsulation

The strict definition of "encapsulation" has sometimes proven too restrictive in object-oriented programming languages. For example, [Stroustrup 1986] proposes the concept of *friends*, a declaration to allow object types to have access to each other's private data. The concept of friends is useful when operations must be defined that span two types, such as integer numbers and real numbers. To convert efficiently an integer to a real number, or vice versa, a method needs knowledge of both representations.

The strict definition of encapsulation can also be too restrictive for object-oriented DBMSs: It is not always desirable to encapsulate data with procedures. [Atkinson et al 1989] and [Ellis and Stroustrup 1990] distinguish a different kind of encapsulation, in which either data or procedures may be in the public and private portions of an object. This definition of encapsulation allows private procedures whose specific details can be modified without affecting procedures outside the object, for example, or public data that can be made visible to methods associated with other objects. We call this definition *external encapsulation,* and the traditional abstract data types *procedural encapsulation.* Programming languages and database systems can be found in both of these categories.

Some ODMSs provide encapsulation at the option of the programmer. Typically, these systems allow the programmer to define methods associated with objects, as well as to define "free" procedures—that is, independently-defined procedures operating on a variety of object types. The database programming languages based on C++ provide free procedures.

4.5.3 Procedures in Functional Models

We saw in earlier sections that functions can be used to represent attributes and relationships associated with objects. They can also be used to represent arbitrary procedures associated with objects.

Data independence in the functional model stems from the fact that how the values of a function are stored, or whether they are stored at all, is transparent to the user.

It is possible to combine the object-oriented and functional data models to give some of the best features of both. Indeed, there is more than one way to do this:

- Starting with a functional data model: The functions associated with an object can be grouped with an object. Functions can also be defined as "private," meaning that only other functions associated with the same object can use them. Work on IRIS [Fishman et al 1987] takes steps in this direction.

- Starting with an object-oriented data model: Methods can be defined as functions, and functional methods can be automatically defined by the DBMS for each object attribute declared by the user, including the inverse attributes used to represent relationships. [Kim et al 1988] take steps in this direction with ORION.

These developments are an improvement over a more primitive data model with no mechanism to layer or group functions according to desired visibility or to associate methods (functions with no values, used only for side effects) with objects. They are an improvement over a purely object-oriented data model, because functions provide a uniform notation, another level of data independence, and a better basis than methods to define a global query language that provides associative access to objects.

4.5.4 Procedures in Extended Relational Models

Another way to incorporate procedures into a data model, besides the object-oriented and functional approaches, is to extend a relational query language to be procedural, or to allow procedures written in a programming language to be invoked from a relational DBMS.

Some DBMSs (for example, SYBASE [Sybase 1989]), take the former approach, extending the SQL language with programming constructs such as variables, for-loops, and procedures. Thus, the programmer can perform computation in the database language instead of in the application programming language, if this is more natural.

POSTGRES [Stonebraker and Rowe 1987] takes the latter approach: It allows arbitrary procedures in a host programming language to be stored as attributes of relations. The procedures are linked and executed in the POSTGRES environment, not in the application environment. They are invoked when an attempt is made to fetch or store from the attribute.

Note that POSTGRES and SYBASE are examples of the *extended database system* architecture we defined at the beginning of the chapter: Computation can be performed in the application environment using the programming language, or in the database environment through the query language.

4.5.5 Active Data

Procedures may be associated with objects or their attributes to define *active* data. We have already referred to this capability in discussing methods, functions, derived attributes, and relationships.

Derived data constitutes only one of many kinds of active data that can be stored in databases. Table 4.2 enumerates many kinds of active data, with the corresponding terminology that has been used in database systems. The figure categorizes active data procedures along two dimensions: the result of the procedure (returning the value of an attribute, making database updates, and performing arbitrary actions), and the way that the procedure is invoked (explicitly by name, by a pattern or predicate becoming true, and as a separate independent process also initiated by predicate).

The most important cases of active data in the table are probably those on the diagonal of the table:

- *Derived data.* As we discussed earlier in this chapter, object attributes or relationships can be defined procedurally in an object-oriented, functional, or extended relational data model. Separate procedures may need to be defined

TABLE 4.2 Common terminology for different kinds of procedures in databases.

		Type of Action		
		explicit invocation, same process	invocation by predicate, same process	invocation by predicate, independent process
Result of Action	field value	derived data	integrity constraint	n/a
	DB updates	DB procedure	rule (trigger)	production
	arbitrary	method	notifier	agent

for update and retrieval operations on the data. Derived data correspond roughly to *views* in the relational database literature, but procedural languages may define more complex derivations than views, and are generally used to define individual attributes rather than relations.

- *Rules:* A pattern–action pair may be activated by a database update that makes the predicate become true. Rules can perform database updates, and are executed under the same thread of control as the triggering process. They are sometimes called *triggers* in relational databases [Eswaran 1976, Date 1988]. Integrity constraints are similar to rules, but they do not perform database updates—they simply return an error condition to the user that modified an attribute incorrectly. Rules are an important and useful way to encode knowledge that would otherwise have to be programmed into application programs. POSTGRES provides a rule mechanism, and [Risch 1989] proposes a rule mechanism for IRIS.

- *Agents:* Actions can be initiated spontaneously like rules, but execute as an independent process, in parallel with the triggering process. Actions by *agents* often differ from rules in another way: they are permitted to perform arbitrary actions in addition to database updates; for example, they may send electronic mail, or put up a new window on the user's screen. Some office-automation environments are implemented through many independent object agents sending one another messages [Ellis and Bernal 1982, Dayal et al 1990, Tsichritzis 1985].

In a database programming language, all kinds of actions are implemented in the same language and environment as the rest of a user's application. In extended database systems, which have a separate execution environment for the database and application, however, actions are generally performed in the database environment. This may reduce their utility somewhat, as they can affect an application only through the values that the application retrieves from the database (derived data and rules) or through interprocess communication (agents).

4.5.6   Other Issues

There are many variations on the specifics of procedures. Some we shall examine in more detail later; others are beyond the scope of this book.

Procedures may be defined and bound at compile time, as is generally the case if the ODMS is built as an extension of a compiled object-oriented language, or it may be possible to define new procedures at run time.

It may be possible (as it is, for example, in POSTGRES), to associate different procedures with different individual objects. In most data models, procedures are associated with types rather than with instances of data. POSTGRES's approach provides more flexibility, since the schema designer does not need to anticipate that an attribute will be defined procedurally. However, there is additional run-time overhead to check for the presence of these procedures.

In most recent database programming languages, including ONTOS, ObjectStore, Objectivity/DB, and VERSANT, procedures are stored in conventional programming-language binary files, not in the database. When opening a new database or when operating on a database with a modified schema, the ODMS must ensure that the application program is using the correct version of the programming environment procedures with database objects. If it is not, portions of the running program may require recompiling, reloading, and relinking. However, this is an implementation issue that should not be visible to the user. Every object type in the database is linked with a single object type in the programming language in these systems, so for most purposes the procedures and data appear as if they are a single type system.

We examine the issues of execution environments and locations where procedures are stored in Section 4.7, in examining programming and query languages. We return to implementation issues for procedures and associated tradeoffs as seen by the user in Chapter 5.

4.6   TYPES AND INHERITANCE

We have now defined objects and their capabilities. We have seen how attributes, relationships, and procedures, which we collectively call *properties*, can be associated with objects. In this section, we study how *types* of objects and their properties are defined. We cover type declarations for objects and variables, type hierarchies, inheritance of properties in a type hierarchy, and changes in type schemas or hierarchies.

4.6.1 Types

In the relational model, tables may be considered to be types. More precisely, the definitions of a table's attributes (columns) are the type definition, and the rows of a table are instances of the type.

Object types are generally called *classes* in object-oriented languages. However, the term *class* has been used with more than one meaning, so we have avoided it in this book. There are at least three meanings that have been associated with "class:"

1. A class defines an object type or *intent*—the structure and behavior of objects of a particular type. For example, all objects of type document have a title and revision date, a set of chapters, a set of methods, and so on. The word "type" is used in this book to refer to intent. Note that the intent includes *structure* (that is, the attributes and relationships in which objects having this type can participate), and *behavior* (that is, the methods associated with the type). There may be multiple implementations of the same external structure and procedures.

2. A class defines an *extent*—the set of objects that have a particular type. This is sometimes referred to as a *classification* of objects, so "extent" might appear to be the most appropriate meaning for "class." However, object-oriented programming languages do not usually maintain the extent of a type (for example, to enumerate all the documents that exist), and some of the object-oriented database programming languages have taken the same approach, on the grounds that this is conceptually cleaner [Bloom and Zdonik 1987] and that is easy for the programmer to maintain the extent when needed.

3. A class defines a *representative:* Types are represented by objects themselves, so the class is an object, or metaobject. This type-representative object has properties (attributes, relationships, and methods) that are used to define the intent of objects with that type.

The name of the type-representative object is generally used to tie together these three aspects of a class. The user can obtain or modify the intent or extent of a type through operations defined on the type-representative object. For example, if **Document** is the representative for type document, the operation

```
Document.create()
```

would create a new document and return a reference to it. The operation

```
Document.members()
```

would return the set of all documents in the database, the extent of the type. The operation

```
Document.add-attribute("best-chapter", Chapter)
```

would add a new attribute to the document type, called **best-chapter**, referencing an object of type **Chapter** (type modification such as this raises new issues that we shall discuss shortly).

It may also be possible to associate *default* and *shared* attribute values with the type-representative object. A default value is fetched from an object's type representative when an application attempts to retrieve the attribute from the object and finds none. A shared attribute value appears in all instances of a type, but all instances reference the same copy, typically stored in the type-representative object.

Types are typically not defined by direct method calls on type representatives, as in our examples; they are defined through a DDL. DDLs are our next topic.

4.6.2   Declarations and Variables

In an ODMS, the traditional distinction between a DDL and a DML is blurred a bit, and may initially be confusing. The DML typically contains both a query-language and a programming-language component. The DDL defines object types in a syntax such as the ones we used in Figures 4.1 and 4.2, as in the relational model. However, the user can also declare procedures and variables associated with object types. To complicate matters further, some systems provide operations that change types at run time, as we just did in the **Document.add-attribute** example, in addition to the language for type definition.

For example, using a syntax similar to C++, we might declare a **SourceProgram** as

```
class SourceProgram: Document {
   private:
      ENUM language;
   public:
      compile(STRING parameters)
         { ... }
   }
```

A variable of type document could be declared as

```
d:  Document
```

or as a set of documents

```
my_books:  SET[Document]
```

Variables such as these are *persistent* in ODMSs such as GemStone; that is, these variables may be stored permanently in a database and retain their name and value from invocation to invocation of application programs. In most ODMSs, however, variable names are transient, and are used only during the program execution.

Even transient variables add considerable expressiveness to the DML (query or programming language) for a DBMS. Relational-model implementations generally do not allow table-valued variables. As a result of this, and of the lack of control constructs, the relational DML cannot express many kinds of database operations. In an object-oriented model, the user may define multiple variables that are collections of type **Document**. In most relational implementations, the only collection of documents that may be referenced on a permanent basis is the extent of type document—namely, the document table.*

Persistent variables add even more capability to a DBMS. They allow objects or collections of objects to be named. Without them, the only naming mechanism available is definition of new types of objects to represent collections, which may not be convenient or appropriate when collections of an existing type are defined, or, to refer to individual objects by use of object keys, which may also be less convenient.

In some object-oriented programming languages, such as Smalltalk-80, variables are not declared; instead, their types are defined at run time. This dynamic definition provides more flexibility than static definitions can offer but may involve substantial run-time overhead. We return to this issue in Section 4.6.8.

Note that the scope of a variable declaration varies across systems, and depends on the type of declaration. A variable may be global or local to a procedure. Because global variables are dangerous in an environment with many users and applications, and local variables do not persist beyond the execution of a procedure, GemStone defines global variables in symbol tables belonging to a particular user or group of users. These variables are a natural extension of the type system, since object types, like tables in most relational databases, are assigned ownership as well.

4.6.3   Literal Data Types

Recall the distinction between *literal* and *entity* data types from Chapter 1: Literal data consist of a simple value such as an integer, date, or string; entity values are a group of values, which we call an object, referenced by an OID. In the object-oriented model, there is often little distinction between the two in the way data are manipulated in the programming language. In the relational model, however, they are quite different. Extended relational systems provide two

---

* A relational view could be defined to include rows in a table that satisfy particular constraints. A view might be regarded as a collection or a new type, depending on the type system.

separate mechanisms for defining new types, one for literals (simple attribute types), and one for entities (object types, or relations).

Literal data types are traditionally built into relational DBMSs. The definition of new literal data types requires information about the amount of storage required to store the values, the procedures required to encode and decode values from an external representation, the collating sequence and other properties required by access methods such as B-trees applied to the values, and so on. It must also be possible to define the semantics of existing operations (such as "+" or "=") on the new data type, and to define new operations.

Extended relational systems and database system generators provide just such a parameterization for literal type definition. Using it, a programmer can define, for example, a new literal data type **point** that consists of two floating-point values, an x and a y coordinate. The operation of subtracting two points could be defined to compute the x, y distance between the points, and equality would demand that both coordinate pairs be equal. The definition of new literal types is not a task suited to the typical user; it requires a good understanding of how data are stored and how access methods work. However, it can be a very useful capability.

In object-oriented database programming languages, the distinction between literal and entity (object) data types is less extreme, because the declaration syntax of object-oriented programming languages already provides for both types of data. The ODMS simply stores literal data in-line, and references objects through OIDs.

4.6.4   Type Hierarchy

Most advanced data models include the concept of *generalization*. Generalization is the idea of a hierarchy of types of objects [Smith and Smith 1978, Bruce and Wegner 1990]. Generalization is also called inheritance, subtyping, or subclassing.

An example of generalization appears in our document database: **SourceProgram** is a subtype of **Document**. This is illustrated with an **ISA** arrow in Figure 1.4, pointing from the subtype to supertype. There are other examples of generalization in the application schemas in Chapter 2.

Because of the different meanings for object "class" we discussed earlier (type intent, type extent, and type representative), there are several different kinds of generalization [Zdonik and Maier 1989, Atkinson et al 1989, Albano and Cardelli 1985]:

- *Specification:* Subtypes may be defined as a type predicate applied to objects, as in some programming languages. The predicate may have to be applied at run time, if the subtype is defined based on particular attribute values. For example, we could define subtypes of **Resistor** in an ECAD application (Figure 2.8) according to its physical properties: a **LargeResistor** might be over 1000 ohms, and a **SmallResistor** under 1000 ohms. The distinction between resistor types could be useful if different fabrication techniques were used for the two.

- *Classification:* Subtypes may simply be used as sets to classify objects—that is, to define different type *extents*. For example, we could classify a **Document** as a **Book**, **Journal**, or **Technical-report** even if all three have the same structure and methods associated with them. Note that classification is really just a trivial case of specification: we could define a special attribute of **Document** that specifies to which subtype they belong. However, this trivial case of subtypes by classification into explicit sets is so common and useful that we consider it separately.

- *Specialization:* Subtypes may add additional attributes or methods to a supertype. For example, **SourceProgram** has a **language** attribute that is not present in other **Document** objects. The different types of document **Component** in the text-processing application (Figure 2.11)—namely **Hypertext-link**, **Formatted-text**, and **Graphic**—have different attributes because each requires different information in order to represent the type.

- *Implementation:* Subtypes may provide different implementations of the methods defined in a supertype. For example, we could define subtypes of **SourceProgram** with different **compile** procedures, depending on whether the language is interpreted or compiled. **Formatted-text** and **Graphic** both have a **display** procedure, but their implementation is quite different. Note that, in these examples, the subtypes have the same specification (the **compile** or **display** procedures appear the same to the caller), but a different implementation. The semantics of procedures with the same name and operand(s) may differ—this is a form of the more general concept of *operator overloading,* in which the effect of an operation depends on the latter's operands.

Note that the uses of subtypes for these four different purposes are not mutually exclusive. Indeed, database systems and programming languages generally do not have different subtype mechanisms for these kinds of generalization: they are all grouped together. For example, **Graphic** and **Formatted-text** subtypes of document **Component** have a different specification, specialization, and implementation. Other subtypes may differ in only implementation, or in only classification. It is important to remember that the different types of generalization are generally provided by the same subtype mechanism.

Subtypes are used in combination with *inheritance* to provide a convenient abstraction mechanism for all four kinds of generalization. A subtype inherits all of the type intent of its supertype. The intent, as we discussed earlier, includes the definition of all of the properties associated with the supertype. For example, an object of type **SourceProgram** not only has a **language** attribute and **compile** method, which make sense only for a source program, but also has all the properties of documents (and of any supertypes of documents that we define). **SourcePrograms** therefore have titles, revisions, and so on. They may also participate in any relationship in which a **Document** could participate; for example, they may have authors.*

In some ODMSs, such as GemStone and ORION, the subtype is permitted to *override* the definition of a property of a supertype. This is done by defining a new component with the same name. For example, a **Transistor** in our ECAD application of Figure 2.8 could be given its own **draw-proc** instead of inheriting the one from **Simple-component**. However, to keep an important feature of the type hierarchy—that any object in the **Simple-component** hierarchy can be treated as a **Simple-component** regardless of to what subtype it belongs—we must define the new overriding component, in this case the **draw-proc**, in a way that is compatible with the parent's definition of the component. That is, we may define a new implementation of **draw-proc** as long as its return value and parameters have the same types as in the original **draw-proc**.

Where the subtype does not override inherited properties, it may be useful to think of a type as the concatenation of its own definition with that of all of its supertypes. As we shall see in discussing implementations, in fact, some systems do just that with the physical layout of a type in memory.

The semantics of subtypes interact with encapsulation. Do methods associated with subtypes have the same privileges to access private data as do the methods associated directly with the supertype? In many implementations—for example, the Smalltalk-80 programming language—they do. [Snyder 1986] argues that they should not, as this makes it difficult to change the implementation of the supertype, thereby losing some of the modularity advantage of the object-oriented approach.

4.6.5   Advanced Hierarchies

Type hierarchies may have semantics more sophisticated than those we have discussed so far. Types may have multiple supertypes, or objects may have multiple types. ODMSs provide different mechanisms to classify objects into subtypes, and different mechanisms to define the subtypes themselves.

Most ODMSs allow objects to be given only a single type, assigned explicitly at the time the object is created. However, as we just discussed in subtypes for *specification*, systems may allow objects to be given types according to a predicate that objects must satisfy. IRIS [Fishman et al 1987] requires explicit specification of type, but allows an object to have more than one type. If objects may have multiple types or object types can be defined by predicates, it may be desirable to have

---

* Our example database definition also allows source programs to have chapters! A more complex schema, perhaps with multiple inheritance as discussed next, would be needed in a real application.

additional integrity constraints in the type system—for example, to define the membership of subtypes to be mutually exclusive *partitions* rather than overlapping subsets. The semantics of systems that allow objects to have multiple types or types defined by predicate are complex, and are relatively rare. For these reasons, we do not cover these approaches further.

Most of the ODMSs we cover allow a type to have multiple supertypes. This feature is generally called *multiple inheritance,* because such a type (and an object of that type) inherits properties of all the supertypes. Multiple inheritance, like the single inheritance provided by single supertypes, is useful in reducing the number of types and complexity required in a data schema and application program.

Multiple inheritance is important when there is more than one orthogonal classification hierarchy for objects. For example, we could define another supertype of **SourceProgram,** a **Program**, that might have another subtype called **ObjectProgram**. All programs may have some common components, such as dependency relationships to other programs, but only a **SourceProgram** would have, for example, the **compile** method and **language** associated with it. In effect, a **SourceProgram** is both a **Document** and a **Program**. Without multiple inheritance, it would be necessary to define the **Document** properties (or the **Program** properties) redundantly in the declaration of type **SourceProgram**.

Although the schema notation we defined in Chapter 1 allows a type to have multiple supertypes (by directing the wide ISA arrows at each supertype), none of the application schemas we examined in Chapter 2 required multiple inheritance. This lack is partly due to the fact that all the data schema examples are necessarily oversimplified; real application schemas might have 30 times as many object types and relationships, and more complex needs for data definition. However, our examples do illustrate that the need for multiple inheritance is much more rare than is the need for single inheritance. Some ODMSs do not provide multiple inheritance for this reason, as well as because it is more difficult to implement (as we shall see in Chapter 5).

4.6.6   Schema Evolution

Many ODMSs allow the user to modify type definitions; they vary considerably in the amount of assistance they offer the user in handling the modifications, however. For example, if a new attribute is added to an object type, is it necessary for the user explicitly to "fix" all the existing objects of that type to have the new attribute? Is it possible to add a new supertype when instances of a type exist? What happens to existing programs that use the old schema?

There are three implications of making changes in a data schema: modification to programs that use the old data schema, modification of existing instances of the modified types, and effects of the changes on the remainder of the schema.

The most substantial implications of schema changes can be for programs. Of course, if strict encapsulation is used, and changes are made to only attributes, the only programs that need to be changed are the methods associated with the modified object type. However, dropping or modifying the interface to an existing method may "break" existing code in other object types, as may changes to attributes not protected by encapsulation or by some other data-independence mechanism.

Most of the ODMSs we cover offer no assistance in modifying existing programs for schema updates. We shall focus on changes to the data and to the schema, and defer further discussion of schema-change implications for programs to Section 4.7, where we cover logical data independence.

[Banerjee et al 1987] define a taxonomy of schema changes. With some simplifications, their taxonomy is as follows:

1. Changes to the components of a type:

    1.1.   Changes to attributes:

        1.1.1.   Add a new attribute

        1.1.2.   Drop an attribute

        1.1.3.   Change the name of an attribute

        1.1.4.   Change the type of an attribute

        1.1.5.   Inherit a different attribute definition through 2

    1.2.   Changes to methods:

        1.2.1.   Add a new method

        1.2.2.   Drop a method

        1.2.3.   Change the name of a method

        1.2.4.   Change the implementation of a method

        1.2.5.   Inherit a different method definition through 2

2. Changes to inheritance graph/tree

    2.1.   Add a new supertype/subtype relationship between types

    2.2.   Remove a supertype/subtype relationship between types

    2.3.   Change the inheritance ordering (multiple-inheritance systems only)

3. Changes to types themselves:

    3.1.   Add a new type

    3.2.   Drop an existing type

    3.3.   Change the name of a type

[Abiteboul and Hull 1988, Penney and Stein 1987, Zicari 1990] define similar taxonomies. We can use such taxonomies to classify database systems according to the kinds of schema changes they permit, whether the changes are permitted at run time, and whether the systems change automatically existing data or programs. Note that changes in relationship definitions were not included in the taxonomy, since relationships were represented as attributes in the database systems that the ORION team [Banerjee et al 1987] had in mind. However, they could be added easily, say as 1.3.

All the systems we cover in this book allow changes 3.1 and 3.2 in our taxonomy. Those with a type hierarchy permit 2.1 and 2.2 on types with no instances. Given these changes, it is possible to achieve any of the other changes "manually," by creating a new type with the desired structure and properties, creating new instances of the type by copying and transforming existing instances as desired, changing references to the old instances to point to the new ones, and deleting the old instances and type.

Many systems allow simple name changes such as 1.1.3, 1.2.3, and 3.3, and adding or dropping properties. The name changes typically involve modifications only to the schema itself, because identifiers rather than names are used to refer to types in the instances themselves. Adding or dropping methods typically affects only the schema, as well. Adding or dropping attributes and relationships often requires more sophisticated techniques, because space is typically set aside for these data in each instance.

Changes can be effected on existing objects either by fixing them immediately, at the time the schema is changed, or by using a type representation that allows object type instances with different sets of attributes or relationships to coexist, and be updated as the instances are used. The latter approach, a form of *lazy evaluation* of schema changes, is more difficult to implement but can be useful in avoiding overhead at the time of the schema modification. We defer discussion of these approaches to fixing existing data to Chapter 5, on implementation issues.

ORION and its follow on, ITASCA, probably have the most sophisticated treatment of schema evolution of any ODMS. They can support all the changes in our schema taxonomy, which was in fact defined by the ORION team. New work is still needed in schema evolution, however—the taxonomy deals with only simple changes to the schema. Most application programs need to deal with arbitrarily complex transformations of the schema—transformations defined using a programming or query language. For example, we might split the **name** attribute of **Person** into **lastname** and **firstname** attributes, and write a program to split the existing **name** data using a simple string-manipulation algorithm.

Because relatively complex schema changes can occur in most applications, it is more important for a system to provide good end-user tools to assist in transforming the schema, data, and existing programs, than to provide incrementally more automatic schema evolution for the simple changes in the taxonomy. Unfortunately, little work has been done in this important area to date [Lerner and Haberman 1990]; we return to the topic in Chapter 5.

4.6.7   Dynamic Type Definition

Related to the issue of schema evolution is run-time types, or *dynamic type definition* [Mathews 1990]. Without dynamic type definition, it is necessary to declare all types a program will use before the program is executed.

There are two problems in dynamic type definition: defining the new schema, and manipulating objects using the new schema. The first problem is easily solved, if the ODMS allows dynamic schema operations such as the `Document.add-attribute` we used in Section 4.6.1. The second problem can be more difficult, for two reasons:

1. As just discussed, existing programs are not aware of new schema definitions. For example, if we changed the type of `Document.title` from a string to an integer, a lot of programs might no longer work! A user should not be permitted to execute inadvertently an old program on a new database structure. Schema and program version/date information can be used by the ODMS to avoid this anomaly. Note that a concurrent user could even attempt to modify type `Document` while a program is manipulating `Document` objects, so schema concurrency control or versions are required.

2. The standard programming interfaces to most ODMSs are compiled, making it impossible to manipulate objects using the new schema except through a special dynamic interface. Some ODMSs provide such a special interface through a run-time library provided expressly for this purpose.

These issues bring us to the topic of *dynamic binding*.

4.6.8   Dynamic Binding

Binding means mapping symbol names in a language to their definitions (the type declarations, for our purposes). For example, `title`, an attribute of `Document`, is bound to a particular physical field and type in the representation of a `Document` object. *Dynamic binding* is the ability to perform binding at runtime, as opposed to *static binding* at compile time. Some authors use the terms *late binding* and *early binding* for these concepts.

Dynamic binding may be applied to type names, variable names, attribute names, method names, or any other symbol mapping in the language. In the case of method names, dynamic binding is sometimes called runtime dispatching. Note that attribute and method names are interpreted in the context of a hierarchy of types, so binding may involve traversing a type hierarchy to find the definition.

There are degrees of dynamic binding depending on the flexibility of the mechanisms. It may be possible to define and bind new symbols, or only to rebind existing symbols. It may be possible to bind symbols to newly-defined dynamic types, only to existing types, or only to subtypes of their current type.

There is debate over the value of dynamic binding versus the cost that it entails, but there are clearly applications where at least some forms of dynamic binding are useful. In an office automation system, for example, dynamic binding allows a document to be refined to a particular document subtype and associated methods at runtime. A user of an MCAD application may redefine a part to have different attributes; dynamic binding allows the new part definition to be used immediately.

Dynamic binding is a programming-language concept, not a database concept, but it must be addressed in ODMSs. In extended database systems, and in database programming language implementations not based on existing compilers, dynamic binding can be provided by the ODMS implementation. Dynamic types and dynamic binding may be difficult to implement in database programming languages that utilize an existing compiler and programming environment that do not support these capabilities. However, if an interpreted query language is available in addition to the programming language, then the query language may be used to manipulate newly-defined symbols and types.

4.7   QUERY AND PROGRAMMING LANGUAGES

One of the most important features of a database system is the language it provides to retrieve, manipulate, and define data. It is in this area that the ODMSs we examine probably vary the most. In relational database systems, we used the term *query language* to refer to this language, with DML and DDL sublanguages. An ODMS provides a *database language* that includes a query language plus programming and other capabilities as well.

To understand more fully the query and programming-language capabilities of ODMSs, we shall contrast these languages along seven major dimensions:

1. *Environments:* Recall that database programming languages are extensions of existing programming languages. Extended database systems, in contrast, have a database language separate from the application programming language, although the database language may have programming capabilities—the two languages execute in different environments. We shall discuss the relative pros and cons of these approaches, as well as the frequently referenced problem of *impedance mismatch* between a database language and programming language.

2. *Query results:* ODMSs differ in the kind of results that can be obtained by nonprocedural or *declarative* queries—that is, queries in a language such as SQL where the user specifies what is to be fetched without saying how to fetch it. Some provide no declarative query language at all; some provide one that produces a set or list of objects; some produce relations, like SQL; and some can produce any type of result.

3. *Encapsulation:* Some ODMSs adhere to strict encapsulation of objects, so that only publicly defined methods are visible to users of the database language. This provides a mechanism for data independence. Other systems violate encapsulation for the purposes of the query language: the query-language user can see all attributes of an object. Some provide no encapsulation mechanism at all.

4. *Virtual data:* Some ODMSs allow data fetched by the database language to be defined using derived attributes and relationships as we discussed earlier in

the chapter. Recall that, when it is transparent to the user whether data are derived or explicitly stored, we call the data *virtual*. Virtual data provide another mechanism for data independence, allowing the conceptual data schema to be changed without modifying existing programs.

5. *Data model:* The database languages provided by ODMSs differ according to data model: relational, functional, or object-oriented. The data model affects the syntax and semantics of the database language.

6. *Extended operations:* In addition to programming-language capability, ODMSs generally extend conventional declarative query languages such as SQL with new operations such as transitive closure, recursion, and rules. We shall define and discuss these new operations, to understand the new capabilities they provide to the user.

7. *Standardization:* An important issue in the use of an ODMS in real-world applications is compatibility with existing query-language standards, such as SQL, and compatibility with other ODMSs, in both programming and query languages. Standards allow users to write programs that can work on more than one ODMS product.

The remainder of Section 4.7 comprises a discussion of each of these dimensions, in the same order as that listed. For our discussion, we shall focus on the first two architectures we introduced in this chapter, extended database systems and database programming languages, because object managers generally do not include a programming or query language, and database generators leave the language(s) to be defined by the database implementor.

4.7.1   Language Environments

The approach taken to many of the language dimensions just enumerated is highly influenced by whether the ODMS was built starting with an existing programming language or query language. Consider how the language design differs between the first two database architectures we discussed in this chapter:

- *Extended database systems* provide a query language and programming language to the user, with separate type systems and execution environments. Both languages typically satisfy *computational completeness* as we defined in Section 4.5; that is, they contain procedural control constructs. However, query-language statements must be embedded in the programming language in order to copy data between the database and programming environments. Program execution may occur in both environments, so applications are effectively written in two different languages. IRIS, SYBASE, and POSTGRES are all examples of the extended database system architecture, although they differ in data model and other respects.

- *Database programming languages* provide only one execution environment, procedural language, and type system. Generally, they have a query language, although some are not yet as powerful as those in extended database systems. The existing programming language is generally extended with query-language syntax; this may superficially seem the same as embedding a query language in the programming language, but differs because the query language has the same type structure as that of the programming language, is executed in the same process, and does not contain its own procedural constructs.

The distinction between these architectures can be subtle. The crucial differentiation between the two is whether the database language has access to all the necessary application variables, operations, and system procedures—that is, whether the language is *resource complete* as well as computationally complete. Can a database language program display graphics in an existing application window, or take user input? Is it an extension of a language with which the user is familiar or which he is willing to learn? Is it a language in which the user is willing to program? Does it run and cache data on the same machine as the application in a client–server environment? If a language fails any of these criteria, then we have a two-environment system: an extended database system.

The existence of two environments in an extended database system can be a problem for the programmer. It is necessary to translate data between the two representations in a database application. The transfer of data or of control between the two environments can be a performance problem, as we shall see in Chapter 5. It is also necessary to learn and use two languages, typically with different manuals, from different vendors.

The problems with using two language environments have been widely cited in the database literature as motivation for database programming languages. The problems have collectively been called the *impedance mismatch* between the application programming language and the database query language [Moss 1988, Ford et al 1988, Bloom and Zdonik 1988, Bancilhon and Maier 1988]. The language impedance mismatch problem can be very important to the applications we studied in Chapter 2; let's look at this problem in more detail.

4.7.2   Issues of Impedance Mismatch

The problem of impedance mismatch between application programming languages and database query languages has been around for a long time. Relational database systems generally provide a declarative query language with no control constructs, variables, or other programming features. The programmer writes applications in a programming language with its own data structures, and uses the query language to transfer data back and forth between the program data environment and the database data environment.

For example, consider a document editing application written in C, using a relational representation of the document database from Chapter 1. In Figures 3.1 and 3.2, we derived relational database tables for this database. The C application would typically represent information about the current document(s) being edited using C data structures; the declarations might look something like the object type definitions in Figures 4.1 and 4.2. Before data could be manipulated in the application program, however, they would have to be translated from the relational-table representation to the C structure representation, and when the application was done with the data, they would have to be translated back again. The two representations of the document database (one in C, one in relations) would have to be kept consistent in the face of concurrent access, as well.

In an extended relational database, or in any ODMS with an extended database system architecture, the problems that arise are the same as those in this relational example. Many approaches have been taken to writing applications to deal with impedance-mismatch issues:

- *Query download:* The most obvious approach may be to write queries that fetch all the objects that are or might be required by an application, to translate these data to the programming-language representation, and to copy them back afterward. This approach allows fast programming-language operation on data, but incurs significant overhead in application startup and completion. More important, it does not allow the power of the DBMS to be utilized during application execution, and it limits concurrent access.

- *Database representation:* Another simple approach is to copy no more than a single data field or object out of the database at a time, operating on the data in the database, instead of in the application program. The problem with this approach, as we shall see in Chapter 5, is the overhead in performing each data operation.

- *BLOBs:* Instead of using a schema such as the one in Chapter 3 for a relational database, all the information about a large object (for example, a document with its index, chapters, and other data) can be encoded as a large data structure in the programming language and stored as a single BLOB field in the database. The BLOB can be fetched and stored reasonably efficiently, since only a single database call need be made. However, most of the advantage of *using* an ODMS is lost, since queries, concurrency, and other operations cannot be performed on the elements of a document using the ODMS; the ODMS is unaware of the internal structure of the BLOB.

- *Procedural database language:* Another approach is to write all or most of the application in the query language, when the query language provides programming language operations, as in SYBASE. This approach is also possible, to a lesser extent, when procedures in a programming language can be called from the query language, as in INGRES, POSTGRES, or Starburst. However, both these approaches suffer from lack of resource completeness: Programs executed in the query language may not have access to important global data or user windows that are available to the application program; the programs may even execute on a database server machine instead of on the application workstation. Also, the programmer may prefer to write more of his application in the programming language, instead of in the database language.

- *Extended programming data types:* Rigel [Rowe 1979] and Pascal/R [Schmidt 1977] extend existing programming languages to make relations behave much like other data structures in the language. However, the database and programming-language data models are still not integrated—relations are added as a new data type, rather than providing persistent programming-language data structures. Also, there are performance problems with this approach as implemented in Rigel and Pascal/R, since the relational model is inefficient for represention of complex data structures.

- *Persistent programming languages:* Recently, progress has been made to provide programming languages with transparently persistent data structures, storing the data in an extended relational ODMS [UniSQL 1993, Persistence 1993, Rowe 1991]. This approach is more promising than the others we enumerated; the result might be called an extended relational database programming language. However, to date, these systems still do not eliminate the language impedance mismatch—when the same data are accessed using the database query language, the user discovers that the data model they use is different from the programming language. This is a problem whenever the programming-language data model is very different from the DBMS data model. It is for this reason that work on database programming languages has focused on object-oriented models that closely parallel popular programming languages.

Thus, many attempts have been made to alleviate the language impedance-mismatch problem in database systems with the extended database system architecture, but none of the approaches to date solve the problem completely. The most important advantage afforded by database programming languages is a reduction of the impedance mismatch. Database programming languages are a step forward, as they make the database language much more powerful. In extended database systems, the programmer writes application front ends in a conventional programming language: only the application back end, which fetches data from the database, is written in the database language. Although the database language may have the convenience of programming constructs or the ability to make calls to procedures written in the application programming language, data retrieved must be translated from the query-language type system to the programming-language type system, and vice versa when data are stored. [Manola 1989, Bloom and Zdonik 1988] provide a good description of these impedance-mismatch issues in more detail.

4.7.3   Query Results

In addition to differences in architecture, ODMSs differ in the type of query language they provide. Some provide no query language, giving up associative data access in exchange for direct access to data from the programming language.

Some provide a query language that is less powerful than a relational one. Others provide one that is even more powerful.

Most of the early ODMSs did not provide the same kinds of nonprocedural, global query languages as do relational DBMSs. Indeed, it was primarily for this reason that criticism was leveled against research in object-oriented database systems as being a step backward in database technology [Laguna Beach 1987, Stonebraker et al 1990]. Without a globally optimized query language, people argued, object-oriented systems do not provide the logical and physical data independence afforded users of relational database systems.

The simplest defense for this criticism is that object-oriented ODMSs provide data independence through *encapsulation*, although they do not provide physical data independence automatically as in a query language that is optimized and translated to an internal level by the ODMS. However, a stronger counter-argument is provided by the recent development of object-oriented database systems with a query language that affords data independence.

ODMSs have generally taken one of four approaches to query languages. The approaches are distinguished by the form of query results:

- *No queries:* Some systems do not yet provide associative lookup of objects through a query language—it is necessary to write programs that navigate access paths manually, as in prerelational DBMSs. However, many early users of these ODMSs have been content waiting for query capability, since queries are a lower-priority application requirement for them. Indeed, in some applications, it is *desirable* to write queries as programs, because that is the more convenient and natural description, or is the only way to obtain the desired performance.

- *Collection results:* Some systems (for example, GemStone, ObjectStore, ONTOS, and ORION) provide a query facility for associative lookup that does not operate on an entire database, as relational languages do. Instead, the queries are used to select objects satisfying constraints from a particular collection of objects. These collections may be retrieved from attributes of objects, or may be the extent of a type, for example.

- *Relation results:* The extended relational DBMSs (for example, POSTGRES and Starburst) provide a query language that results in relations. In contrast to collection-result queries, the results can be constructed from any data in the database; they need not be selected from objects of an existing type or collection. These query languages equal or exceed the expressive power of SQL and other relational query languages.

- *Open results:* The O_2 system and the ODMG standard provide a query language that can result in any type of data—for example, a literal value, an object, a list or set of objects, or a tabular array of data. Collection-result and relation-result queries can produce single data elements as a special case, and POSTGRES can return multiple relations, but an open-result query language can be distinguished by its symmetry with respect to data types.

ODMSs with collection-result queries can be further subclassified according to whether they permit *value joins* or only *entity (reference) joins,* as defined in Chapter 3: Reference joins are joins to objects with explicitly defined relationships to objects in the query collection—for example, joining **Chapters** to the **Document** that they reference.

Reference joins are so called because they follow references between objects; in fact these joins are performed whenever the "dot" notation is used to fetch fields of related objects, as in the examples in Section 4.3:

```
D1.borrowed.who
```

Value joins are joins based on arbitrary comparisons of attribute values. For example, in Figure 2.4 a value join would be required to find **Programmers** whose skill-level is greater or equal to the **skill-req** for a **Work-item**. In ObjectStore, you might write this query for **Work-item W** and **Programmers** on a **Project P** as follows:*

```
P.prog_team[: skill_level >= W.skill_req :]
```

All of the relation-result and open-result query languages permit both value and reference joins. Note that collection-result query languages, even where they permit both types of joins, are restricted to *semijoins*: the join restrictions can only be used to filter out elements of a collection, not to create a new relation or type whose elements contain attributes "joined together" from existing relations or types.

It is an application-dependent decision which form of query results is needed, or whether queries are required at all. Collection-result queries with semijoins may be adequate for most applications. Open-result queries subsume all the others, so should cover any need.

Data independence is another important feature of a query language. On what data may queries operate? Are the private data visible to queries, or do the queries operate on methods instead of attributes? To what extent does the query language hide physical representation? We address these issues in Sections 4.7.4 through 4.7.6.

4.7.4   Encapsulation

There are two ways to provide logical data independence in a query language. One is through object-oriented encapsulation. The other is through virtual data. Both encapsulation and virtual data were covered earlier, in our discussion of

---

*   More complex value-joins can also be performed with ObjectStore, for example,

```
S.Work-items[: W = this,
   ! Programmer::extent[: skill_level >= W->skill_req :] :]
```

would find **Work-items** on a **Schedules** for which no programmer exists with the required skill level. However, explanation of this and other query language syntax is beyond the scope of this book.

procedures. Now, we look at these concepts in the context of query languages. We focus on encapsulation in this section, and on virtual data in the next.

Encapsulation provides data independence through the implementation of methods, allowing the private portion of an object to be changed without affecting programs that use that object type. It is important to note that there are two requirements for encapsulation and the data independence it affords:

1. *Hiding:* Some components of an object must be public, while others are private.

2. *Mapping:* Methods must define a mapping between the public and private components.

Any ODMS that provides encapsulation satisfies these two requirements. Note that a system with hiding and mapping also provides logical data independence, because the hidden components can be changed and the mapping redefined.

In the strict definition of encapsulation, as exemplified by Smalltalk, there are several restrictions:

1. Only procedures (methods), not data, may be in the public portion of an object.

2. Methods are defined in a procedural language.

3. Methods can see and manipulate only data within the object.

We shall relax somewhat all three of these restrictions on encapsulation for the purposes of this book.

In keeping with [Atkinson et al 1989], we relax the first restriction, allowing data to be in the public portion of an object. Note that C++ also allows data in the public portion of an object. Data independence can still be achieved with data in the public portion if the language allows virtual data. We discuss this topic in the next subsection.

With a database language that provides both procedural (programming language) and declarative (query language) features, we modify the second restriction. Methods may be defined in either or both types of language. The use of a declarative language is important for *physical* data independence.

The third restriction on encapsulation needs to be relaxed somewhat to remedy the shortcomings of the object-oriented paradigm: for example, operations that involve more than one type of object cannot be expressed cleanly. The operation "+" can be defined on real numbers and on integers, but what happens when we want to multiply an integer and a real number? Do integer objects need to know about the implementation of real objects, or vice versa? We cannot even convert an integer to a real number without writing a procedure that is dependent on both representations.

To remedy this shortcoming, the C++ notion of object type has three portions: public, private, and protected [Ellis and Stroustrup 1990]. The public portion is globally visible. The protected portion is visible only to subtypes. The private portion is visible only to methods defined within the class, or to classes or procedures declared to be *friends* of the class. The notion of friends and of protected portions allows groups of classes to cooperate more flexibly in the implementation of an abstraction.

As noted earlier, encapsulation places restrictions on the use of a query language. Traditional query languages are designed on the assumption of a simple, uniform, and visible structure for the objects on which they operate. A strict object-oriented approach dictates that the attributes and relationships associated with objects be invisible to the user; the query language must operate only on methods.

Some ODMSs avoid the problem by violating the object-oriented paradigm for the purpose of the query language, or at least for use of the query language by the end user, allowing object attributes and relationships to be visible through the query language just as they would be through a method on the object. These systems provide *partial hiding:* The private implementation of an object is hidden from programs, but not from queries. The justification behind this approach is that the query language is for ad hoc end-user access, so logical data independence is less of an issue [Bancilhon et al 1989].

Of course, programmers could avoid the encapsulation issue by defining methods for all the attributes that they want visible to the query language. Or, the ODMS could provide retrieval-only access or automatically derived attribute-fetch methods for selected classes of objects.

4.7.5   Virtual Data

As we noted in Section 4.2, the notion of derived data is analogous to that of relational views. Derived data may be useful for many purposes, but the most important use is probably to define virtual data, for logical data independence: When a data schema is changed, derived data can be defined for old attributes and relationships, so that existing programs and queries continue to work.

The data models differ in their approach to virtual data. The idea of relational views is adapted and expanded in extended relational models. Derived data defined using object-oriented methods in a procedural language can be more powerful than relational views, because separate actions can be specified for retrieval and update, and arbitrary computations can be specified.* [Gilbert 1990] discusses derived data in object-oriented models. The functional data model is ideal for defining virtual data, because *computed* functions associated with objects are indistinguishable from *stored* functions (that is, ordinary attributes).

Relational views, functions, object-oriented methods, or any other form of virtual data are not sufficient for logical data independence; they provide *mapping*

---

* Object-oriented query languages may allow derived data through a query language, as well as methods. For example an ObjectStore programmer could write `set <person*> trusted = people[:age()<30:]` to define a derived collection.

but not *hiding*. Many ODMSs as well as traditional DBMSs provide mapping without hiding. For example, most relational products do not provide hiding, although they will probably eventually support hiding through the external and conceptual levels we defined in Chapter 3. The functional model DBMSs we discuss, IRIS and PROBE, do not provide hiding.

Although most of the object-oriented DBMSs we have discussed provide hiding, the *mapping* mechanism is often weaker than that in relational views. As we have noted, in many object-oriented DBMSs, both data and procedures are accessed using dot notation, but it is *not* transparent to the user whether data or procedures are being accessed. Procedure calls are followed by parentheses, whereas a variable access is not. Thus, it is bad practice to place variables in the public portion of a type definition, as the variables cannot later be redefined procedurally without all references to the variable being changed. Perhaps the inability to provide procedurally defined fields transparently will be corrected in a future version of C++, providing convenient logical data independence analogous to that afforded by relational views.

To provide *full* logical data independence, the mapping mechanism must work for both storage and retrieval of data values, not just retrieval. We have already seen some of the limitations of relational views used to provide logical data independence. Views cannot always be used to update data, because the mapping is not necessarily reversible. The same will be true of derived data defined in *any* declarative language with sufficient expressive power [Keller 1985], and certainly of derived data defined in procedural languages.

An alternative to deriving update methods automatically for derived data would be to allow the user explicitly to specify procedures to fetch and store derived data values. This is not yet implemented in the ODMS prototypes and products we discuss.* Also, user-defined fetch and store procedures are not guaranteed to be correct—a surprised user may find that an attribute to which he assigned the value 3 has the value 4 when he fetches it, if the procedures are not properly implemented!

4.7.6 Data Independence

In summary, we have seen that virtual data and encapsulation are both useful to provide logical data independence, but that they cannot do so unless they provide both *hiding* and *mapping*. Hiding and mapping were provided in the relational model through the three-level schema architecture [Tsichritzis and Klug 1978] and relational views [Date 1990] we discussed in Chapter 3. These requirements also can be satisfied in more advanced data models:

* In a functional or extended relational model, functions or views defined in a database language can provide mapping, but the mapping must be invertible

---

* Of course, as we have noted, the user may define and invoke separate **set** and **get** methods for each attribute, but this is neither convenient nor as amenable to use in a query language.

for full logical data independence, and both external and conceptual schema levels must be defined to provide hiding—it must be possible to define public components whose interface will not change, and private components with restricted access.

- In an object-oriented model, it is useful to weaken the strict definition of encapsulation, to allow data in the public portion of an object, to allow more flexible sharing of private data, and to define "function" methods that act as virtual attributes. Again, these functions must be invertible, or else both fetch and store semantics must be defined.

The most important factor for *physical* data independence is the use of a declarative query language in programs and methods. Declarative languages specify the data that the user wants without specifying how to obtain them. As a result, the query optimizer can determine automatically whether indexes, links, or other access methods exist on stored attributes and, transparently to the caller, can choose the most efficient technique to fetch the objects satisfying the query. If the physical structure is later changed—for example, if an index is added—the new structure will be used and the programs do not need to be changed. Since most ODMS database languages are designed by combining procedural control constructs and a query language, this physical data independence can be lost, because the resulting language is not amenable to the simple algebraic transformations that can be made to optimize operations such as relational selections, projections, and joins.

Note that the level of physical data independence provided by query optimizers for declarative languages is not unlimited; perhaps a higher level of physical data independence can be provided for procedures defined in a mixture of procedural and declarative languages through future research combining traditional programming-language optimization with query-language optimization. However, the algebraic simplicity of optimizing languages that are "more" declarative than procedural will always remain a factor.

Note that encapsulation provides a level of physical as well as logical data independence, even using method definitions in a programming language. Encapsulation allows the private data structures associated with an object to be changed arbitrarily. However, when changes are made, the programmer must modify manually all the methods affected by the change. Also, the advantage of encapsulation to limit the repercussions of changes to private data structures are reduced as encapsulation is weakened to encompass operations that span object types—for example, joins.

4.7.7 Issues in Data Models

Another dimension on which ODMS database languages differ is in the data model used for the language: extended relational, object-oriented, or functional. Generally speaking, since most of the ODMSs we consider have computationally complete database languages, the data model affects the syntax more than the semantic power of the system: the programming-language portion can be used to overcome any shortcomings in the query language. However, the expressive power of the declarative query language is still an issue, as we shall discuss in Section 4.7.8, and the user may find the query language used in one data model more natural than that used in another. For example, the use of functional notation and operators may be more natural to a user than are relational query languages. Since object-oriented DBMSs vary widely in the query languages provided (for example, ONTOS uses a variant of SQL, whereas ObjectStore uses a notation based on an algebra derived from C++ expressions), user convenience might be an issue even between ODMSs with different variants of the same model.

Depending on the data model, the query and programming languages may be combined in more than one way. If an ODMS does not provide the ability to call the query language from the programming language, as well as vice versa, then some applications may be awkward or less efficient to encode using the ODMS.

The choice of data model is perhaps the most controversial issue in object data management: Determining the most natural representation and syntax for an application is often a subjective process. Unfortunately, every ODMS we cover has a quite different query language, so it is not feasible to provide examples of all the alternatives here. Examine the Appendix and the references cited in the bibliography to see some of the approaches.

4.7.8 Extended Operations

The expressive power of the query language may vary across ODMSs. Additional expressive power is important because it allows more of the application to be encoded in the declarative language, which may be more concise or provide a higher level of physical data independence than the programming language [Lindsay and Haas 1990, Stonebraker and Rowe 1986, Khoshafian et al 1990, Beech and Ozbuton 1990].

For example, some ODMSs include some form of *transitive closure* in the query language. Transitive closure allows relationships to be traversed iteratively to find all objects reachable from a given starting point through specified relationships. POSTGRES provides transitive closure through use of a "***" specification:

```
retrieve * into Subordinates (E.name, E.manager)
from E in Employee, S in Subordinates
where E.name="Jones" or E.manager=S.name
```

This query, when executed on a relation defined by

```
create Employee
   (name=char[20], salary=int[7], ... manager=char[20])
```

retrieves all of the subordinates of employee `Jones` and stores them in the new relation `Subordinates`. The `retrieve` command is repeated for new employees `E` until no more changes are made to the `Subordinates` relation.

Another useful extension of query languages is text pattern matching [Itasca 1990]. The SQL query-language standard has limited capability for regular expression pattern matching in strings, and ODMSs lend themselves to applications such as office information systems where text search can be as important as structured queries.

4.7.9   Rule Systems

In addition to query-language enhancements for transitive closure, text matching, and other operations, a useful ODMS feature is a *rule system*. As we noted in Chapter 1, a rule system is the essential ingredient to allow an ODMS to be used for *knowledge management*, in addition to data management and object management.

POSTGRES is the only ODMS we cover that incorporates rules in the query language. It allows commands of the form:

```
on {retrieve, replace, delete, append, update, new}
to object where POSTQUEL-Condition
then do POSTQUEL-Commands
```

The `POSTQUEL-Commands` may also qualify data fetches with `new`, `old`, or `current` to refer to data before or after execution of the POSTGRES transaction invoking the rule. The transaction may also be refused altogether. This feature allows for more convenience and power in specifying actions.

For example, the rule

```
on new Employee.salary where Employee.name="Jones"
then do replace E (salary = new.salary)
using E in Employee where E.name="Smith"
```

updates Smith's salary to keep up with Jones's whenever Jones's salary is changed. A simple rule on our example database might be something like

```
on update Chapter
then do Chapter.doc.revision = Today()
```

to update a document-revision date whenever one of the chapters is modified.

Rather than incorporating rules directly into the ODMS as in POSTGRES, another approach is to build an expert-system shell on top of the ODMS. [Ballou et al 1988] report on work in this direction, using the PROTEUS expert-system development facility on top of MCC ORION, storing knowledge and rules in the ODMS. The advantage of this layered approach is that it allows the expert system and ODMS to be developed, maintained, and optimized separately. The disadvantage is that it is more difficult to deal with functionality or performance issues that span the two; the ODMS must provide the necessary "hooks" for the expert system—for example, a notification mechanism powerful enough to detect when rule predicates must be re-evaluated.

In the future, much more complex operations and rule systems may be incorporated into query languages. Other work on rule systems includes the logic database language (LDL) system [Chimenti et al 1990] and NAIL! [Morris et al 1987]. These languages have not yet been integrated with a database system. [Cacace et al 1990] describe work in progress toward combining expert-system rule systems with an ODMS in LOGRES. Eventually, all the power of logical inference from deductive database research [Zaniolo 1990, Brodie et al 1990, Kim, Nicolas, Nishio 1990] will be incorporated into the ODMS itself, or ODMSs will be designed such that they can support expert-system shells efficiently and conveniently to the user.

4.7.10   Standards Issues

The invention of ODMSs introduces a variety of standards issues. The SQL query-language standard [Date 1987, X3H2 1986] has been important to the success of relational DBMS products. Standards are just beginning to emerge for ODMS products.

There are four standards issues for ODMSs:

1. *Data model:* As we noted in Chapter 1, there has been no single "object-oriented data model;" there are many such models, depending on the kind of encapsulation, inheritance, procedures, and other features provided. Similarly, there are many extended relational and functional data models. Although each family of data models shares common features (for example, basic relational capabilities in extended relational systems or the features [Atkinson et al 1989] define for object-oriented models), there is little common basis for these models.

2. *Query language:* Even with a common data model, there has been no equivalent of a standard query language for any of the models. No two ODMS products have the same query language at the time of this writing. Thus, it has not been possible to write queries, either in a program or by an end user, that can operate on more than one ODMS.

3. *Programming language:* For those extended database systems that provide query-language extensions for procedural capabilities, or database programming languages that provide programming-language extensions for database

operations, there is a new standards issue that did not arise in traditional DBMSs: a standard is needed for these extensions, to allow programs to be portable across systems. Also, a data-model standard is needed that works with multiple languages, at a minimum allowing interchange of data between languages as is possible with SQL today.

4. *SQL:* SQL is a standard for relational DBMSs, and it is currently the only standard for database access that is widely implemented and recognized. Thus, it affects new ODMS products as well.

Extended relational database systems have advantages in all these dimensions of standards, since they share a common relational model supported by standards groups. However, progress on relational standards has been slow, and almost none of the current systems fully support the SQL standard. The extensions embodied by POSTGRES, Starburst, and extensions to existing relational systems such as INGRES and SYBASE are not standardized.

You might be surprised by inclusion of SQL in the list of standards for the next generation of database systems, since SQL is a relational standard. However, SQL will be important to ODMSs for three reasons:

- *Heterogeneous database access:* In a typical customer site, different types of data in different departments will be stored in separate DBMSs. It is necessary to speak SQL to fetch data from another repository, or to allow another DBMS to fetch data from the ODMS.

- *Familiarity:* There are already many database application programmers who are familiar with SQL syntax and semantics.

- *Standard:* SQL is standardized, whereas standards are just emerging for the more powerful query capabilities of ODMSs.

Thus, SQL is a natural starting point for further standardization efforts. However, it is difficult to extend SQL to incorporate the semantics of ODMSs. Already, extensions made to SQL by different DBMS vendors such as SYBASE, INGRES, and ORACLE are not compatible. The most important influence of SQL on ODMSs is probably the first one we listed: heterogeneous database access. New standards for a more powerful "OQL" for ODMSs are emerging, but we also will need to fetch data out of existing SQL-based DBMSs as part of an ODMS query, and, possibly, to fetch data out of ODMSs from relational DBMSs. Little progress has been made on these problems, although attempts to build object-oriented models on top of relational models may offer some help [Premerlani et al 1990, Wiederhold 1986], a few ODMS projects have successfully used an SQL derivative as a query language (IRIS, ONTOS, Objectivity/DB, VERSANT), and gateways have been built to allow relational database access within an ODMS (Objectivity/DB, GemStone, VERSANT, ONTOS).

Standards are important to the acceptance of new ODMS technology, mainly because of the portability issues with programming-language and query-language standards. Many of the new ODMSs are products from small companies that may not be around in a couple years; software developers are hesitant to write a lot of code that is not portable to other products.

Recently, substantial progress has been made toward standards for both extended relational (SQL3) and object-oriented (ODMG-93) DBMSs. We shall cover this work in Chapter 6.

4.8   PERSISTENCE, CONCURRENCY, AND RECOVERY

Object data management raises entirely new issues in concurrency and recovery for databases, because ODMSs are intended for users with new kinds of concurrency requirements: Data may be checked out for long periods of time, multiple versions of the same objects may be stored in a database, and known semantics of objects may influence the most desirable granularity or type of concurrency control.

In relational database systems, the transaction mechanism provides both concurrency-control and recovery mechanisms that are normally adequate for business applications. ODMSs use enhancements of transactions, as well as new techniques such as versions.

4.8.1   Persistence

Concurrency, recovery, physical integrity, and logical integrity are important because data in a DBMS are *persistent;* that is, the data remain after a user session or application program execution [Khoshafian and Valduriez 1990]. Because ODMSs may differ from traditional DBMSs in allowing both persistent and transient data, a few comments on persistence are appropriate before we proceed.

Transient data last only for the invocation of a program. Persistent data are retained until they are no longer used; then, they are deleted. In traditional DBMSs, transient data are stored in programming-language variables, and persistent data are stored in the database (generally speaking—some relational databases do provide a mechanism for temporary tables).

The ability to manipulate transient data can be useful for a variety of applications. In the CASE programming-in-the-small application we considered in Chapter 2, for example, it may be desirable to use a transient database to represent information about a program the user is currently manipulating, storing data persistently only after the changes have been completed and checked, and storing only a subset of the transient data (information indicating where data objects are displayed on the screen in a graphical representation may no longer be needed at the end of a session, for example). The data-modeling and query-language facilities of the ODMS can be applied to the transient data, whereas they cannot be applied to the transient data stored in conventional programming-language variables.

ODMSs may differ in how an object actually becomes persistent. In fact, a single ODMS may offer more than one choice for persistence:

1. *By type:* An object may be made persistent when it is created, based on its type (persistent types versus transient types), as in Objectivity/DB or ONTOS. The type might be identified as persistent in the declaration, or by being a subtype of a system-supplied persistent object type.

2. *By explicit call:* The user may explicitly specify persistence of an object, as in ObjectStore. This call may be performed at the time the object is created, or, in some systems, it may be performed at any time.

3. *By reference:* A few systems automatically determine persistence of objects by *reachability* from certain globally known persistent root objects. This approach, used by GemStone and PS Algol, is analogous to that in garbage-collected languages such as LISP or Smalltalk.

The arguments for approaches 2 and 3 are generally ones of convenience. Persistence is naturally orthogonal to the type of an object, and mixing the two in 1 overloads the meaning of type. Persistence by reference (3) is the most powerful approach, in some sense: it frees the user from thinking about persistence for each data item.

The convenience of 2 or 3 may not be justified by the implementation overhead, however. Implementations for persistent objects typically require that objects be stored in a special area of memory, thus requiring that objects be copied when they become persistent. Determining persistence by reference can involve significant overhead. It also may not be consistent with the data model, since, in most database systems, unlike in programming languages, *all* objects can be retrieved according to their type and attribute values, regardless of whether they are referenced explicitly by other objects. We discuss the implementation issues further in the next chapter.

4.8.2   Transactions

ODMSs generally do not discard transactions as a concurrency and recovery mechanism; instead, they merely augment transactions, to allow *long* transactions and *nested* transactions. Long transactions are transactions that may last for hours, or days. Nested transactions are transactions that allow a group of updates in an existing transaction to be committed or aborted without committing or aborting the surrounding transaction.

Let's look at the motivation and definition for these kinds of transactions in more detail. There are generally two uses for transactions in the applications we covered in Chapter 2:

1. Transactions may be used for concurrency control in some cases. If portions of a database have access characteristics similar to traditional business applications—that is, frequently accessed data that are shared between users—then traditional short transactions are good for concurrency control. However, when a transaction continues for hours or days, then new approaches are needed—it would be disastrous to lose days of work because of a lock conflict with another user, for example. Two solutions that have been suggested for this longer-term concurrency control are *conversational transactions*, which allow data to be checked out for a long period [Lorie and Ploufe 1986], and *versions*, which we discuss in Section 4.8.3.

2. Transactions are important for recovery and for performing a group of operations as an atomic action. Recovery is particularly important when a database session lasts for long periods—the life of a database is typically just as long as in business applications. Traditional short transactions are sufficient for performing atomic actions, as well as for recovery in most cases. However, if conversational long-term transactions are used for concurrency control, it may be necessary to nest transactions within the long-term transaction for recovery purposes.

Most traditional DBMS products cannot handle transactions that last for hours or days — such transactions may be aborted spontaneously, or may exhibit poor performance. This problem with long-lived transactions is primarily one of implementation, as we shall see in the next chapter; with the appropriate techniques, transactions may last for days or weeks. Another issue with long transactions is that data may be locked for long periods, making it impossible for other users to complete their work. This problem demands other solutions, such as *soft* locks that send notification when broken. Researchers have investigated long transactions for object data management [Korth et al 1988, Skarra and Zdonik 1988, Khoshafian and Valduriez 1990, Lorie and Ploufe 1983].

Nested transactions can be used for both recovery and atomicity in CAD applications, where a long design session consists of many individual design changes [Moss 1981]. Each individual change can be either committed to disk, or backed out in its entirety, in the event of an error. The entire session may also represent a change of a much larger magnitude that should be completed correctly or backed out. Transactions can be nested many levels, as needed by the application; a transaction abort at one level does not affect a transaction in progress at a higher level.

Nested transactions are generally not implemented in the ODMSs we discuss in this book, although some systems have a partial implementation, and relatively little has been written about nested transactions and transaction requirements for CAD, CASE, and other new applications [Bancilhon et al 1985, PCTE 1989].

Nested transactions apparently have been a lower-priority requirement for engineering applications to date.

ODMSs may also implement *optimistic* as opposed to traditional *pessimistic* transactions. Optimistic transaction implementations are more efficient when concurrency conflicts are rare—the system does not check for lock conflicts with other users until transaction-commit time. Since optimistic concurrency is an implementation and performance issue, it is deferred to Chapter 5.

4.8.3 Object Versions

Although transactions will probably continue to be useful for recovery purposes, there is an alternative to conversational and nested transactions for concurrency-control purposes that is gaining popularity: versions. The use of multiple versions of objects to allow coordination among multiple users and different copies of objects has received some attention in the literature [Beech and Mahbod 1988, Kim and Chou 1988, Katz 1985, Tichy 1982]. Versions have been implemented in a number of products and prototypes, although their semantics currently differ widely. With time, perhaps a standard set of features for versions will evolve.

The most basic functionality required for versions is creation and deletion of object versions. ORION, ITASCA, VERSANT, ObjectStore, Objectivity/DB, and ONTOS provide the capability to create and destroy object versions, for example. A user or program may create new versions of objects explicitly, or under certain circumstances—for example, for an object declared to be *versioned*—a new version may be created implicitly whenever the object is modified. Of course, it must also be possible to destroy or archive old versions of objects when they are no longer needed.

Versions in an ODMS can greatly simplify applications that must maintain multiple versions of data; without this functionality, the application must implement version semantics and maintain version information explicitly in the database. For example, in the CASE application of Figure 2.3, a database of programs and modules, we explicitly maintain generic **Configuration** and **Module** objects, as well as multiple versions of these objects, called **Config-vers** and **Module-version**, respectively. To access the multiple versions, we must maintain **version** and **latest-vers** relationships between them. If an ODMS implemented versions, this schema could be greatly simplified.

Very complex *version histories* can result for a particular object. We illustrate version histories for hypothetical objects X, Y, and Z in Figure 4.4; these objects might be **Cells** in our ECAD database example, for example. The figure illustrates that new versions of an object need not be created in a strict linear sequence. We may create new versions of an object X_1, X_2, X_3, X_4 by sequentially modifying the latest version of the object X, but we may also go back to an earlier starting

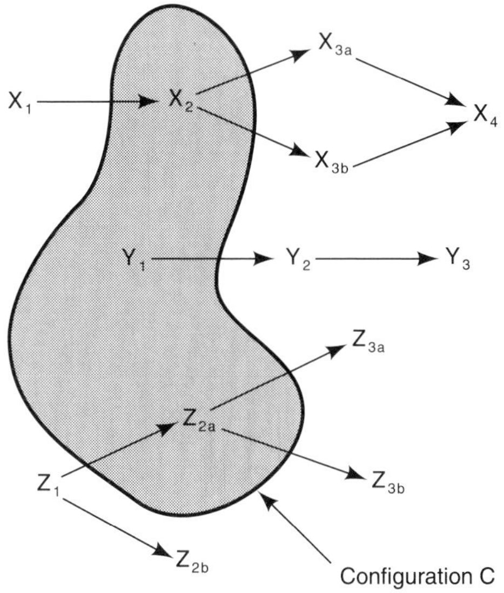

FIGURE 4.4   Version history for three objects X, Y, and Z in a database. The configuration C represents a group of object versions that are a mutually consistent view of the database; other such configurations may be defined.

point and create *branching* versions X_{3a} and X_{3b}, both derivatives of X_2. These versions may later be subsumed by a *merged* version X_4.

Branching versions—that is, two or more independent new versions of any object—can be useful in a design environment when two or more engineers must work independently on revisions that involve some of the same objects. Eventually, the engineers must merge their work together; that is, they must create a single new version of an object that supercedes their separate, branched versions, in order to build a consistent design from their work. Thus, the version history will contain both branch and merge points.

All the ODMSs with versions provide mechanisms to examine this version history, and most allow version histories with branching and merging. In some systems, versions may be classified as *transient, working,* or *released.* A transient version is promoted to a working version visible to other users at the end of a session, and a working version is promoted to a released version when objects are frozen for use.

Versions may also be applied to composite objects, to create new versions of a group of objects at once. An ODMS may also allow versions to be applied to the schema itself, thus simplifying the schema-evolution problem we discussed in Section 4.6.

Object versions introduce a problem: references to an object must be updated when a version of the object is created or destroyed. When a new version of an object is created, do references to it elsewhere in the database get updated to refer to the new one, or do they continue to refer to the old one? More generally, how does the user know which versions of which objects belong together in a consistent *configuration* of objects in an entire database? We address these questions next.

4.8.4   Configurations

A *configuration* is a collection of versions of the objects in a database that are mutually consistent. For example, if updates are made to 20 software modules to create a new version of an operating-system release, then these 20 new object versions, plus the existing versions of all the other modules in the operating-system release, represent a configuration. References between objects in a configuration—for example, to modules defining common data structures—must be maintained to the appropriate versions of objects in the configuration when object updates are made. In Figure 4.4, object versions X_2, Y_1, and Z_{2a} represent one consistent configuration. A reference between X and Y, when dereferenced by an application program from X_2, must therefore yield Y_1.

There are two approaches to configurations in an ODMS:

1. The ODMS may provide a *mechanism* but not a *policy* for configuration management, leaving the configuration-management problem to be solved by the user. This approach is taken by Objectivity/DB, for example.

2. The ODMS may implement configurations automatically, with some policy options specified by the user. ObjectStore, for example, uses this approach.

In the first case, the ODMS must provide sufficient mechanism to implement configurations in an application conveniently. For example, in Objectivity/DB, composite objects may be used to represent configurations. Objectivity/DB gives the user three version-maintenance options for relationships between objects: *move, drop,* and *copy.* An inverse attribute representing a relationship in a versioned object is tagged with one of the options; when a new version of the object is created, the corresponding action is taken.

*   *Move*: The reference should be moved to the new version of the object, and should be set to NIL in the old version.

*   *Drop*: The reference should stay with the old version, and should be set to NIL in the new version.

*   *Copy*: Both the new and old versions should have the same reference in them.

For example, consider what happens to the `doc` attribute of a `Chapter` in our document database when we create a new version of the `Chapter`: The reference to the chapter's document can be moved to the new version, leaving no connection (a NIL value for **doc**) in the old chapter; it can be dropped, with a NIL value for **doc** in the new chapter; or it can be copied, so that both the new and old versions appear as chapters of the same document.

A variety of other approaches has been taken to maintaining consistent references to versions. An ODMS may provide *static* and *dynamic* references to objects; static references "stick" to the current version of the referenced object when a new version is created, whereas dynamic references always point to the most recent version. The user may specify a *default* version of an object to be used for all references unless otherwise specified. In ORION, an application can request *change notification* when a new version of an object is created.

The set of these mechanisms that an ODMS provides to maintain consistency in version references, together with composite objects and user-defined methods associated with objects that can implement application-specific version semantics, provide mechanisms for the programmer to implement a variety of basic configuration-management policies. There are differences in the functionality provided by the ODMSs (for example, ORION provides only *move* and *drop* semantics for references, and VERSANT does not have composite objects), but the general philosophy of these systems is the same: Users define their own configuration management on the primitives provided.

The second alternative for configurations is to build configuration management into the ODMS. There are many ways in which this can be done, depending on the policy for treatment of versions, references, and queries. However, the approach taken in ObjectStore is probably simplest; it works as follows:

1. Configurations are represented as special objects, with an OID, name, or other means for identification.

2. There is always a *current configuration* in a database session; the user may open an existing configuration or create a new configuration to change the current configuration.

3. Whenever an update is made to a database, it is made in the context of the current configuration. New object versions created as a result of updates in a session are tagged with the configuration under which they were created.

4. Any reads of data during a session are done in the context of the current configuration. That is, when an object is retrieved by the user, the version of the object in the current configuration, or in the most recent configuration in a partial ordering of configurations defined by the user, is returned to the user.

This implementation of configurations represents a "snapshot" of a database that can be modified by the user. These configurations might be likened to a "transaction in a suitcase"—that is, they are analogous to updating a database under a transaction that can be put away and brought back later for reuse. (Note, however, that transactions as we have defined them are orthogonal to configurations—either or both can be used in an application, for different purposes.)

As an example of the use of built-in configurations, consider the database of three objects X, Y, and Z in Figure 4.4. Until the user specifies otherwise, all updates to the database are performed under an initial default configuration, let's call this C_1, containing X_1, Y_1, and Z_1. In fact, if the user never creates a new configuration, then all the data in the database will be in configuration C_1, no new versions of X, Y, and Z will be created, and the user does not even need to be aware of versions (this is analogous to use of a default transaction in traditional DBMSs—the user does not need to be aware of them).

Now, suppose the user creates a new configuration C_2 and makes it be the current configuration. At this point, it appears to the user as if a copy has been made of the entire database. New versions of X, Y, or Z will be created in C_2 if and when these objects are modified. If object X references object Y, and the user updates object Y_1, creating new version Y_2, then a subsequent fetch of the reference attribute of X_1 will return the new, updated version Y_2. However, if configuration C_1 is re-established as the current configuration, the user will see the old X_1 and Y_1.

When we say that it *appears to the user* that a copy of the entire database is made when a new configuration is created, we mean this in the same sense that it *appears to the user* that a copy of a database is made when a *transaction* is opened; it is unlikely that an ODMS would implement configurations this way! For example, an ODMS could chain together X_1, X_2, and other versions of an object X, resolving a reference to X to the version in the current configuration at run time.

References are not the only way to retrieve objects—objects may be retrieved using a query language. It is easy to see how queries, including both retrieval and update, can be performed under a particular configuration when they are built in to the ODMS. In the case of a user-defined configuration policy, the query language would require hooks to specify which object versions should be retrieved—for example, the query language could always operate on default object versions, such as the most recent version. ObjectStore's query language permits the programmer to specify explicitly versions of objects in a query, or to perform the query in the context of a configuration.

Configurations may also have other uses, regardless whether they are built in or are constructed by the user. For example, they could be used as a basis for authorizing access to different versions of data.

4.8.5   Object-Based Concurrency Semantics

Another approach to concurrency in ODMSs is based on an elaboration of transactions utilizing user-defined object concurrency semantics. This approach takes advantage of the fact that objects can be updated only through methods, which comprise a specific set of known operations. Because all the possible operations on objects are known, the kinds of conflicts between potential updates can be predetermined.

Such an approach can allow more concurrent access than can traditional transactions based on *read–write semantics*. In read–write transaction semantics, as discussed in Chapter 3, any data read or written are implicitly locked (with a shared or exclusive lock, respectively); it is assumed that, if a user reads any datum, the updates performed depend on the datum read and the transaction is invalidated if another user updates the same datum.

Method-specific concurrency control allows conflict semantics to be more flexible than for straight read–write conflicts. [Weihl 1988, Skarra and Zdonik 1988, Herlihy 1986] and other researchers have investigated concurrency-control mechanisms based on object and method semantics. However, to date, such concurrency mechanisms have not been implemented in database prototypes, so we do not discuss them further here.

4.8.6   User and Time Data

POSTGRES [Stonebraker and Rowe 1988] provides a novel capability that can be used for concurrency or for versions. Objects can be "stamped" to identify which user last updated them, and at what time they were updated.

This user–time stamp can be fetched from a record just like any other attribute, and can be used in queries to examine database history. For example, in the text-processing application we introduced in Figure 2.11, a user could request all the document components modified by a coauthor since the last date the user read the document. More complex operations are also possible, such as restoring to their previous states the components modified by a particular user in the last hour.

User–time stamps add a new dimension of capability to an ODMS, although they are generally not a replacement for versions, transactions, or locking for concurrency control. They are particularly useful for historical queries. As such, user–time stamps are as useful in traditional business applications, particularly in decision support, as they are in the new applications we discussed in Chapter 2.

4.8.7   Concurrency Granularity

The concurrency-control mechanisms we have discussed can operate at the granularity of objects, generally by performing object locks. However, they may also operate at other granularities.

It may be more efficient to operate at a physical granularity, with pages or segments. An object lock may be automatically "promoted" to lock an entire page, for example. Physical locks such as these should generally be transparent to the user, and we defer their discussion to Chapter 5. However, for efficiency, logical units such as composite objects or entire type extents may be specified explicitly to be units of lock granularity by the database designer.

4.9   OTHER TOPICS

In this section, we discuss some remaining topics in object data management not covered by the earlier sections: user interfaces, distributed data access, performance, and protection.

4.9.1   User Interfaces

This chapter has covered only the object data management "engine," not the end-user tools built on top of it. Of course, application-specific end-user tools, such as CAD tools, are the responsibility of the application, and are not part of the ODMS. However, the ODMS may provide a 4GL or application-generation system to assist the application writer in building end-user tools, and may provide *generic* end-user tools that are application independent.

User interfaces to ODMSs are an interesting topic, but little work has been done—too little to provide a basis for a section in this book. Recent ODMS products are aimed more at a programmer than at an end user. However, the user interfaces in initial releases of ODMS products, including ObjectStore, Versant, GBase, Itasca, Objectivity/DB, and others, generally include two tools:

- *Graphical schema editors:* Tools to manipulate a schema diagram similar to the one we introduced in Chapter 1 are very useful in visualizing and modifying the schema for a database. Such schema editors generally produce declarations in the underlying DDL as output, and are able to accept existing schemas as input as well.

- *Object browsers:* Another useful tool is a simple browser to examine and modify database objects. Such a tool may allow the user to follow connections to other objects by selecting the objects on the screen.

An ODMS that does incorporate a graphical application-generation system, as well as the end-user tools we discussed, is O_2 [Cazalens et al 1990]. Servio has recently released an application-development toolkit for GemStone, as well, and other companies have such products planned.

4.9.2   Distribution

Distributed databases, distributed computation, and remote database access are designed to be as transparent as possible to the user; thus there are only a few data-modeling issues associated with them. These topics have therefore been deferred to the next chapter, on implementation.

4.9.3   Protection

We have not discussed *protection* of data from unauthorized or inadvertent access. It might be argued that protection is less important in the applications that motivated object data management. However, many of these applications do require protection; we have not covered protection because very little new work has been done in this area of object data management [Rabitti, Woelk, and Kim 1988].

We define *protection* as having two components: *safeness* and *security*. "Safeness" means that a user cannot corrupt physical data structures through the programming language, query language, or end-user tools. "Security" means that a user cannot access data for which they have no authorization. Safeness is a necessary prerequisite to security.

Traditional solutions to protection do not generally apply to ODMSs, as a result of performance considerations. For example, ODMSs with good performance generally cache objects in the same process data space as is used for the application program, typically copying physical units (pages) directly from the disk. In most programming environments, no data that are in the same process data space are "safe" from user programs, because it is possible to examine objects physically adjacent to those fetched by probing memory. In any case, any data cached on a workstation that is physically in control of the user is ultimately not safe from tampering.

ODMSs with an extended database system architecture may solve the protection problem in the same way that traditional relational DBMSs do, by placing sensitive data on a database server in a locked room that can be accessed only over the network through a query-language processor residing on the server. If the query processor is "safe"—that is, if it cannot be compromised by the user through direct access to physical memory locations or bypass of the normal data-access features—then the only objects that can be downloaded on the user's machine are those to which the user has access. However, protection at a query-language level may be too inefficient for many ODMS applications, particularly if the objects retrieved by a query were already in the workstation cache—any extraneous computation must be avoided.

ODMSs with a database programming language architecture can still provide a degree of protection if the database programming language is safe: The compiler can generate code to check access authorization. It might at first appear that protection based on a safe programming language is the same as protection based on a query-language processor in an extended database system architecture; however, for security purposes, this is true only if the user is restricted to execute on a server machine or on some other machine to which physical access is limited.

In either architecture, arbitrarily complex predicates for authorization to access data can be defined. Access to particular attributes, relationships, or methods may be limited to specific users, and a method may restrict user operations based on access lists attached to each object, or even by time of day. Security is more complicated than in a relational DBMS, since authorization may be based on methods, composite objects, versions, and hierarchies of types. The unit of authorization may be object types, composite objects, or individual objects. In addition to, or instead of, authorization to access object data, an ODMS may authorize access to object methods. Note that in a type hierarchy, access to one object type does not imply authorization to access its subtypes.

An efficient protection methodology that *can* be provided in database programming language architectures is based on physical units, such as pages, segments, or files. In such a scheme, objects must be placed in physically separate areas for different authorization, and logical "on-the-fly" authorization on the basis of object characteristics is not provided; the server machine simply checks access to each physical unit according to user ID or group. GemStone does this at a segment level, and allows objects and object attributes or methods to be placed in different segments. Thus, even though the granularity of protection is physical, an ODMS may present to the user the illusion that protection is based on logical units such as object types, attributes, methods, or individual objects. Despite the drawbacks of protection based on physical units, this approach may be adequate for most of the applications that we discussed in Chapter 2, and its performance is probably much better for simple kinds of protection.

4.9.4   Performance

Performance is an implementation issue, not a conceptual issue, so discussion of performance is deferred to the next chapter. It is important to understand, however, that an order-of-magnitude performance difference between systems can effectively constitute a *functional* difference, because it is not possible to use an ODMS at all if the system's performance is too far below the requirements.

A common mistake in industry is to create a "requirements list" for an application and to weight most of the requirements equally in choosing a DBMS solution. Performance requirements are difficult to specify precisely, and cannot be compared on a checklist from the vendor. However, performance can be the most important feature for the applications we discussed in Chapter 2.

For example, traditional relational database servers can require minutes to perform operations that must be performed in seconds for reasonable user feedback in CAD applications [Cattell and Skeen 1991]. This performance is more a problem with the database implementation than with the relational model, but it puts the relational servers in a different functional category—the language impedance mismatch and distributed architecture implementation are not simply an inconvenience.

4.10   SUMMARY

In this chapter, we covered all the major functional characteristics of ODMSs, particularly the *data model*. We examined three important families of data models in some detail: object-oriented, extended relational, and functional. We discussed four major *database architectures*: extended database systems, database programming languages, database system generators, and object managers. We defined five overall *ODMS approaches*: object-oriented database programming languages, extended relational database systems, extended functional database systems, database system generators, and object managers. The Appendix to the book provides examples of ODMS prototypes and products organized according to these five categories.

Regardless of approach, the new ODMSs generally provide similar functionality for new database applications—functionality not provided by current relational systems. The most important new functionality includes object identity; object references based on OIDs; BLOB-valued attributes; collection-valued attributes including sets, lists, and arrays of literal or reference values; composite objects and operations; type hierarchies with inheritance; procedures used for encapsulation and active data; more powerful query languages integrated with programming languages; versions; and new transaction mechanisms.

The most important functionality advantages of ODMSs over relational DBMSs are the closer association between programming language and database system, including the ability to associate procedures with database objects, and the more complex data structures for objects, including complex attributes, aggregation, generalization, and rule systems. In other areas, such as query capability, end-user tools, distributed databases, and authorization, only a few ODMSs compete with relational systems in terms of capabilities.

To present a clean and simple presentation of functionality, we have avoided discussion of implementation details. However, these details can be as important to someone choosing or using an ODMS as they are to someone studying or building one. The implementation issues are the topic of the next chapter.

CHAPTER

5

Implementation Issues

5.1 INTRODUCTION

In this chapter, we focus on implementation issues for ODMSs. The chapter does not constitute a complete description of how to build the functionality described in Chapter 4, since relatively little work has been reported on complete implementations. However, we touch on most of the problems, particularly where such an implementation differs from the traditional techniques we covered in Chapter 3, and where there are significant performance implications. We cover issues for the application implementor as well as those for the ODMS implementor, to help in choosing which ODMS or which ODMS feature to use to satisfy application needs.

5.1.1 Chapter Overview

In this chapter, we cover the following:

- Object storage, including the representation of object identifiers, keys, and attributes, and storage on disk, in caches, and application programs

- Representation of relationships and references, on disk and in main memory, and techniques for redundant storage
- Implementation of methods and derived data
- Techniques for clustering objects, including composite objects and segments
- Object type representation and schema evolution
- Query-language implementation, including indexing techniques
- Versioning, long transactions, and recovery techniques
- Remote data access, distributed databases, and distributed computation
- Important overall performance considerations

These topics are covered in Sections 5.2 through 5.10. Sections 5.2 through 5.8 parallel the discussion of database functionality in Chapter 4; the last two sections cover new topics.

5.1.2   Implementation Approaches

The data models and database architectures we introduced in the previous chapter substantially affect implementation difficulty and issues. The data model primarily affects syntax implementation for the query language and programming language. The database architecture primarily determines the number of layers in the implementation. The layering of the architectures defined in Figure 4.1 may or may not mirror the actual implementations, but we can utilize the layering to simplify the study of implementation issues for the architectures:

- *Object manager* functionality is common to all the database architectures. Our discussion of object managers, including storage management, caching, and access method implementation, is independent of data model and database architecture.
- *Extended database systems* provide a powerful data model and query language. Our discussion of extended database system issues, including query-language optimization and schema evolution, is common to all the systems but object managers. Traditional database systems might be thought of as somewhere between an object manager and an extended database system, providing a simpler data model and query language.
- *Database programming languages* enhance extended database systems, integrating database access with a programming language. The implementation could be based on translating programming-language operations into query operations in an extended database system, but current implementations are generally based directly on the object manager level.
- *Database system generators* are left out of the layering of database architectures, since database system generators are designed to produce all these architectural layers. We shall discuss these systems only briefly, but more detailed examples are given in the Appendix.

5.2   OBJECT STORAGE

We first focus on the implementation of objects themselves: object identifiers, attribute layout, and efficient object fetches. The implementation of objects is one of the most important factors in the performance of an ODMS.

5.2.1   Object Identifiers

A number of approaches have been taken to object identifiers (OIDs). [Khoshafian and Copeland 1986] survey some of the alternatives.

OIDs may be *physical* (that is, they may contain the actual address of the object) or *logical* (that is, they may be mapped through an index to obtain an object location). There is more than one approach to both physical and logical identifiers, resulting in at least four kinds of OIDs:

1. *Addresses:* The simplest way to identify objects is the one traditionally used in programming languages: the physical address of the object. The address is generally 32 bits or less, and is the most efficient representation to get to the object information quickly. Physical addresses are rarely used in database systems, however, because they do not allow an object to be moved or deleted without all existing references to the object being found and repaired.

2. *Structured addresses:* One of the most popular approaches in relational, extended relational, and object-oriented database systems is to use an address with both a physical and a logical component. As discussed in Chapter 3, such identifiers typically contain a segment and page number in their high-order bits, which can be used to determine quickly the correct disk read to perform to fetch the object, and a logical slot number in the low-order bits, used to determine the precise location of the object. We can delete or move an object within a page by updating the slot array at the beginning of a page, or can move it to another page by using a forwarding address.

3. *Surrogates:* A purely logical OID can be generated, using any algorithm guaranteed to produce unique IDs (for example, time and date, or a monotonically increasing counter). These surrogate OIDs must be mapped to the physical address of an object, typically through an index.

4. *Typed surrogates:* A variant of surrogate identifier contains both a type ID and an object ID portion. The object ID portion is generated by different counters for each type, segmenting the address space. In some cases, it could be useful that typed surrogate identifiers allow the type of an object to be determined without fetching it.

OIDs are typically used to refer to objects both in application programs and in references between objects (attributes representing relationships). OIDs must therefore be unique over an entire database. In some cases, they are unique over an entire database for all time (that is, deleted OIDs are not reused), and, in a distributed database, OIDs must be unique over a number of databases on a network.

5.2.2 Identifier Performance

Because of the widespread use of OIDs, the choice for their representation can be a critical factor in the performance of an ODMS. The most important performance factor is often the number of disk accesses required to retrieve an object given its OID.

As we just discussed, addresses are the fastest way to retrieve an object, but addresses are generally not used for OIDs because they do not allow objects to be relocated.

It is generally possible to obtain an object from disk using a structured address OID in a single page access. In the worst case, this approach requires two disk reads to obtain an object. This would be the case if the object had been moved to a different page—for example, because it became too large to fit with the other objects on a page. Depending on the implementation of references, as we shall see shortly, it may be possible to find all references to an object and to make them point directly to the new location, avoiding the second page lookup. ONTOS, Objectivity/DB, and other recent ODMS products use this technique.

Surrogate OIDs often have poorer retrieval performance; they are typically mapped to addresses using a hash index. In the best cases, however, with a well-balanced extensible hashing function using the object pages themselves as hash buckets, it is possible to retrieve most objects in a single disk access. GemStone and POSTGRES use surrogates for OIDs.

Typed surrogate OIDs, such as those used in ORION and ITASCA, have performance characteristics similar to those of surrogate OIDs. The ability to determine type from an OID is possibly useful, but is probably not that important—an object's type usually can be determined from the reference context in which the OID appears. Also, it is more difficult to change the type of an object when typed surrogate OIDs are used. The ability to segment the OID address space by type is potentially useful for distributed databases, but there has been too little experience with distribution of objects on networks to say whether it is in fact useful, at this point.

Another performance factor to consider is the OID size; OIDs longer than 32 to 48 bits can have a substantial effect on the overall size of a database, particularly because many of the databases with which we are dealing contain complex heavily interrelated objects. In theory, 32 bits is adequate for about 4 billion objects, allowing a reasonably large database. However, OIDs 64 bits or larger may be necessary for a variety of reasons:

- In systems where it is not practical to find all references to an object, OIDs must be unique for all time, so that dangling references can be recognized.

- If OIDs are surrogates generated by a monotonically increasing function, it is generally not practical to reuse "holes" produced in the sequence by OIDs no longer (or never) used.

- In a distributed environment, it may be necessary to prefix the OID with a machine or database identifier to make the OID universally unique.

- If the OID is divided into parts, as with typed surrogates or structured addresses, there is typically some waste in not using the full range of each portion.

Tricks can be used to make OIDs shorter in some cases. A flag may be used to indicate "local" OIDs, for example, which are short references within a single database, segment, or other group of objects [Moss 1988]. Since there is almost always significant locality of reference in databases, this trick can decrease database size, with only a small time overhead.

Many implementations convert OIDs used for references between objects into memory addresses when objects are fetched from disk, to make reference-following fast. That is, all references to an object's OID in currently cached objects are replaced with the object's address when the object is brought into memory. ObjectStore even uses a virtual memory address form in the *disk* representation of OIDs. The replacement of OIDs with addresses, called *swizzling,* can be exercised regardless of which OID representation is used. We shall study swizzling in Section 5.3.4.

5.2.3   Object Buffering

Another important factor in ODMS performance is the technique for caching and accessing objects in main memory after they have been fetched from disk. Data-buffering requirements for ODMSs can be quite different from those of traditional DBMSs. Main-memory buffering is crucial in the common scenario where there is locality or repetition in the objects referenced by an application, or the entire database working set fits in main memory. To illustrate this point, Figure 5.1 shows a traditional and a more recent approach to buffering objects in main memory.

Traditional DBMS techniques, illustrated in Figure 5.1a, have relatively high overhead for access to objects. There are several points to note about this approach:

1. Disk pages are copied into a DBMS buffer, not directly into application memory, and then data must be copied into an application program's variables.

2. Individual fields or records are copied into application variables from the DBMS buffer, rather than entire complex objects being copied.

3. A conversion may be necessary from the programming-language representation of literal data (for example, real numbers) to the DBMS representation.

Application program memory

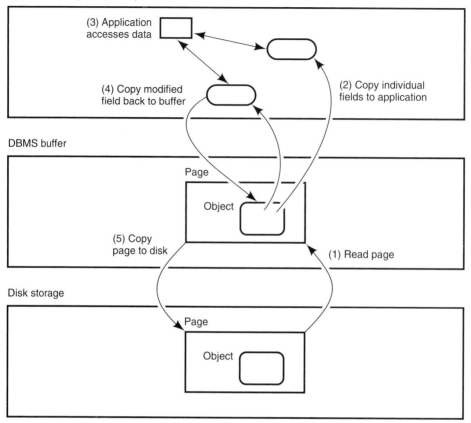

FIGURE 5.1 (a)   Steps in accessing an object using traditional DBMS techniques.

4.   The DBMS and application run in different processes, so an interprocess call is necessary to retrieve additional related objects or to modify them.

5.   When an application updates data, then the overhead of points 1 through 4 must be repeated to get the new data back into the database, in addition to concurrency-control overhead. We return to concurrency later.

In Figure 5.1b, the overhead has been greatly reduced by copying data pages directly from disk to application memory, making any conversions necessary to the representation "in place." We call this the *disk-image* approach; it is used by Objectivity/DB, ONTOS, POET, O$_2$, and ObjectStore, and is generally not used in the extended database systems. In the disk-image approach, the main-memory representation of objects is typically designed to be identical to that of an existing

Application program memory

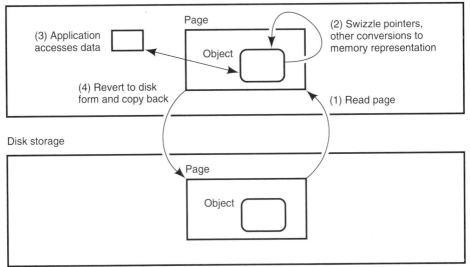

FIGURE 5.1 (b) More efficient steps to reduce copying and interprocess communication for object data management.

programming language, but a number of conversions may be necessary:

1. References between objects may be swizzled (converted in place from OIDs to pointers, as just discussed).

2. Minor structural changes may be necessary—for example if the programming language requires a type code or size at the beginning of an object.

3. In a heterogeneous hardware or programming-language environment, the representation of literal data (numbers, strings) can be different on the server disk from in the client memory, so a conversion may be necessary. To minimize this problem, it is important to keep the disk representation in the most frequent client's representation.

Note that, in both the disk-image and traditional approaches, the caching of disk objects in main memory requires the appropriate locking of objects or groups of objects on disk, and copying data back to disk must be performed in concert with a transaction or versioning mechanism. Also, a database may be located remotely over a network, requiring remote disk or DBMS access. We shall see that concurrency and remote-access considerations do not invalidate the arguments we make here, but they do bring up additional performance issues; more on these issues later.

At first glance, the difference in overhead between the traditional and disk-image approaches might appear to result in a speed difference of perhaps a factor of two, because of the copying and interprocess calls. However, the performance difference may be much more in a typical case, because application operations may be executed repeatedly on objects cached in memory. Nowadays, workstation memories are large enough that several megabytes can be dedicated to a database cache. In such a case, the entire database working set that an application uses—for example, a portion of a circuit design or document—may fit in memory and be checked out of the database for hours or days. Since interprocess calls typically take milliseconds, particularly over a network, and operations on data in program memory typically take microseconds, there can be a difference in performance of a factor of *1000*. The points in the figure can thus be important to ODMS design [Cattell and Skeen 1991, Maier 1988, Hardwick 1987, Franklin 1993].*

Some ODMSs take a hybrid approach, between that of Figures 5.1a and 5.1b. Instead of transferring *pages* from server to client as in the disk-image approach, they transfer objects (ORION, ITASCA, UniSQL, VERSANT) or the results of queries (Persistence). [Dewitt and Maier 1990] call these three architectures a *page* server, *object* server, and *query* server, respectively. Most ODMS vendors have chosen a page server (disk-image) approach, since it avoids the overhead of copying and translating objects and processing queries.

However, in cases where network overhead is high and objects cannot be clustered on pages, object or query servers could conceivably be faster. The page server approach might provide less performance advantage for applications that can encapsulate their operations on data in a query language, rather than operating directly on objects. In a networked environment, some applications could be considerably slower using this approach, because it is more efficient to ship the operation (query) to where the data are stored, rather than shipping all the data to a workstation to perform the operation. However, in the applications we discussed in Chapter 2, the application operations typically cannot be performed in a high-level query language, and data are often "checked out" for an extended period. Besides, "batch" operations that are executed more efficiently on the server can be executed as a separate program or procedure in both disk-image and traditional implementations.

Thus, the benefits of the traditional approach are not lost in an ODMS providing the disk-image alternative; rather, there is a new optimization option: executing operations on the application workstation or the server machine. These alternatives were not available in the traditional approach. Note that this optimization choice is not straightforward, however—executing a query on the server when data have been cached on the workstation may involve flushing the cache, or performing a distributed query decomposed between cache and server. If the cache is not transparent to query execution—that is, if different run-time calls and representations are used for cache data and disk data—then a cache flush or distributed query processing may be needed simply to execute the query on the workstation [Banerjee et al 1988].

---

* It may appear that many of the benefits of the disk-image approach can be achieved through an application implementing its own cache; however, as we shall see in Section 5.10, there are problems associated with use of an application cache.

5.2.4   Data Integrity

A factor of 1000 performance improvement is not obtained for free, or it would have been achieved in DBMSs long ago, and extended database systems would use it as well. The biggest disadvantage of the disk-image approach is probably that it provides less protection for data integrity.

Protection is particularly poor if the programming language is not "safe"— that is, if it is possible for the application to examine or modify any memory location inadvertently or maliciously. There are three consequences:

1. Reliable protection and authorization must be based on physical data units such as segments or files protected by an operating system or server, because any data copied from disk can theoretically be accessed.

2. An application program may compromise the logical integrity of the database, by bypassing the methods or other integrity-constraint mechanisms provided by the ODMS.

3. Worst of all, the application may destroy the physical integrity of the database by changing random memory locations, causing arbitrary actions at a later date by applications accessing incorrect pointers, type specifications, or other data.

The loss of physical integrity is a significant issue, particularly given the persistence longevity of databases as opposed to program variables. As a result, unsafe languages, or the use of unsafe features in an otherwise safe language, do not mix well with object data management. Traditional interpreted languages such as LISP and Smalltalk, and some more recent languages such as Modula-3, are safer than languages such as C or C++. Relatively safe programs can be written in a subset of C++, but none of the C++ based ODMSs that we cover check automatically for such a subset at this time.

5.2.5   Run-Time Object Information

In addition to maintaining the objects themselves, an ODMS must maintain run-time information for the objects in main memory—for example, to determine which objects are currently cached, or whether OIDs have been swizzled. Some of this information may be maintained in in-memory tables, some may be maintained with the object itself, and some may be maintained in *object descriptors*. An object descriptor is simply a record in memory used to keep information about an object; it is useful in disk-image buffering we discussed earlier, for example, where there may not be space in the object itself for this information. When an object is fetched by an application program, the ODMS returns a pointer to the object descriptor, instead of returning the object itself. The object descriptor in turn points to the data [Objectivity 1990, Kim et al 1988].

If the programming language provides "smart-pointer" capability—that is, it gives the ODMS control when a pointer is dereferenced—then it may be possible to make object descriptors invisible or less obtrusive to the application program. Of course, the introduction of object descriptors entails additional overhead—for example, to allocate and free the descriptors—so their benefit for storing temporary information (and possibly other benefits, such as the protection afforded by not giving the application pointer a pointer directly into the disk buffer) must be weighed against the cost.

In-memory tables, object descriptors, or additional bits in an object may be used for many purposes, including these:

• *OID to address mapping:* The ODMS must maintain a "resident object table" to determine quickly whether an object with a given OID has been fetched from the disk, locked, and cached in memory, and if it has been, where it can be found.

• *Dirty bits:* A "dirty bit" indicates that an object has been updated since fetched from disk, and so it must be written back at the end of a transaction. The dirty bit could be maintained on a per-page basis.

• *Reference count:* A single object descriptor may be shared by all application variables referencing an object, using a reference count in the descriptor. When the reference count reaches zero, the descriptor may be freed and the object is eligible to be removed from main memory.

5.2.6   Collections and Iterators

Collections in object data management systems, including lists, sets, and arrays, may require special treatment for good performance. Collections may result from a number of sources:

1. Parameterized types may permit sets, lists, and arrays of simple values, such as integers, to be stored in object attributes.

2. The representation of many-valued relationships as attributes results in attributes whose values are lists or sets of object references.

3. The extent of a type is a collection, whether it is maintained automatically or manually.

4. The result of a query produces a collection of objects.

In all four cases, the resulting collections may contain thousands of elements. In such cases, it is more efficient to return an *iterator* to an application program, instead of materializing the entire collection requested. An iterator produces elements of the collection only as they are requested by an application program. Also, an iterator makes it possible to lock only data currently in use, instead of the entire collection.

An iterator is a temporary object of its own, providing a method to produce the next element of a collection, a method to close the iteration when complete, and some internal state used to keep track of the current position in the collection.

The iterator may contain additional methods—for example, to go backward to the previous element, to reinitialize to the beginning, or to jump to a particular ordinal position in the collection.

Iterators may be available directly in an object-oriented database programming language, and may be used internally at the access-method level of an ODMS in computing the result for an ad hoc query. In the former case, of course, the use of iterators is not transparent to the user: in fact, object types and methods for collections are typically part of the programming language or standard libraries, as they are in C++. In POSTGRES, *portals* are provided to allow more flexibility in iterating through the results of queries. In ObjectStore, a *foreach* statement is provided to iterate through the results of a query or other collection in the programming language, or methods associated with built-in collection types may be used to enumerate elements directly. We return to these constructs in examining queries.

Although the use of iterator methods could be regarded as less convenient than direct access to a collection in memory, the performance advantages can be substantial. The encapsulation of collections through iterators allows many different implementations to be used according to the size and properties of a collection. A collection could be implemented via a list, an index search, an array, or any other technique. The iterator implementation can be designed to interact efficiently with object buffering, fetching or prefetching portions of a collection according to the granularity stored on disk.

5.2.7   Object Keys

In most of the ODMSs we cover, objects may be referenced either by OID or by an object key. The implementation of object keys in ODMSs does not generally differ from the implementation of primary keys in the relational model. A hash or B-tree index can be created mapping keys to OIDs. A B-tree index allows objects to be enumerated sorted by key.

In an object-oriented model, new methods or syntax must be provided in the language to allow access by key. For example, Objectivity/DB supplies a `lookupObj` method on a class. ObjectStore extends C++ to allow expressions of the form:

```
Document[:title=="Object Data Management":]
```

The ObjectStore syntax can be used for a wide variety of queries, not just lookup by key, as we shall see later.

Note that, in extended relational DBMSs, the query language must be extended to allow access by OID, just as object-oriented languages are extended to allow value-based access by key (and other associative access). The extended relational database system POSTGRES, for example, provides a built-in `oid` attribute in every tuple.

Since by our definition object keys are the primary keys, objects may be clustered by object key. In fact, objects could be stored directly in the leaf pages of the B-tree, as in clustered relational indexes, instead of storing the OID in the index and invoking an OID lookup to map to the actual object; however, the ODMSs we cover do not do this.

5.2.8   Property Lists

The simplest implementation of object attributes is similar to that for relational records discussed in Chapter 3. In defining an object type, a layout is automatically chosen for an object of that type by concatenating the object attributes, allowing a fixed-sized field for each attribute.

Simple concatenation of fixed-sized fields is an efficient implementation of attributes. However, there are several cases where fixed-sized fields are not adequate:

- *Variable-sized attributes:* Attributes may vary in size; for example, a variable-length string or list cannot be stored in-line. We discussed alternatives for dealing with variable-size attributes in relational DBMSs in Chapter 3, storing the attribute value (or the portion of the attribute value that does not fit in a small fixed-sized area) as a separate object. The OID for the separate object can then be stored in the attribute. Note that the variable-sized object may not be visible to the user as an object; it is system-defined.

- *Collection-valued attributes:* As noted earlier, attributes that represent relationships may be variable-sized collections. Collections of literal data values may also expand and contract; they can be handled similarly to other variable-sized attributes.

- *New attributes:* It is not possible to add new attributes to existing objects when the data schema is changed if fixed field locations are used for attributes, unless additional storage space happens to be available at the end of an object, or each object is identified with the version of the schema under which it was created and the version is checked whenever attributes are accessed.

- *Sparse attributes:* In some databases, a particular attribute may almost always have a null value. It is a waste of space to provide a fixed field for it in all objects, because it is generally not used.

The latter two cases, new attributes and sparse attributes, are often implemented using *property lists*. Property lists are a different physical representation for attributes in an object, using a sequence of pairs of attribute identifiers and values.

Variable-sized objects consisting of a sequence of fields are generally stored as shown in Figure 5.2. The **attr** field in the figure is some kind of identifier indicating which object attribute is stored, the **size** is the number of bytes stored (this may be omitted when the attribute is of fixed size), and the **value** is the variable-sized value of this attribute for the object. The detailed implementation of variable-sized

FIGURE 5.2 A sequence of fields of this form is used for property lists.

objects differs among systems, but the basic concepts are similar. For example, ORION stores all the `attr` information together at the beginning of the record, with pointers to the `value` fields that are all stored at the end of the record.

Property lists are more flexible than a fixed size and offset for attributes in several ways. The same attributes may have a different size in different objects, the attributes may be stored in different physical positions, and all objects of a type do not need to have the same set of attributes (although they must all be a subset of those defined in the object type definition). As a result, object type definitions may be changed without the need to fix all existing objects to match the new set of attributes. When an attempt is made to retrieve or assign a field that does not yet exist in an object, a schema-modification module can be called to transform the object to the new schema representation on the fly. The property-list representation is also useful when attribute values are sparse—that is, when most of them have null values. Null-valued fields do not need to be stored, saving space and time.

The main disadvantage of property lists is that they are slow to use. To fetch or store a particular attribute value, it is necessary to search the entire list of attributes to find the correct one. Also, it may be necessary to translate the property-list format to a different representation for program access if the DBMS is to be integrated with an existing programming-language implementation.

An ODMS may provide a hybrid of fixed and property-list representation of attributes [Objectivity 1990, Batory 1985]. The representation to use may be declared by the database administrator when the attribute is defined.

5.2.9 Attribute Inheritance

In the presence of a type hierarchy, it is necessary to store not only the attributes defined for an object type, but also attributes of supertypes.

In a strict hierarchy—that is, one without multiple inheritance—an object layout can be constructed by concatenating the fields for the object's attributes, its parent's attributes, and so on, as shown in Figure 5.3. This approach is adequate,

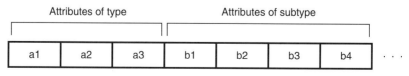

FIGURE 5.3 Attributes of object types can be concatenated down the type hierarchy, starting with the highest ancestor type.

since variable-sized attributes are stored separately from the object using the schemes we discussed.

Note that, with fixed-sized attributes, the offset of a field in this representation is always the same, even in a subtype. For example, if the title of a document is stored in bytes 10 through 40 of a **Document** object, then it will be in the same location in objects of the **SourceProgram** subtype, since the **SourceProgram** attributes are appended on the end. The fixed field offset simplifies compilation of programs when the specific type in a hierarchy is not known until run time.

In a type system that permits multiple inheritance, an object type may inherit attributes from more than one chain of supertypes, so a more complex scheme must be used for fixed-sized attributes. For example, suppose **SourceProgram** has multiple inheritance, from both **Document** and **Program**. The **title** of a **Document** may be stored at an offset of, say, 6 bytes from the beginning of the object, but the **creation-date** might be stored at that same offset in a **Program**. Only one attribute may be stored at byte 6 in a **SourceProgram**. A variety of implementations may be used to remedy this difficulty; for example, a property-list format may be utilized for attributes, or separate objects may be chained together, each storing fields associated with one supertype [Atkinson et al 1983].

5.2.10   Large Attributes

There are several implementation techniques for very large variable-sized attributes, or BLOBs, such as images or large text values stored as a single attribute value [Lehman and Lindsay 1989, Carey et al 1986].

The simplest technique is to treat large attributes just like variable-sized attributes—that is, to store them out-of-line as a separate object, as discussed in Chapter 3, but to use a different method for materializing the value: Instead of requiring that the entire value be produced in main memory for storage or retrieval of the attribute, a *stream* interface is used. The stream concept is similar to that of iterators, in the sense that a stream avoids materializing an entire attribute value at once via a stream object that provides specific methods for accessing an attribute. Streams simply provide a different abstraction from that provided by iterators.

A stream object value provides several methods to its user:

- **Position(place)**: Set current position in stream to a particular integer position.
- **Read(size, block)**: Read a block of data bytes at current position.
- **Write(size, block)**: Write a block of data bytes at current position.

A stream interface such as this is typically most convenient for dealing with large attribute values such as images or blocks of text. It is also efficient, because only the required data need to be placed in contiguous main memory.

The stream interface is easy to develop on top of the variable-sized attribute implementations we have already discussed. If the large values are stored contiguously, then it is adequate simply to maintain state variables for current position and overall size of the attribute value. If the values are broken up into separate segments on disk, then the implementation is only slightly more complex.

Instead of streams being used, BLOB values may be demand-paged [Object Design 1990]. That is, the entire BLOB value may be "returned" to the application program at a particular virtual memory location, but materialized only one page at a time, as accessed by the program. The demand-paging alternative has the advantage that existing code for manipulating images, text, or other BLOB data may require little change to work on data fetched from the database. Also, direct memory mapping of the BLOBs may be more convenient for the programmer in general.

On the other hand, stream implementations are more amenable to extensions to allow "editing" of BLOB values. For example, a stream can provide variants of the **Write** procedure that allow data to be inserted or deleted at the current position:

- **Delete(size)**: Remove bytes at current position, moving the remaining data forward.

- **Insert(size, block)**: Insert bytes at current position, moving the remaining data back.

We call streams that provide these additional operations *piece streams*. Piece streams are convenient in a number of applications—for example, in a text editor where it is necessary to insert and delete bytes from the middle of a block of text.

Piece streams are more difficult to implement than are simple streams. However, several systems, including EXODUS and ORION, provide piece streams by using tree structures to point to the segments of the data. [Carey et al 1988] describes such an implementation, using B-trees indexed by byte position in the BLOB. Each B-tree entry represents a contiguous segment of data; the B-tree maintains the segments in the proper order, and insertions and deletions in the BLOB result in modification of the entries. For example, deletion of 100 bytes in the middle of a 1000-byte B-tree segment entry might split the B-tree entry into a 400-byte segment and a 500-byte segment.

5.3 RELATIONSHIPS

In this section, we cover issues that arise in the implementation of relationships: representation, referential integrity, ordering, and swizzling. For the most part, these issues are the same in all the data models we cover, although the manifestation of relationships to the user may be relations, attributes, or functions.

5.3.1 Representation

Relationships bring up an issue that does not arise with attributes. Relationships are logically associated with more than one object, whereas attributes are associated with only one. For this reason, it is necessary to represent relationships with inverse attributes in the object-oriented models, by multiple functions in functional models, and by relationship tables in relational models.

Although a relationship may be materialized as attributes to the user, the relationship does not need to be actually stored with objects in the same way that the user sees them. In fact, in functional and extended relational models, and for ternary relationships in object-oriented models, relationships are generally implemented as separate data objects.

Consider the one-to-many relationship between chapters and documents in our example database. There are many different ways this relationship could be represented:

- *Collocation:* The chapter objects for a document could be stored physically following the document object. Relationships have traditionally been represented this way in the hierarchical data model. However, this implementation is generally not as flexible as are other alternatives. It is difficult to represent more than one relationship for the same object this way. However, in the case of one-to-one relationships, such as the document–index relationship, this approach may be ideal.

- *Indexing:* The chapter and document objects may be stored separately, building B-tree or hash indexes to provide mapping between documents and chapters. This is the approach typically taken in relational systems, as noted in Chapter 3: We can index chapter objects according to the document to which they belong, using the **DocID** attribute. There must also be an index on documents (on **DocID**), so that the ODMS can produce the document quickly given one of its chapters. In an ODMS where documents have object identifiers, we can use a similar scheme by using the document OID for the index instead of the **DocID** relational key. The index on documents is not necessary in this case, since the index or other access method is provided by the OID mechanism itself.

- *Links:* The most common implementation of relationships in ODMSs is some variation of the parent-child links discussed in Chapter 3; links are rarely used in relational systems. [Carey et al 1990] found links to be efficient for join operations on relationships. A link implementation may mimic the attributes we defined in Chapter 4 to represent the relationship—that is, an OID-valued **doc** attribute of chapters, and a **chaps** attribute for documents that is a variable-sized array of OIDs, analogous to the scheme shown in Figure 3.4b. Or, a list rather than array may be used, as in Figure 3.4a. In the case of a binary many-to-many relationship, such as **references** between **Documents**, two list-valued (or array-valued) attributes may be used, one for each participating object type. In any case, keep in mind that the implementation of the relationship is independent of how that relationship is materialized to the user, particularly if an iterator is used to materialize set-valued attributes for the user.

- *Multilevel:* In the case of a relationship of degree higher than two, the previous approaches will not work. It is necessary to define an intermediate object to represent the relationship, decomposing the relationship into a set of binary relationships between the participating object types and the new intermediate object type. These relationships can in turn be implemented using one of the previous schemes.

Multivalued (collection) attributes may be sets, arrays, or lists. In the case of the latter two, an *ordering* is thereby defined on the relationships. This is an important aspect of relationship semantics that differs from relational DBMSs; let's look at ordering in more detail.

5.3.2 Ordering

Any of the implementation methods we just described can also be used for *ordered* relationships. For example, some B-tree implementations allow an ordering to be placed on multiple entries with the same key. However, the simplest implementation for ordered relationships is probably that using parent–child linked lists.

In systems where a query language for associative lookup is implemented in addition to a programming language, the ordering should be visible through the query language, not just through explicit list operations on attributes in the programming language.

It is possible to define ordering of objects by attribute values—for example, by chapter number in our example database. Indeed, this is the *only* way to define ordering in a relational model. However, such an ordering may not be as convenient to the user as is an explicitly defined ordering. For example, if the user inserts new paragraphs in the middle of a chapter, it is undesirable to force reassignment of remaining paragraph numbers.

In the CODASYL model [DBTG 1971], an ordering by attribute values is called an *automatic set*; explicit ordering is called a *manual set*. It is important to understand that there are cases where each type of ordering is needed: automatic ordering by chapter number works well, if chapter numbers must be maintained anyway; manual ordering is better for paragraphs. The need for manual ordering is not exclusive to new applications such as those in Chapter 2; traditional business applications may require this feature. The need for automatic ordering is not exclusive to business applications; it can be useful in CAD, CASE, and other new applications.

Unfortunately, most ODMSs we cover do not provide both manual and automatic ordering. Exceptions are ONTOS, ObjectStore, and Gemstone, which provide manual ordering through the programming language, and automatic ordering through the query language.

5.3.3   Referential Integrity

In an object-oriented model, referential integrity is maintained for relationships through the maintenance of inverse-attribute pairs. That is, whenever an attribute such as the **doc** attribute of a chapter is updated, the inverse attribute must be updated—in this case **chaps** for its corresponding document. If the inverse attributes are mapped by the ODMS into a single underlying representation of the relationship, the maintenance problem is simple. For example, if relationships are represented using parent–child links, then all the references to an object can be located and corrected quickly when an object is deleted.

In a functional data model, similar statements apply to maintaining inverse functions. IRIS maps the multiple functions representing a relationship onto one underlying stored function implemented as a relational table. In an extended relational model, referential integrity for relationships based on OIDs is the same as for traditional methods for foreign keys.

In ODMSs where it is not possible to find all uses of an OID quickly, such as in GemStone, it is difficult to provide full referential integrity. However, reference *validation* is performed, since objects are not deleted until there are no more references to them. Reference validation can be provided in any ODMS implementation with OIDs that are never reused, since references to objects that are deleted can be recognized when the programmer attempts to follow the reference. At that time, the reference can be set to NIL and an error (attempt to use NIL reference) can be returned to the user [Servio 1990, Versant 1990].

As mentioned in the previous chapter, some ODMSs give the user the choice of whether to perform relationship integrity. ONTOS, for example, provides high-performance *TRefs* as well as associations with relationship integrity.

In any model, there are cases where referential integrity may be more complex. For example, as we shall see in our discussion of distributed DBMSs, OIDs may be guaranteed to be unique only over a single database, or over a distributed database with the same address space for OIDs. The data schema may span a larger number of databases. Thus, it is not always possible to create a reference from a **Chapter** to a **Document**, if the two are stored in different databases.

5.3.4   Swizzling

Recall that relationships are represented by references, and references are generally represented by OIDs. As mentioned earlier, references between objects may be *swizzled*—that is, turned into physical pointers—when objects are stored in memory.

Consider the tradeoffs involved in swizzling. The advantage of swizzling is that pointer-following is many times faster than is OID lookup for following references between objects. If a "working set" of objects fits in virtual memory, then access between objects can approach the speed of conventional programming-language data structures. Note that swizzling is not necessarily good, however; the overhead of converting the OIDs to pointers and back again may exceed the benefits of faster reference-following.

[Moss 1991] proposes an analytic model to indicate whether swizzling is worth the overhead for a specific application. There are many parameters for the model, and the decision depends on the performance characteristics of the particular ODMS in use. However, it is safe to say that in applications in which objects have a significant chance of being swapped out of main memory, or in which references are not followed at least several times on average, efficient tables to map OIDs to object addresses in memory, such as those used by Objectivity/DB, are more efficient than swizzling. Mapping tables have other advantages as well; for example, they allow objects to be moved in memory without reswizzling of references to the object. Thus, swizzling is useful only in some applications.

Swizzling is generally used in combination with the *disk-image* approach to storing objects, so swizzling must be performed *in place*. That is, the object field that contained an OID must be physically written over with the pointer. This is generally not a problem, because OIDs are longer than memory pointers, and 1 bit can easily be reserved to indicate whether an OID has been converted to pointer format (or an auxiliary data structure can be used to track converted OIDs). Note that, before a modified object is written back to disk, however, it is necessary (1) to find all swizzled OIDs in the object, and (2) to convert them back to OIDs, typically by following the pointer and fetching the OID of the referenced object.

Different approaches may be taken to determining when the swizzling is performed:

1. References can be swizzled at the time an object is first fetched by an application. This demands changing all references from the object to other objects in memory, and vice versa.

2. References may be swizzled the first time the reference is followed. This is not difficult to implement if the language provides "smart pointers" that can perform checks and have run-time side effects.

3. References in an object can be converted when requested by an application program, by explicit call to the ODMS run-time system.

4. References may be maintained in swizzled form at all times. This is done in ObjectStore by assigning database objects to fixed addresses in contiguous segments of virtual memory at the time the objects are created. The next time objects in a segment are brought into memory, ObjectStore attempts to map them to the same virtual-memory locations; only if this is not possible must the objects on the page (and references to them) be reswizzled to place them in another virtual-memory location.

A choice of more than one of these methods may be best, particularly if the application program or schema can be used to provide "hints" as to when swizzling is appropriate, because no one approach is universally best. Swizzling references when an object is fetched into memory is suboptimal when objects are not referenced frequently. Swizzling at application request requires additional programming. Maintaining swizzled references at all times limits the total number of objects in a database to what can fit in virtual memory.

5.3.5 Access Methods

In Sections 5.2 and 5.3, we have covered the basic storage and implementation of attributes and relationships. More sophisticated semantics can be built on top of these basic mechanisms:

- *Indexes:* Attributes or relationships may be indexed for fast access to objects.

- *Replication:* Attributes or relationships may be replicated to avoid following references.

- *Derived data:* Attributes or relationships may be defined procedurally.

We defer discussion of these more advanced topics to later in the chapter, although they also constitute part of the implementation of attributes and relationships; indeed, all three should be designed to be transparent to the user accessing attributes and relationships. We return to indexes, replication, and derived data in our discussion of query processing in Section 5.7.

5.4 COMPOSITE OBJECTS AND CLUSTERING

One of the advantages of the composite-object concept in ODMSs is that it provides a basis for clustering for better performance. Composite objects are the first topic of this section; clustering is the second topic.

Because there are many kinds of clustering possible in an ODMS besides composite objects (grouping objects by type, by indexes, and by relationships, for example), and the various clustering schemes interact (an object generally can be clustered with only one group of objects), we consider all kinds of clustering in this section.

5.4.1 Implementation

As we discussed in the previous chapter, an ODMS user defines composite objects by declaring aggregation relationships explicitly, or through using a built-in **PART-OF** relationship. In some systems (for example, VERSANT and Objec-tivity/DB), a closely related construct, a *container*, can also be defined. A container is a degenerate case of composite object that is simply a set of objects—the aggregation relationship is simply set membership in the container.

Regardless how composite objects are defined, the implementations are similar. There are several aspects of aggregation relationships, and the composite objects these relationships define, that must be dealt with in an implementation:

1. It must be possible to query and modify aggregation relationships. This is accomplished through the same mechanisms used for other relationships. Our discussion of relationships and their representation in Section 5.3 therefore addresses aggregation as well.

2. The operational semantics of composite objects must be preserved. When a composite object is deleted or a new version is created, for example, it is generally necessary to treat all the subobjects as a single unit. We discuss the semantics of composite objects in Section 5.4.2.

3. Often, composite objects are most efficiently stored contiguously. Therefore some systems either optionally or automatically attempt to place subobjects on the same physical page or segment of a database. We discuss clustering in Section 5.4.3.

5.4.2   Semantics

Operations such as deleting objects and creating new object versions may have special semantics when applied to composite objects. As we discussed in Chapter 4, the user may request that these operations be applied recursively to composite objects. When a composite object is deleted, its subobjects can be deleted automatically. If they, in turn, are composite objects, then their subobjects are deleted as well, and so on.

Deleting a composite object can thus be time consuming, unless objects are clustered by the aggregation relationship such that a group of objects may be deleted together. Consider a document defined as a composite object containing chapters, with chapters containing sections, and sections containing paragraphs. In the definition of the **Document** type, or for a particular document, the user may inform the ODMS that a document and its components (that is, the composite object) should all be stored in a single database *segment*. Since, as you may recall from Chapter 3, a segment is a logically contiguous set of pages, the document and all its components can be deleted by removing this set of pages from the database.

A segment may be removed from a database quickly, by changing the segment table to remove a range of page addresses. However, references to objects in the segment may need to be changed elsewhere in the database as well. For example, it may be necessary to follow back-references to other objects to delete references. Even in systems with surrogate OIDs that are never reused, where it is possible to let references simply "dangle" until they are next used (and recognized as nullified), it is generally necessary to remove the surrogate OIDs from a hash table. Also, the semantics of the data model may require that other dependent objects be deleted, outside the aggregation. However, despite the overhead to maintain referential integrity and other constraints, composite objects can provide a more efficient as well as more convenient mechanism to delete a set of related objects.

Storing composite objects in segments may also make other operations on the composite object more efficient—for example, copying or creating a new version. For example, the entire segment may be block-copied. Again, indexes and references between objects must still be "repaired" individually in the copied segment.

As noted in Chapter 4, some ODMSs allow "multiple parents" in an aggregation hierarchy; that is, an object may be part of more than one composite object. For example, there may be an independent bill-of-materials hierarchy and physical subassemblies hierarchy. With multiple-parent composite objects, the efficiency advantages of aggregation are more limited, since it is possible to cluster composite objects in only one hierarchy.

5.4.3 Clustering

Clustering can have substantial impact on ODMS performance. [Chang 1989] finds that a factor of three improvement can be achieved by proper ODMS object clustering for some CAD applications. Clustering can actually be performed in many different ways in an ODMS [Chang 1989]:

- *Composite objects:* As we discussed, objects can be clustered according to aggregation relationships. Such clustering may be defined at run time, by identifying particular composite objects to cluster, or the ODMS may be given a "hint" in the schema definition that clustering should be performed using particular aggregation relationships, for example to collocate **Modules** with the **Configuration** of which they are a **part** in the CASE application of Figure 2.3.

- *References:* Some ODMSs allow objects to be clustered according to relationships with other objects. Composite object clustering is, in fact, a special case of this, clustered by the aggregation relationship. Clustering could be performed, for example, according to the **references** relationship, so that documents that are referenced by a given document are more likely to be nearby.

- *Object types:* Objects may also be clustered by their type. For example, the user may specify that all objects of type **Document** should be stored in the same segment. If there is a generalization hierarchy, subtype instances may also be clustered in the same segment. ORION allows a subgraph of the type hierarchy to be clustered. Most relational DBMSs cluster by type (relation) by default; however this form of clustering is usually not useful unless repeated access is expected to objects of just one type.

- *Indexes:* As in relational DBMSs, it may be possible to cluster objects by an index on their attributes. For example, documents may be clustered using an index on their titles. This can be efficient if documents are accessed frequently in alphabetical order.

- *Custom:* Some ODMSs allow clustering to be performed "on the fly." In Objectivity/DB, for example, an existing object may be supplied as a parameter to the new-object procedure, and the system attempts to create the new object physically close to the existing one.

Unless objects are stored redundantly, an object can generally be clustered according to only one of these rules. Where the rules do not conflict, however, it is possible to follow multiple clustering rules. For example, chapters may be clustered within a single segment for objects of type chapter, and within the segment according to the document to which they belong.

This example illustrates that clustering may be performed at two levels:

- *Pages:* Objects may be clustered according to the smallest physical unit read from disk, which normally is a page. This type of clustering can produce the greatest gains in performance when a "working set" of objects cannot be precisely specified for all applications. Page clustering is most useful for clustering by index, reference, and composite objects.

- *Segments:* Objects may be clustered in larger units, when the user is able to specify a meaningful logical grouping for segmentation. Segment clustering is most useful for type clustering. It may also be used for composite objects, if used at a sufficiently course grain.

The largest performance gains are generally afforded by page clustering, since pages are the unit of access from the disk, and a "working set" of pages is selected dynamically according to the access characteristics of an application program. Segment clustering produces efficiency gains only if relatively large contiguous units are transferred from disk, or when efficiency gains can be made through grouping operations—for example, for composite object deletion described earlier.

Note that efficiency gains are realized not only by reading a page (or segment) when an application program explicitly fetches an object from it; in addition, a lookahead can be performed to fetch data likely to be required next. The simplest form of lookahead is to use a larger page size than is normally fetched by the hardware and operating system, or to fetch entire segments, to take advantage of object clustering. Although some of the ODMSs we cover allow control of page size, none of them perform lookahead in a more complex manner—for example, by following references. Little is known about performance characteristics of more complex lookahead mechanisms; they could decrease performance in many applications, by causing additional I/O. However, the use of a large page size when objects are known to be clustered along frequently used access paths almost always provides an improvement.

5.5   PROCEDURES AND PROGRAMMING LANGUAGES

In the previous chapter, we discussed dimensions in which ODMS query and programming languages differ: execution environment, query scope, virtual data, encapsulation, new operations, and data model. We identified the two most important approaches to database architecture: *extended database systems,* based on query languages, and *database programming languages,* based on programming languages.

In both architectures, both a declarative query language and a procedural programming language can be used to code application semantics. In both architectures, the query language may be invoked by the programming language, and the programming language may be invoked by the query language. However, in the database programming language architecture, the user may access the database from either the query language or the programming language.

The approach taken substantially influences the difficulty and type of implementation, particularly the execution environment and query scope. In this section we address the implementation issues associated with the programming language; we defer discussion of the query language to Section 5.7.

5.5.1   Language Integration

The database programming language approach faces a unique difficulty: integrating database-access primitives into an existing language and compiler. Programming languages have not been designed with database concepts such as persistence and concurrency control in mind, so these features must be retrofitted.

In many cases, the ODMS implementor does not have control of the programming-language compiler, so extensions to the syntax or semantics must be made through preprocessors or through the existing language mechanisms to define new types, to overload operators, and to add new run-time libraries. Remember that an important advantage of the database programming language approach is compatibility with the user's existing programs and language expertise, so it is preferable to define *extensions* rather than *changes* to the language and compiler. Unfortunately, maintaining compatibility with the existing language and compiler makes integration with the ODMS difficult.

Important integration issues include the following:

- *Type declarations:* The data schema is shared by the ODMS and the programming language compiler. This sharing is usually achieved by preprocessing the DDL, which is a superset of the programming-language declaration syntax, and automatically generating the programming-language declarations as well as the database calls to generate the schema.

- *Object storage format:* If objects are stored in disk-image format, as discussed in Section 5.2, then the layout of database objects on disk must be consistent with the representation used by the compiler.

- *References:* Reference-valued attributes (OIDs) appear as pointers to the programmer. When the user attempts to dereference a pointer, it may be necessary to fetch the referenced object from disk and to replace the OID attribute with a pointer to the object in memory.

- *Concurrency control:* For the system to operate properly with a transaction or version check-out mechanism, it is necessary to lock objects when they are first retrieved by an application. If the objects are to be updated, it is necessary to obtain an exclusive, rather than a shared, lock. Like most implementations of transactions, a "default lock" mode is desirable, in which the programmer does not need to make explicit calls to obtain these locks. The first reference and the first update of objects under a transaction or new version must be recognized at run time by the ODMS.

- *Dirty bits:* It is necessary to monitor updates to know what must be written back to the database when a transaction or session ends. A change to the value of any object attribute must therefore mark the object, or the page on which it resides, as being dirty. A "dirty bit" can also be useful in the "first update" run-time check just mentioned for concurrency.

- *Multiple programming languages* Some recent ODMSs with a database programming language architecture, including GemStone, VERSANT, and O_2, have been integrated with more than one programming language. To store persistent objects from more than one programming language in a database, yet share data structures between the languages, requires mapping all data structures in one into data structures in the other. This is a difficult problem; generally, the ODMS will be better integrated with one, primary, language and allow more limited interoperability in others.

The difficulty of ODMS integration with the programming language can be greatly simplified by use of appropriate "hooks" in the language. For example, smart pointers in C++ make it possible to check automatically whether objects are already in memory in a reference-following operation, or whether an OID must be used to fetch the object, perhaps swizzling the OID into a pointer for the next use. However, if it is impossible to distinguish between an assignment or a fetch in the implementation of smart pointers, update operations cannot be trapped to set dirty bits or exclusive locks.

5.5.2   Execution Environments

As we discussed in Section 4.7, procedures are executed in one of two environments:

- *Application environment:* In database programming languages, procedures execute in the same environment as the rest of the application program, with access to application state and resources such as global variables, procedures, and user interaction.

- *Database environment:* In extended database systems, procedures execute in the database environment, with side effects limited to changes to the database. Remote procedures generally cannot "call back" to the procedures in the application program that invoked them.

In both cases, the procedural language is *computationally complete,* in contrast to relational query languages; that is, the languages are capable of expressing any computation that can be executed in programming languages. However, the language is *resource-complete* only in the case of database programming languages, where the procedure has access to all the same state as does any other part of an application program.

In an ODMS with a client–server network architecture, where the database resides on a machine different from the application, the application-environment and database-environment cases involve execution locally and remotely, respectively. That is, application-environment procedures execute on the client machine with the user and application program, and database-environment procedures execute on the server machine.

It might seem that, in the new world of distributed computation, remote procedure calls, network file systems, and client–server database architecture, it should be of little importance where and in what environment a procedure executes. This is true to the extent that all the resources a procedure might require are defined as network resources. However, computing "at arm's length" is not always the most effective way to decompose computation.

Generally speaking, ODMSs taking the database programming language approach execute procedures on the client machine, and ODMSs taking the extended database system approach perform remote execution on the server. However, this is not always the case:

1. It is generally easy to provide remote computation in an ODMS with application-environment procedures, by using a remote procedure-call mechanism. That is, the programmer may deliberately distribute an application program among client, server, or other nodes on a network, using remote procedure calls. The shared database can be used as a communication medium between the distributed procedures.

2. New extended database systems could allow procedure execution on any machine on the network. If the language is powerful and convenient enough, and the user is not predisposed to using an existing programming language, then the application can be written in the database language, running on the client machine.

5.5.3   Rules

As noted in Chapter 4, a procedure may be invoked by satisfying a predicate rather than being explicitly invoked by name. For example, in an MCAD application, we may wish to trigger a new structural analysis whenever certain critical components in the design are modified. Recall that a procedure invoked by a predicate is called a *rule*.

Rules may be written in a programming language, a query language, or a logic language, depending on the system. POSTGRES [Stonebraker et al 1990] is an example of an ODMS with rules defined in a query language; thus, the logic and database capabilities are combined in the implementation. LDL [Chimenti et al 1990] and LOGRES [Zicari 1990] define rules in a logic language, although only limited experience has been had to date with layering these systems on top of a database system. In object-oriented database programming languages, it may soon be possible to define rules in a combination of the query and programming languages; however, none of the object-oriented ODMSs provide rules yet.

We focus on the POSTGRES work in this subsection, but most of the implementation techniques in POSTGRES should be applicable to rule implementations in other systems, regardless whether a logic language, query language, programming language, or some combination is used for rule definition. Additional implementation issues will arise in systems layering the logic language on top of the database language, but there is little experience to report in this area yet.

The most difficult part of implementing a rule system efficiently is determining when the predicates for rules are satisfied. There are two main approaches to this problem: *rewrite* and *marking*. The *rewrite* approach is analogous to query modification in traditional database systems: Database-language statements that could potentially update objects on which the predicate might depend are recognized and rewritten by the database-language processor, which adds code to check whether updates have caused the predicate to become true. This added code invokes the rule action if so, as an "invisible" procedure call from the database-language statement.

The *marking* approach to matching predicates is data-driven. Objects on which a rule depends are tagged with a special bit or a special kind of lock that is checked whenever the object is updated. After the update is performed, the lock manager (or the code examining the special bit) invokes the associated rule for the object. In this approach, the triggered code must first check to see whether any predicate constraints are satisfied, execute the rule's action if it is, and return.

The marking approach can be much more efficient than the rewrite approach, because predicates need to be reevaluated only when specific objects are modified, rather than on any update to objects of a type. The marking approach also has the advantage that triggers can be added at run time without recompiling existing procedures to perform the rewrite process. The rewrite approach requires that the programmer specify the predicates when the programs and their queries are compiled. When new rules are introduced, it is necessary to recompile programs that may be influenced by them.

On the other hand, the marking approach can perform badly when there are large numbers of marked objects, since it requires additional run time and space for locks or tag bits. More important, the marking approach may be less convenient for the user, who must explicitly identify objects on which a predicate depends.

The first implementation of the POSTGRES Rule System, called PRS I, introduced *automatic marking,* a novel solution to the latter problem. POSTGRES analyzes the data dependencies of a rule and automatically marks data objects for which updates may trigger the rule. The programmer specifies rules by supplying POSTQUEL statements that should always (or never) be true. A sophisticated automatic marking algorithm determines objects on which the truth of the predicate depends, and marks them. Thus, in PRS I, the programmer is given the best advantages of both automatic and manual marking.

The POSTGRES implementors had difficulties with the PRS I implementation, however; they found it complex and inefficient. They have now introduced PRS II, giving the programmer the option of using automatic marking or query rewrite. The user specifies rules in this form:

```
ON operation TO object(s)
WHERE predicate
THEN DO action
```

5.5.4   Agents and Productions

Thus far, we have dealt with code that executes within one overall thread of control. That is, when an application program invokes a procedure or rule, whether it be by explicit call or pattern match, whether it be written in a separate database language or in the same language, and whether it be on the same machine or executed by remote procedure call, the execution of the application program is suspended until the procedure or rule execution completes.

Recall from Table 4.2 that code may instead be executed in a separate process. In the case of procedures—that is, code executed explicitly by name—we referred to the separate processes as *agents.* In the case of rules—that is, code executed by pattern match—we referred to them as *productions.*

In the database programming language approach, the ability to implement agents and productions may be limited by the language or operating-system support for parallel (multithreaded) computation. In most modern systems, however, there is some facility for parallel processing.

A number of implementation issues with agents and productions concern efficiency: Most implementations of parallel processes are relatively expensive. The overhead to invoke a new process, for example, can be hundreds or even thousands of machine instructions. If parallel processing is combined with distributed computation, by invoking remote processes, the overhead is even higher.

The pattern-match portion of productions can be implemented analogously to rules, through marking or rewrite techniques. Productions differ only in that the code can be "fired" in parallel with continuing the invoking code.

Another implementation consideration is sharing data between independent processes. ORION allows code in parallel processes to execute under the same transaction and locks. However, ORION shared transactions work on only one machine; in the case of processes executing on different machines, it is hard to see how fine-grain data sharing could ever be implemented efficiently. This restriction limits what an application programmer can do with agents or productions; however, agents or productions can still be useful in a distributed application environment.

Since the ODMSs we discuss provide only the basics for agents or productions, at best, we do not study these features further here. Concurrent processing is less important than other features to most database applications, so the subject has usually been deferred to future research. However, as noted earlier, agents have proven useful in office-automation applications.

5.5.5   Derived Data

As we discussed in the previous chapter, derived attributes or relationships require that the database language compiler or interpreter be modified to translate a fetch or store of derived data into calls on user-defined procedures, much as relational DBMSs implement relational views by replacing them with their definition in a query. We used the example of a **Document.revision** defined in terms of **Document.creation**.

There are several implementation issues associated with derived data:

- *Syntax:* In the database programming language architecture, the implementation of derived data is limited by the features of the underlying object-oriented language—as we noted, the language may not provide a syntax to invoke procedures transparently through operations on attributes. In such cases, the syntax may have to be preprocessed to invoke procedures.

- *Update:* The ODMS may allow updates on derived data, through algorithms to invert the mapping specified by derived data definition in a query language. Otherwise, the ODMS must disallow updates, or allow a programmer to specify update semantics manually.

- *Caching:* It is possible to increase the efficiency of a derived attribute implementation, by storing the derived values to avoid recomputation. Such an implementation requires a marking scheme such as the one we discussed for rule systems, in order to know when to invalidate the cached values. Using rules, an application programmer could implement caching of a derived attribute manually.

Unfortunately, few implementations of derived data have been done in ODMSs, and no work has yet been reported on caching and update. We therefore defer further discussion of derived data to Section 5.7, where we cover the query language and data independence.

5.5.6   Dispatching

Dispatching is the process by which a call on a method, for example

```
obj.meth(a, b)
```

is bound to a particular implementation of the method (`meth`). A variety of issues arises in dispatching:

1. Some systems allow free procedures that are not bound to particular object types. If invocations of methods and free procedures are not syntactically distinguished as they are in our example, it is necessary to look first for a free procedure called `meth`.

2. There may be many methods with the name `meth`; it is necessary to execute the one associated with `obj`'s type.

3. The method may not be associated directly with `obj`'s type; it may be a method inherited from a supertype. The method may even have more than one definition in the type hierarchy—for example, in `obj`'s parent as well as grandparent. In this case, the definition in the most immediate ancestor of `obj`'s type overrides more general ones.

4. The definitions of types are dynamic in some systems: `meth` may be redefined at any time. This is a special case of *dynamic binding,* which we discuss in Section 5.6.3. To allow this late binding of methods, we can perform dispatching "on the fly" at run time. However, it is generally preferable to perform dispatching at compile time for efficiency; this demands that existing programs be repaired when a method definition is changed.

[Manola 1989] discusses some of the performance tradeoffs in dispatching. Again, in the database programming language approach, the existing programming language generally already addresses dispatching issues in a particular way, so dispatching is not an ODMS issue. In extended relational database systems, procedures rather than methods are generally provided, so dispatching is again not an issue. However, in extended database systems such as POSTGRES, or in object-oriented database programming languages not based on an existing programming-language compiler—for example, Gemstone OPAL—these issues must be addressed by the ODMS.

5.5.7   Procedure Storage

Two approaches have been taken to storing procedure definitions in ODMSs:

1. Procedures may be stored and dispatched in the existing programming-language environment, as mentioned. In this case, procedures are stored using the conventional programming-language files; they are merely associated with object types in the database by the declarations in user programs. Recent object-oriented ODMS products have taken this approach.

2. The source code, and optionally a compiled binary form of the code, may be stored in the database itself. This approach is used in extended database systems such as POSTGRES, and also in ORION and GemStone. O_2 [Bancilhon et al 1989] also uses this approach: CO_2 or other programming-language source code is stored in the database and is dynamically compiled, linked, and loaded into memory of the existing programming environment.

The second solution is more elegant, and may appear more powerful. However, either of these alternatives is viable; the differences lie in the performance and difficulty of the implementation.

The second alternative makes it easier to share new procedures among multiple users on a network; the first alternative requires a network file system with pointers to file names and versions in the database schema.

Since method definitions are normally compiled, both alternatives require that modified procedures be recompiled and stored back when modified, and relinked with running programs if currently in use (if dynamic binding is permitted). The first alternative may be more efficient when dynamic binding is not required, if the implementation loads a module with many procedures instead of one procedure or type at a time.

Both alternatives must maintain integrity when types or procedures are modified—procedures must not be executed on objects of the wrong type. The ODMS implementation of type integrity is more difficult but not impossible when procedures are stored in files with unique identifiers and creation times.

Both alternatives face special problems if procedures contain code in multiple programming languages. An environment and procedure-invocation interface that supports cross-language calls might be constructed, but little experience with the multiple-language problem has been reported.

5.6   OBJECT TYPES

In this section, we consider the implementation of object type information: representation of object types and the type hierarchy; the internal data schema, including indexes; and schema evolution, the process of changing object types and revising existing data to match the new schema.

5.6.1   Schema Representation

In most ODMSs, the data schema (object types) are represented as objects, as we discussed in Chapter 4. This self-representation is convenient for the user in examining the data schema. However, the system cannot allow direct updates to this representation since the integrity of the database may be compromised. Instead, the user generally defines the schema using declarations written in a data definition language, in an extended database system architecture, or an extension of the programming-language declaration syntax, in a database programming language. These schema declarations are then translated into calls to run-time procedures that create the schema objects themselves.

In the database programming language approach, the preprocessor that reads the user's schema declarations must not only generate calls to create the database schema, but also generate the declarations used by the programming-language compiler for the data objects in memory. These two representations of the schema do not need to be visible to the user, however.

In any one of the approaches, changes to the schema result in two different representations of the schema: the old one, stored in the database, including instances of these old object types, and the new one, described in the data definition language. This brings us to our next topic, schema evolution.

5.6.2 Schema Evolution

Some authors claim that the schema changes more frequently in applications to which ODMSs are addressed, so it is especially important to be able to modify the schema easily. However, there are relational database applications where schema changes are equally frequent. In any case, schema evolution is an important problem, and is more complex in advanced data models because of the number of features and possible schema transformations [Skarra and Zdonik 1987, Banerjee et al 1987, Panel 1989].

There are four main approaches to maintaining data instances under schema modification:

- *Write-once types:* The simplest approach is to disallow type modification once instances have been created. If a user wishes to define a new attribute or otherwise change a type in such a system, then a new type must be defined and the old data must be copied to it.

- *Immediate update:* In the immediate-update approach, a change to the schema immediately affects existing data of that type [Penney and Stein 1987]. For example, if a new attribute is added to an object type, all existing objects of that type are updated automatically to have a null value for that attribute. This approach is most common among the ODMS products.

- *Lazy update:* Another approach is to defer updates to objects of a type until the next time the objects are used [Kim and Chou 1988]. When objects are fetched into memory, a tag associated with the objects indicates whether they have been updated to the latest type definition. If the schema has changed (for example, an attribute has been added), the update is done at that time. In this approach, historical schema information and conversion procedures must be maintained by the ODMS until all instances of a given type have been converted to the new representation. [Harrus, Velez, and Zicari 1990] study the performance tradeoffs of lazy versus immediate update.

- *Schema mapping:* The most extreme approach would be to delay updates to existing objects indefinitely, or until a reorganization is requested explicitly, maintaining a *mapping* between the current representation of types and all previous versions [Ahlsen et al 1984, Skarra and Zdonik]. Like the lazy update approach, schema mapping requires maintaining multiple versions of the schema. If a mapping is maintained between all versions of the schema pairwise, users may view the same objects through different versions of the schema. Schema mapping is very difficult, and is not implemented in any of the systems we survey.

In general, all ODMSs degenerate to the first approach (defining new types and copying) for sufficiently complex schema changes. Many systems can handle simple changes such as adding or dropping an attribute, relationship, or method, or even adding or removing subtypes. However, even in systems such as ORION that can handle all the changes in our taxonomy of Section 4.6, the vast majority of changes not covered by the taxonomy require that the user write a program to create new types and perform transformations of the data from the old schema to the new one. Even simple semantic rearrangements of attributes may require writing a program or query:

- Changing a **parent** relationship into a **mother** and **father** relationship according to the sex of the related **Person** object
- Changing **SourceProgram** objects into **CompiledLanguageProgram** or **InterpretedLanguageProgram** objects, depending on the language in which they are written
- Changing a string-valued **part-type** attribute into a reference to a **PartType** object with the string as its key

As we noted in Chapter 4, rearrangements such as these are common in database applications, as is a host of other changes that no current ODMS can handle automatically. Probably the majority of real-world schema modifications are transformations that will require programming in an ODMS, and future research into more sophisticated schema-transformation algorithms, although academically interesting, will probably not change this situation much.

It would therefore be more useful to put future research effort into more sophisticated tools to aid the user in schema modification—for example, graphical transformation tools or languages to simplify a large class of transformations—rather than making incremental improvements to the schema-modification features of the ODMS itself. Unfortunately, relatively little work has been done in this area [Lerner and Haberman 1990, Zicari 1989]. At least, the introduction of more powerful query languages and more convenient database programming languages simplifies updates to existing data somewhat; this is the approach taken in most traditional database systems. Note that the user must also deal with compatibility of existing programs using the old schema, a problem we return to later in discussing data independence in Section 5.7. Thus, there is much work still to be done in schema-modification research.

5.6.3   Dynamic Binding

An advantage of many ODMSs is that they allow *dynamic binding*. That is, the precise type or semantics of a symbol may not be known until run time. One example of dynamic binding is run-time dispatching, as discussed earlier. Another example is run-time mapping of attribute and variable names to their types and values.

Some systems, such as Smalltalk-based ones, do not require that variables be declared at all. In others, such as those based on C++, it is possible to achieve some of the effect of dynamic binding by declaring a variable to be of a type that is a supertype of all types. We call this all-inclusive root type **ANY**. When possible, it is even better to use a supertype over exactly those types a variable's value can vary.

The advantage of dynamic binding is convenience to the programmer. For example, dynamic binding makes it possible to write a generic print routine taking a variety of data types as argument, rather than calling a different print routine depending on the type of variable. Another common example is the ability to define procedures on derived types such as lists, without knowing the types of elements in the list, using **LIST[ANY]** as their argument.

The convenience of dynamic binding does not come for free: When a variable of a more general type is passed to a procedure or operation requiring a specific type, it is necessary to perform a run-time check on the object in order to coerce it to the more specific type. [Mathews 1990, Manola 1989] discuss some of these implementation issues. If used carefully, however, dynamic binding can greatly simplify code with negligible performance degradation: A more general type should be used only when required, and coercion of objects into more specific types should not be performed repeatedly.

5.7   QUERY PROCESSING

In Section 5.5, we discussed procedures and the programming-language implementation. In this section, we cover the query language and its implementation, including its integration with the programming language, and the selection of indexes and other access methods for query processing.

5.7.1   Approaches

As discussed in Chapter 4, ODMSs differ in the kinds of query languages they provide. Recall the most important dimensions we covered:

- *Environment:* The query language may share the same data space with the programming language, or it may require that data be copied back and forth between the two.

- *Query scope:* Queries may result in collections, relations, or any type of data. They may permit value joins, where objects may be matched by literal attribute values, rather than by a reference between the objects.

- *Encapsulation:* The query language may violate encapsulation, or it may provide access to only public properties.

- *Virtual data:* The query language may operate on procedurally defined data, as well as on stored attributes and relationships.

The extended relational database systems, extended functional database systems, and database system generators all provide a relation-result query language or equivalent implementation that can perform value joins between types. This implementation executes in an environment separate from that of the application program. The query language can generally be used directly by the end user for ad hoc queries, or can be embedded in the programming language to copy data into application variables.

Some of the current database programming languages have weaker query languages. However, even a collection-result query language without value joins may be able to handle the vast majority of queries application programs require, since relationships are generally defined in the schema where joins will be required between objects. For example, in the application schemas in Chapter 2, it is hard to conceive of useful joins except along the "arrows" connecting object types.

We shall focus on the implementation of open-result and relation-result query languages. The query-processing implementations for collection-result query languages generally use a subset of these techniques.

Objects can be thought of as approximately analogous to records in a relational model. Object attributes may be queried by the language. Thus, algorithms used for relational query processing can generally be applied to query processing in an ODMS, as well. However, queries in an ODMS can be more complex to process than those in a relational system, because the data model is richer. This is true regardless of whether the ODMS has a functional data model, extended relational model, or object-oriented model. The introduction of a hierarchy of types in any of these models, for example, requires that query processing search subtypes in determining the response to a query request. Since we assume a background in relational query processing, we shall focus on cases where data model extensions result in new query-processing issues.

5.7.2   Procedures and Queries

In both an extended database system and a database programming language architecture, users are given two languages in which to code their applications: a declarative query language and a procedural programming language. Although the two might be somewhat more closely integrated in the database programming language approach, since the programming language has the same type system and has direct access to the database, in both approaches the users must choose how to decompose their application problem into a "query" component and a "programming" component. In most of the ODMSs, it is possible to invoke the query language from the programming language, as well as vice versa—perhaps even nesting calls, from the programming language to the query language and back again, in complex cases.

For example, in the text-processing application of Figure 2.11, consider a program to perform a reasonably complex function: (1) find all documents belonging to the user's project, (2) for those whose abstracts match a text search pattern specified by the user, print the title and the line of text where the match occurred, and (3) similarly print titles and matched text for documents referenced by these documents that contain the search pattern. The structure of the program might look something like this:

```
projectdoclist =
  SELECT FROM Document
  WHERE userproject IN Document.projects;
w = createscrollablewindow(); /* to display answer */
FOREACH d in projectdoclist
  IF regularexprmatch(d.abstract, pattern, bytepos)
     addline(w, d.title, getline(d.abstract, bytepos));
  FOREACH r IN d.references
     IF regularexprmatch(r.abstract, pattern, bytepos)
        addline(w, r.title, getline(r.abstract, bytepos));
displaywindow(w);
```

This program is written in a database programming language—we perform direct access to the database by using expressions such as **d.references**. In an extended database system, such expressions would require additional query-language calls. In an extended relational model, where the references might be represented by a separate **references** relation with **source** and **dest** attributes, rather than by the multivalued attribute **references**, we might replace **d.references** with

SELECT source FROM references WHERE reference.dest=d

If an ODMS offers a sufficiently powerful query language, it may be possible to express the entire computation in the query language. For example, POSTGRES allows calls to procedures such as **regularexprmatch** and **addline** to be part of a query; that is, they may be nested inside complex **SELECT** expressions. The advantage of the POSTGRES approach is that relational query optimization is well understood, and a declarative language, in which the user specifies the desired result without specifying how and in what order to achieve that result (as in a procedural language), can be optimized by simple algebraic transformations. The selection, projection, and join operations of relational query languages have simple well-defined optimization rules; this is not true for procedural languages.

The fact that query languages are easier to optimize than are programming languages is an argument for providing more powerful declarative query languages. It is also an argument for writing as much of an application program as possible in the query language. The same program could be written in many different ways in a database programming language architecture, since the query language frequently can be used interchangeably with the programming language. Note that the fact that query languages are easier to optimize is *not* an argument for a particular architecture or data model, since the query language can be made equally powerful regardless of overall approach.

For sufficiently complex queries, the query language is inadequately expressive, so it will always be necessary to fall back on a programming language at some point. In addition, there may be restrictions on procedure calls that can be embedded in the query language. For example, in extended database system architectures, the procedure **addline** is not permitted access to global variables such as the window **w**, and the procedure **regularexprmatch** would not be able to prompt for user input—say, to allow the user to accept or reject particular documents. In extended database system architectures such as POSTGRES and IRIS, the query language and embedded procedures are executed on a server machine, and the rest of the application program is executed on a client machine, so there can be substantial performance implications to how a program is organized and optimized.

Unfortunately, little research has been reported on optimizing database programming languages. Traditional programming-language optimization techniques should be applicable in many cases, but no research has been reported on optimizing the *combination* of query and programming languages. Coverage of these optimization topics therefore is not possible at this time. This is an important and difficult area for future research, because it spans programming language and database systems disciplines.

5.7.3 Value Joins and Selections

As in relational DBMSs, there are two kinds of joins in ODMSs: value joins and entity joins. The latter are also called *reference* joins, since they follow OID-valued object references. Relatively little work has been reported on joins and query processing in ODMSs; the ORION and O$_2$ papers cover issues in object-oriented query languages. We discuss some issues associated with value joins in this section; reference joins are covered next, in Section 5.7.4.

Indexes are used for value joins and selections, as in relational DBMSs. However, the existence of a hierarchy of types makes testing of attribute type compatibility and selection of indexes more complex. As in relational systems, a B-tree or hash index on objects in a collection or on all objects of a type can be used to enumerate objects with specific attribute values (selections), or to match objects with the same values in corresponding attributes (joins). B-tree indexes may even be clustered as in relational implementations, although as we have noted there are many other ways to cluster objects in ODMSs. However, B-trees on a hierarchy of object types introduce a new issue not present in relational systems: When an object type has subtypes, do we create a separate index for each subtype, or a single index for a type and all of its subtypes?

A single index on a type T is most efficient for queries on objects of that type, but can be used for queries on T's subtypes only by doing the lookup and rejecting entries from other subtypes. Separate indexes for each subtype are useful for queries for any type in the hierarchy, but are somewhat less efficient to search all objects of type T—we must search all the subindexes.

For example, the object type **Simple-component** in the ECAD example of Figure 2.8 has three subtypes: **Transistor**, **Capacitor**, and **Resistor**. We could create an index on the **orientation** attribute of a **Simple-component** to find all components in a particular range of orientation coordinates. Or, we could create three separate indexes, one for each subtype. The latter would be more efficient to find all **Resistors** in a region, and the former would be more efficient to find all **Simple-components** regardless of subtype. However, either approach would be sufficient to answer any query on coordinates, as follows:

- *With three indexes:* A query requesting **Simple-components** with a particular **orientation** can be satisfied by doing a lookup on all three indexes and taking the union of the results. Requests for **Capacitors** with a particular **orientation** can be processed by a single index lookup.

- *With one index*: A query on all **Simple-components** can be satisfied by a single index lookup. A query specifying **Capacitors** alone can be processed by an index lookup on the **Simple-component** index, rejecting index entries not of type **Capacitor**.

Depending on the mix of lookups expected, either of these approaches could be more efficient. [Banerjee et al 1988, Maier and Stein 1986, Kim, Kim, and Dale 1989] discuss the use of indexes on type hierarchies in ODMSs. The latter article provides a model for comparing the costs of the different approaches. Note that the issue of indexing type hierarchies occurs in any data model with subtypes, not just in object-oriented data models.

5.7.4   Reference Joins

We have seen how reference-valued (OID) attributes add new capability to ODMSs, beyond the capabilities of foreign keys in the relational model. Reference-valued attributes may be accessed directly—for example, fetching the document for chapter **x** with **x.doc** in a database programming language, as we have discussed. They may also be used to perform joins; thus, their implementation is important to the discussion of query processing in this section.

Reference-valued attributes in objects have been implemented in two ways:

1. *Parent–child links:* References may be represented directly by pointers, or by pointer equivalents such as physical OIDs. Parent–child links are used in database programming languages such as ONTOS, Objectivity/DB, ObjectStore, and O_2 to support OID references and joins.

2. *Surrogate indexes:* References may be implemented by storing OIDs that are not pointers, using a hash index on OIDs to get to the referenced object. These are called *identity indexes* in Gemstone [Maier 1986]; they are also used in POSTGRES.

There is little research on the performance tradeoffs between these access methods. However, one might expect parent–child links to be more efficient for reference-following and joins than are index-based approaches, since they require only a single page access to reach a related object, whereas the index-based approaches may require intermediate index page fetches. [Carey et al 1990, Cattell and Skeen 1990] present evidence to support this conclusion.

Of course, logical references between objects can also be supported in ODMSs through user-defined foreign and primary key values instead of OIDs, when user-meaningful unique values are defined. Note that these keys, like OID-valued references, can be implemented by either parent–child links or indexes. [Carey et al 1990] discuss the relative efficiency of these approaches in performing joins. We covered both indexes and parent–child links in the relational model in Chapter 3. There, parent–child links are updated automatically to reflect changes in key values rather than OID updates being made directly. However, the relative efficiency of the underlying access methods is the same, whether the access methods are used for keys or for OIDs.

5.7.5   Nested Attribute Indexes

Nested attribute indexes [Maier and Stein 1987, Kemper and Marcotte 1990] can be used to avoid reference-following altogether in some cases. Consider an object of type T that references objects of type U. We shall call the attributes of type U *nested attributes* of type T. In our example database, the attributes of a **Document** are nested attributes of a **Chapter**. We may index objects of type T on a nested attribute. For example, chapters could be indexed according to their document's **revision** date, to make finding chapters in a particular revision faster. Nested attribute indexes can be used to avoid following reference-valued attributes to fetch objects, when the referenced objects are needed only to obtain the nested attribute value.

A special case of nested attribute is that where the nested attribute is the primary key of the referenced object; in that case, the index is identical to a *foreign key index* as described in Chapter 3. Indeed, foreign key indexes may be the most common use for nested attribute indexes, and they may be used to support referential integrity as well as to make queries faster on nested attributes.

The main disadvantage of nested attribute indexes is that they are expensive to maintain when attributes are updated—all indexes that contain the attribute must be fixed. Compare this to the cost of changing a primary key in the relational model; the key may be stored in a variety of fields and indexes in the database. There is also space overhead associated with maintaining the nested attribute index.

Little research has been done on the benefits of nested attribute indexes; the costs may outweigh the benefits for most applications. Even if objects are fetched half the time merely to obtain a single attribute value, the time and space costs to maintain the indexes might be too large to justify use of this method. Performance models and comparisons are needed.

5.7.6 Nested Attribute Replication

Nested attribute values can be replicated in an object. For example, we may frequently fetch the `Document` for a `Chapter` simply to obtain its `title`; if we store both the OID and the `title` of the `Document` in the `Chapter` objects, it is not necessary to fetch the `Document` whenever the `title` is required.

As with nested attribute indexes, the idea of attribute replication can be generalized to replicate any field of a referenced object, not just a primary key. [Shekita and Carey 1989] discuss approaches to implementing replicated attributes, and develop a simple analysis of performance benefits. They recommend that a database administrator be able to specify replication selectively on sets of object instances, rather than in the type declaration.

Nested attribute indexes and replicated attributes are sometimes called *precomputed joins* in the context of the relational model, because they obviate the need for additional index lookups and sorting using traditional join methods.* Nested attribute indexes and replication are most useful in applications where the most frequent reason for following a reference is to fetch the nested attribute of the referenced object.

The pros and cons for attribute replication, like those for nested attribute indexes, are not well understood. Attribute replication is probably less important than object clustering and disk-image objects in producing good performance. Attribute replication can considerably increase the size of a database; a smaller database increases the benefits of clustering, so the referenced object is more likely to be in memory. Avoiding disk I/O by finding the referenced data in memory is, as we discussed earlier, the most important performance objective. Also, replication increases the overhead in performing updates, because a change (for example, to the `title` of a `Document`) must be made in more than one place. The ODMS must maintain this consistency automatically, so it must be efficient to find references to an object that may entail replicated data—parent–child links, indexes, or some other access method must be maintained to enable fast access.

---

* Parent–child links are sometimes called precomputed joins. However, links do not avoid the overhead of fetching the referenced object to retrieve data—they simply reduce it.

5.7.7   Custom Access Methods

There are some cases where hash indexes, B-trees, and parent–child links all fail to give fast access for the kinds of use expected; new access methods may be required. In database system generators such as EXODUS and GENESIS, and in extended relational database systems such as POSTGRES and Starburst, it is possible to add new access methods; in the case of object-oriented database programming languages, it is possible to write custom methods to utilize new access methods.

One important use for custom access methods is for a *multiple range query*, which is a lookup in which more than one attribute is constrained. As an example, consider a graphics application where we wish to find all the objects in a particular rectangular "window" of x,y coordinates. B-trees can be used to find objects in a range of x or a range of y coordinates, but not in both ranges simultaneously.

Various multidimensional indexes have been developed for these cases. [Samet 1990, Rosenberg 1985] provide a good survey of these. Multidimensional access methods may appear in commercial DBMS products in the 1990s. They are essential for spatial databases, and they are also useful for multiconstraint queries in traditional applications—for example, to find employees making less than $50,000 in the age range of 30 to 40 years. Multidimensional indexes are therefore a candidate for inclusion in relational database systems as well as in ODMSs. Multidimensional indexes may also be useful in indexing a hierarchy of types; however, this idea has not yet been explored.

It is generally not easy to implement custom access methods for an ODMS. The POSTGRES manual contains an extensive explanation of how to install them. The only frequently cited uses for new access methods are for multidimensional indexes and for text pattern matching. One could argue that it would be good to add these two features to existing ODMSs, rather than to put substantial effort into extensible storage and query algorithms. However, extensibility is useful in research into new database capabilities, and it is difficult to anticipate the needs of the wide range of applications now exploring ODMS alternatives, so for now programmer-defined access methods appear to be a useful feature.

5.8   CONCURRENCY AND RECOVERY

Concurrency control and recovery in ODMSs require the invention of new techniques, because traditional methodology is based on different assumptions: short transactions, high likelihood of access conflict between users, a single version of the database, a need for fast recovery times, and a heavy premium placed on loss of data. These assumptions typically hold for few if any of the data in the applications we address.

In this section, we cover these new techniques: long transactions that may last for days, and long-term checkout of object versions. Keep in mind that traditional concurrency and recovery techniques may also find use in ODMSs, so the new techniques are additions rather than replacements for these techniques.

Lock mechanisms are required for both versions and transactions, so let's look at them first.

5.8.1   Locking

As in traditional lock implementations, there may be many kinds of locks, including read (shared) locks, write (exclusive) locks, and intent-to-write locks. Some ODMSs introduce "monitor" or *soft* locks that can be "broken" by another process, notifying the application program.

Locks may be performed at a variety of granularities: objects, composite objects, or all objects of a type. It is also common to lock physical units such as pages or segments. Physical locking is normally performed transparently to the user—a page is locked automatically when an object on the page is locked by the user, or a segment is locked when a composite object or type stored in the segment is locked by the user.

The performance advantage of physical locking can be substantial. The advantage is not simply one of placing fewer locks because of larger units, or placing locks more quickly because of a simple, uniform lock table. The biggest speed improvement probably results from the fact that locking is performed on the same physical units that are transferred between disk and memory, and the same physical units that can be cached conveniently by the ODMS [Dewitt and Maier 1990].

Note that, when all objects of a specific type (class) are locked, then objects of subtypes must be locked as well. Similarly, when a composite object is locked, all its subobjects must be locked, and their subobjects, and so on. The propagation of locks down aggregation or generalization hierarchies is a feature that does not enter into relational-database locking; lock propagation in ODMSs must be implemented carefully to avoid substantial overhead.

5.8.2   Transactions

Recall that there are two uses for transactions: concurrency control and recovery. Traditional transactions are generally useful for concurrency control in ODMSs only when application data have traditional access characteristics—that is, for short transactions. If there were potential for concurrency conflict in a transaction lasting for hours or days, then substantial amounts of work could be lost if the conflict occurred and the transaction was backed out.

Transactions are still important in applications such as those in Chapter 2, for several reasons:

- *Recovery:* Most important, transactions are essential for recovery, to reestablish a consistent database state in the face of system failures. It would be disastrous to lose a week's worth of work on the set of objects a user has checked out of the database.

- *Undo:* In many applications, it is convenient to use transactions as an undo facility, so that database updates can be backed out to a consistent state in case an error is detected by the user or application program. "Undo" might be considered a special case of recovery, for correcting logical, rather than physical, errors.

- *Short-term concurrency:* In cases where a separate database or a portion of a database is subject to only traditional short-term sessions, transactions may still be used for concurrency control. For example, in an office information system, documents may be checked out for weeks, but transactions to send electronic mail may be short.

When transactions are used for the first two reasons, it is important that transactions be capable of lasting for long periods. Thus, the transaction implementation in an ODMS must be capable of dealing with what we call *long transactions*.

Transaction implementations using traditional logging and locking techniques generally perform poorly for long transactions, for at least two reasons:

1. Locks are acquired on the user's first attempt to read or write each datum; if lock conflicts are extremely rare, then these lock requests represent substantial overhead that is not required until the transaction is committed.

2. The log file can become arbitrarily long, containing entries for uncommitted transactions from days earlier, since a single log file is used for all users. The old entries cannot be thrown away, yet there may be many millions of bytes of log records that have been written after them. The log will overflow, using up all disk space.

The first of these problems can be remedied through an *optimistic* locking technique: the database system can wait to acquire some or all locks as a single "batched" request just before transaction commit. The choice of optimistic or pessimistic locking can be given to the application, as in GemStone and Objectivity/DB, so that the user can weigh the additional overhead cost against the risk of aborting a transaction after substantial work: in optimistic locking, the user may not discover conflicts with other users until he attempts to commit the transaction and his transaction is aborted.

The second problem can be remedied in several ways. Multiple logs may be used, or, when the log gets too big, the old entries for uncommitted transactions may be rewritten into a new, condensed log, and the old one thrown away. Another remedy is to use a variation on the traditional technique of *shadow paging*. In shadow paging, a new database page is allocated whenever a database page has been modified and must be written back to disk. The segment table, which maps logical to physical page numbers on disk, continues to point to the old database pages until the transaction is committed. Updated pages need not be written back to the disk until transaction commit, as long as there is space in the main-memory cache. At transaction-commit time, all updated pages are flushed to disk and the segment table is updated to replace old pages with the new pages. The header page of the segment table is written as a single atomic disk update, causing all the new pages to become visible.

Shadow-page implementation of transactions can be less efficient than is logging, since more data are copied for updates [Astrahan et al 1976]; in the case of ODMS applications, however, shadow pages might be quite good, because they mesh well with long-term checkout of data and database-caching techniques. GemStone uses shadow paging.

Yet another approach to transaction implementation is to store time stamps with objects, instead of using a log to record all updates to a database. In this approach, used in POSTGRES [Stonebraker et al 1990], existing objects (extended relational records) in the database are never changed when an update is made; instead, a new version of the object is written elsewhere, with a new time stamp. Multiple updates of an object can be made to the new version of the object, up until the transaction is closed, at which time that version of the object and the associated time stamp are frozen forever.

The POSTGRES transaction implementation eliminates the need for a log for all but some bookkeeping information on the status of transactions in progress, and has a substantial side benefit: keeping a complete historical record of changes to the database. As we noted in Section 4.8.6, POSTGRES allows you to query the state of the database as of any previous date and time, and since the identity of the user as well as the time is stored with the updated objects, it is even possible to query object versions according to who created them. It is also very fast to back out transactions, as in the shadow-page implementation, because the new objects can simply be thrown away.

Although innovative, the time-stamp implementation has its drawbacks. First, since objects are constantly being replaced with new versions on other disk pages, it is hard to cluster objects and to keep the newest, most frequently accessed versions quickly accessible. POSTGRES will perform automatic reclustering, but this introduces additional overhead. Second, in a distributed system, time stamps are hard to maintain consistently. Third, a very large quantity of historical data can be generated in some cases. POSTGRES uses a background process called the *vacuum cleaner* to move historical records to an archival store, such as a low-cost write-once read-many (WORM) drive, but the vacuum cleaner can become overloaded when small changes are made to a large number of objects. Future research in POSTGRES, or in other systems using its approach to transactions, will hopefully show whether and how this approach will be practical.

As we have noted, long transactions have limitations for use in concurrency control, because locks are held for the entire duration of the transaction, limiting other users' data access for long periods. The possibility of conflicts and deadlock is increased. POSTGRES time stamps are useful in this context, as are soft locks and change-notification mechanisms in ODMSs such as ORION. However, a better alternative may be to abandon the use of transactions for concurrency control altogether, in favor of long-term checkout of versions.

5.8.3   Versions

Some ODMSs provide facilities to track multiple versions of objects [Objectivity 1990, Object Design 1990, Ontologic 1990, Beech and Mahbod 1988, Chou and Kim 1985, Katz and Lehman 1984, Versant 1990]. There are three implementation issues for object versions: when to create a new version, how to represent the version, and which versions in a database represent a consistent *configuration* of objects. Configurations are discussed in Section 5.8.4; we focus on the object-version questions here.

The user may specify that an object is *versionable*—that is, that the ODMS should maintain multiple versions of the object—in the object type declaration or at the time the object is created. Objectivity/DB allows the user to do either. If an object is versionable, a new version of the object can be created when the object is checked out for update, when the object is first updated, or when it is closed by the application and is written back to the database.

More than one strategy may be used to represent multiple versions of an object:

1. Most commonly, new object versions are created by copying the object and chaining the old object (and any older versions to which it has been chained) behind the new version. Note that a different OID is associated with the new version of the object; however, references to the most recent (or specified default) version can be maintained by using the OID of a special "generic" representative for the object that is always updated to contain the OID of the desired version.

2. Time stamps or version numbers may be associated with every attribute or relationship for an object, and the attributes and relationships may be chained together in historical order. The result is a single object and OID, with the versions actually associated with the attributes. A fully specified reference to an object must then consist of both an OID and a time. An OID by itself references the most recent versions of all attributes. Whenever an attribute is fetched in this scheme, the list of historical values associated with the attribute must be searched to find the correct version; the most recent version may be placed first for efficiency.

The first approach is currently taken in all the ODMSs we cover, probably because it seems more efficient to track versions at the granularity of objects rather than of attributes. However, if the objects are large and changes are made to only a few attributes, the latter approach could have advantages. No performance study has been performed on these alternatives.

It may be important for the user to get at the version history for an object— that is, to examine the attribute values for earlier versions of an object. The version chains used in the representations of versions we mentioned must therefore be doubly linked, or must offer some other mechanism to get from any object version to the entire version history. The user must then be provided operations to follow these connections. In ODMSs that permit an object version history with branching and merging of versions as in Figure 4.4, the history storage and access mechanisms must also support these capabilities.

Given some implementation of object versions and histories, the next problem is which version to use for what. For example, when a new version of the object is created, should existing references be updated automatically to point to the new version, or should they be left pointing to the old one? When the user looks up an object by a primary key value, is he given the most recent version, or a user-specified default version? As we noted in Chapter 4, these questions are addressed by *configurations.*

5.8.5   Version References and Configurations

Versions, as we have so far described them, have some utility. However, versions are more powerful when mutually consistent versions of the many objects in a database can be grouped as configurations. You might think of a configuration as a version of an entire *database,* although it needs to reference only the portion of the database that has changed. For the purposes of concurrency control (but not recovery), a configuration is much like a transaction that can be put away and picked up later, as we noted in Chapter 4. The configuration is an object in itself, representing a version of the database.

Recall that there are two approaches to implementing configurations in an ODMS:

1. The ODMS may provide *mechanism* but not *policy* for configuration management.

2. The ODMS may implement configurations automatically.

In the previous chapter, we described mechanisms such as Objectivity/DB's versionable objects and move, copy, and drop semantics for relationships, which can be used to implement configurations. To clarify these mechanisms, consider the simple ECAD database in Figure 2.8, consisting of **Cells** (capacitors, resistors, transistors, or composite components made from these) with **Ports** (terminals) connected by **Net-Lists** (wires). The declarations

```
Cell: Versioned Object [
   ...
   ports: LIST[Port] DROP <-> on-cell ]

Port: Object [
   ...
   on-cell: Cell <-> ports
   ... ]
```

create a `Cell` object type that is versioned, so that a new instantiation is created whenever a `Cell` object is modified, and the `Ports` on that cell continue to reference the old `Cell` statically; that is, the relationships to `Ports` are dropped when a new `Cell` version is created.*

The built-in configuration semantics we described in Chapter 4 may be implemented quite simply by utilizing object history chains, tagging each object in the history with a configuration identifier. A single OID is used to reach a default representative of the object; for optimum efficiency in most applications, this representative should be the most recent version of the object. The ODMS then follows the version history to find the version of the object in the current configuration, or the version in the most recent preceding configuration. In this implementation, it is not necessary to maintain a nonlinear partial ordering of object version history as we described in the previous subsection. Instead, this ordering is kept in one place, to maintain the version history of configurations and configuration identifiers. If an object is always retrieved by using the default OID, whether through the query language or through following a reference, then this implementation of built-in configurations can be used in all cases where object versions are retrieved.

There is some debate as to whether it is appropriate to implement configurations in an ODMS, since applications may have very different policies for configuration semantics, and basic mechanisms can be provided to allow users to implement their own configurations. Indeed, there is even debate as to whether ODMSs should implement object versions at all: user-defined methods can be used to implement any version semantics desired. However, there is no question that both version and configuration management in the ODMS, if they do what an application requires, can be a significant benefit—substantial programming may be required otherwise. Implementing versions with methods or implementing configurations with composite objects and custom relationship semantics can be error-prone or awkward. Version and configuration management can be implemented with negligible performance impact on application programs that do not use them, so there is no argument to isolate the implementation in applications for performance reasons. In future research and products, the debate over version and configuration management will hopefully be resolved in the form of least common functionality that is widely accepted as appropriate in an ODMS.

5.9 DISTRIBUTION

The final function of ODMSs that we cover in this chapter is distribution of programs and data. We will focus on three major areas: accessing remote data, distributing data across multiple databases, and distributing computation across multiple sites.

---

* Rather than specifying versionable object types and reference semantics in the declaration, in Objectivity/DB we can specify version semantics at run time when objects are created or references are modified. The syntax shown is a simplified form of Objectivity/DB's.

5.9.1   Remote Databases

A majority of the applications we covered in Chapter 2 run on personal workstations or are otherwise distributed on a network such that the application code runs on a computer different from the one where the data are stored. Thus, remote database access and its performance are important differentiators between ODMSs.

There are several important decisions in the implementation of remote database access:

- *Access units:* Data may be transferred over a network as objects, pages, composite objects, or segments. Data may be cached on the local machine in the same units, if concurrency control operates at the same granularity.

- *Representation and translation:* Data may be represented in a format on the disk different from that used in memory, and may be represented in different formats in a heterogeneous hardware network. Data must be copied and translated between these representations.

- *Transport protocol:* Another implementation choice is the transport mechanism used to transfer data: remote procedure call, a protocol on top of a transport such as TCP/IP, a networked file system, or other techniques.

The first of these decisions probably has the most profound impact on performance. To understand this fact, consider rough figures for the operations involved on typical workstation–server technology:

- Fetching a page from disk might take about 30 milliseconds, depending on disk seek time and operating-system overhead.

- The shortest roundtrip communication on a network might take about 10 milliseconds, depending on network and transport. Note that this limit determines the minimum time to perform a lock or other concurrency-control operation, since data are shared over the network.

- Translating or copying an object representation might take 1 millisecond, mainly dependent on CPU speed. Processing a declarative query takes longer.

- Fetching an object that has been found in the local cache might take 1 microsecond (0.001 milliseconds), with an efficient OID and object-handle mechanism.

It is immediately apparent from these figures that the most profound performance improvements come from avoiding both network and disk over-head, arranging for objects to be found in memory frequently when fetched by an application program. Frequent cache hits also require that objects be clustered according to frequently used access paths. To take advantage of that clustering, however, we must fetch entire pages or larger units over the network. In addition, concurrency control must be performed at the same granularity as data fetch over the network so that data may be cached—object locks must be promoted to page locks, or entire composite objects or segments must be locked.

A disk cache on the remote server does not make nearly as much sense as does a cache on the workstation. If a database can be cached such that 99 percent of objects accessed are already in the cache, for example, then 1000 object accesses from an application program require about 0.4 seconds with a local cache, and 11 seconds with a remote cache, using the figures just cited. This is a factor of 25 difference in speed! However, note that if objects cannot be clustered to produce more than a 10-percent hit rate, then 1000 object accesses will take about 1 minute in either case, which is over 100 times slower than the efficient local cache.

There is an important exception to the advantages of caching data sent over a network. If it is more efficient to send the operation to the data, rather than the data being sent to the operation, as we shall discuss in Section 5.9.3, then significant overhead can be avoided. However, this approach puts more load on the resource shared with other users (the server), and access to resources on the workstation (including the end-user's screen) is less efficient or impossible to perform from the program when executing on the server. Thus, it is better to execute database applications on the workstation when reasonable database performance can be obtained there.

We can draw other conclusions from our rough technology parameters:

1. It generally does not make sense to send an object at a time over the network, if a group of objects (a page, a segment, a query) can be sent that is likely to be used in the same session. [Dewitt and Maier 1990] provide concrete evidence for this conclusion.

2. Even the overhead of copying and translating data—for example, by sending queries over the network and packing the objects that satisfy the query into packets to be returned—may add substantial cost compared to simply returning disk pages. A well-controlled study of applications is needed to evaluate the benefits of selective queries versus the server and client processing overhead that the latter entail. The extended relational database systems we study use queries, whereas the object-oriented database programming languages use pages.

It is important to note that the observations we have made will generally become *more* true with evolution of current technology. CPU speeds are increasing faster than network speeds, and faster than disk speeds. In particular, caching data and minimizing the number of network packets will become even more important.

5.9.2   Distributed Databases

Data may be distributed over multiple databases in many ways.

*   *Federated databases:* Data may be split across DBMSs from different vendors, or with different data models. A *gateway* may be built between two DBMSs to allow data in one to be accessed by applications in another. *Federated databases*

provide gateways between multiple DBMSs and databases, providing a mapping between the data schemas in each.

- *Conventional distributed databases:* Data may split across multiple databases using a single data model, from a single vendor.

This section discusses the latter. We do not cover federated databases in this book; little work has been done on this topic in the context of ODMSs. However, several of the ODMS products have gateways to ORACLE or SYBASE.

Distributed databases are important in object data management for many of the same reasons as they are in relational databases. Probably the most common case is when different data are administered and controlled by different organizations; since databases are the unit of data administration, schema definition, and crash recovery, the data must be placed in separate databases for each organization. Application programs must be able to query and update data across organizational boundaries.

Another reason to use distributed databases is performance. The data may be placed on the machine where they are queried most frequently, and applications that operate on more than one database can sometimes be decomposed to multiprocess, distributing the computation between machines. However, as in relational distribution, performance can also suffer, so careful analysis is necessary before splitting a database up in the hopes of improving application run time.

Distributed database implementations in ODMSs face many of the same issues as in relational databases. Network overhead typically dominates, particularly in a wide-area network. Two-phase commit is required for consistent multisite updates.

Like relational DBMSs, two strategies can be taken to distributing ODMSs; we will call them *local-schema* and *global-schema* distributed databases. The two approaches differ in the degree to which participating databases are interdependent.

In local-schema distribution, each database has its own schema. The generation of unique OIDs may also be localized to databases in this approach. A schema mapping is defined between databases on a type-by-type basis, however, so that objects may be referenced in another database. For example, type **Document** and **Chapter** in database A may be mapped to type **Document** and **Chapter** in database B, if the types and their attributes are defined compatibly, so that application programs may operate on documents as if the databases were merged. Relationships (references) may span local-schema databases in this way as well. Note, however, that OIDs in the foreign database must be tagged explicitly by the ODMS in some way, so that, when an OID is dereferenced, it is mapped to an object in the proper database context.

If the types in the two databases are not identical, the mapping between local schemas must define how types in one schema are to be mapped to the other. Some form of derived data mechanism is useful to define such mappings; in INGRES-STAR, a local-schema distributed relational database, relational views are used for this. A limited form of local-schema distribution can be provided in an ODMS *without* a mapping mechanism by permitting references to equivalent types in another database only when they are identical to local types.

In global-schema distribution, one or more database resources are centralized. A shared data schema unites all the databases in a single global domain. Object types and attributes in the shared schema are valid over all of the databases in the domain. A networkwide mechanism for OIDs must be provided so that OIDs are unique over the entire network as well. A single network OID generation process may be used, or OIDs may be made unique by prefixing them with a machine ID, distributed type ID, or other distinguishing string. Objectivity/DB and ORION/ITASCA provide global-schema distribution.

The difference in the two distributed database approaches is primarily one of early versus late binding of database schemas. The global-schema approach guarantees that types are compatible across databases in an organization, but it requires that the organizations coordinate on the schema definition. The local-schema approach is more flexible, as each database schema may evolve independently, but if and when it is desired to access data in another database, the mapping between the schemas must be defined.

5.9.3   Distributed Computation

An important feature of object data management is the ability to perform *distributed computation,* to split an application into multiple cooperating processes on one or more machines on a network.

The object-oriented approach provides a particularly clean way to decompose distributed computations, treating objects as independent *agents* cooperatively computing by sending each other messages to execute associated methods, as we discussed in Section 4.5. The agents may execute on the same machine, on a client and server machine, or on any number of machines on a network.

Because the ODMS provides a shared database environment independent of the machine where the procedures actually execute, it is relatively easy to distribute or redistribute computation. The ODMS needs only to provide some mechanism to specify where computation is to be performed.

To date, relatively little work has been done on distributed computation in ODMSs, and no ODMS product provides this facility except for the client–server machine split, which is not transparent. However, the important ODMS feature for distributed computation is not the remote procedure call or other mechanism to invoke actions across process or machine boundaries. These calling mechanisms are already provided by many operating systems, and it may not be important for an ODMS to provide them. What the ODMS provides is an environment to make distributed computation feasible—a shared data environment so that the processes can cooperate. A "poor man's" version of an ODMS with distributed computation using remote procedure calls can be just as useful, particularly when distributed computation is important in only a few instances.

On the negative side, a distributed database does not solve all the problems associated with distributed computation. Other resources, such as communication with the user, ordinary files used by the application, global variables in an application program, and any other program state used by application procedures must also be accessible across a network. Database objects must be defined for these resources, or other mechanisms must be provided for distributed access to them; otherwise, these resources cannot be used in distributed computation.

5.10   PERFORMANCE

Although we have touched on performance issues throughout this chapter, in this final section we focus specifically on performance, to emphasize its importance. We consider both database size and access speed in our consideration. We give priority to the latter, because speed is most frequently the limiting factor in application performance.

We cover two kinds of performance issues:

- *Model-based:* In some cases, performance is limited by the data model, regardless of how good the implementation. For example, relational-model implementations have an impedance mismatch between programming and query language, forcing an application to represent a list (such as the chapters of a book) as a table, and to copy the data wholesale from the table to a list in the programming language at run time in order to manipulate the elements efficiently.

- *Architecture-based:* As noted throughout this chapter, the implementation of specific ODMS features can have major performance implications. In some cases, the implementation choices for two particular features, such as concurrency control and remote databases, can interact favorably or very badly for overall speed. Thus, it is important to consider the overall view.

After covering some general considerations in comparing ODMS performance, this section focuses on the most important performance issues for overall application speed. We cover both model-based and architecture-based issues in the process, and identify them as such as we proceed.

5.10.1   Understanding Performance

Little work has been done on performance in the field of object data management, despite its importance to most applications [Maier 1988, Hardwick 1987]. It is not possible to compare the performance of different implementations through abstract analysis except in some simple cases. However, some benchmarks have been proposed for ODMSs [Anderson et al 1989, Cattell and Skeen 1991, Carey, Dewitt, Naughton 1993]. We briefly consider the OO1 (Object Operations, Version 1) benchmark [Cattell and Skeen 1991] to illuminate performance issues.

The OO1 benchmark is intended as a generic measure of ODMS performance; it is designed to replicate operations most frequently performed by applications such as those in Chapter 2. A simple database of parts is used with a many-to-many connection relationship between the parts. Three kinds of operations are performed on the parts and connections:

- *Lookup:* Fetch 1000 parts given randomly selected primary keys for the parts (part numbers).

- *Traversal:* Find all parts connected to a random part, all parts connected to one of those parts, and so on, to seven levels deep (obtaining 3280 parts, since each part is connected to three others).

- *Insert:* Create 100 new parts with randomly distributed attribute values and 300 randomly selected connections to them, and commit these updates to disk under a transaction.

In a CASE application, where the parts in the database might correspond to program modules and the connections to compilation dependencies, the lookup operation is analogous to finding program objects given the program name, the traversal is analogous to building a compilation plan for a system from the dependency graph, and the insertion is analogous to adding new program modules to the database. In an ECAD application, where the database might represent electrical connections between components, the lookup is analogous to finding parts the user references by name on the screen, the traversal is analogous to finding electrically connected parts to minimize wire lengths, and the insert is analogous to adding new components and connections to a circuit.

Figure 5.4 shows the results of running the OO1 benchmark operations on a new object-oriented database product with a database programming language architecture, labeled OODBMS, and a state-of-the-art relational database product, labeled RDBMS. The benchmark operations were run with these systems on a small database of approximately 4 megabytes, containing 20,000 parts and 60,000 connections between parts. The database was accessed over a network. The left side of the figure shows the results of the benchmark from a "cold" start, the right side shows the asymptotically best results achieved when database caching is permitted.

Note the significant differences between the RDBMS and OODBMS systems, particularly on the "warm" results: the OODBMS is as much as 30 times faster overall. The lookup and traversal operations, which do not require disk updates when data are cached (the insert requires a transaction commit), can be over 100 times faster. Even on the "cold" results, the traversal operation is several times faster for the OODBMS than RDBMS. These differences stem from database architecture, data models, and other issues [Dewitt and Maier 1990, Carey 1990, Moss 1991]. We refer to these results as we proceed through Section 5.10.

In 1989 and 1990, the OO1 benchmark was run on the object-oriented database programming languages Objectivity/DB, ONTOS, ObjectStore, VERSANT, and GemStone, and both the SYBASE and INGRES relational database products. OO1

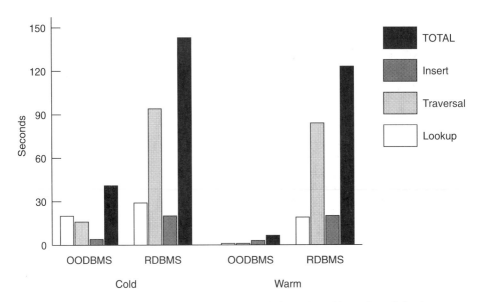

FIGURE 5.4 Comparison of traditional relational DBMS against object-oriented database programming language on the OO1 engineering database benchmark. Initial "cold" results are shown
on the left; "warm" results after caching are shown on the right.

has subsequently been run on many other systems. The results for the database
programming languages have been consistent with the results for OODBMS
shown in the figure, and the results for relational systems have been consistent
with the RDBMS results shown in the figure. Thus, the differences seen in the
figure are not an accident of particular implementations.

On the other hand, the differences between the relational and object-oriented
systems should *not* be attributed to a difference between relational and object-
oriented models. There is reason to believe that most of the differences in this
particular benchmark's results can be attributed to *architecture-based*, rather than to
model-based, differences. [Winslett and Chu 1990] report that a relational DBMS
with the right architecture can perform adequately for a CAD application, using a
version of MAGIC that has been modified to store data in the UNIFY relational
DBMS. They speculate on several reasons that UNIFY might have performed well:

1. UNIFY ran on the same machine as the application and was linked directly
    with the application program, thereby caching data in the client process. In
    contrast, all major RDBMS products use client–server architectures.

2. UNIFY provides parent–child links that can be used to represent relation-
    ships, unlike other relational DBMSs.

3. The CAD application was programmed directly to the access-method level of
    UNIFY, bypassing the SQL processor.

    It is also important to note that the CAD application was programmed to use
"batch" interaction with the DBMS. That is, all the data were dumped from UNIFY

to the application data structures at the beginning of a session, and were copied back at the end of a session. In contrast, OO1 was defined using "interactive" interaction with the DBMS; that is, the benchmark operates directly on data stored in the DBMS, rather than caching them in application data structures.

There is not consensus in the literature as to whether the batch or interactive models are more representative of future engineering applications. However, a reasonably strong argument can be made that the trend is toward the interactive model. Although many engineering applications operated in a batch mode using files, they did so out of necessity—implementing interactive database capability was intractable. If application programmers are to convert to using an ODMS, they probably will want to take advantage of the power that the ODMS provides for queries, integrity constraints, object identity, relationships, and other capabilities that would have to be redundantly implemented on application data structures in the "batch" approach. Database programming languages can now reach the speed of programming languages on cached objects, making the interactive approach feasible without penalty.

[Carey, Dewitt, Naughton 1993] have recently improved on OO1 with a new benchmark, OO7, based on a much more comprehensive array of DBMS measures and a more complex database. OO7 was designed for detailed comparisons of OODBMS products, as opposed to the rough overall measures we just examined. However, in interpreting any generic benchmark, and in considering the generic performance guidelines in the following sections, keep in mind that the best measure of application performance is to test parts of the application itself against the target DBMS. Generic data may not be applicable.

5.10.2   Data Types and Language

Many performance limitations may result from model-based issues. There are two common cases:

- *Limited data structures:* If the ODMS does not provide a mechanism for ordering (lists), random access (arrays), or other data structures required by application semantics, data access can be inefficient. In the example using relations for chapters of a book, ordered access to the chapters always requires sorting the chapters by number.

- *Language impedance mismatch:* If the ODMS requires a language different from the application programmer's language for database access, then a significant amount of execution time can be wasted copying data from the database language to the programming language and back again.

Unfortunately, no study has been performed to quantify the severity of these effects on application performance. Some of the performance difference between the relational and object-oriented results in Figure 5.4 may be a result of the language impedance mismatch; using the relational model in an interactive mode, it is necessary to fetch objects in the query language and to operate on each one in the programming language. However, there are many other differences. An equally likely candidate for the discrepancy is the difference in the way data are cached and remotely accessed, our next topic.

5.10.3 Caching and Remote Access

Another factor that can substantially affect performance is the use of main memory to cache data. The effect is large for several reasons:

- *Disk access:* Random access to main memory is over 10,000 times faster than random access to disk.

- *Network access:* When data are stored on a server machine, a cache on the client workstation can avoid costly network overhead.

- *Representation:* Translation overhead in converting from the disk representation of objects to a more efficient main-memory representation can also be substantial.

In CAD, CASE, and other design applications, it is common for all or most data used during a session to fit in several megabytes of main memory storage on a workstation. An engineer may check out a portion of the design for several days to work on it, or a design-automation program may spend minutes or hours optimizing a portion of the design. Thus, such applications are ideally suited to a main-memory cache—for the duration of a session, they act primarily as a "main-memory database." As noted earlier, many of these applications were built to load main-memory data structures from a disk file, and to dump them back at the end of a session. ODMSs can now automate this process and provide much more flexibility as well. Substantial conversion overhead may also be eliminated, using a disk-image in a database programming language.

Note that it is not possible to cache data unless other users are prevented from modifying the data during the session. Thus, the concurrency-control mechanisms of the ODMS must mesh efficiently with caching. Objects, pages, or segments in the cache must be locked on the server in some fashion, typically through a checkout mechanism or through creation of a new version of the data. Automatic locking by long-term transactions can also be used. Concurrency control at this granularity might seem too restrictive, but the performance gains to be had usually outweigh the drawbacks of excluding other users from write access to the data.

To get an idea of the kinds of performance improvement to be had, you should refer back to Figure 5.4, comparing the right and left sides of the figure. The OODBMS system is significantly faster after it has been given an opportunity to cache data in main memory. The RDBMS does not do local caching, so shows only a small difference in speed. As we noted earlier, the RDBMS's disk cache on the server has negligible performance impact due to the network and other overhead in getting to this data.

5.10.4   Compile-Time Binding

Another important factor in ODMS performance is elimination of run-time overhead that can be incurred at compile time. There are many ways this can be done.

The most obvious optimization is to use a compiled rather than interpreted database and programming language. All the ODMSs we cover use compiled languages; however, some may still incur overhead each time a program is executed, by compiling a set of commands the first time they are executed. Ideally, programs are compiled only one time, and the only run-time check performed is to ensure that the schema version or date with which the program was compiled matches that of the database at the time the database is opened.

Overhead can also be incurred by the need to perform type checks on variables and objects at run time, or to perform dynamic binding of methods. In languages with untyped variables and object references, such as Smalltalk-80, it may not be possible to infer types at compile time, so the type checks are unavoidable.

5.10.5   Translation and Copying

Given an efficient data-access language, a good caching scheme, and minimal run-time system overhead, the next most important performance issue is probably minimizing the translation and copying of data.

As we discussed in Section 5.2, many levels of translation and copying may occur. Some common cases for optimization are these:

- *Operating-system buffers:* If data are read from a file using traditional file I/O, data pages may be copied from disk to operating-system buffers, and then copied a second time into the application process address space. It is better to avoid this second copy if the operating system allows us to do so.

- *DBMS buffers:* If the disk representation of objects can be made compatible in size and structure to the application representation of objects, so that only minor adjustments such as swizzling are required, another copying step can be avoided by making the DBMS and application buffers the same. Note that, even if this copying is required, minor restructuring of objects is much simpler than that required by the language impedance mismatch discussed earlier.

- *Heterogeneous hardware:* If a DBMS allows data to be accessed from computers with different data representations, it is usually necessary to translate the representation of integers, reals, strings, and so on. If the DBMS is designed carefully, however, the most common representation can be used for the database, to minimize the need for conversion.

Together, these optimizations could turn several data copy and translation steps into one. This improvement will be particularly significant if an application is performing relatively few operations on each object—for example, examining and modifying a single attribute. Of course, in the common case of a remote database, a minimum of two copying steps will be required anyway: one from the disk to server memory, and one from server to client-machine memory; in addition, the disk and network overhead is larger than that for a memory-to-memory copy or translation. Thus, the optimizations discussed here are less important than those in the previous three sections.

5.10.6   Other Performance Factors

We have covered the factors that most frequently affect ODMS performance. However, in special cases, other factors can have substantial effects on performance.

The existence of special access methods is important where the methods can be applied usefully. For example, the two-dimensional indices discussed in Section 5.7 can substantially improve object lookup in spatial or graphical applications.

Space efficiency can differ substantially between DBMSs. The OO1 benchmark, in results on seven different systems, was found to require a range between 4 and 20 megabytes in size! These differences may be due to tradeoffs between clustering and internal fragmentation; the size of OIDs and references; overhead for segment, page, and object descriptions; and other factors. Space differences not only affect the amount of disk memory—they significantly affect the access speed as well, if the working set of data no longer fits in a main-memory cache. A larger database representation will also use more disk space and incur slightly higher network-transfer overhead.

There may be substantial performance differences between ODMSs depending on the implementation of lock and transaction management. These differences may be particularly noticeable at the time updates are made or transactions are committed.

Any number of other factors may be important to performance for any particular ODMS. Generally speaking, more mature products have had much more performance tuning than new ones, but any ODMS may have particularly inefficient behavior for a specific application.

Performance is important—typically more important than most of the functionality provided by an ODMS. Many kinds of functionality can be added in an application on top of an ODMS, but poor performance generally cannot be improved at the application level.

5.11   SUMMARY

This chapter covered implementation issues that you should consider in building, using, or choosing an ODMS. It is too early to provide a complete guide to implementing an ODMS, because none of the ODMS products or prototypes have all the functionality we covered in Chapter 4, and very little has been written about complete implementations. However, we touched on the most important and difficult issues.

Storage management for an ODMS requires many of the same features as does relational DBMS storage management, such as indexes and allocation of records on pages, but an ODMS requires new capabilities as well. The implementation of OIDs is much more important than that for relational record identifiers, since OIDs are the primary method by which a user refers to database objects and establishes relationships between objects; in a relational system, these references are value-based. The implementation of clustering is more complex than in relational DBMSs, because the data model is much richer: objects may be clustered according to aggregation, generalization, or other relationships.

Query processing in ODMSs has much in common with relational DBMSs, since the optimization and access methods for the most basic operations, such as selection, projection, and join, are similar. However, ODMS query languages include generalization, aggregation, lists, arrays, and other new semantics in the data model, so query processing can be much more complex. Also, the close integration between programming languages and query languages, particularly for ODMSs taking the database programming language approach, make the implementation of an ODMS much more difficult than is implementation of a relational system.

Although the use of transactions for atomic operations and recovery can be carried over from relational DBMSs to ODMSs, new implementation issues arise in concurrency control as a result of the introduction of long transactions and nested transactions, and, more important, versions and configurations. Little research has been done on these implementation issues, particularly in the context of composite objects, main-memory caching, remote databases, and other features essential to object data management.

Performance is crucial in the implementation of an ODMS. This fact is not widely understood, perhaps because much of the work in object data management thus far has been in academic and research environments, where the initial focus has been on functionality, or because performance issues for the applications in Chapter 2 are quite different from traditional on-line transaction processing or decision-support applications, and are not well understood. Performance is so important that many users would *give up* most of the functionality described in the previous chapter in order to allow simple database operations to be accomplished in fractions of a millisecond instead of fractions of a second. Some features, such as the level of protection afforded by relational DBMS through manipulating data in a separate process or separate machine, may not be possible to implement in the context of these performance requirements.

The most important performance issues arise in the use of main-memory caches for data, the ways remote access is performed, the integration of the ODMS with the programming language, the implementation of concurrency control, and the availability of new semantic constructs, such as lists and two-dimensional indexes, that an application cannot emulate efficiently on top of relational or other simpler models.

You should now have a good understanding of the major implementation issues in current ODMS products and prototypes, to augment the conceptual framework provided by Chapter 4. You may also wish to examine particular systems and their functionality in the Appendix. In the remaining three chapters of this book, we look at future directions for object data management: future standards, goals for the ideal ODMS, and expected directions for research and the marketplace.

6

Future Database Standards

6.1 INTRODUCTION

In this chapter, we look at future standards for ODMSs. Standards are a more important part of the study of ODMSs than they are for the study of traditional database systems: ODMS standards are necessary to complete the picture, because ODMSs differ so much in their programming models and their languages. Standardization of these systems is a major effort that is essential to the viability, understanding, and acceptance of this new database technology.

ODMS standardization allows this chapter to go into more detail than in Chapters 4 and 5, where the different syntax and semantics of ODMSs prevented a system-independent coverage at this level. We shall examine database application examples coded using these standards.

6.1.1 Chapter Overview

This chapter is organized around the major standards activities relevant to object data management. In Section 6.1, we examine the important groups involved in object and database standards. In the remainder of the chapter, we look at the major activities in more detail:

- Sections 6.2 and 6.3 cover work by the Object Database Management Group (ODMG). The ODMG standard is designed for object-oriented DBMSs (database programming languages).

- Section 6.4 covers the SQL3 work in progress for extended relational database systems. SQL3 is not yet a draft standard; this section describes the best understanding of SQL3 directions available at the time of this writing.

- Section 6.5 covers other relevant standards work in programming languages and object environments. The Object Management Group (OMG), ANSI X3J16 (C++), and other groups impact the standardization of ODMSs.

In Section 6.6 we examine the future of standards activities, and consider how ODMS standards are most likely to evolve.

6.1.2   Importance of Standards

It is not widely appreciated that the lack of a standard for ODMSs has been a major limitation to their more widespread use. The success of relational database systems did not result simply from a higher level of data independence and a simpler data model than previous systems. Much of their success came from the *standardization* that they offer. The acceptance of the SQL standard allows a high degree of portability and interoperability between systems, simplifies learning new relational DBMSs, and probably most importantly, represents a wide endorsement of the relational approach.

All of these factors are important for ODMSs as well as relational systems. In fact, these factors are even more important, because most of the products in this area are offered by young companies: portability and endorsement of the approach are essential to a customer. In the case of database programming languages and to some extent extended database systems, the ODMS scope is more far-reaching than that of relational DBMSs, encompassing all of an application's operations and data. A standard is critical to making such applications practical.

6.1.3   Major Standards Activities

As noted in earlier chapters, the two most popular approaches to object data management have been object-oriented and extended relational ODMSs. It is therefore not surprising that the the major standards activities have been with these approaches, in the ODMG and SQL3 groups, respectively.

The ODMG group has defined a standard, ODMG-93, designed for object-oriented DBMSs. Their architecture is based on a database programming language architecture, with bindings to provide transparent persistence and database capability in object-oriented programming languages such as C++ and Smalltalk. We shall examine the ODMG-93 standard, with particular attention to the C++ binding.

For ODMSs using the extended relational database architecture, the ANSI X3H2 (SQL) group has begun work on SQL3, which is almost to "draft standard" stage. The vast majority of the work on SQL3 is aimed at object data management capabilities, extending the type system and adding procedural capability to the SQL language. We shall examine the current state of the SQL3 designs with respect to these capabilities.

Keep in mind that this chapter represents the best knowledge of these activities available at the end of 1993. These standards and standards groups are likely to change. References are provided in the following sections to obtain the latest status and information on these activities. We will look at likely future directions at the end of the chapter.

6.2   ODMG

We begin with the work of Object Database Management Group, whose activities are centered on object-oriented DBMSs (ODMG calls these object database management systems).

Our study begins with the history, scope, and architecture of ODMG, to put the work into perspective. In the remainder of this section, we look one by one at the central components of the ODMG-93 framework. Then, in Section 6.3, we look at the most important programming language binding, for C++.

You are encouraged to read the specification for more information. It is only possible to give an overview of the standard here. The examples and some of the following text is derived from the full ODMG specification [Cattell 1993], with the permission of the publishers. You should consult the latest ODMG specification for the most recent information; the following material is based on the status at the end of 1993.

6.2.1   Background

ODMG was conceived because no progress had been made towards standards for object-oriented DBMSs several years after their successful deployment. OMG had formed a database special interest group and had begun work toward database-related standards in the Object Services Task Force; ANSI had formed an Object-Oriented Database Task Force which resulted in ANSI X3H7; and various ad hoc attempts were made between vendors, but nothing resulted in standards for these products. A standard was very important because the existing products were only roughly similar, and acceptance of this technology depended heavily on agreement and portability between vendor products.

There are some lessons to be learned about technology and the standards process from this history, but these are beyond the scope of this book. Suffice it to say that it is very difficult to do substantial creative work within a standards group, given the number of people and the amount of politics involved. It is generally necessary to choose a *de facto* standard as a starting point, and then make incremental modifications. Unfortunately, unlike SQL in the relational DBMS world, no accepted starting point existed. Instead, the ODMG work is derived by creatively combining the strongest features from a number of products currently available. These products provided implementations of the standards components that had been tried in the field.

ODMG was formed in late 1991. Most of the ODMG work was done by a small group of five vendor employees who committed one week per month to the ODMG work. As a result, the work progressed very quickly compared to traditional standards groups. A first draft for all the major components was produced during 1992, and the accepted version was published in 1993 [Cattell 1993]. The intense ODMG effort gave the object database industry a "jump start" toward standards that would otherwise have taken many years.

The ODMG authors and reviewers were from Object Design, Ontos, O$_2$ Technology, Versant, Objectivity, Digital Equipment, Hewlett-Packard, Itasca, Intellitic, Poet Software, Servio, and Texas Instruments. Nearly all of these companies are committed to support the ODMG-93 standard by the beginning of 1995; thus ODMG-93 is likely to become a de facto standard for the object-oriented DBMS industry.

ODMG plans to submit its results to OMG, ANSI, and other groups; in fact, ODMG may join with one of these groups, since the standard is now at a stage where it is amenable to a larger group of people making further improvements. At present, ODMG continues as a separate entity, but it is loosely affiliated with OMG.

6.2.2   Architecture

Keep in mind that the focus of the ODMG is on an object-oriented database programming language approach, more informally called an object-oriented DBMS. Rather than providing only a high-level query language such as SQL for data manipulation, an object-oriented DBMS transparently integrates database capability with the programming language.

As a result, the ODMG standard must encompass a larger scope of application development than relational or extended relational DBMSs. There is some overlap with extended relational DBMSs, since the ODMG group wanted some compatibility with the current SQL standard. However, the ODMG standard must provide an integrated binding with existing programming language syntax, semantics, and compilers. The object-oriented DBMS extends the language with transparently persistent data, concurrency control, data recovery, associative queries, and other database capabilities. Embedded database statements alone are insufficient.

The first step for ODMG was to agree on a common architecture for database programming languages. Figure 6.1 illustrates the agreed upon architecture. The programmer writes declarations for the application schema (both data and interfaces) plus a source program for the application implementation. The source

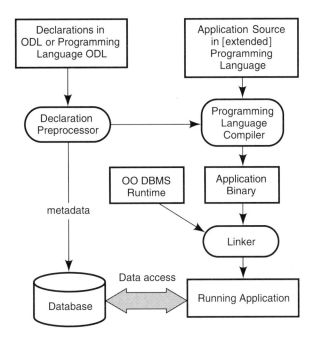

FIGURE 6.1   ODMG DBMS architecture. The programmer's ODL and OML are combined with the DBMS runtime to produce the running application.

program is written in a programming language such as C++, which has been extended to provide a full database manipulation language including transactions and object query. The schema declarations may be written in an extension of the programming language syntax, labeled programming language ODL (object definition language) in the figure, or may be written in a programming language-independent ODL. The latter ODL might be used as a higher-level design language, or to allow schema definition independent of programming language.

The declarations and source program are then compiled and linked with the DBMS to produce the running application. The application accesses a new or existing database, whose types must conform to the declarations. Databases may be shared with other applications on a network; the DBMS provides a shared service for transaction and lock management, allowing data to be cached in the application.

6.2.3   Components

The ODMG-93 standard is composed of two parts:

- *Framework:* A portion of ODMG-93 that is common to all programming languages defines an architecture, object/data model, declaration language, and declarative query language common to all programming languages.

- *Bindings:* Since ODMG deals with a database programming language architecture, a binding must be defined for each programming language in which the ODMS will be used. ODMG-93 currently includes a C++ and Smalltalk binding. These bindings are an extension to the language semantics and syntax—quite different from a SQL "binding".

The remainder of Section 6.2 covers the ODMG framework. This common framework consists of three components:

- *Object Model:* ODMG defines a common data model to be supported by object-oriented DBMSs. A subset of the object model provides interoperability across programming languages, e.g., allowing the same database to be shared by a C++ and Smalltalk program.
- *Object Definition Language:* ODMG defines an object definition language (ODL) as a syntax for the object model. ODL may be used to define an application schema; the schema can subsequently be translated into declarations in the desired programming language.
- *Object Query Language:* ODMG defines a declarative (nonprocedural) object query language (OQL) for querying database objects. OQL can be used by end-users or from within a programming language.

The ODMG currently defines language bindings for C++ and Smalltalk. Bindings for C, LISP, and OMG IDL are also being considered. In Section 6.3 we will give an overview of the C++ binding and an example of its use. This binding consists of the C++ OML, or object manipulation language, and the C++ ODL for declarations. There are plans for a C++-specific syntax for OQL as well.

In the remainder of this section we look at the ODMG framework (object model, ODL, and OQL) in more detail.

6.2.4   Object Model

The ODMG object model is derived from a number of sources; it is designed to be a superset of the OMG object model. Since the ODMG terminology is very similar to that used in this book, the basic elements of the model can be described reasonably easily:

- The ODMG model is based on *objects,* with *object identifiers.*
- Objects can be categorized into *types.* All objects of a given type exhibit common behavior and a common range of states.
- The behavior of objects is defined by a set of *operations* that can be executed on an object of the type.
- The state of objects is defined by the values they carry for a set of *properties.* These properties may be either *attributes* of the object itself or *relationships* between the object and one or more other objects.

- Human-meaningful *names* may be given to objects. An object will have a single object identifier, but it may have more than one name. A name must refer uniquely to a single object within the scope of the definition of the name; currently the only name scope defined is a *database*.

- *Operation signatures* define the operations that objects of a given type support. Each signature defines the name of the operation, the name and type of any arguments, the name and type of any returned values, and the names of any *exceptions* (error conditions) the operation can raise.

- Attributes of object types are similarly specified with *attribute signatures*. Each signature defines the name of the attribute and the type of its legal values. Attributes take *literals* as values, e.g., strings, numbers, etc.

- Relationships in which objects of a given type can participate are specified as a set of *relationship signatures*. Each signature defines the type of the other object or set of objects involved in the relationship and the name of a *traversal function* (inverse attribute) used to refer to the related object or set of objects. Relationships are binary and are defined between two types of objects (as opposed to attributes that are defined between an object and a literal). The cardinality of the relationship can be one-to-one, one-to-many, and many-to-many.

- A number of collection types are defined in the model: sets, bags, lists, and arrays. Named instances of these types can be used to group objects, for example, **senior_employees** might be the set of employees whose **years_experience** exceeds 10.

- Object types are related in a *subtype/supertype* graph. All of the attributes, relationships, and operations defined on a supertype are inherited by the subtype. The subtype may add additional properties and operations to introduce behavior or state unique to instances of the subtype. It may also "refine" the properties and operations it inherits to add new semantics. Multiple inheritance is supported.

- An *extent* set can be declared to contain all the instances of a given type. The type programmer can request that the system automatically maintain a current index to the members of this set by including an extent declaration in the type definition. The maintenance of the extent is optional.

- In some cases the individual instances of a type can be uniquely identified by the value they carry for some property or set of properties. These properties or sets of properties are termed *keys*, as in relational DBMSs.

The full type hierarchy for the ODMG object model is shown in Figure 6.2.

A full explanation of the object model is beyond the scope of this book. Most of the model is a straightforward completion of the overview just given. However, a few items are worth special note in the type hierarchy figure.

First, note that ODMG supports both **Structures** and **Collections**. A **Structure** is what programming languages typically call a **struct** or **record**.

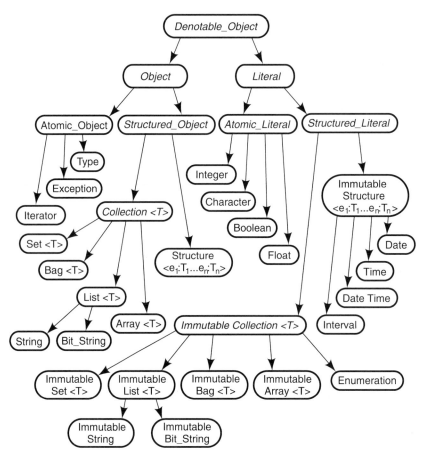

FIGURE 6.2   The ODMG built-in type hierarchy. The types shown in italics are not directly instantiable; objects must be defined on one of their subtypes instead.

It has a fixed number of named slots, each of which contains an object or a literal of a specified type. A **Collection** contains an arbitrary number of elements, does not have named slots, and contains elements that are all instances of the same type. Four kinds of collections are supported: **Set, List, Array,** and **Bag** (a **Bag** is a **Set** allowing duplicates). **Collections** and **Structures** may be freely composed: The model supports sets of structures, structures of sets, arrays of structures, and so on.

Another important thing to observe is that there are two main subtrees in the ODMG type hierarchy, labelled **Object** and **Literal**. An **Object** has an object identifier, and therefore can be referenced in more than one place in a database. If an attribute of an object changes, all references to the object see the change. In contrast, the identity of a **Literal** *is* its value — you cannot change the value of a literal, because the result would be a different literal. For this reason, the ODMG specification (and most of the type hierarchy shown) refers to the types in the `Literal` subtree as *immutable*. For example, `Immutable_Collection` and `Immutable_Structure` are the direct analogues of the `Structured_Object` types, `Structure` and `Collection`, except that they are immutable.

The distinction between immutable (literal) and mutable (object) types gives the ODMG model some added power. For example, the result of a query can be either a set of records (as in the relational model) or a set of objects. For an attribute that takes a structured literal as its value, it is possible to replace the value of the attribute with a new structured literal, without affecting any other uses of the same structure. Thus, attribute values can either be "shared" or "independent" of other attribute values.

The treatment of databases and transactions in ODMG is mostly similar to traditional databases. Transactions are units of atomicity, consistency, and integrity. A database provides storage for persistent objects of a given set of types, called the database *schema*. A single (logical) database may be stored in one or more physical databases.

Unlike traditional DBMSs, there is an explicit object type **Database** and **Transaction**. Nested transactions are permitted. The names of the types in the schema and their associated extents are global to the database, and become accessible to a program once it has opened the database. A database may also contain named objects, often called "root objects," that can be referenced by a program once it has opened the database. These three kinds of global names—type names, extent names, and root object names—provide entry points into the database. Other objects can then be found by navigation of relationships or by associative retrieval. In contrast, the type names, extent names, and root names are all one and the same in relational systems: they are the table names.

6.2.5   Object Definition Language

The ODMG object definition language (ODL) is the syntax for the object model we just covered: ODL is ODMG's language for describing database schemas. ODL is intended to define object types that can be implemented in a variety of programming languages. Thus, it is not tied to the syntax or semantics of one programming language.

There are a number of benefits of ODL:

- ODL allows the same database to be shared across multiple programming languages, and allows an application to be ported to a new programming language without rewriting the data schema description.

- ODL can also be used by design and analysis tools that must describe an application's data and operations independently of programming language. The resulting design can then be used directly or translated into a data description language of the programmer's choice.

- A schema specified in ODL can be supported by any ODMG-compliant ODBMS.

In addition to the programming-language independent ODL defined here, the ODMG programming language bindings (currently C++ and Smalltalk) describe optional ODL syntaxes designed to fit smoothly into the declarative syntax of their host programming language. Due to the differences inherent in the object models native to these programming languages, it is not always possible to achieve 100% consistent semantics across the programming-language specific versions of ODL. ODMG's goal has been to maximize database schema portability across programming languages. In the ODMG specification, each programming language binding documents any extensions or shortfalls with respect to the common ODMG framework.

ODL's syntax is based on IDL—OMG's Interface Definition Language developed as part of the Common Object Request Broker Architecture (CORBA). ODMG used IDL rather than invent yet another language syntax. IDL was itself influenced by C++, giving ODL a C++ flavor. ODL adds to IDL the constructs required to specify the complete semantics of the ODMG Object Model.

As an example ODL definition, consider the university database schema shown in Figure 6.3. In the figure we use the same schema notation defined in Chapter 1, except that role names (traversal paths) have been added to the relationship arrows because they are required by ODL.

To define object type **Course** you begin with the following ODL syntax:

```
interface Course {
    extent courses;
    keys name, number;
```

The interface keyword is used for consistency with OMG IDL. The extent and keys for **Course** are specified. The attributes of **Course** are defined as follows:

```
attribute string name;
attribute string number;
```

The relationships between **Course** and other object types are defined with a **relationship** keyword, and an **inverse** keyword that specifies the inverse attribute of the related object type. These attributes and inverse attributes represent the traversal paths defined in the object model, and are consistent with the inverse attribute concept we introduced in Section 4.2 and the role names we introduced in Section 1.3.2.

```
relationship List<Section> has_sections
        inverse Section::is_section_of;
relationship Set<Course> has_prerequisites
        inverse Course::is_prerequisite_for;
relationship Set<Course> is_prerequisite_for
        inverse Course::has_prerequisites;
```

The **relationship** keyword (and **attribute** keyword) is optional, since it can be inferred from context. As with **interface**, these keywords are used to maintain consistency with OMG IDL.

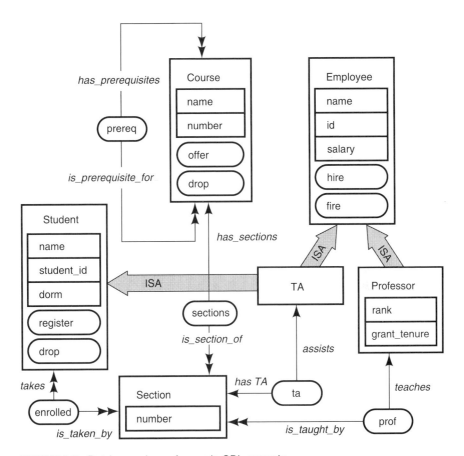

FIGURE 6.3   Database schema for use in ODL example.

Finally, we define the operations associated with a `Course`:

```
    offer (in Semester) raises (already_offered);
    drop (in Semester) raises (not_offered);
}
```

This completes the definition of type `Course`. The other object types in Figure 6.3 can be defined in a similar fashion:

```
interface Section {
    extent sections;
    key (is_section_of, number);
    attribute string number;
    relationship Professor is_taught_by
      inverse Professor::teaches;
    relationship TA has_TA inverse TA::assists;
```

```
        relationship Course is_section_of
          inverse Course::has_sections;
        relationship Set<Student> is_taken_by
          inverse Student::takes;
     ...
  }

  interface Employee {
      extent employees;
      key (name, id);
      attribute string name;
      attribute Integer id;
      attribute annual_salary Integer;
      hire (in Person);
      fire (in Employee) raises (no_such_employee);
  }

  interface Professor: Employee {
      extent professors;
      attribute enum rank {full, associate, assistant};
      relationship Set<Section> teaches
        inverse Section::is_taught_by;
      grant_tenure () raises (ineligible_for_tenure);
  }

  interface TA:Employee, Student {
      relationship Section assists inverse Section::has_TA;
      ...
  }

  interface Student {
      extent students;
      keys name, student_id;
      attribute string name;
      attribute string student_id;
      attribute struct<string college,string room_number>
        dorm_address;
      relationship Set<Section> takes
        inverse Section::is_taken_by;
      register_for_course (in Course, in Section)raises
        (unsatisfied_prereqs,section_full,course_full);
      drop_course (in Course)
        raises (not_registered_for_that_course);
      ...
  }
```

6.2.6   Object Query Language

Information may be retrieved from a database through navigating relation-ships in an object manipulation language (OML) as we shall describe in Section 6.3, or through the object query language (OQL), by identifying objects through predicates defined on their characteristics. A predicate is a boolean conjunction or disjunction of operations supported by the object types that appear within the predicate.

In the simplest kind of queries, a predicate is applied to a collection to select the members of a collection that satisfy the predicate. However, more complex queries may be performed: OQL can perform the equivalent of relational joins, and more. OQL need not produce an object or a table—it may result in an integer, a list of object references, a structure, a set of sets of real numbers, or any data structure that can be defined in the object model.

As a stand-alone language, OQL allows you to query denotable objects starting with their names, which act as entry points into a database. A name may denote any kind of object: atomic, structure, collection, or literal. As an embedded language, OQL allows you to query denotable objects which are supported by the native language through expressions yielding atoms, structures, collections, and literals.

ODMG's OQL design is based on the following principles and assumptions:

- The ODMG object model is used as the basis for OQL. The semantics of OQL are formally defined.

- OQL is a declarative query language; it is not computationally complete. OQL can be easily optimized by virtue of its declarative nature.

- OQL has a concrete syntax that is based on SQL, because of the prevalence of this language in the DBMS world. However, ODMG did not feel constrained to SQL syntax or semantics in cases where it would compromise the simplicity or power of OQL.

- Other concrete OQL syntaxes will be defined in order to merge the query language into programming languages. For example, ODMG plans to define a syntax for preprocessed C++ that is a natural extension of the language as opposed to an embedded foreign syntax.

- OQL provides high-level primitives to deal with collections of objects but does not privilege the set construct as in SQL. Thus, it also provides primitives to deal with structures and lists, and treats all such constructs with the same efficiency and convenience.

- OQL does not provide explicit update operators. It relies on methods defined on objects for that purpose.

In the remainder of this section, we look at some examples of OQL in order to illustrate its characteristics. A full description of the language is beyond the scope of this book, but these examples give a feel for the majority of the language.

Probably the most common query is a predicate applied to a collection. A simple case of this is selecting an object that has a particular value for one of its properties from the extent of a type. For example, the query

```
select distinct x.age
from x in Persons
where x.name = "Pat"
```

selects the set of ages of all persons named Pat. Thus, this query returns a literal of type `set<integer>`. (The `distinct` keyword removes duplicates; a `bag<integer>` would normally be returned.) The query

```
select distinct struct(a: x.age, s: x.sex)
from x in Persons
where x.name = "Pat"
```

does about the same, but for each person, it builds a structure containing **age** and **sex**. It returns a literal of type `set<struct>`, that is, a "table" in the relational sense (relational DBMSs generally cannot return a list, an array, an object, a string, a structure, or the other data structures we discuss in this section). The query

```
select distinct struct(
   name: x.name,
   hps: (select y from y in x.subordinates
      where y.salary >100000))
from x in Employees
```

is the same type of example, but now we use a more complex function. For each employee we build a structure with the name of the employee and the set of the employee's highly paid subordinates. For each employee **x**, to compute **hps**, we traverse the relationship **subordinates** and select among this set the employees with a salary greater than $100,000. The result of this query is therefore a literal of the type `set<struct>`, namely:

```
set<struct (name: string, hps: bag<Employee>)>
```

OQL also permits a `select` operator in the `from` part:

```
select struct (a: x.age, s: x.sex)
from x in
   (select y from y in Employees where y.seniority ="10")
where x.name = "Pat"
```

You do not always have to use a select-from-where clause. If **Chairman** is an entry point in the database (a *name* in the object model), then the following is a complete query:

```
Chairman
```

The following query retrieves the set of subordinates of the chairman:

```
Chairman.subordinates
```

The following query retrieves the set of all persons:

```
Persons
```

OQL supports both types of denotable objects in ODMG's model: mutable (i.e., having an OID) and literal (identity is the value), depending on the way these objects are constructed or selected.

A type name constructor is used to create an object with identity. For instance, to create a **Person** you can simply write

```
Person(name: "Pat", birthdate:"3/28/56", salary: 100,000)
```

The parameters in parentheses allow you to initialize certain properties of the object. Those which are not explicitly initialized are given a default value.

Objects without identity are created using **struct**. For instance,

```
struct (a: 10, b: "Pat")
```

creates a structure with two fields named **a** and **b**. Of course, the values **10** and **"Pat"** (and the values in the **Person** constructor above) could be queries rather than literals.

In summary, queries may return:

- A collection of objects with identity, e.g., **select x from x in Persons where x.name ="Pat"** returns a collection of persons whose name is Pat.

- An object with identity, e.g., **element (select x from x in Persons where x.passport_number=1234567)** returns the person whose passport number is 1234567.

- A collection of literals, e.g., **select x.passport_number from x in Persons where x.name="Pat"** returns a collection of integers giving the passport numbers of people named Pat.

- A literal, e.g., **Chairman.salary**.

In contrast, in ODMG notation a relational DBMS always returns a **set<struct(...)>** as the result of a query.

6.2.7   Relationship to Other Standards

A number of standards are related to ODMG, though they do not deal with the same object-oriented DBMS problems addressed by ODMG.

Since ODMG is based on a database programming language architecture, it is heavily dependent on programming language standards, in particular C++ (ANSI X3J16) and Smalltalk (X3J20). Since object-oriented programming languages were designed without persistence in mind, there are some shortcomings in these language standards with respect to ODMG's extensions. As an appendix of the ODMG-93 Version 1.0 specification, the ODMG group suggests some "hooks" that would be valuable in ANSI C++ in order to simplify the task of the object-oriented DBMS vendors and to improve the integration that can be achieved between programming language and database from the programmer's perspective.

The ODMG members are also OMG members, and ODMG took special care to address its relationship to OMG standards. We will cover OMG standards in more detail later, but the important points to note are the following:

- The ODMG object model is designed as a superset of the OMG object model. This is in keeping with OMG's architecture where groups of vendors can define application-specific *profiles* for the object model. An appendix to the ODMG specification describes this profile in the terminology of the OMG object model.

- The OMG defines an object request broker (ORB) whose functionality overlaps somewhat with object-oriented DBMSs. An appendix to the ODMG specification describes how object-oriented DBMSs can fit efficiently and productively into the ORB environment.

- The OMG defines an interface definition language (IDL), based on operations on objects. IDL defines the signatures for object types for the purposes of invocation through the ORB. Rather than define a completely new language or use SQL, ODMG chose IDL as the basis for the object definition language (ODL).

Finally, the ODMG-93 standard is related to SQL3; we will return to this comparison after we have had a chance to look at SQL3.

At the time of this writing, the ODMG members are considering merging or affiliating with some of these other standards groups, and are working on future releases of the ODMG specification. To determine the latest status of the ODMG effort, you should send electronic mail to:

> info@odmg.org

6.3   ODMG C++

This section is an overview of the ODMG's C++ binding. ODMG's sense of "binding" is quite different than a SQL binding for a language. The ODMG binding is based on using a programming language's syntax and semantics in order to provide database capabilities rather than embedding statements in SQL or another language.

There are three components to the C++ binding, as with any ODMG language binding: OML, ODL, and OQL. The C++ binding of ODL is expressed as a class library and an extension to the standard C++ class definition grammar. The class library provides classes and functions to implement the concepts defined in the

ODMG object model. The OML, or object manipulation language, is used for retrieving and operating upon objects from the database. The C++ OML syntax and semantics are those of standard C++ in the context of the standard class library. The C++ OQL provides a way to retrieve data based on predicates.

In Section 6.3.1, we overview the general approach to the ODMG C++ binding. In Sections 6.3.2 through 6.3.4, we discuss the C++ ODL, OML, and OQL, respectively. In Section 6.3.5, we look at a C++ example.

6.3.1 Architecture

It is the goal of an ODMG programming language binding that the programmer feel there is one language, not two separate languages with arbitrary boundaries between them. This goal results in several general principles:

- There is a single unified type system across the programming language and the database; individual instances of these common types can be persistent or transient.

- The programming language-specific binding for ODL, OML, and OQL respects the syntax and semantics of the base programming language into which it is being inserted.

- The binding is structured as a small set of additions to the base programming language; it does not introduce sublanguage-specific constructions that duplicate functionality already present within the base language.

- Expressions in the OML and OQL can be composed freely with expressions from the base programming language and vice versa.

There was considerable debate in ODMG over how far they should go with these principles in the first version of the standard. A completely seamless interface between C++ and the ODL, OML, and OQL would require a preprocessor, given the constraints of the current C++ language. In the future, ODMG hopes to influence the C++ standard to include hooks that would make a completely seamless interface possible without a preprocessor, or at least to standardize the preprocessor such that existing compilers and programming tools would integrate well with object-oriented DBMSs.

For now, the ODMG group elected for a two-step approach:

1. The current standard, ODMG-93, requires only an ODL preprocessor. A nearly seamless OML solution is possible without C++ changes, and a short-term OQL solution is possible with procedure calls. This allows vendors to get a standard API out quickly to customers, and to get some experience with it.

2. In the next release of the standard, ODMG members plan to define a fully seamless interface (all C++ operations and data structures supported with transparent persistence), and to define a natural extension to C++ syntax for declarative lookup. We will examine some of these future features here; the main differences are in object queries and support for C++ pointers.

The current C++ OML is called the *Ref-based* approach, because programmers refer to objects using a C++ class **Ref<X>** provided by the ODL preprocessor for each database class **X** defined in the schema. These database classes are distinct from the normal classes defined by the C++ language, all of whose instances are transient; C++ class instances don't outlive the execution of the process in which they were created. Database class instances may be persistent or transient. Instances of database classes are referenced using parameterized references, e.g.,

```
Ref<Professor> profP;
```

Standard C++ operations work on references declared in this way.

The future binding, by contrast, allows any C++ class to have both persistent and transient instances and allows the programmer to use the same pointers and C++ reference syntax that have always been used to refer to transient classes:

```
Professor* profP;
```

ODMG allows instances of database classes to reference transient objects, but only during the execution of a transaction (they are set to **NULL** at transaction commit). Transient objects are not subject to transaction semantics in the current specification. All access, creation, modification, and deletion of persistent objects must be done within a transaction on an open database. Operations are defined on predefined **Database** and **Transaction** types. For example, the following method invocation locates the named database and makes the appropriate connection to that database:

```
database->open ("name");
```

Additional optional parameters to the open method allow implementation-specific features.

A database application generally will begin processing by accessing one or more critical objects and proceeding from there. These objects are in some sense "root" objects, in that they lead to interconnected webs of other objects. The ability to name an object and retrieve it later by that name facilitates this start-up capability. Named objects are also convenient in many other situations.

6.3.2 Object Definition Language

The C++ ODL provides a description of the database schema as a set of object classes—including their attributes, relationships, and operations—in a syntactic style that is consistent with current C++ language syntax. Instances of these classes can then be manipulated through the C++ OML. C++ ODL declarations may be generated automatically from the framework (programming language-independent) ODL described earlier, or the programmer may use the C++ ODL directly. The latter is the more likely case when an entire application is coded in C++.

Operation declarations are identical to C++ member function declarations. Attribute and relationship declarations are similar to C++ data member declarations. Relationship declarations are syntactically distinguished by the presence of an **inverse** clause. At present, this relationship syntax is the only major ODMG extension to standard C++ declarations.

The following is an example C++ declaration for the type **Professor** that we defined in ODL in Section 6.2.5. Again, this declaration could be written by a programmer, or a vendor's ODL processor could be used to generate this declaration from the framework ODL.

```
class Professor : public Pobject
{
  public:
    // properties:
      int age;
      int id_number;
      String office_number;
      String name;
      Ref<Department> dept inverse professors;
      Set<Student> advisees inverse Student::advisor ;
    // operations:
      void grant_tenure ();
      void assign_course (Course&);

  private:
    ...
}
```

The ODMG object model includes collection type generators, collection types, and collection instances. Collection type generators are represented as *template classes* in C++, e.g., **Set<T>**. Collection types are represented as collection classes, e.g., **Set<Professor>**. A particular set of professors would be a collection instance:

```
Set<Ref<Professor>>faculty;
```

The subtype/supertype hierarchy of collection types defined in the ODMG object model is directly carried over into C++. The standard C++ syntax and semantics for inheritance are supported. A class is made persistent by inheriting from **Persistent_Object**.

6.3.3   Object Manipulation Language

The C++ OML is the syntax used to create, delete, identify, reference, get/set property values, and invoke operations on a persistent object. A single expression may freely intermix references to persistent and transient objects.

Objects, whether persistent or not, may refer to other objects via object references. In C++ OML object references are instances of the templated class

`Ref<T>`. All accesses to persistent objects are made via methods defined on class `Ref` and the class `Persistent_Object` inherited by persistent objects. The dereference operator `->` is used to access members of the persistent object "addressed" by a given object reference. How an object reference converts an object's database address (its OID) to a memory address is up to the ODBMS implementor.

Standard C++ access syntax works on persistent objects, for example:

```
profP->grant_tenure();
profP->age = 35;
deptRef = profP->dept;
```

Objects can be created, deleted, and modified. Objects are created in C++ OML using the **new** operator, which is overloaded to allow additional arguments specifying the database or clustering.

A dereference operation on an object reference always guarantees that the object referred to is returned or an exception is raised. If an object (persistent or transient) refers to a second, persistent, object that is not in memory when the dereference is executed, the second object, if it exists, will be retrieved automatically from disk, mapped into memory, and returned as the result of the dereference. If the supposedly referenced object does not exist, an appropriate exception is raised. References to transient objects work exactly the same (at least on the surface) as references to persistent objects.

There is only one area where the current Ref-based C++ OML deviates significantly from ODMG's goal of making operations on persistent objects identical to those on transient objects: persistent objects that have been modified must communicate to the runtime ODBMS process the fact that their states have changed. The ODBMS will then update the database with these new states at transaction commit time. Object change is communicated by invoking the `mark_modified` member function defined on all persistent objects:

```
profP->mark_modified();
```

As a convenience, the programmer may omit calls to **mark_modified** on objects whose classes have been compiled using an optional C++ ODL preprocessor switch; the system will automatically detect when the objects are modified. In the default case, **mark_modified** calls are required, because in some ODMG implementations performance will be much better when the programmer explicitly calls **mark_modified**. The **mark_modified** call will not be needed in ODMG's future binding.

The ODL specifies which relationships exist between object classes. Creating, traversing, and breaking relationships between instances are defined in the C++ OML. The integrity of relationships is maintained by the ODBMS.

A template class, `Iterator<T>`, defines the generic behavior for iteration. All iterators use a consistent protocol for sequentially returning each element from the collection over which the iteration is defined. The type parameter supplied is the type of the collection elements. A template class has been used to give type-safe iterators. Type-safe iterators are guaranteed to return an instance of the type of the element of the collection over which the iterator is defined.

6.3.4 Object Query Language

There are generally two options for binding a query sublanguage to a programming language: loosely-coupled or tightly-coupled. In the loosely-coupled approach query functions are introduced that take strings containing queries as their arguments. These functions parse and evaluate the query at runtime, returning the result as the result of the function. In the tightly-coupled approach the query sublanguage is integrated directly into the programming language by expanding the definition of the nonterminals `<term>`, `<expression>` as defined in the BNF of the programming language. The tightly-coupled approach allows queries to be optimized at compile time; in the loosely-coupled approach they are generally optimized at execution time. The C++ binding for OQL supports two variants of the loosely-coupled approach:

*   a `query` method defined on the generic class `Collection`
*   a free-standing `oql` function not bound to any class

In the future C++ binding, a tightly-coupled approach is anticipated. Both of the loosely-coupled variants as well as the tightly-coupled future binding are discussed in this section.

To support the first loosely-coupled variant, each collection class comes with a `query` member function whose signature is:

```
int query(Collection<T>& result,const char* predicate);
```

This function filters the collection using the predicate and assigns the result to the first parameter. It returns a nonzero value if the query is not well formed. The predicate is given as a string with the syntax of the where clause of OQL. The predefined variable `this` is used inside the predicate to denote the current element of the collection to be filtered.

Given the class `Student`, as defined in Section 6.2.5, with extent `Students`, we can compute the set of students who take math courses as follows:

```
Ref<Set<Student>> mathematicians;
Students->query(mathematicians,
  "exists s in this.takes: s.section_of.name=\"math" ");
```

In contrast, the `oql` function allows the programmer to gain access to the whole functionality of OQL from a C++ program. It is a free-standing function, not part of any class definition. It takes as parameters a reference to a variable to receive the result, the OQL sentence, and a variable length list of C++ expressions whose values are input operands for the query. Inside the query these operands are identified with the syntax given below. The function returns a nonzero result if the query is not well formed.

As an example, the following code finds the set of professors assisted by math students who are teaching assistants and earn more than x. We suppose there exists an extent for teaching assistants which is called TA.

```
Set<Student> mathematicians; // computed as above
Set<Professor> assisted_profs;
double x = ...

oql(assisted_profs, "select t.assists.taught_by \
    from t in TA where t.salary > $1r and t in $2k",
    x, mathematicians);
```

The future binding planned for C++ OQL achieves more complete integration with the language by extending the definition of expressions in the grammar of the base programming language to support identification of objects by descriptions as well as by variable names. These descriptions are in the form of predicates defined on the attributes of objects, on their relationships to other objects, and on the results of operations applied to objects. This means that C++ expressions can be used freely within the query sublanguage, and vice versa.

As an illustration, our earlier example of fetching students who take math courses might look something like this in the future binding:

```
mathematicians = Students[
    exists s in this.takes: s.section_of.name="math"];
```

As part of the future binding, ODMG also plans to define a derivative to the OQL syntax that is more "C++ like," supporting all C++ expressions and providing operators for longer keyword-based expressions like **select from where**.

6.3.5 Example

We now look at a complete example of a small application using the ODMG C++ ODL, OML, and OQL binding. Our example application manages records representing people. People are entered into the database, and then special events are recorded: marriage, the birth of children, moving to a new address. The application consists of two parts: the first part populates the database, while the second part consults and updates it.

We will first define the schema of the database, as C++ ODL classes.

The structure **Address** is used in a variety of places. It contains a reference to a **City** object, which is defined shortly. The two address constructors referenced here, for creating a new address and for copying an address, will be defined shortly.

```
struct Address{
  int number;
  String street;
  Ref<City> city;

  Address(int, const char*, Ref<City>);
  Address(const Address&);
  Address() : number(0) {};
};
```

Class **Person** is defined as follows. For our example, we simply make all of its properties public. Notice the relationships to other **Person** objects defined using the **inverse** keyword: **spouse, children,** and **parents.** Operations are defined to create new **Person** objects and to update them in various ways. The extent of the class **Person** is called **people.**

```
class Person : public Persistent_Object {
public:
// Attributes
  String name;
  Address address;
// Relationships
  Ref<Person> spouse inverse spouse;
  List<Ref<Person>> children inverse parents;
  Ref<Person> parents[2] inverse children;
// Operations
  Person(const char* name); // constructs new Person
  void birth(Ref<Person> child); // creates child
  void marriage(Ref<Person> with); // creates marriage
  Ref<Set<Ref<<Person>>> ancestors(); // ancestors
  void move(Address); // changes Address
// Class extent
  static Ref<Set<Person>> people;
};
```

Class **City** is similarly defined. It contains an attribute **population** that contains the set of people in the city (this is not defined as a relationship, so no integrity is maintained on this attribute).

```
class City : public Persistent_Object {
public:
// Attributes
  int city_code;
  String name;
  Ref<Set<Ref<Person>>> population;
// Operations
  City(int, const char*) // constructor
// Extent
  static Ref<Set<Ref<City>>> cities;
};
```

We now define the code for the operations declared in the schema. This is written in plain C++. We assume that the C++ ODL preprocessor has generated a file which is called "schema.hxx" which contains the standard C++ definitions equivalent to the C++ ODL classes, and that this file is included when compiling.

The operations on address structures are as follows:

```
Address::Address(
    int number, const String street, Ref<City> city) {
// Constructs an Address
    this->number = number;
    this->street = street;
    this->city = city;
}


Address::Address(const Address& copy){
// Copies an Address
    number = copy.number;
    city = copy.city;
    street = copy.street;
}
```

The operations on **Person** are defined as follows:

```
Person::Person(const String name) {
// Constructs a Person with no address.
    this->name = name;
    people->insert_element(this);
}


void Person::birth(const Ref<Person>& child){
// Adds a new child to the children list
    children.insert_element_last(child);
    if(spouse != 0)
      spouse->children.insert_element_last(child);
}
void Person::marriage(const Ref<Person>& with){
// Initializes the spouse relationship
    spouse = with;
    // with->spouse automatically set to this Person
}
```

```
Ref<Set<Ref<Person>>> Person::ancestors(){
// Constructs the set of all ancestors of this Person
   Ref<Set<Ref<Person>>> the_ancestors =
   new Set<Person>;
   int i;
   for(i = 0; i < 2; i++)
     if(parents[i] != 0){
        // ancestors = parents union ancestors(parents)
        the_ancestors->insert_element(parents[i]);
        Ref<Set<Ref<Person>>> grand_parents =
          parents[i]->ancestors();
        the_ancestors->union_with(grand_parents);
        grand_parents.delete_object();
     {
   return the_ancestors;
}

void Person::move(const Address new_address&){
  // Updates the address attribute of this Person
    if(address.city != 0){
       address.city->population->remove_element(this);  }
    new_address.city->population->insert_element(this);
    address = new_address;
    mark_modified();
  }
}
```

Finally, the operation to create a `City` is defined as follows:

```
City::City(int code, const String name){
// Constructs a City Object
   city_code = code;
   this->name = new char[strlen(name)+1];
   strcpy(this->name, name);
   cities->insert_element(this);
}
```

This completes the schema definition. We now define the two parts of the application itself. The first part populates the database. It begins by creating extents for **Person** and **City**, giving them names, and creating three instances of **Person**:

```
static Database dbobj;
static Database * database = &dbobj;

void Load(){
  Transaction load;
  load.start();
```

```
Person::people = new(database) Set<Ref<Person>>;
City::cities = new(database) Set<Ref<City>>;

database->set_object_name(Person::people, "people");
database->set_object_name(City::cities, "cities");

Ref<Person> God, Adam, Eve;

God = new(database) Person("God");
Adam = new(database) Person("Adam");
Eve = new(database) Person("Eve");
```

Then, we create addresses and children for the **Person** objects **Adam** and **Eve**, and commit all these updates to the database:

```
Address Paradise(7, "Apple",
  new(database) City(0, "Garden"));

Adam->move(Paradise);
Eve->move(Paradise);

God->birth(Adam);
Adam->marriage(Eve);
Adam->birth(new(database) Person("Cain"));
Adam->birth(new(database) Person("Abel"));

load.commit();
}
```

The second part of the application consults the database and does some updates. First, we define a **print_persons** procedure, and then we use it to print four lists of people: all of the people in random order, people sorted by name, people with two children living in the city named Garden, and people that are ancestors of Cain.

```
static void print_persons(const Set<Person>& s){
  Ref<Person> p;
  Iterator<Person> it = s.create_iterator();
  while(it.next(p))
    printf("— %s lives in %s",
      p->name, (p->address.city != 0)
      ? p->address.city->name: "unknown" );

};
```

```
void Consult(){
  Transaction consult;
  consult.start();

  database->lookup_object(Person::people, "people");
  database->lookup_object(City::cities, "cities");

  printf("All the people ....:\n");
  print_persons(Person::people);

  printf("All the people sorted by name ....:\n");
  oql(s, "sort p in people by p.name");
  print_persons(s);

  printf("People with 2 children in Paradise:\n");
  oql(s, "select p from p in people \
      where p.address.city != nil and \
      p.address.city.name = \"Garden\"\
      and count(p.children) = 2");
  print_persons(s);

  printf("Cain's ancestors ...:\n");
  Ref<Person> Cain =
    Adam->children.retrieve_element_at(0);
  print_persons(Cain->ancestors());
```

Finally, we update the database to move Adam and Eve to a new address:

```
  Address Earth(13, "Macadam",
    new(database) City(1, "St-Croix"));
  Ref<Person> Adam;
  oql(Adam, "element(select p from p in people \
    where p.name = \"Adam\"")));
  Adam->move(Earth);
  Adam->spouse->move(Earth);
  consult.commit();
}
```

The main program for ODMG's example application opens and closes the database, and invokes the parts of the application we just described:

```
main(){
  database->open("family");
  Load();
  Consult();
  database->close();
}
```

6.3.6   Conclusions

In summary, the ODMG C++ binding maps ODMG's programming-language independent framework (object model, ODL, and OQL) into C++. With only a couple exceptions, this mapping remains faithful to the goal of integrating database functionality seamlessly with native C++. A Smalltalk binding can also be found in the ODMG-93 specification, and other programming language bindings are now planned. However, this overview of the C++ binding should be sufficient to get a feel for the form of the ODMG standard programming language bindings, and the philosophy behind them.

6.4   SQL3

The other important standard for object data management, SQL3, is most relevant for ODMSs using the extended relational database system approach. However, with the ubiquity of SQL this standard could have impact on all approaches.

In this section, we look at the historical and technical background for SQL3, and then examine the type system extensions and procedural extensions in SQL3 as envisioned at the time of this writing.

6.4.1   Background

The SQL standard is published by the ANSI X3H2 group and by ISO [X3H2 1992, ISO 1992]. ANSI X3H2 (the Database Languages Committee) has over 30 members, including all the major relational DBMS vendors (16 vendors!). ANSI provides input to the international database languages committee ISO/JTC1 SC21/WG3 DBL, which includes 11 national bodies. ANSI SQL is generally identical to, or a superset of, ISO SQL functionality; most of the ISO SQL direction to date has come from ANSI.

In all of its incarnations, SQL is based on an architecture in which SQL statements are mixed with programming language statements in a source program. A preprocessor removes the SQL statements and produces source for the native programming language compiler in which the SQL statements have been replaced with calls to a (nonstandardized) SQL runtime system.

The first version of the SQL standard was SQL-86. This version was largely based on the SEQUEL language developed as part of IBM's System R project [Chamberlain et al 1976]. A revised version of the standard was published in 1989, adding referential integrity, and another revision, SQL2, was published in 1992.

SQL2, also known as SQL-92, included a dozen new features: integrity assertions, domains, temporary tables, new join operations, schema updates, new cursor capabilities to move through the result of a query, and many other capabilities. SQL2 is not fully implemented in relational database products at the time of this writing.

Work is now underway on SQL3. Except for a few capabilities deferred from SQL2, such as triggers, the thrust of the SQL3 work is on two kinds of capabilities: a more powerful data model, allowing the representation of data that do not fit well into the traditional tabular format of relations, and procedural capabilties, to make SQL computationally complete (like a programming language).

The comments on SQL3 in this book are based on the current direction for this standard, which may change. In fact, major changes were made in 1993, and it is still unclear how some of the SQL3 functionality will work. SQL3 is not yet to official "draft standard" stage.

6.4.2 Abstract Data Types

The most important data modelling construct introduced in the current SQL3 draft is an abstract data type, or ADT.

An ADT is roughly analogous to a class definition in an object-oriented programming language: it specifies a set of *attributes* and *routines*. All instances of an ADT share these attributes and routines. The routines may be procedures or functions. Attributes and routines may be public, private, or protected, as in C++.

For example, we might declare an **employee** ADT as follows:

```
CREATE TYPE employee UNDER person(

PRIVATE
  birthdate DATE CHECK (birthdate < DATE '1992-01-01'),
PUBLIC
  name VARCHAR,
  id INTEGER NOT NULL,
  annual_salary INTEGER,
  boss employee,
  age UPDATABLE VIRTUAL GET WITH get_age
SET WITH set_age,
EQUALS DEFAULT,
LESS THAN NONE,
CONSTRUCTOR FUNCTION employee (E EMPLOYEE,
  N VARCHAR, B DATE, ID INTEGER, S INTEGER);*
  BEGIN
  SET E.name= N;
  SET E.birthdate= B;
  SET E.id= ID;
  SET E.annual_salary= S;
  RETURN E;
  END,
```

---

* SQL2 syntax requires a ":" before variable names; SQL3 will probably not, pending final resolution. In the current SQL3 definition, a new (empty) employee is passed *in* to the constructor function.

```
      DESTRUCTOR PROCEDURE remove_employee(E employee);*
        BEGIN
        -- Various cleanup actions, as required
        ...
        DESTROY E
        END,
      ACTOR PROCEDURE hire(P person);
        BEGIN
        -- Operation to create employee from person
        ...
        END,
      ACTOR PROCEDURE fire(E employee);
        BEGIN
        -- Operation to remove employee data
        ...
        END,
      ACTOR FUNCTION get_age(E employee) RETURNS INTEGER;
        RETURN -- Calculate age from birthdate
        END,
      ACTOR PROCEDURE set_age(E employee, A INTEGER);
        RETURN -- Set birthdate based on age
        END FUNCTION
  );
```

This example illustrates the use of both *public* and *private* attributes. Private attributes may only be used by routines nested within the ADT definition. By default, the visibility (public or private) of an attribute is the same as the visibility of the immediately preceding attribute. The first attribute of an ADT, if not otherwise specified, is public. The **birthdate** in our example is private.

Routines need not be nested inside an ADT definition as we have shown here; nesting is required only to give the routines access to the ADT's private attributes. SQL3 uses a complex algorithm to perform method dispatching, unlike C++ and Smalltalk, in which the class of the first parameter of a method always determines where to look for the method (in that class definition). We discussed dispatching algorithms in Section 5.5.6; coverage of SQL3's algorithm is beyond the scope of this section.

The example illustrates the use of both *stored* and *virtual* attributes. A stored attribute is the default case: these attributes are simply fields of the instances that are fetched and assigned by the DBMS. The **age** attribute is declared to be virtual; it is computed using the **get_age** function and assigned using the **set_age** procedure. It is transparent to the caller whether an attribute is stored or virtual, so virtual attributes provide logical data independence, as we discussed in Section 4.7.5.

---

* The current SQL3 syntax uses a destructor FUNCTION, but this will probably be changed to a PROCEDURE since no return is needed.

Attributes may be declared to be **UPDATABLE, READONLY**, or **CONSTANT**. By default attributes are updatable. Read only attributes cannot be updated, and constant attributes may be updated only when instances are created.

An attribute may be of any built-in type, such as **INTEGER** or **VARCHAR**. An attribute may also refer to an instance of an ADT, for example the **boss** attribute which references another **employee**. References to ADT instances (objects) are through an object identifier (OID). As in other ODMSs, and unlike relational foreign keys, the OID value is independent of the values of the object attributes.

Instead of indicating in the attribute declaration whether an ADT instance's value or a reference to the value (an OID) should be stored (as in ODMG-93), the current SQL3 draft requires that the ADTs referenced by OID be declared differently, for example:

```
CREATE TYPE employee WITH OID
```

This causes all attributes of type **employee** to be *references* to **employee** instances instead of storing the **person** record in-line. This is the desired intent in the above example, with the **boss** attribute of **employee**. The **WITH OID** tag also allows the OID of an instance **e** of type **employee** to be referenced as a read-only attribute, e.g., **e.OID**.

SQL3 defines three kinds of routines that can be associated with an ADT: *constructors, destructors,* and *actors.** Constructors initialize instances of the type, destructors release instance resources,† and actors perform all other operations on instances of the type. In our example, **employee** and **remove_employee** are constructor and destructor routines, respectively, and **hire** and **fire** are actor routines.

Note that the functions on virtual attributes, **get_age** and **set_age**, are also actor routines. The declaration of an ADT may also specify actor functions for comparison operations such as **LESS THAN** or **EQUALS**. In our example, **LESS THAN** is declared to be undefined on **employee** instances.

6.4.3   ADTs versus Tables

The relationship between ADTs and tables in SQL3 requires some explanation. Because of the desire to remain compatible with SQL2, these two concepts are not as integrated as you might like in the current SQL3 specification.

As noted earlier, ADTs are similar to class definitions in object-oriented programming languages and databases. However, they are different in an important respect. Although you can use ADTs in SQL3 routines for parameters and variables, the only way you may use an ADT in a database is as the type of an

---

* We assume that these are functions, procedures, and routines (can be procedure or function), respectively, but this is not yet finalized.

† You might expect constructors and destructors to actually create and destroy the instances, but in the current specification this is done outside of these functions.

attribute of a table. You cannot create a "top level" instance of an ADT, in the sense that a SQL table is "top level."

For example, you can define a **workers** table with an ordinary string-valued attribute and two ADT attributes containing a photo and the other information that we defined in the **employee** ADT.

```
CREATE TABLE workers(
  ssn VARCHAR,
  photo image,
  info employee );
```

If all of the information about an employee is in the ADT, however, you would need to define a one-attribute table like this:

```
CREATE TABLE workers(
  info employee );
```

You would need to write **name(w.info)** to refer to a worker **w**'s name.*

You might think of **CREATE TABLE** as defining a record type, plus a named collection (an instance of a multiset of that record type). However, unlike an ADT, this record type cannot currently be used elsewhere in the data schema, e.g., to define the type of an attribute or variable. Another table with the same attribute names and types can be defined with SQL's **LIKE** keyword, but this keyword is essentially a macro that copies the column definitions (minus any constraints); type checking is performed only at the level of individual attributes. For example, a **SELECT** from the rows of a table can be stored in another table that has the same attribute type, and so can the result of a join that produces a record with the same attribute types.

Keep in mind that the SQL3 specification is still under development; one change that was considered but has currently been rejected is to allow a declaration of the form:

```
CREATE TABLE employees OF employee;
```

This would allow the rows of a table to be ADT instances.

Since SQL3 tables and the ADT type subsystem are currently not fully integrated, there must be parallel subtyping and collection mechanisms for the two. We look at these next.

6.4.4   Subtypes and Collections

SQL3 incorporates the notion of a hierarchy of ADT types using the **UNDER** clause:

```
CREATE TYPE employee UNDER person
  . . .
```

---

* The mix of parentheses and dot notation is currently necessary to avoid ambiguity with SQL's **schema.table.column** notation.

This defines employees to be a subtype of person. Employees inherit all the attributes and functions defined on persons. Employees may also redefine attributes or functions by associating a new definition with the same name: dynamic binding is supported.

Multiple inheritance is also supported, for example:

```
CREATE TYPE teaching_assistant UNDER employee, student
  ...
```

This allows a teaching assistant to inherit properties from both employee and student ADTs.

For tables, you can define a new table that inherits all the attributes of an existing table using the **UNDER** clause in conjunction with **CREATE TABLE** (as opposed to **CREATE TYPE** used for ADTs).

```
CREATE TABLE professor UNDER worker;
```

SQL3 provides a parameterized type mechanism for ADTs, similar to that provided by object-oriented programming languages and databases. For example, a type **point** can be defined to have two coordinates of any specified type:

```
CREATE TYPE TEMPLATE point (T TYPE) (
  xval T, yval T,
  EQUALS DEFAULT,
  LESS THAN NONE,
  CONSTRUCTOR FUNCTION point (x T, y T) RETURNS
  GEN_TYPE
    ...
    END,
  DESTRUCTOR PROCEDURE remove_point(p GEN_TYPE)
    ...    END,
  ACTOR FUNCTION distance
    (from GEN_TYPE, to GEN_TYPE) RETURNS REAL;
    ...
  END   );
```

Built-in parameterized types are provided for ADT lists, sets, and bags (multisets).

There is no parameterized type mechanism for tables. However, there are corresponding built-in list, set, and bag constructs which can be used (for collections of tuples, at the top level only). The **CREATE TABLE** command already discussed creates a bag of tuples (the original relational model defined this as a set, but SQL allows duplicate rows). You can declare sets and lists of tuples as follows:

```
CREATE SET workers ( ... )
CREATE LIST workers ( ... )
```

Keep in mind that these **SET** and **LIST** constructs define a new top-level entity in the relational schema (**workers**), while the parameterized types **SET** and **LIST** are different: they can take any ADT as argument, and they produce a new ADT; they do not produce a new top-level collection instance.

6.4.5   Procedural Extensions

SQL3 introduces many procedural constructs to a formerly declarative SQL language; you use these constructs to define functions and procedures. The constructs include compound statements, looping statements, conditional statements, assignment statements, and error signalling.

Local variables may be defined in a compound statement. Their values may be changed with assignment statements and conventional SQL statements. For example:

```
BEGIN
DECLARE x INTEGER;
DECLARE y STRING;
SELECT COUNT(*) INTO x
  FROM employees WHERE age>60;
revise_retirement(x);
SET x = x - 10;
UPDATE employees ...;
SELECT name FROM course INTO y WHERE number='CS101';
...
END;
```

SQL3 defines syntax and semantics for exceptions and signals in compound statements.

Two forms of familiar conditional statements are defined: **CASE** statements and **IF** statements. A **CASE** statement looks like this:

```
CASE SUBSTRING (course FROM 1 FOR 2)
  WHEN 'CS' THEN
    ...;
  WHEN NULL THEN
    ...;
  ELSE
    ...;
  END CASE;
```

An **IF** statement looks like this:

```
IF x > 100 THEN
  ...
ELSEIF x > 10 THEN
  ...
END IF;
```

A **WHILE** and a **FOR** statement are supported for looping:

```
WHILE n > 0 LOOP
  INSERT INTO enrollment
    VALUES ('Jones', 'Robert', 'CS101');
  SET n = n - 1;
  END LOOP;

FOR enroll AS EACH ROW OF SELECT * FROM enrollment
    WHERE lname = lname AND fname = fname DO
  IF result <> '' THEN
    SET result = result || ', ';
    END IF;
  SET result = result || enroll.course;
  END FOR;
```

SQL3 also extends SQL2's capabilities for defining and calling procedures, functions, and modules. Functions and procedures may be written in SQL or in programming languages; the latter are called *external*.

6.4.6   Conclusions

SQL3 will add important object-oriented features to SQL's type system, and will make SQL3 into a programming language that is computationally complete. Some aspects of SQL3 are still unclear at the time of this writing, in particular how the new type system introduced by ADTs will be connected to the old type system represented by tables, and the extent to which queries can span the two.

Note that both SQL3 and ODMG-93 define database access languages. A large portion of ODMG-93 does not fit within SQL3's scope, since X3H2 is not dealing with a database programming language architecture (extending programming languages with database capabilities). However, there is a direct overlap with respect to OQL, because both OQL and SQL3 provide constructs for declarative object access.

Although ODMG chose SQL as a starting point for much of OQL's syntax, 100% compatibility with SQL2 was deemed too constraining in producing a clean query language that would be simple to understand and powerful enough to retrieve any type of data structure. In support of ODMG's position, it should be noted that successful relational DBMS products have not been 100% compatible with SQL. Nevertheless, X3H2 opted for compatibility with SQL2, and this compatibility is a powerful argument: existing queries continue to work. It is possible that X3H2 and ODMG proponents will get together and try to produce a "best of both" merger, however some technical compromises would probably be necessary in doing this.

SQL3 will probably be completed as a standard around 1996, with full implementations a few years after that.

The SQL3 draft is quite long—over 1000 pages—and it is being regularly updated by the committee. SQL2 (ANSI X3.135-1992), and SQL3 when it becomes a standard, can be obtained as standard ANSI documents from:

ANSI Sales Department
1430 Broadway
New York, NY 10018 USA
Phone: +1-212-642-4900

6.5   OTHER STANDARDS ACTIVITIES

In this section, we consider other standards activities that are important to ODMSs, even though they are not directly aimed at database standards.

6.5.1   OMG

The first consortium to consider is the Object Management Group (OMG). OMG was formed in 1989 by HP, Sun, and a dozen other companies. It now has nearly 400 members, including practically all the major software vendors, hardware vendors, and large end-users.

OMG's stated goal is to standardize and promote object technology in all forms. The OMG operates through a technical committee which spawns task forces to focus on specific standards. The task forces operate using RFIs (requests for information) and RFPs (requests for proposals) to get input and proposals on technology components, then voting on the resulting alternatives.*

There are three OMG task forces to date:

- ORBTF: The object request broker (ORB) task force is focussing on an object definition and invocation mechanism that spans programming languages, networks, and vendors. The ORB is the topic of the next section.

- OSTF: The object services task force is focussing on various software services that would be invoked through the ORB, including a persistence mechanism, transactions, event notification, and others. We consider the OSTF in Section 6.5.3.

- OMTF: The object model task force has defined a core object model to be used by the ORB, object services, and other components of the OMG environment. This model is then extended with a *profile* for each application domain. For example, the ODMG model was designed as a profile for object databases.

The OMG architecture is illustrated in Figure 6.4. The core components are the object request broker (ORB), which provides the communications "backbone" of

---

* To date, most of the agreement has been obtained through asking submitters to merge the best of their proposals into unified submissions, instead of voting.

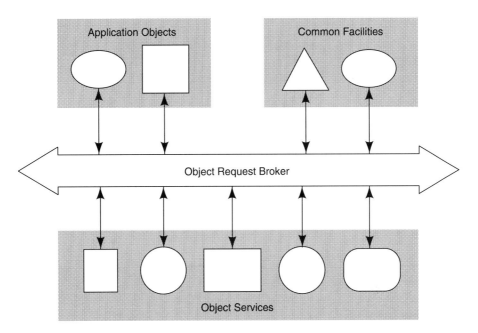

FIGURE 6.4 OMG Architecture: The ORB and object services support applications and common application facilities.

the system, and the object services, which augment the ORB to create a complete object environment. The other components, application objects and common facilities, are not part of OMG's object foundation; they are constructed as objects using this foundation. *Application objects* are exactly that: they are components of applications, e.g., a spreadsheet program, decomposed into objects, e.g., spreadsheet cells or display components. *Common facilities* are objects that are useful to a variety of applications, e.g., fonts, text windows, or relational DBMS gateways. These objects are carefully defined to be re-useable in many contexts.

A more complete description of the OMG architecture, covering the object model and the relationship between the ORB, object services, and other components, can be found in a specification called the *Object Management Architecture (OMA) Guide.* This specification, as well as the *Common Object Request Broker Architecture (CORBA)* and other OMG documents, can be purchased from OMG:

> Object Management Group
> Framingham Corporate Center
> 492 Old Connecticut Path
> Framingham, MA 01701
> E-mail: omg@omg.org
> Phone: +1-508-820-4300

6.5.2   OMG ORB

The first technology component that OMG adopted was the object request broker (ORB). This component is sometimes called CORBA, since the specification is entitled the *Common Object Request Broker Architecture* [OMG ORBTF 1992].

The ORB provides a number of functions for OMG objects:

- *Distribution:* The ORB supports distribution of objects over a network.
- *Description:* The ORB provides a way to describe object types using IDL, the interface definition language.
- *Identification:* The ORB provides an identifier for objects, called an *object reference*.
- *Registration:* Objects make themselves known to the ORB through an interface called an *object adaptor*. A basic object adaptor (BOA) is part of the specification.
- *Location:* The ORB can locate objects based on their identifiers (object references).
- *Invocation:* An object can invoke another object's methods through the ORB.
- *Translation:* The ORB translates the format of data types across the network, across programming languages, and across hardware representations.

Briefly summarized, there are three main parts of the CORBA specification: IDL, the BOA, and the ORB. IDL is used to declare types, the BOA is used to define object instances, and the ORB is used to invoke objects.

Like object-oriented DBMSs, the ORB must provide a programming language binding in order to be used. An IDL compiler produces classes (or the equivalent) in the programming language for each IDL type, so that ORB calls can be sent and can be received by objects in the programming language. The CORBA also defines a dynamic invocation interface (DII) based on character strings passed at runtime, to allow dynamic calls where object types are not known at compiletime.

Thus, the steps in using the ORB are roughly these:

1. An IDL interface is defined for an object type. This interface may be compiled to create programming language stubs for calls to objects of that type, or programming language skeletons for instances of that type.
2. An instance of the object type is created using the BOA, and an object reference is generated.
3. A call is made to the object through the ORB, using the object reference. The binary representation of parameters to the call may need to be converted across machine or programming language boundaries.
4. The ORB locates the called object, invokes the requested operation, and returns the result. This may require the cooperation of other ORBs.

As illustrated in Figure 6.5, there is overlap between the functionality of the ORB and the functionality of a DBMS, particularly with respect to an object-

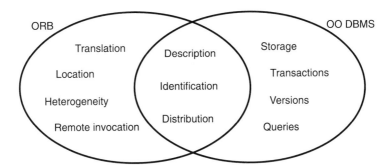

FIGURE 6.5   Overlap of ORB and distributed object-oriented DBMS functionality.

oriented DBMS. There has been some confusion about how DBMSs and ORBs fit together in a distributed object environment, and as a result it has been unclear how the OMG standards impact database standards. In fact, the situation is even more complex than the figure shows, because object-oriented programming languages offer a third environment whose functionality overlaps with the two in the figure. A fourth component, OMG object services, overlaps further with DBMS functionality; we will discuss this overlap in the next section.

In an appendix to their specification, the ODMG explains how ODMSs can fit into the OMG ORB environment such that the two systems complement each other's capabilities. The main issues to address in a successful integration of ODMSs with the ORB are the following:

- ODMSs should utilize the ORB to enable multi-vendor distributed databases. ORB object references could serve as a common denominator that allows selected object references and invocations to span database boundaries. An ODMS may also use the OMG services such as location and distributed name services.

- ODMSs should utilize the ORB for distributed method invocation. OO DBMSs normally delegate method invocation to a programming environment. Through use of the ORB, methods or entire objects could be invoked in the most appropriate site on a network.

- ORB implementations and ORB clients could profitably use ODMSs for storage of distributed object data that they manage. ODMSs might be invoked through the ORB, or through direct APIs.

- The BOA or an alternative object adaptor needs to support high performance access for lightweight objects managed by an ODMS, allowing objects to be cached in the caller's environment. If every ODMS object that an application wanted to reference were individually registered with the ORB or if every request to those objects in the ODMS went through the BOA, the overhead would be unacceptable.

- The object space managed by the ORB must permit subdomains of object identifiers managed by an ODMS, and the ORB must know how to invoke objects managed by an ODMS.

In summary, the ORB acts as a communication mechanism to provide distributed transparent dispatching of requests to objects among applications and service providers. An ODMS acts as manager of a collection of objects, most of which are fine-grain application objects for which high-speed transparent distributed access must be supported. There is functional overlap between the two in various aspects of the object paradigm. However, an ODMS and an ORB are mostly complementary, and the union of the two allows distributed database capability and allows the programmer to choose the best invocation mechanism for each granularity of object. More work in both standards and implementation are needed to realize this integration of ODMSs and OMG ORBs.

6.5.3   OMG Object Services

While continuing work on ORB standardization, for example on interoperability and additional programming language bindings, OMG moves forward in a parallel task force to define object services [OMG OSTF 1993]. The object services utilize the ORB for communication; they are the first services OMG has defined using IDL interfaces for operations on objects and associated services.

The scope of object services is difficult to define. Briefly, object services provide what the ORB is missing to provide a complete object environment. In many software systems, including DBMSs and operating systems, the functionality of object services might be part of the "base level" system: that is, object services would be in the CORBA specification. However, OMG chose a more flexible architecture in which the CORBA contains only the minimum functionality to allow object invocation. Everything else has been separated out into services that are invoked through the ORB and defined through IDL interfaces. In contrast to "built-in" services in the system, this architecture allows many different implementation and interface styles to be supported.

The object services task force has identified a long list of object services. Many of these services overlap with ODMS functionality:

- *Life cycle:* IDL interfaces have been defined for creating, deleting, moving, and copying OMG objects.
- *Naming:* IDL interfaces have been defined to associate names (character strings) with objects, and to map these names to objects using name *contexts*.
- *Events:* The ORB provides only a synchronous call-return mechanism; IDL interfaces have been defined to allow objects to register interest in events and to be notified asynchronously when these events occur.

- *Persistence:* OMG is defining interfaces to allow objects to store their persistent state in a simple fashion. The state might be stored in files or in database systems.

- *Properties:* IDL allows the definition of object attributes.* OMG also recognizes the need for properties that are not part of the object's interface, for example to attach additional information of which the object is not aware.

- *Relationships:* Interfaces are being defined to provide referential integrity and to allow selective propagation of operations such as copy and delete according to the type of relationship between two objects.

- *Externalization:* Mechanisms are being defined to allow objects to be transformed into external strings that can be used to recreate or store the object state elsewhere.

- *Concurrency:* Locking protocols are being defined to allow cooperation between objects in a distributed multi-threaded environment.

- *Transactions:* Protocols analagous to X/Open XTP for distributed transaction commits are being defined for the OMG ORB environment.

- *Security:* Security authorization facilities based on object services and the ORB will be defined.

- *Queries:* OMG recognizes the need to find objects in the distributed ORB environment based on predicates; interfaces for queries are in the future object services plans.

- *Versions:* Versioning is needed for both objects instances and IDL definitions; this is also in the plans.

Together, the object services provide all the functionality of an ODMS, and more. As such, you could consider the OMG object services as another standard for future ODMSs, like SQL3 and ODMG-93. Indeed, ODMG plans to work on IDL-based bindings for the ODMG functionality. However, the OMG object services differ from database standards in an important way: OMG is trying to allow all of these services to be provided *separately* by different vendors or different implementations, defining the interfaces between them so that the sum total still operate correctly.

This is a more ambitious goal than the SQL or ODMG groups set out to tackle. It may require some trade-offs in performance and flexibility, particularly to achieve this goal in a distributed, multi-vendor, multi-language environment. Thus until proven otherwise, there will be a need for database standards that define one interface that provides most of the same functionality.

---

* IDL attributes are virtual; that is, they map onto get and set procedures and they may or may not be stored as object state.

6.5.4 ANSI Programming Languages

For ODMSs based on a database programming language architecture, another important standards arena is object-oriented programming languages, particularly C++ and Smalltalk. The features of these languages are important because the "hooks" these languages provide make a big difference in the level of integration that can be provided with programming languages.

We noted some of these needed hooks for C++ in Chapter 5. For example, current C++ syntax doesn't allow logical views of attributes analogous to views in relational DBMSs. In an object model, views would be classes based on selected member fields or combinations of member fields that are computed (intentional) rather than stored (extensional). You would like to be able to use the expression `object.field` for either a computed or stored value.

C++ permits you to overload the C++ access operators ("." and "->"), allowing you to write expressions like `object.field` to invoke a method defined in the class definition, but the class implementor cannot tell whether the expression is being used to fetch or to store a value. This limitation makes it difficult to automatically generate write locks or to set a dirty bit, as required by DBMSs. Other solutions exist, but are less efficient or less integrated.

ANSI X3 documents, including SQL specifications (X3H2), Object Information Management (X3H7), the X3/SPARC/DBSSG OODB Task Group Report (contact fong@ecs.ncsl.nist.gov), the C++ standard (X3J16), and the Smalltalk standard (X3J20), can be obtained from:

X3 Secretariat, CBEMA
1250 Eye Street, NW, Suite 200
Washington, DC 20005-3922

6.5.5 Standards in Application Domains

In a number of application domains, standards groups have defined functionality that overlaps with database standards. These include:

1. CFI, the CAD Framework Initiative, for electronic CAD,

2. PDES/STEP (Product Data Exchange using STEP, the STandard for Exchange of Product data) for mechanical CAD, and

3. PCTE, the Portable Common Tools Environment, a repository for CASE information.

All three of these standards are designed to integrate and to facilitate communication between various tools in their respective application domain. They generally bear a lot of similarity to ODMS data models and data manipulation interfaces such as ODMG-93. In fact, some object-oriented DBMS vendors are building implementations of these interfaces on top of database standards. This layering approach is probably the most promising way to deal with these interfaces in the context of database standards.

6.6   SUMMARY

In summary, the most important groups to the future of ODMS standards are ANSI X3H2 (SQL3) and ODMG. Standards in the ODMS area are still in a state of flux. The SQL3 standard is likely to differ in important ways from what is described here, since it will be some time before it is finalized and implementations are on the market. The ODMG-93 specification has been finalized, but future revisions are anticipated. The future of both the ODMG and X3H2 groups are still uncertain: For example, ODMG could find a new home that influences its direction, the two groups could merge query languages, relational vendors could reject the more ambitious SQL3 changes, or these standards may be implemented more quickly or more slowly than anticipated.

Other influential groups are the OMG, which has focussed on object standards of all kinds, other ANSI groups including X3H7 and the programming language standards committees, and application-specific standards groups such as CFI, PDES, and PCTE.

7

Goals for Object Data Management

7.1 INTRODUCTION

So far in this book, we have learned about the need for ODMSs providing capabilities beyond traditional DBMSs, discussed the different approaches to ODMSs, examined the features typically provided by these systems, studied implementation issues, and looked at emerging standards. In this chapter, we now critically examine the work in object data management, arriving at a definitive set of features that every ODMS should provide.

Strictly speaking, an ODMS can be evaluated only from the perspective of the intended application. However, a number of generic arguments can be made in object data management, on the basis of generally desirable properties of an ODMS from a user's perspective, or on the basis of needs shared by a large set of applications, such as those in Chapter 2. This chapter is based on these generic arguments.

7.1.1   Feature Comparison

This chapter covers object data management features in approximately the same order as in Chapters 4 and 5: objects and their properties, procedures, type system, programming and query languages, and database architecture. Unlike in Chapters 4 and 5, we mix conceptual and implementation aspects, and there is an element of opinion as well as fact in the discussion.

This element of opinion is unavoidable in any discussion of what computer software "ought" to do; there is disagreement over the best approach to object data management. The debate goes on in research conferences as well as in the DBMS marketplace, and is nowhere near resolution at the time of this writing. The topics of discussion—the ODMS products and prototypes—are rapidly moving targets. Indeed, much of the debate stems simply from confusion between initial prototypes and longer-term intent.

This chapter takes a stand on most of these controversial issues. However, since object data management is a fast-changing field, you are urged to take this chapter as being less "textbook" like than the rest of the book; the ideas expressed herein are *not* universally accepted truths. Do your own reading, form your own opinions. This chapter provides a position against which you can compare your conclusions.

7.1.2   Basis for Conclusions

Before we begin our comparison of object data management features, some ground rules are important.

First, the statements made are based on *demonstrable systems.* Much debate has gone into the discussion of an approach in *theory* versus what has successfully been produced in *practice.* There is no general agreement on what can be done, say, integrating an extended relational model with a persistent programming language. Our "show me" ground rule reduces speculative argument. In some cases, we may need to interpret the rule with careful thought, but using it makes for more objective conclusions.

Second, the conclusions are based on the applications covered in Chapter 2. Without a concrete group of applications, we could argue endlessly on the merits of ODMS approaches, inventing new needs as we go. As we have noted, however, different environments require a different mix of applications. Thus, again, this ground rule must be interpreted carefully.

Third, we cover both conceptual and implementation issues, because the two are inseparable in any real evaluation of object data management approaches. Demanding particular features may cause significant performance degradation, for example.

7.1.3   Background

Papers have been written contrasting the merits of the various approaches and features for object data management systems. Much of the debate over the next generation of DBMSs has focused on the two most popular data models: object-oriented and extended relational.

A basis for definition of the object-oriented approach can be found in [Atkinson et al 1989], which describes an agreement by several leading researchers in the field on what constitutes an object-oriented database system. [Stonebraker et al 1990] have criticized the statements in that paper and in others on object-oriented databases, claiming that extended relational systems are preferable. Both papers provide a list of tenets specifying properties that the next-generation DBMSs should and should not have.

We shall arrive at our own tenets in this chapter, mostly variants from these and other papers on the merits of different DBMS approaches. Our tenets are concerned with the integration of programming and database languages, the level of data independence provided by the DBMS, the use of object identifiers and references, the capabilities of the type system, the properties of the query language, and other issues.

Some features are required; without them, we would not have an ODMS. Others are desirable; that is, they simplify the development of many applications. In specifying our tenets, we shall distinguish explicitly those features that an ODMS *must* have from those that it *should* have. The desirable tenets are distinguished from the required ones by being marked with an asterisk (*).

7.2   DATABASE FUNCTIONALITY

Before we have an ODMS, we must have minimal database system functionality. We therefore begin by specifying basic requirements for data storage and access for any database system. These requirements distinguish a database system from a programming language or operating system, for example.

7.2.1   Data Storage

A database system provides the ability to deal with persistent, structured, large databases:

- *T1: Persistence.* An ODMS must store data that persist beyond the execution of an application program.
- *T2: Schema.* An ODMS must provide a schema for the data. Users must be able to examine the schema as persistent data, and to create and destroy types.

- *T3: Secondary storage.* An ODMS must provide the capability to deal efficiently with large volumes of data, through secondary-storage management, indexes, links, and other techniques.

7.2.2   Data Access

A database system provides basic data-access features for concurrency and access control:

- *T4: Transactions.* An ODMS must provide transactions or an equivalent mechanism for concurrency control and recovery.
- *T5*: Security.* An ODMS should provide mechanisms to authorize users and to control access to data.

All five of the data storage and access tenets are required of an ODMS, except for security (T5), which is optional since many of the applications we considered do not have strong security requirements.

7.3   OBJECTS AND PROPERTIES

First, consider the definition of objects and their properties. Recall from Chapter 4 that objects may have unique identifiers, and their properties may be attributes, relationships, or procedures.

7.3.1   Object Identity

There is general agreement in the field that OIDs are a good idea. There is some disagreement about whether they should be required for all object access. We take the position that the use of OIDs should be optional; if a convenient primary key exists, the user may prefer to use it. Also, if there is overhead associated with creating and maintaining OIDs in the system, then the ODMS implementation needs to know when OIDs are not required.

- *T6: Objects.* An ODMS must provide the ability to store objects, and the user must be able to refer to these objects by a primary key and by a system-generated unique OID.

Note that, although the use of OIDs or primary keys is optional, the ODMS must provide an implementation of both.

It is not necessary that OIDs extracted from the ODMS remain valid in a later session, and there are no other requirements on the implementation of OIDs. However, we note that the utility of OIDs decreases rapidly with additional disk accesses required to fetch an object using an OID, so structured or possibly hashed surrogate OIDs are the only efficient representations.

7.3.2   Attributes

A major difference between ODMSs and traditional relational DBMSs is that object attribute values may be drawn from a wide variety of types, unlike attributes of records:

- *T7: Attributes.* An ODMS must allow object attributes that can be simple literal values such as integers and strings, large values such as bitmaps and text, and collection values including sets and lists.

Object-oriented systems generally provide all these attribute types. Extended relational and functional models also support these types [Zaniolo 1983], but list-valued attributes have been somewhat of a problem because the declarative query languages generally do not support ordering [Stonebraker 1983]. This is particularly important for the representation of ordered relationships, as we shall see in the next section.

We do not require that attributes be accessed syntactically in any way, such as by functional or "dot" notation.

7.3.3   Relationships

There is debate as to whether it should be transparent to the user whether a reference is by OID or by primary key. We do not require transparency, since transparency can be accomplished using virtual relationships.

- *T8: Relationships.* An ODMS must provide a mechanism to represent relationships between objects. It should be possible to define related objects by primary key or by OID.

If relationships are not represented by attributes, then T7 must also apply to relationships: it must be possible to create relationships between objects and literal values such as integers, and it must be possible to specify an ordering on relationships. In our example document database, for example, ordered relationships are important to define the chapters for a document; without them, chapters must be sorted on a chapter number every time they are enumerated.

We need another tenet for relationships:

- *T9: Referential integrity.* The mechanism for representing relationships must maintain referential integrity, avoiding update anomalies on deletion of objects or redefinition of the relationship.

Object-oriented systems without inverse attributes do not satisfy this tenet because there can be two independent representations of the same relationships. Many relational products still do not implement referential integrity, either.

7.3.4   Composite Objects

Aggregation of objects into composite objects is a desirable feature, although it is not necessary, since it can be accomplished by an application program:

- *T10*: Composite objects.* An ODMS should provide the ability to aggregate objects for the purposes of operations such as deletion, copying, and concurrency control. If aggregation is provided, then it must be usable for purposes of physical clustering. The application of operations—for example, deletion—to the entire aggregate must be optional.

7.3.5   Procedures

In addition to attributes and relationships, objects may have associated procedures:

- *T11*: Procedures.* It should be possible to associate procedures with object types.

As we shall see in Section 7.5, procedures may be called directly, used to define virtual attributes, or used in the query language.

7.4   TYPE SYSTEM

In the previous section, we considered important issues in the type system for object properties. In this section, we shall consider the important features of a type system for the objects themselves.

7.4.1   Type Representation

It is a corollary of T2 that an ODMS type system should be visible from both the programming language and query language used by the application programmer. For example, an ODMS could allow abstract data types in the language to be stored as attributes of objects, but if it is not possible to examine all the data in the abstract data type in a query, then there is still a language impedance mismatch.

On the other hand, it *is* necessary to extend the type system of programming languages to provide a data model satisfactory for database systems. For example, programming languages typically do not provide associative operations on a type required in a query language, such as fetching all objects of a type that have a value between 4 and 15 in an integer-valued field. Indeed, most programming languages do not allow enumerating the instances of a type, with or without such associative constraints.

7.4.2   Inheritance

A tenet on which almost everyone agrees is that type inheritance is useful:

- *T12: Inheritance.* An ODMS must allow inheritance of properties from supertypes. Optionally, it may allow multiple inheritance, multiple types for an object, or instance exceptions (one-instance types).

Inheritance is important in essentially all the applications we considered; without it, many more types may be necessary in the schema, and operations on the types are much harder to specify. The optional extensions beyond inheritance provide additional richness, but all of them add complexity to the data model and implementation that may not justify the gain. Multiple inheritance is probably the most likely to gain acceptance; however, as we discussed in Chapter 5, multiple inheritance can reduce efficiency for property access, so should be used only when necessary.

7.4.3   Run-Time Types

In some applications, it is important to be able to bind to types and to define new types of data at run time. This capability is also useful in writing programs to change the data schema.

- *T13*: Run-time types.* An ODMS should allow dynamic binding and simple changes to types.

Note that, in database programming languages based on compiled languages it may be necessary to use a special programming interface to access objects when their types are defined at run time—for example, through database language strings interpreted by a run-time library. Because of the additional complexity associated with type changes and binding at run time, and the more limited number of applications requiring these features, they are classified as desirable rather than required.

7.4.4   Schema Evolution

Given logical data independence in a database system, the problem of changing the schema is greatly simplified. It is still a major issue, however, given the longevity of databases. This problem does not arise in programming languages, where types outlive data, rather than data outliving types.

In Chapter 5, we discussed some of the research into schema evolution in a database system. We shall *not* require sophisticated schema-evolution capabilities in an ODMS, however, because no schema-evolution capability will be satisfactory to include many of the transformations that will be required: the important features are those that make it easier to program schema transformations.

- *T14*: Schema Evolution.* An ODMS should provide tools to assist the user in schema transformations.

A declarative query language can go a long way toward satisfying T14, but graphical tools or a language specifically oriented toward describing transformations would be more useful. No ODMS provides such tools at present, however.

Run-time capability to rename, add, and drop properties of object types, and to add and drop object types themselves, are the important features required in T13 in order to support T14 and ad hoc programs to perform schema transformations. Without these simple run-time type capabilities, it would be necessary to define both the new and old schema statically in the transformation program.

7.5   PROGRAMMING AND QUERY LANGUAGES

We consider the programming and query languages together, because there are tradeoffs and interactions between the use of procedural and declarative capabilities.

7.5.1   Query Language

There are two important purposes for a query language: (1) to provide physical data independence, and (2) to provide a convenient higher-level language to express data manipulation.

Direct access to data in a programming language does not provide either of these. Note that a query language provides a higher-level language for the programmer, embedded in a programming language, or for the end user, for ad hoc data manipulation.

Query languages have also been used for other purposes. For example, they may be extended into a 4GL for writing simple programs, or for linking screen forms to databases. These uses of a query language are not of importance for the purpose of our tenets, however.

Our basic tenets for query languages are as follows:

- *T15: Query language.* An ODMS must provide a declarative DML that may be used for ad hoc operations by an end user.

- *T16: Physical data independence.* The query-language processor must provide a high degree of physical data independence, automatically selecting physical access methods to use to satisfy a query.

- *T17: Queries in programs.* An ODMS must support a programming language that includes the query language as a subset. It must be possible to invoke the query language from the programming language, and the programming language from the query language.

7.5.2 Query Optimization

It is difficult to write an ODMS query processor that optimizes across the barrier between the query and programming language. A declarative query language can be optimized by simple algebraic transformation, whereas programs with control constructs cannot. This is the essential difference between the two, and is the reason for the following tenet:

- *T18*: Queries preferred.* Programs should specify data access in a query language rather than directly in a programming language, when it is practical to express the set of operations and objects desired in the query language.

Application of this tenet can increase the physical data independence, efficiency, and readability of an application program. When data access is expressed in a query language, the entire query can be optimized according to the current structure of the database and shipped to the database engine (possibly remotely located), and the set of data satisfying the query can be returned efficiently as a single unit. A programming language does not provide a query language's support for physical data independence, except in a limited way through encapsulation: Encapsulation allows the physical implementation of a property to be changed without affecting programs that use the property, but it is necessary to rewrite the property implementation manually. The query-language processor automatically provides the best implementation for a property based on the access methods defined.

T18 was one of the original motivations for the relational approach, as opposed to earlier navigational access at a physical level. Navigational access is sometimes cited as a major step backward in the object-oriented approach [Stonebraker et al 1990], because the relational model made navigation details transparent to the user. However, since a number of the object-oriented database programming languages we examined provide an embedded query language with at least the power of relational systems, and nearly all these ODMSs have query capability in the plans, this criticism is undeserved.

Also, this tenet needs to be applied carefully. There are cases where a program can be more readable when written in a programming language, and a satisfactory level of physical data independence can be achieved through encapsulation. There are also cases where the programmer may produce a better result than the query optimizer on a critical portion of a CAD, CASE, or similar application.

7.5.3 Query Capability

A less well-understood area in comparing ODMSs is in the power of the query language. In relational systems, the notion of *relational completeness* [Date 1990] can be used to gauge query language power. With the addition of capabilities such as collection-valued attributes, procedures, and queries on arbitrary types, models of completeness are not yet well developed.

The query languages in some ODMSs operate on only collections, and do not provide the equivalent of relational joins between object types unless an explicit reference attribute has been defined between the types. In contrast, the query language in O₂ [Bancilhon et al 1989] is much more powerful than the relational calculus. It provides constructors and operators on sets, lists, and tuples, and may produce intermediate or final results of any type.

We require that the DML be as powerful as SQL applied to collections, and that all data be accessible through the DML:

- *T19: Query-language completeness.* The DML must provide at least the capability of the relational calculus with collection-results, and should allow access to all data structures, including collections.

This capability is probably adequate for most of the applications we studied. It could be made stronger when a better model of query-language power is available.

7.5.4   Programming Capability

T17 introduced a programming language with the query language as a subset; now, we further specify the capabilities of the programming-language component. Note that the programming language may be a database query language with control constructs, application programming-language procedure calls embedded in a query language, or a unified database programming language.

The first issue with the programming language is what you can do with it:

- *T20: Programming-language completeness.* An ODMS language must support programming capability that is computationally complete and resource-complete.

This tenet addresses one of the most misunderstood areas in advanced database systems. Although, as specified in T18, it is desirable to use the query language whenever possible to express application operations, to provide a higher level of physical data independence, the declarative query language is generally not sufficient to express all operations. Where it is not, it is necessary to call on the programming language.

Recall that *computational completeness* is the ability to perform an operation that can be expressed in the application programming language, whereas *resource completeness* means that the computation must have access to all the same environment as the application program—for example, global variables and the user's screen.

In the database programming language approach, a single language with programming and query capabilities is provided. Thus, this approach provides a well-integrated language that provides both forms of completeness.

In the extended database system approaches, computational completeness can be provided in two different ways: by adding control constructs to the query language, or by allowing embedded calls to the application programming language from queries. However, the former does not provide resource completeness, and the latter provides resource completeness only if the application calls are executed in the same environment as the application program.

7.5.5   Programming-Language Integration

We see that programming capability may be provided in an ODMS in a variety of ways. However, the integration between the programming and query capabilities as seen by the application programmer may differ substantially. The ideal solution is simply integrating queries and other database functionality into the application programmer's existing language:

- *T21*: Programming-language integration.* An ODMS should be integrated with an existing programming-language environment, to provide a persistent superset of an application programming language with which users are already familiar.

This tenet deals with the often-referenced impedance-mismatch problem between the application programming language and DBMS. In a system that provides good integration, the programmer has only one language to learn, and does not need to split the execution of application code across two environments.

It is possible to underestimate the importance of this tenet. Application programmers have accepted the impedance mismatch in business applications for many years, so it may not seem a major issue. However, integration with an application programming language that is already in wide use may be a powerful force in the marketplace.

Let's look at how programming-language integration is dealt with in the different database architectures. Note that, in any case, it is necessary to express queries in a programming language, and to call programs from a query language. Indeed, it may be important to nest calls recursively between query and programming languages, to an arbitrary depth. However, the architectures differ in how they achieve this nesting.

7.5.6   Database Architectures and Integration

The database programming language approach was specifically aimed at the programming-language integration problem; in fact, that is one of the biggest strengths of the approach, as noted in Chapter 4. Often, it is not just the language that is familiar to the application programmer—the same debugger, compiler, libraries, and any other tools developed for the programming language are automatically available in the database programming language.

Because the data model of the ODMS is a carefully designed superset of the programming-language data model (type system) in this approach, it is difficult to achieve close integration with more than one programming language. Only the

GemStone and O$_2$ work has explored building several persistent programming languages on the same ODMS to date. In fact, the difficulty of close integration with multiple programming environments is the main drawback of database programming languages. On the other hand, other approaches to date have "solved" the problem by providing close integration with *no* programming language. It would seem that integration with one is better than integration with none.

In the extended database system architecture, there are two ways to provide programming capability: extending the query language with control constructs to make it computationally complete, or providing the capability to call the application programming language from within a query. In either case, or even if both capabilities are provided, there is no integration between the type systems of the database and programming language. The programmer must copy data explicitly between the two representations. This is the major drawback of the extended database system architecture.

As we noted in Chapter 4, the distinction between extended database system and database programming language architectures can be subtle. For example, in a DBMS such as SYBASE, in which control constructs have been added to the query language, it might be possible for an application programmer to write the entire application in the extended SQL. Thus, like the database programming language approach, there may be only one language to learn and use. Also, among the systems we have classified as object-oriented database programming languages, some systems have much better integration with the programming language than with others, and some do not provide 100 percent compatibility with existing programs in the language, or with existing programming tools. Thus, the distinction between database programming languages and extended database systems must be treated as a continuum. Whether a database programming language solves the language impedance-mismatch problem must be judged by the users.

7.5.7   Logical Data Independence

Recall from Chapter 3 the distinction between the external, conceptual, and internal levels for a database, and remember that *logical data independence* is the ability to support multiple distinct external views of a database on a single, frequently changing conceptual view of the database. The conceptual level is generally defined by a database administrator, and the external levels are defined by application programmers.

Logical data independence is very important, because it allows the conceptual structure of the database to be modified without changing existing application code. It also allows different applications to see the same data in different ways.

Recall from Chapter 4 that an ODMS must provide two features of logical data independence: *hiding* and *mapping* of object properties. Hiding and mapping are tenets T22 and T23.

- *T22: Property hiding.* An ODMS must allow properties (attributes, relationships, or procedures) that are externally visible to be distinguished from private ones.

T22 allows the schema designer to distinguish common, private properties on which external ones can be defined. This is important for logical data independence because it limits the number of properties affected by a change in representation.

This tenet generally applies to any access to data, whether through a declarative query language or through a programming language. However, we could relax this tenet somewhat for direct query language access by end users, since the primary purpose of property hiding is to avoid rewriting programs.

Many implementations of relational views do not provide hiding. At a minimum, it is necessary to distinguish views that define the public, external level, from those at the private, conceptual level. The view-layers problem is not simply one of access control, assigning different authorization constraints to different views and relations. It is necessary to *group* views such that they are presented to users in levels.

Encapsulation in the object-oriented approach provides hiding: The private portions of objects represent the conceptual level, and the public portions represent the external level. As we noted in Chapter 4, however, it is useful to broaden the traditional definition of encapsulation used in object-oriented programming languages, where procedures are public and data are private. In a database system, it should be possible to place either procedures or data in the public portion, and either procedures or data in the private portion.

An ODMS may have *more* than two access levels for properties, but it must have at least two (public and private). An ODMS that provided an arbitrary number of logical levels, rather than simply public (external) and private (conceptual) levels, could be useful in several ways. For example, it is helpful in some applications to define *three* logical levels: one level shared by all applications, one level that is visible to groups of applications, and one level for specific applications. However, we require only the public and private levels.

We state the tenet for mapping, the second requirement for logical data independence, in a strong form that is not satisfied by most of the ODMSs we cover:

- *T23: Property mapping.* An ODMS must allow a user to define procedurally *virtual* properties of a database object. Virtual properties are properties that can "hide" other properties. It should be transparent to the user whether a property is virtual or is stored directly.

There is a variety of reasons that existing ODMSs fail to fully satisfy this tenet:

1. If there are two different languages in an ODMS, a programming language and a query language, then this tenet must apply to the use of virtual properties in both contexts. That is, mappings defined in either language must be accessible in the other. Hiding must also work in both contexts.

2. Many object-oriented systems do not allow virtual attributes because they use a different syntax for method and attribute access. Only procedure mapping, or encapsulation, may be used in these systems, and the query language can be used on object attributes only from within a method of that object. Encapsulation is more useful if there is a duality between procedures and data, so that the user at a higher level can use the "attribute" abstraction without regard to procedural versus stored attribute semantics (as in O_2).

3. The property mapping may not be *invertible;* that is, the ODMS may not be able to use property retrieval mappings to perform property updates. Relational views are not always transparent for this reason. [Stonebraker 1986, Dayal and Bernstein 1982, Furtado et al 1979, Keller 1985] made some progress on updateable views, but a complete practical solution is yet to be demonstrated. In database programming languages, a separate specification of retrieval and update operations may be required to provide transparent mapping.

If it is not possible to redefine any visible property transparently, then changes to the property will require that existing programs or queries be rewritten. To the extent that the tenet is not satisfied—for example, if there is transparency for only read access—there is less logical data independence in the system. However, partial satisfaction of the tenet is better than nothing.

Note that the ability to define virtual relationships allows the user to specify relationships procedurally or in a declarative language. These relationships define what have traditionally been called *automatic sets,* as opposed to *manual sets*—relationships that are individually created and deleted by the user. Automatic sets are one of the advantages of the relational model over earlier models based on explicit user-defined sets, because sets can be maintained automatically by the system based on object properties; ODMSs based on other models can also provide automatic sets through virtual properties. However, there are cases where manual sets are also needed—for example, when it is desired to maintain an ordering on a set and there are no natural attributes of the objects that lend themselves to definition of an automatic set (for example, paragraphs in a document). We require both automatic and manual sets.

7.5.8   Standards

Standards in database systems are important mostly because they make it easier to write applications that can be converted to a different ODMS. Conversion may be desirable for many reasons: better performance, reliability, support, availability, or just because a vendor went out of business.

*   *T24*: Portability.* An ODMS should provide the ability to write programs that will also run on other ODMSs.

Portability requires a standard for both the query language and programming language. Particularly in a database programming language, where the programming language has been extended with database capabilities, the entire language, or at least a procedure library, must be standardized to allow portability to another system. We covered some of the object data management standards work in Chapter 6. Even in relational database systems, a query language standard without a standard for how it is embedded in a programming language is not useful.

There is already a standard for query-language access to relational databases: SQL [Date 1987]. It is unlikely that an ODMS, even one with considerably more functionality than existing relational systems, can ignore this standard. As we noted in Section 4.7.9, SQL is important for a variety of reasons, such as user familiarity and interfaces to existing databases. We therefore add the following tenet:

- *T25*: SQL compatibility.* An ODMS should provide backward compatibility with SQL, or gateways to and from SQL database systems.

This tenet may seem too restrictive to people in database systems research, but history has shown that conversion to new technology is very slow unless there is some form of compatibility with existing technology. It is generally not practical to move all the data in a company into an ODMS, even if the ODMS supports all the transaction-processing, decision-support, and application-development capabilities of the existing DBMS. Industry has only just begun to convert to relational database systems!

Unfortunately, this tenet will be difficult to satisfy fully. Some capabilities of an ODMS, such as lists and procedures, cannot be mapped into SQL easily. Access to a relational DBMS from an ODMS will not be transparent, since the relational DBMS provides less capability. Conversely, the relational DBMS may not be able to access all the information or capability in an ODMS through SQL. Therefore, there are only degrees of conformance to this tenet.

7.6   DATABASE ARCHITECTURE

The architecture and implementation of the ODMS are almost entirely independent of the data model, but they are also important to us, because many of the applications we have considered have strong performance requirements and need functionality such as remote data access.

7.6.1   Access Overhead

It is important that the query language and programming language provided by the ODMS have minimal overhead for the kinds of operations required by the applications. For example, if data can be accessed only through a query language, and an interprocess call plus data copying is necessary to obtain data in the programming language, then applications that must make thousands of data accesses per second are not practical, as we noted in Chapter 5.

- *T26: Minimal access overhead.* An ODMS must minimize overhead for simple data operations, such as fetching a single object.

Compile-time type checking, a single-process architecture, programming language integration, efficient mapping from object handles to data, swizzling references to pointers that are frequently accessed, and other techniques can be used to satisfy this tenet.

It is also desirable to minimize execution time for complex queries, but the performance differences in this area are generally not so dramatic as to determine whether an application can be used at all.

7.6.2   Caching and Clustering

The next most important performance factor is eliminating disk accesses. The two most important approaches to doing this are generally caching and clustering:

- *T27: Main-memory utilization.* An ODMS must maximize the likelihood that data will be found in main memory when accessed. At a minimum, it should provide a cache of data in the application virtual memory, and the ability to cluster data on pages or segments fetched from the disk.

This tenet is interdependent on other requirements; for example, the concurrency control mechanism must allow long-term checkout so that a main-memory cache can be utilized. Note that, to date, the database programming language and object manager implementations generally satisfy T26 and T27, whereas extended database systems do not.

7.6.3   Distribution

We have two requirements for distributed databases. The first is remote access:

- *T28: Remote operations.* It must be possible to access data located on another machine with an ODMS. It must also be possible to execute operations remotely, if this capability is not conveniently provided through operating-system features.

Nearly all the systems we covered in Chapter 6 provide transparent remote data access. Only a few provide remote execution; the choice of sending the data to the operation (remote data access) or the operation to the data (remote execution) must be made on an application-specific basis, so this is an important factor. However, remote procedure call (RPC) mechanisms are improving to the point where remote execution (and distributed execution in general) is relatively convenient to perform without the aid of the ODMS.*

Note that we do not require that SQL or another query language be the medium of network communication between application front end and database back end, for remote data access. Some researchers have claimed that using a query language over a network is better than remote page access or other techniques. However, as we saw in Chapter 5, the performance advantage can also weigh substantially in the other direction. More research is needed to understand these tradeoffs.

The second distributed capability that is important is the ability to break up data across independently administered databases:

- *T29*: Database distribution.* An ODMS should provide the ability to execute queries and programs that access more than one database. Objects in a database should be able to reference objects in another database.

References between databases must be made on the basis of some human-meaningful key, unless surrogate OIDs are provided that are unique for all time and all databases.

7.7 OTHER ISSUES

In this final section, we cover remaining features that do not fall into the data-modeling and database-architecture categories we have considered.

7.7.1 Concurrency

We required the implementation of transactions in T4. However, there is no general agreement on more sophisticated mechanisms for concurrency control.

Some provide long-term transactions, some propose transaction concurrency mechanisms based on object type semantics. We shall not propose any specific requirements for more sophisticated semantics, but, on the basis of what we have learned, we can specifically include the requirement for long-term locking:

- *T30: Locking.* An ODMS must provide a locking mechanism, at the granularity of an object or page, that allows data to be checked out for long periods.

---

* Often, it is not essential that the distributed computation all be performed under the same transaction. More sophisticated distributed database capabilities will be necessary for applications that require distributed transactions.

We do not specify whether the locking mechanism is used directly by the user, or in conjunction with whatever transaction or version mechanism is provided by the system.

Most of the applications we covered have some requirement for versions and configuration management. Again, however, there is no widely accepted paradigm for how versions should *work* in a way that all these applications would be satisfied. We therefore include versions as an option, without specific requirements:

- *T31*: Versions.* An ODMS should provide primitives to manage multiple versions of data. It may provide configuration-management capabilities as well.

Research in version management for ODMSs is proceeding quickly; it is likely that some scheme for versions will become more widely accepted in a few years.

7.7.2   Rule Systems

Although knowledge-management capabilities are not required for many applications, and can often be incorporated in an expert system when they are required, many applications have a need for simple rules triggered by predicates. Some proponents of the object-oriented approach claim that such rules can simply be incorporated in the methods associated with an object type; although this is true, this approach makes it much more difficult to ensure that particular constraints are satisfied as the system changes. Thus, rules are a desirable feature:

- *T32*: Rules.* An ODMS should provide a rule invocation mechanism, to execute actions when specified predicates become true. The action associated with a rule may be an arbitrary procedure (triggers) or an error condition (constraints).

Note that only the predicate evaluation needs to be provided by the ODMS; the action might be specified in a programming language or another host environment. As we discussed in Chapter 4, it remains to be seen whether complex knowledge bases with a large number of rules and a sophisticated scheme for efficient rule evaluation will become very important in ODMS a decade from now—large numbers of rules can be more difficult to understand than procedural specifications.

7.7.3   High-Level Tools

Our last, but certainly not least important, requirement for an ODMS is for end-user and programmer tools. These are among the most important features of any database system, to increase productivity.

- *T33*: Tools.* An ODMS should provide high-level tools to allow data and schema access, and to assist the programmer in application generation.

The development of these tools is a significant effort in a database product, as witnessed by current relational systems. In fact, the existence of these tools is sometimes cited as a reason to start with current relational products as a basis for object data management. However, most of the existing work on these tools is not relevant, since the tools must be discarded in favor of a whole new generation of tools based on graphical user interfaces and more sophisticated data models.

7.8   SUMMARY

There has been disagreement in the database literature on what the next generation of database systems, focusing primarily on object data management, should provide to their users [Stonebraker et al 1990, Atkinson et al 1989, Laguna 1989, Silberschatz 1990]. The purpose of this chapter has been to propose a specific set of features for a next-generation database system. Remember that the tenets we have derived are not based on consensus in the research and development communities. Until more widespread agreement is reached, you must exercise your own judgment.

Our 33 tenets provide a basis for evaluating any particular ODMS, focusing primarily on the 20 tenets a system "must" satisfy, and on tenets important to any specific intended application. Remember that, although the ODMS features described by these tenets add significant new capability over traditional database systems, they also add more complexity to implementation and learning of a database system, so the inclusion of the optional features and the tradeoffs for your own application must be considered carefully.

The required tenets were those for persistence, on-line schema, secondary storage, transactions, objects, attributes, relationships, referential integrity, inheritance, query language, physical data independence, queries in programs, query-language completeness, programming-language completeness, hiding properties, virtual properties, minimal access overhead, main-memory utilization, remote operations, and locking. The additional, desirable features are specified in the tenets for security, composite objects, procedures, run-time types, schema evolution, preference for queries, programming-language integration, portability, SQL compatibility, database distribution, versions, rules, and end-user tools.

Our tenets, along with observations made throughout the book, provide a basis for comparing the approaches to object data management we have examined. In the final chapter of the book, we shall reexamine what we have learned, and shall draw conclusions about the most promising approaches for future work in object data management.

8

Conclusions

8.1 NEEDS FOR OBJECT DATA MANAGEMENT

In this final chapter, we review application needs for object data management, examine how to evaluate your own application requirements, compare and review the approaches to object data management, and look at directions for object data management in research and in the database marketplace. In this first section, we focus on application needs.

8.1.1 New Application Requirements

In Chapter 2, we examined many application databases that are not addressed by traditional DBMSs: electronic or mechanical designs, software-engineering projects or programs and their components, documents in an office, scientific data, and others. We can now see that the new ODMSs satisfy the needs we identified for these applications.

The most important features of ODMSs for these applications are these:

*   *Performance:* Most of the ODMSs we covered offer many times better performance for applications where data are checked out for long periods with relatively little contention among users, there is locality of reference so that data can be cached in workstation memory, and very little overhead can be tolerated for simple database operations.

*   *Procedures:* ODMSs offer the ability to mix a query language and programming language to perform database access, reducing language impedance mismatch in applications where data access is needed for programming as well as for queries.

*   *Object semantics:* ODMSs allow the user to group related data as objects, to reference objects by OIDs as well as traditional keys, to aggregate related objects as composite objects, and to generalize common object type features through inheritance of properties.

*   *Rich data structures:* ODMSs provide new data structures for these object data, including lists, arrays, sets, BLOBs, and custom user-defined types. Tables in the relational model, although conceptually simpler, are too weak to represent these more complex data.

*   *New concurrency control:* ODMSs provide new mechanisms to share data among users, including long-term and nested transactions, multiple versions of data, and configurations to maintain consistent groups of data versions.

These new capabilities allow applications previously forced to use hand-crafted representations of data to benefit from the productivity gains and additional functionality provided by a database system, by using ODMSs.

8.1.2   Evaluation of Application Requirements

The new capabilities in ODMSs represent a new generation of database systems. However, it is still important to examine your specific application requirements to determine whether an ODMS is a better choice than traditional or hand-crafted databases for its specific needs, and if so, which ODMS product is the best fit.

There are several questions to answer in evaluating a particular application and choosing a database solution that satisfies its requirements:

*   What portion of the data is persistent? Can the database, or most of the data that will be used in one session, fit in main memory?

*   Can the high-level operations required by the application be expressed in a query language, or will it be necessary to decompose them into simple operations for which a programming language is more appropriate?

*   How many of these operations must the application perform per second? Must this rate be achieved accessing data on disk over a network, or is there

significant locality of reference? Will new data be accessed randomly and incrementally, or will an entire design or other group of data be loaded into memory at once?

- Does the application require ad hoc queries or associative lookup of objects by complex constraints?

- Are application programs expected to evolve over a long period, so that physical and logical data independence are important?

- In what language will the application be written? Can it be programmed entirely in a new database language? Are there existing application libraries that must be used? What resources must be available in the language?

- What level of concurrent access is expected for the database? Will portions of the database be checked out for long periods? If so, is a versioning facility needed to track changes or to allow concurrent design work? How will versioning be used?

- Is remote access, distributed data, or distributed computation required? What level of support is needed in the database system for these features?

- How complex is the data schema? Is there a need for inheritance or multiple inheritance to simplify its description? Will the schema change frequently, or dynamically during execution of a program?

- Does the application require lists, arrays, sets, relationship and reference integrity, large text or binary fields, or custom-defined types such as x,y coordinates?

The answers to these questions should be matched against the features and performance of candidate database systems, so that you can choose approaches by considering general characteristics of the application database. If there are no requirements for concurrency control, queries, or a large quantity of data, then you may question whether a database system is needed at all—a custom-crafted solution using conventional programming-language data structures may be the best solution. If application operations can be expressed in SQL, and the database can be represented in tabular form with only modest extensions such as BLOBs and simple embedded procedures, or if many users are anticipated in an on-line transaction processing context, then one of the most recent relational DBMSs may be the best choice. If more substantial extensions are required to the data model, then an extended relational, functional, or semantic database system should be considered, according to your preferences in language syntax and relational compatibility. If close integration with a programming language is an issue, or if your applications check out objects that are used for more than a few seconds and the performance of the other approaches is unsatisfactory for this, then an object-oriented database programming language should be considered. If none of these alternatives work for your needs, then you should consider crafting your own database solution, through use of a database system generator or by building on top of an object manager.

8.2   OBJECT DATA MANAGEMENT APPROACHES

Chapters 4 and 5 introduced the approaches to object data management and contrasted aspects of each in covering the features and implementation issues. Chapter 7 enumerated the most important features and implementation requirements for object data management. Now, let's bring together what we have learned in a summary of the approaches, examining how each fared overall as a result of our observations.

8.2.1   Database System Generators and Object Managers

Database system generators and object managers are the most flexible solutions to object data management, but require the most effort on the part of the user. Generally, their users are database implementors, who in turn may produce systems for application programmers or end users.

Object managers generally provide most of the features we described in Chapter 4: basic object storage, attributes, and object references, an object type hierarchy, and simple concurrency control and versioning primitives. More sophisticated features, such as query and programming languages, relationship and composite object semantics, and end-user tools, are left to the database implementor.

The main benefit of an object manager is that it does not include time and space overhead for higher-level semantics when such features are not needed, or when they are not the right high-level semantics for an application. Object managers are useful for applications in which simple object-management facilities are required, to provide services to application-programmer clients. Examples are the system service applications for network management, electronic-mail routing, and application-integration frameworks we covered at the end of Chapter 2. Object managers can also be used to build database systems; in fact, there is an object manager at the core of every one of the other approaches to object data management, as we noted at the beginning of Chapter 4.

Database system generators make it easy to implement all the functionality in Chapter 4, including query and programming languages and high-level semantics. Using an object manager, the languages and semantics would have to be built from scratch, and using one of the other ODMS approaches, the database implementor would be constrained to use the languages and semantics built in to the ODMS, with only limited extensibility for user-defined operations and types.

Database system generators are most useful in applications where unusual or custom capabilities are required. For example, if you want to design your own database query language, specialized to an application such as image recognition or statistical operations on matrices, then a database system generator is probably the best starting point for your work.

Object managers and database system generators are both very useful for custom applications for which existing ODMSs are not a good fit. However, they require a more sophisticated user than that needed for the other approaches, and require more effort when one of the other approaches already provides a satisfactory solution. Their user audience is therefore a small fraction of that for the other approaches. For this reason, these approaches received relatively little attention in this book.

8.2.2 Extended Functional and Semantic Database Systems

Extended functional and semantic database systems incorporate objects, generalization, aggregation, and other data-modeling capabilities. In extended functional database systems, functions are used to represent attributes, relationships, and procedures associated with objects, and objects are represented as unique IDs. Functions may also take literal values as parameters, or produce them as values. The functional query language can be embedded in application programs, and calls to functions written in the application programming language can be embedded in the query language.

Only a few ODMSs have been built based on a functional or semantic data model. These approaches do not share the compatibilities afforded the object-oriented database programming languages (many existing programming languages have been based on the object-oriented model), or the compatibilities of the extended relational database systems (many existing database systems have been based on the relational model). At their current level of popularity, these data models are least likely to become the basis for next-generation database systems. However, we have included them in this book because semantic data-modeling ideas were historically the basis for much of the more recent work in database systems, and functional models provide a particularly simple and powerful notation for many of the capabilities we have described, particularly for virtual data and composition of operations.

8.2.3 Extended Relational Database Systems

Extended relational database systems augment the relational model with the ability to invoke programming-language procedures from the query language or to write procedures in the query language itself. Since no standard has been established for extensions to the relational model, a wide variety of features may be incorporated in different ways in extended relational ODMSs, including a hierarchy of relation types with inheritance of attributes, object IDs for tuples, query-language extensions for transitive closure, rules, and the ability to define new literal data types.

Only a few ODMSs have been built based on an extended relational model, and the extensions made to relational database products to date have been quite modest. However, this approach has wide support from the large relational database industry and research communities [Stonebraker et al 1990]. This approach benefits from the substantial existing investment in relational database research and existing applications. Extended relational database systems are therefore quite likely to see further research and development in this decade.

8.2.4   Object-Oriented Database Systems

Object-oriented database systems add database capabilities to existing object-oriented programming languages. They typically incorporate similar features: objects, object IDs, object references, composite objects, a hierarchy of object types, collections, BLOBs, and methods to provide procedural encapsulation. Most of the object-oriented database programming language products are based on C++; they have also been built on Smalltalk and CLOS. Some provide interfaces to more than one language.

The strengths of object-oriented database systems lie primarily in the convenience and performance advantages afforded by a single language for database and programming operations, and the wide popularity of the object-oriented approach in programming at this time. A weakness of object-oriented database systems is that relatively little experience and development effort has gone into these ODMSs; relational DBMSs have been widely used since the early 1980s. Nevertheless, the wide popularity of object-oriented models for database systems suggests that they, along with extended relational models, are the leading contenders for next-generation database systems.

8.3   FUTURE DIRECTIONS

In this final section, we examine issues in the future of object data management, in both products and research: What is the future of object data management? Is it a passing fad in data management research? Is it simply a set of features to add to existing database products? Will it spawn a whole new generation of database systems?

In the research domain, object data management encompasses most of the research work done in database systems in the 1980s and 1990s. As such, object data management is not a passing fad, although particular terminology, such as "object-oriented," may well be.

In the marketplace, the future of the recent ODMS introductions is unclear. There are many object-oriented DBMS products, considering the size of the CAD and CASE market, and the companies do not have established customer bases. However, modifications of existing relational database products, allowing them to compete in the same market, will be difficult to achieve without a complete rewrite of these products.

8.3.1 Marketplace

As we discussed in the first chapter, there is more than one scenario for the future of object data management technology. One is that traditional data management and new object data management capabilities will be integrated into a single system. Another is that ODMSs will be used for only the applications we discussed in Chapter 2, and that traditional DBMSs will be used for only business applications.

Much of the relational database research community seems to believe the former scenario, and these researchers probably will prove correct in the long run. However, the "long run" could be very long in practice, because the market is generally driven by the needs of each application niche, and we are a long way from building DBMSs that can satisfy data-, object-, and knowledge-management needs simultaneously.

Granted, some simple object- and knowledge-management capabilities—such as BLOBs, user-defined types, and basic rules—have already been added to relational DBMSs. Also, the designers of most ODMSs have included basic data management capabilities, such as a query language. However, combining the two requires much more than providing all the required features in one database system. Satisfying both object-management and traditional business-application needs with one DBMS will be difficult for at least two reasons:

1. Such a DBMS must be able to change its own architecture—for example, to optimize for access characteristics of long-transaction design applications on workstations versus short-transaction on-line transaction processing on servers. Such changes have effects throughout the implementation of the database system.

2. ODMSs are substantially more complex for a user to understand than are relational database systems. Where this additional complexity is not needed, it will be very difficult to hide; the user will prefer a traditional relational database system.

Thus, there will probably be a separate market for ODMSs and relational DBMSs for some time to come. ODMSs will address a "niche" market defined by the applications in Chapter 2. There will be a need for gateways for information transfer between DBMSs focused on satisfying different mixes of object, data, and knowledge management. In a time frame of 5 to 10 years, however, you may see systems that satisfy both application categories.

Note that there are other possible scenarios as well. ODMS products may fail altogether; perhaps only modest extensions will be made to traditional DBMSs, and applications such as CAD and CASE may continue to use custom internal data managers. ODMS startups could displace large relational database vendors. There generally is no agreement on the future of this technology.

8.3.2 Research Topics

In studying object data management, we have uncovered a variety of areas where research is needed for future progress, in all the data models and database architectures we considered.

Database programming languages have brought up new issues that span both database and programming-language research. In the past, when database query languages were embedded in programming languages, research and development of programming and query languages could proceed independently. Now, programming languages may need new syntax to allow features such as virtual data fields or associative lookup of objects (queries). Perhaps new ways will be found to decouple the database and programming portions of a language by providing "hooks" in a compiler to add database language syntax and semantics.

The different data-access characteristics of the new applications we studied will motivate new research and performance studies for database architectures for efficient clustering, caching, and translation of data from its persistent representation. Swizzling, replication, and new access methods also need further study, and we do not yet understand how to implement object versions and configurations efficiently. Ultimately, research in database architectures will probably lead to a single database system that can be configured to support different access characteristics, as opposed to the current state of affairs, with object-oriented database programming languages optimized for checkout of data for long periods, and relational systems optimized for on-line transaction processing or decision-support users.

New end-user and application-development tools will be required to exploit the functionality of new ODMSs in all data models, supplanting the current 4GLs and tools in relational database systems and better exploiting the graphical and computational capabilities of new workstations. Application-development tools must be expanded to provide much more powerful schema-evolution tools to assist in transforming existing data and programs when complex schema transformations are performed, not just simple addition and removal of object properties.

New, more powerful query-language features will be developed, along with implementation techniques for their optimization. These query languages will support lists, arrays, recursion, embedded procedures, and other new capabilities not present in SQL and in similar relational languages.

New research in concurrency control is needed. Flexible version and configuration mechanisms are important; hopefully, a consensus will develop for the best approach to these problems. Time stamps and object-based concurrency semantics need more exploration. Performance models for transaction implementations in the context of versions, object-based concurrency semantics, and a mixture of optimistically and pessimistically locked data are needed in order to make the right implementation choices.

New work in knowledge management needs to be integrated with the object- and data-management capabilities we have covered in this book, combining expert systems with database systems. This will require extending query-language optimization into the domain of rule-based search, a complex optimization problem. Few researchers have expertise in both knowledge systems and database systems—interdisciplinary research is required.

The need to exploit distributed and parallel computers will motivate new work in distributed database and computation, and decomposition of computation into object agents communicating through method calls. Also, federated databases consisting of relational, object-oriented, and other databases will require more study.

8.4   SUMMARY

We have seen how object data management provides substantial new functionality and performance for engineering, scientific, and office applications, as well as for new generations of traditional business applications. The new ODMSs are sufficiently advanced over current DBMSs to constitute a revolution in database research and development.

Whether new object data management technology will prevail over current relational DBMSs through evolution of current relational DBMSs or through replacing them is still a matter of debate. Most likely, both of these things will happen: research and development of extensions to current relational systems will proceed, and new ODMSs will find research and product audiences as well. Eventually, the multiple avenues of research and development may come together, as ODMSs capable of supporting a wide range of applications are designed with the best features of relational, object-oriented, and other approaches.

One thing is clear: object data management has been a very popular and fast-moving area. A book such as this one is very difficult to write at this stage of development: the products, vendors, prototypes, and research in the area are tentative steps in a new direction, and it is not yet clear what the overall direction will turn out to be. Nevertheless, the consolidation and comparison of work in this area we have done is essential to further progress. You should continue your own reading and analysis of the work introduced in this book, as different approaches to object data management evolve.

Products and Prototypes

A.1 INTRODUCTION

In this appendix, we study in more detail the approaches to object data management defined at the beginning of Chapter 4 , by examining examples of the approaches and their implementation in research prototypes and commercial products.

A.1.1 Database Architecture, Model, and Approach

We defined four database architectures for object data management: extended database systems, database programming languages, database system generators, and object managers. The latter two have only a limited data model; in the database programming language architecture, only object-oriented systems have been built. Thus, only the first architecture—extended database systems—has been used with different data models.

Since we cover only approaches that have been taken in actual research prototypes and commercial products, we defined just five basic approaches to object data management: object-oriented database programming languages, extended relational database systems, extended functional database systems, database system generators, and object managers.

A.1.2   Using the Appendix

This appendix is organized into top-level sections covering each of the approaches to object data management:

- *Object-oriented database programming languages:* ODMSs constructed as an extension of an object-oriented programming language used to define and store the procedures associated with object types

- *Extended relational database systems:* ODMSs based on extensions of a relational query language, adding procedures and other capabilities

- *Extended functional database systems:* ODMSs based on extensions of functional query languages, adding procedures and other capabilities

- *Database system generators:* Systems allowing a user to build an ODMS tailored to particular needs, typically with a custom data model and database language

- *Object managers:* Packages that developed as extensions of existing file systems or virtual memory

For each approach, we present examples of systems that fit in that category. We also include brief summaries of each approach; however, the more detailed descriptions and comparisons of the merits of the different database architectures, data models, and features can be found in the text of this book. References to the systems we describe can be found in the System Bibliography. By looking up the same reference in the Annotated Bibliography, you will find a brief description of the system, other references on the system, and references to related systems.

A.2   OBJECT-ORIENTED DATABASE SYSTEMS

We consider object-oriented database programming languages first, since this approach has been so popular in research prototypes and products. Again, the proponents of these systems use the somewhat less precise term "object-oriented DBMS," so we will follow suit where there is no ambiguity. Object-oriented DBMSs differ from the others we cover in two important aspects: use of the object-oriented data model, and integration with existing programming languages.

A.2.1   Introduction

Most of the concepts covered in Chapter 4 were common to extended relational, functional, and object-oriented data models: objects, OIDs, inheritance, procedures stored in databases. However, the object-oriented DBMSs can be distinguished through their use of some of the more advanced features of object-oriented models, such as the notion of encapsulation of behavior with methods. The object-oriented model differs in syntactic representation of attributes from the functional approach, and differs in semantic representation of relationships from the relational approach.

All the systems we categorize as object-oriented DBMSs have the common thread of objects as the basic data structure, public methods (and, in some cases, attributes) associated with objects as the mechanism to operate on objects, private attributes (and, in some cases, procedures) associated with objects as the underlying representation, inheritance of attributes and procedures from supertypes, the ability to define dynamically new simple attribute types as well as new object types, and the representation of relationships by attributes.

The database programming language architecture used in these systems means that the data model used by the ODMS maps directly onto that used by the programming language, most frequently with C++ [Ellis and Stroustrup 1990]. The database system augments the programming language by providing persistence, concurrency control, a query language, and other DBMS capabilities. The application programmer may access database objects directly using the data-access operations in the programming language, or may perform associative lookups of objects using the query language. As we noted in Chapter 5, the implementation of object-oriented database programming languages is complicated by the desire to operate transparently within the existing programming-language environment.

A.2.2   Variations

Two important differences among the object-oriented DBMSs are their choice of query language and their choice of programming language.

The variations in the programming-language base for the object-oriented ODMSs are important, due to the close integration of the ODMS data model with the language. We cover a number of example systems, each with a different programming language base:

1. *ONTOS* is based on C++, and stores the binary code for methods associated with objects in C++ binaries rather than the database, linking the methods with object data when objects are accessed. ONTOS operations are invoked by calls on a run-time library, and persistent application classes inherit methods from an ONTOS-supplied persistent object class.

2. *ObjectStore* is also based on C++, with methods stored in binary files, but is syntactically integrated with the language, thus demanding preprocessing or compiler changes; persistence is orthogonal to type.

3. O_2 was originally based on its own object-oriented derivative of C, called CO_2. O_2 has also been integrated with other programming languages, including LISP, C++, and Basic. O_2 stores binary code in the database, rather than in files.

4. *GemStone* was designed based on a derivative of Smalltalk called OPAL. However, it has subsequently been integrated with C++ as well.

5. *ORION* was designed around extensions of Common LISP, as is the product followon, ITASCA. LISP methods are stored in the database, and are invoked by the system.

6. *ITASCA* is a commercial product based on extensions and improvement on the ORION system.

7. *Objectivity/DB* is designed based on C++, with code stored in programming language binaries.

8. *VERSANT* supports C++ and Smalltalk interfaces, with C++ code stored in programming language binaries.

9. *POET* is based on C++, with code stored in C++ binaries.

All of these systems provide a C library that can be used to invoke database operations as well. However, since C is not object-oriented, this library cannot provide the close programming-language integration that makes database programming languages interesting.

Variations in query languages are important as well as the programming-language differences, because the systems differ substantially. The large differences probably result from the fact that the object-oriented DBMSs started with programming languages for their model of data—a declarative query language was sometimes introduced after the initial implementation, and there is no standard or formal background for object-oriented query languages. The differences in query-language syntax, completeness, SQL compatibility, and treatment of encapsulation are noted in the summaries.

The product descriptions that follow were the latest available at the time of publication; contact the vendors for the latest information. Nearly all of these vendors plan to move to an ODMG-93 compliant implementation with time.

A.2.3   ONTOS

ONTOS [Ontos 1993], a product of Ontos of Billerica, Massachusetts, is one of several new commercial products based on making C++ into a database programming language. ONTOS replaced an earlier product from Ontologic, VBase, which used the object-oriented model with proprietary languages COP and TDL. The nonstandard languages and performance shortcomings of the VBase architecture led Ontos to introduce the new ONTOS product.

ONTOS provides a persistent object store for C++ programs. It is integrated with the language through the introduction of new, persistent classes, all defined as subclasses of **Entity**. Methods can be invoked through conventional compiled C++ calls, and ONTOS also provides facilities to invoke methods by interpretation of name strings at run time.

Objects exist in two states: *deactivated*, stored on the disk, and *activated*, as ordinary C++ objects in an application program. Objects are activated automatically when an application program first attempts to fetch them, and are deactivated, and written back to disk if changed, at the end of a transaction. There is overhead in activating an object, not only in converting to the in-memory representation, but also in swizzling any OIDs for objects already in memory into C++ pointers to the objects.

Concurrency in ONTOS is provided by conventional transactions. Locking may be performed at the granularity of individual objects, pages, or entire segments. ONTOS provides caching of objects (locked under transactions) on the client workstation in its client–server architecture.

ONTOS incorporates a variant of SQL as a query language, making attributes of objects visible to the query-language user. Like other object-oriented DBMSs, the ONTOS query language is not constrained by the encapsulation semantics of C++; it makes all the attributes of an object visible to the user.

Other ONTOS features include the following:

- *Inverse-attribute pairs:* ONTOS automatically maintains inverse OID-valued attributes, single-valued or multivalued, that represent a single relationship.

- *BLOBs:* Attribute values too large to fit in a single page are stored using a B-tree representation similar to EXODUS, which we describe in Section A.5.3.

- *Versions:* Multiple versions of objects are supported.

- *Administration tools:* ONTOS provides an interactive browser to examine and modify the data schema, commands to modify the physical data clustering, and a **Make** tool to keep application programs synchronized with schema changes.

A.2.4   ObjectStore

ObjectStore [Object Design 1993], a product of Object Design of Burlington, Massachusetts, is also a commercial product based on making C++ a database programming language. ObjectStore provides object identity, inverse attributes, multiple inheritance, large objects (BLOBs) accessed one page at a time, an interactive database browser, and an interactive schema designer. A library of collection types is provided, including sets, bags, and lists.

ObjectStore provides both DML and library interfaces to C++ and C. The DML interface uses extensions to the C++ language, whereas the library interface works entirely through a library of C++ functions. The comments in this subsection refer to both interfaces unless otherwise specified.

In the DML interface, queries are provided as a new kind of language expression. A query expression consists of a collection object (such as a list or a set) and a C++ Boolean-valued subexpression. The value of the query expression is the subset of elements of the collection for which the subexpression is true, with the value of the C++ **this** variable being set to each element. Queries are also supported by the library interface. The query expression is passed as a string to query construction, binding, and evaluation functions. The syntax of the quoted expression is exactly the same as in the DML. Index maintenance and optimization-strategy formulation are performed automatically by the system; the programmer specifies which data members, or, in general, paths to data members, should have indexes, and whether they are B-tree or hash-table indexes. Queries obey the rules of C++ encapsulation; that is, private members cannot be accessed unless the function doing the query is itself a member of the class.

The DML interface makes ObjectStore more closely integrated with the C++ programming language than other ODMS products. No special base class is used, as it is in ONTOS. Any C++ data, not only objects can be persistent. Accesses to data from objects use exactly the same C++ syntax, data structures, and memory layouts that would be used for ordinary C++ programs; "handle" objects and operations to the "activate" objects are not required. Object persistence is specified by a parameter to **new** operation, saying in which database an object should reside, and optionally specifying clustering information.

On the negative side, ObjectStore's convenient DML extensions to C++ requires Object Design to maintain its own C++ preprocessor or compiler changes to support the syntax, making a port to a new compiler a more difficult exercise. The compiler dependencies may also limit the use of customer-supplied compilers. On the other hand, any of the database programming languages supporting C++ object-layout conventions must also deal with compiler dependencies. Also, the programmer can always use the library interface, which, like other C++ ODMS products, does not require special C++ syntax.

Another interesting feature of ObjectStore is its implementation of interobject references using direct virtual-memory pointers—that is, 32-bit pointers are used directly as OIDs. ObjectStore reverts to longer, structured OIDs for special purposes, such as conveying object ids between processes or to external (non-ObjectStore) repositories.

Like the other database programming languages we cover, ObjectStore maintains a cache of objects in application memory. When the target of a reference is not in the client cache, the virtual-memory system signals a page fault, which the operating system reflects to ObjectStore. Subsequent accesses to the data run as fast as they would for ordinary C++ objects.

Short-term concurrency and recovery are provided by conventional transactions, implemented with page-level two-phase locking and a write-ahead log. Objects are cached on the client workstation, and can remain in the cache even from one transaction to another.

Long-term concurrency and recovery are based on a version-control mechanism. Configurations of objects can be checked out into private "workspaces," modified, and then checked back into shared workspaces when the changes are complete. Thus, the granularity is by object. Concurrency control can be either pessimistic or optimistic. When a configuration is checked out, other users can be forbidden from checking out the same configuration, or they can be allowed to check out an alternative version. If two users change the same data, rather than forcing a long transaction to abort, ObjectStore allows the users to operate simultaneously on parallel versions of the data, and later to merge their changes.

The version-control mechanism can be used for simply recording history, as well as for long transactions.

A.2.5 O_2

The O_2 object-oriented DBMS, a research prototype [Bancilhon et al 1991] that has been transformed into a commercial product, was developed by the Altair research consortium in France from 1986 to 1990. Since 1991, it has been marketed and developed by O_2 Technology in Versailles, France. O_2 is implemented in C++, with some parts developed in O_2 Technology's O_2C language. It is currently available on SUN, HP, IBM, BULL, and DEC Unix platforms.

O_2 consists of a database engine, O_2Engine, on which three layers of tools are available:

1. Language interfaces: C and C++, a 4GL, O_2C, an object query language, O_2SQL, and a low level application programming interface, O_2API.
2. GUI tools: a GUI generator, O_2Look, and a graph manipulation package, O_2Graph.
3. Environment tools: a graphical programming environment, O_2Tools, and a set of reusable components, O_2Kit.

We begin by discussing the O_2Engine; then we proceed to these three layers of tools on top of the database engine.

O_2Engine fulfills the functions of a database engine: it supports distribution and has a client/server architecture, distinguishes between physical and logical object management, and provides concurrency and recovery services, indices, query optimization, data placement and clustering, and method storage, manipulation and execution. It is composed of three main layers:

- The upper layer of the system is the *Schema Manager*. It is responsible for monitoring the creation, retrieval, update and deletion of classes, methods and global names. It is also responsible for enforcing the semantics of inheritance and for checking the consistency of a schema.

- The *Object Manager* is the mid layer. It handles objects with identity and passes messages to objects. It supports the reachability model of persistence, and implements indexes and clustering strategies based on complex objects and inheritance.

- The innermost layer, O_2Store, an extension of WiSS [Chou et al 1985] is the *Disk Manager*. O_2Store provides record-structured sequential files, B-tree index files and long data items. All these structures are mapped into pages, the basic persistence unit. O_2Store provides full control of the physical location of pages on disk. Locking is used for concurrency control, and a write-ahead log (WAL) technique is used for rollbacks and recovery. Among the extensions provided to the original WiSS package are (a) client/server split (see below), (b) rollbacks and crash recovery, and (c) multi-thread support for the server.

The client/server architecture is a "page server." The client/server split is performed at the O_2Store Level, which deals with pages. O_2Store is split into a client process and a server process in the following way: the server process consists of the I/O levels and the page-cache level, concurrency control and recovery services. Concurrency control is handled by a hierarchical, two-phase locking protocol on pages and files. Recovery is provided by the WAL protocol.

The server deals with multiple threads of execution, one for each client request, and these threads are non-blocking with respect to I/O, as these operations are handled by dedicated I/O processes. In addition, parallel disk I/O can be performed on different volumes by different I/O processes. The client process consists of a page-cache level plus all the higher object management levels, including index management and the query optimizer. Some transaction management occurs also on the client.

The log volume is a per-object redo log; that is, it describes the effects of an operation on a particular object after applying the operation (the client process generates redo log records as the transaction progresses). The database pages are not forced to disk at commit time, only the log is forced. No disk page has to be undone if the transaction rollbacks or if there is a system crash. This is because in the (rare) case in which such a ("dirty") page P would be eligible for replacement both at the client and the server process, instead of writing P to disk, it is written into a temporary shadow page P'. If the transaction aborts, the temporary shadow page is discarded. If the transaction commits, page P' must be read from disk and its contents interpreted as the contents of page P. This technique allows the system to avoid computing undo log records for all kind of transactions, with the hope that only very few transactions will need to use this temporary shadow mechanism.

However, log records are not all "redo-only", because operations on volumes, files, and pages (such as file creation and page allocation), need to have an undo log record. These log records are generated on behalf of the transaction that allocated these resources over the server process.

Record identifiers are used as (persistent) identifiers for objects. On disk, records storing objects refer to each other by physical identifier, that is, identifiers reflecting disk locations. The O_2Store 64-bit record identifiers are used directly. The record identifiers contain a volume identifier (2 bytes), a page identifier within a volume (4 bytes), and a slot-number (2 bytes) which indirectly addresses a record within a page.

In memory, O_2Engine uses a two-level addressing mechanism: the client modules of O_2Engine are given *handles* to identify objects. Each handle denotes a distinct record containing an object. Handles are only valid within a transaction. They are a uniform means to reference persistent or temporary objects. This uniformity allows a temporary record storing an object to get promoted to persistent space at commit time or at some point in between (depending on whether clustering information exists for this object or not). If early promotion occurs, the persistent identifier is generated and stored within the (parent) record that transmitted persistence to the promoted record. Otherwise, the handle is stored within the parent record, and replaced with its persistent identifier later.

As cluster trees, indexes represent physical schema information attached to a database. Indexes may efficiently support retrieval from a collection of those members meeting a predefined selection criteria. The O_2Query optimizer recognizes the existence of indexes and uses them to optimize queries.

Indexes may be defined on named collections on a composition path that may traverse tuples or collections. The system allows, however, indexing a collection of objects on a path ending at an object-valued field (for an index on object identity). Because of the no-sharing semantics of object values, index maintenance in O_2Engine does not require all the apparatus that appears in indexing mechanisms using composition paths traversing objects. In fact, there is no need to index on segments of the path or to keep back pointers up the path, because there is no sharing of subpaths.

The O_2 data model supports complex objects: *atomic objects* such as integer, real, boolean, strings and bits (for large objects), and *object constructors* such as tuple, sets and bags, and insertable array. It offers persistence by reachability: to become persistent in a database, an object must be attached directly or transitively to a persistent "root". These roots are declared in a schema by giving a name to them. From a data manipulation point of view persistence is transparent.

O_2 provides encapsulation at three levels: class, schema, and database.

- The first form, class encapsulation, is classical in object-oriented models.

- The second form extends this notion to a set of classes, called a *schema*. A schema may *export* some classes and thus allows other schemas to reuse (import) them.

- The last form provides encapsulation of a *database* itself, the actual data. An application running on a particular database may access another database by invoking a method which will run against this "remote" database.

The C++ interface allows direct development of applications in C++ or the reuse of existing C++ applications. It enhances a standard C++ environment by providing 4 new features:

- *Persistent pointers* allow transparent access to any persistent object. A persistent pointer is predefined as a template that implements the syntax and behavior of a standard C++ pointer.

- *Generic collections* offer management of persistent or transient collections: lists, sets, bags, and arrays.

- *Persistence roots* are named objects to which a transient C++ object may be attached directly or transitively and then become persistent.

- *Database support* includes transactions, indexing, embedded O_2SQL, and C++ object editing through O_2Look.

The C++ classes get the persistence property after being parsed by an O_2 utility which imports them into an O_2 schema. A Makefile is automatically generated which enables incremental compilation of C++ application.

O_2C is O_2's 4th generation language. The O_2 data types and operators are basic features of this language which is a superset of the C programming language and whose compiler generates standard C code. O_2C includes the query language and the O_2Look primitives. O_2C handles directly memory management, supports persistence by reachability, provides high level primitives to manipulate the structured data types of the data model. It is smoothly integrated with O_2SQL and with the GUI tool O_2Look. It allows the incremental compilation of applications.

O_2SQL is an SQL-like query language extended to deal with complex objects. It may be used as an *ad hoc* interactive query language or as a function callable from C, C++, or O_2C.

All O_2 data types and operators, including methods, are allowed inside a query.

O_2SQL has primitives to manipulate every object constructor. It uses select-from-where clauses to manipulate collections. It generalizes the SQL approach to complex objects and allows the creation of arbitrarily complex structures in a natural manner.

O_2Look is a Motif toolkit extension designed to meet the O_2 programmer requirements in terms of end-user interaction. O_2Look addresses two problems:

- It allows the programmer to create simple user interfaces quickly by means of predefined generic dialogue components or *widgets*. This is done without drawing or programming.

- It allows the programmer to customize these predefined widgets to match the requirements of specific applications. This is usually not taken into account in traditional database programming environments.

Any O_2 object can be presented and edited dynamically without requiring any programming. O_2Look consists of an extensible set of widgets tailored to graphic and interactive manipulation of data.

O_2Tools is a graphical programming environment supporting the development of O_2 applications. It allows the programmer to browse, edit, and query the data and the schema; and to edit, test, and debug methods and programs. It also provides tools to simplify the programmer's work.

Finally, O_2Tools contains a toolbox, O_2Kit, of predefined classes and objects which the programmer can use as software components. O_2Tools can be also used by the casual user who wants to interact with the database. This novice user can browse, query, and edit both the database and the schema.

A.2.6   GemStone

GemStone [Maier and Stein 1987, Servio 1993] is a product of Servio Corporation of San Jose, California and Beaverton, Oregon. GemStone was one of the first object-oriented DBMS products, along with VBase from Ontologic and GBase from Object Databases.

GemStone originally evolved in an effort to make the Smalltalk programming language and system into a DBMS. The query and programming language for the system, OPAL, is very close to Smalltalk-80. Like O_2, GemStone provides its own programming-language implementation; it does not operate with an existing Smalltalk compiler or interpreter.

GemStone has subsequently been integrated with C++; it is the first database programming language product with close integration with two languages. GemStone provides a mapping between C++ object data structures and OPAL data structures stored in the database, and transparently fetches and translates objects when a C++ application references them. However, only OPAL methods are stored in the database; C++ methods are stored and invoked through the existing programming-language mechanisms.

The architecture of the GemStone system includes two processes, called *Gem* and *Stone*. The Stone process is the data manager, providing disk I/O, concurrency control, authorization, transactions, and recovery services. The Stone process typically resides on the server machine, accessing the disk through the operating-system calls. This architecture is similar to those of the other object-oriented database programming languages.

The Gem process provides compilation of OPAL programs, user authorization, and a predefined set of OPAL classes and methods for use by the user program. The Gem process may reside on the server or on a client workstation. Thus, there is interprocess communication, possibly over a network, among the user program, the Gem process, the Stone process, and the operating system, in that order. The Gem process may fetch, lock, and cache objects, pages, or whole segments of data at a time over a network, so it can be optimized to application needs.

Concurrency control in GemStone may be performed by either optimistic or pessimistic methods. In the pessimistic scheme, a traditional transaction implementation is used, as described in Chapter 3. In the optimistic scheme, a shadow copy of the user workspace is taken at the start of a transaction. When the client requests transaction commit, a check is made for conflicts with other transactions that have committed since the transaction began. If any data read or written by the transaction have been modified by another transaction, the shadow copy is thrown away and GemStone informs the client that the transaction is being aborted. Otherwise, the shadow copy replaces the original.

OPAL does not provide a global query language, but does provide associative access to objects in a single collection, according to their attribute values. This associative lookup is performed with a **select** command:

```
Chapter select: { aChap | aChap.number = 1 }
```

So that encapsulation will not be violated, objects may be associatively retrieved only within a method that has access to the attributes (however, this is true only when OPAL is used; the C procedure-call interface can violate this rule). B-tree indexes may be created on attributes to allow efficient associative access on attributes; the **select** operation transparently utilizes these B-trees when they are present, resorting to sequential search of the collection otherwise. Note that GemStone does not support the level of data independence of the relational model with B-trees—if no B-tree exists, and the programmer does not explicitly enter objects in a collection in the "create" procedure for a type, then there is no way to enumerate all of the objects of a type.

Although only a single type of object may be queried, the equivalent of relational joins between types can be performed in cases where a relationship is defined explicitly as a reference in the object type definition. For example, the following query would require a join between chapters and documents in a relational query language:

```
Chapter select: {aChap | aChap.doc.title = "Databases"}
```

Data may also be fetched and stored from GemStone using procedure calls from C or Pascal application programs. In the case of Smalltalk programs, however, a more closely integrated interface has been implemented, automatically coercing Smalltalk objects into GemStone objects when appropriate. Persistent types can be defined that are identical to any type existing in a Smalltalk program. In addition, OPAL is similar enough to Smalltalk that Smalltalk programs can typically be made to run in the OPAL environment with few changes (which is why GemStone is classified as a database programming language).

Other GemStone features include these:

- *Relational gateway:* GemStone provides a gateway to fetch data from SYBASE.
- *BLOBs:* A portion of large persistent objects may be paged in at a time.
- *Multiple name spaces:* Object type names as well as attribute and method names are interpreted in context.
- *Garbage collection:* As in Smalltalk, objects are not deleted explicitly; an object is deleted automatically when it is no longer reachable through any global variables. Surrogate OIDs are used for objects.
- *Schema evolution:* Simple changes may be made to a class definition with automatic conversion of existing class instances.
- *User interfaces:* Browsing, forms, schema design, and programming tools have also been developed for GemStone.

In addition to GemStone, Servio sells Geode, a powerful graphical application construction based on plugging together object-oriented components.

A.2.7   ORION

ORION is an object-oriented ODMS built at MCC in Austin, Texas. A commercial product version of ORION is being marketed as ITASCA, from Itasca Systems of Minneapolis, Minnesota. Our comments about ORION generally apply to ITASCA as well. ITASCA is described in the next section.

ORION incorporates object identifiers, multiple inheritance, composite objects, versions, indexing, queries, transactions, distributed databases, dynamic schema evolution, and access authorization. It is implemented in LISP. Several applications have been built on ORION at MCC, so ORION has seen some use even though it was constructed as a research prototype. More than one version of the ORION system was built; we cover the one described in [Kim et al 1988].

The version of ORION in [Kim et al 1988] extends LISP with object-oriented capabilities, with database calls for navigational or query access, and for definition of data types. Like GemStone, the ORION query model currently implemented allows queries on only one object type at a time [Banerji 1988]; that is, joins may be performed only in cases where a "join" already exists in the schema in the form of a reference from the queried object type, as described earlier.

Object identifiers in ORION differ from those in most other systems in that they incorporate both the object type and an instance identifier, and use an extensible hashing technique to map to physical addresses. Object identifiers are not reused when an object is deleted; the instance identifier number is monotonically increasing. The tradeoffs in this approach were discussed in Section 5.2.2.

ORION does not incorporate the concept of *inverse attributes* as described in Chapter 4, except for composite objects. Reference attributes are unidirectional, and a list of references to an object is not maintained automatically. However, invalid references are recognized when an attempt is made to use them, since object identifiers are not reused, so referential integrity is maintained. Also, ORION allows the programmer to redefine the class methods that create objects and assign attribute values, so referential integrity can be added on a case-by-case basis. Unless auxiliary data structures are maintained in this way, there is no efficient way for the user to locate references—for example, all the **Chapters** for a **Document** in our example database.

In addition to object access through references, ORION implements B-tree indexes, and provides a flexible object-clustering technique allowing the user to give hints as to where to place an object (with other objects of the same type, or with other objects that reference it, for example). The B-trees are *class hierarchy* indexes; that is, a single B-tree is constructed for an attribute, even if the attribute is inherited by many subtypes (see Section 5.7.3).

ORION implements versionable objects and references using time stamps. ORION time stamps can be used as a notification mechanism, allowing arbitrary code to be invoked when new versions of data are created.

ORION allows BLOBs, like most other object-oriented database systems, but provides an additional capability for "multimedia" values such as images, audio, or text: the values may be accessed and manipulated in either one or two dimensions.

An area where ORION has put more emphasis than other systems is distributed databases. ORION implements distributed two-phase commit, and can process queries that span databases. Because ORION's OID contains the object type ID in the upper-order bits, OID generation is provided by a separate OID generator for each type, and can be distributed on a network.

Another area that ORION has emphasized more than have other systems is schema evolution. [Kim 1988] discusses *schema versioning,* a technique to allow multiple versions of the schema to be maintained simultaneously. Objects are identified with the version of the schema with which they are currently constructed. A mapping can be maintained from the old schema to the new, and an object can be converted automatically to the new schema format at the time it is accessed, rather than immediately on schema update. At the time of this writing, however, schema versioning has not yet been implemented in ORION or ITASCA.

A.2.8   ITASCA

ITASCA, a product of Itasca Systems, Inc. of Minneapolis, Minnesota, is a commercial ODMS based upon the ORION prototypes developed at MCC in Austin, Texas. Development of ORION began at MCC in 1985 and prototypes were delivered in three phases through 1989. The first release of ORION was a stand-alone system. The second release featured a single-server, multiple-client (remote access) architecture. The third release featured a multiple-server, multiple-client (distributed database) architecture. ITASCA is based upon this final release of ORION and has been shipping since August 1990.

ITASCA incorporates traditional database features such as transactions, concurrency control, clustering, indexing, queries, and recovery. It also supports object system features like object identifiers, multiple inheritance, polymorphism, data abstraction, and encapsulation. Advanced features of ITASCA include distributed databases, data migration, shared and private databases, dynamic schema evolution, multimedia support, access authorization, composite objects, versions, and change notification. ITASCA has application programming interfaces for C++, C, CLOS, Lisp, and Ada. ITASCA stores objects in a neutral format so that objects may be shared among applications written in different languages.

The distributed database architecture of ITASCA is based upon multiple servers and multiple clients. The object identifier contains the instance id, the type id, and the location at which the object is created. Because objects may be migrated from one server to another, the system maintains an object directory. The combination of the object identifier and the object directory allows for transparent access to data anywhere in the distribution—it is not necessary to know where an object physically resides in order to access it.

ITASCA supports shared and private databases. The shared database provides a global repository for objects that are shared among all users and applications. Private databases provide personal workspaces for individuals or groups of individuals. The shared database spans across all servers in a distribution, whereas private databases are local to a given server. ITASCA provides checkin and checkout facilities to move objects between private databases and the shared database.

An area on which ITASCA places a great deal of emphasis is dynamic schema evolution. The system allows users to dynamically modify the schema without forcing them to offload/reload the data or to shutdown and recompile applications. The modifications are allowed anywhere in the inheritance hierarchy and encompass the taxonomy of schema changes found in Section 4.6.6.

Multimedia data like images, video, sound, and text are supported by a subsystem called the Long Data Manager. The Long Data Manager stores and manages multimedia data (BLOBs) as objects, just as it does "traditional" data. As such, multimedia data can easily be associated with other data through object references.

Selected data access may be restricted from specific users by using the ITASCA authorization system. The authorization system is based upon roles that users assume. Access for users of a given role can be restricted to an entire private database, a class definition, all instances of a given class, a single instance, or a single attribute value of a single instance. Access authorization can be set up in a positive fashion (granting access privileges) and in a negative fashion (restricting access privileges).

ITASCA supports the notion of composite objects. By default, reference attributes are unidirectional, but when an attribute is defined as a composite (containment) reference, an inverse attribute is automatically maintained. Through the composite object support, a user can specify whether a component object is dependent upon the existence of the composite object and whether a component object is exclusive to a given composite object.

ITASCA provides the fundamentals for a configuration management system through support for versioned objects and change notification. Version trees may be built by creating new versions and alternative versions of existing objects. The system associates time stamps with each versioned object. Objects and applications may reference a specific version in a version tree through a generic reference. The generic reference can then be changed to a different version within the version tree, eliminating the need to modify all referencing objects and applications. Change notification is supported through passive and active mechanisms. When an object is modified, all users responsible for referencing objects are notified of the change. Passive change notification is flag-based. When an object is changed, a flag is raised indicating potential inconsistency. A user may then query the database for raised flags. In contrast, active change notification is message-based. When an object is changed, a method is executed to carry out a programmatic resolution to the change. The programmatic resolution can be customized by the user.

ITASCA's query language may be executed interactively or it may be embedded within a program. The query functions accept a class target and a query expression. Several operations are provided for use within the query expression, but user-defined functions are allowed as well. This allows the query language to be extended by a user. In addition, the query expression may be constructed dynamically. The scope of a query may be restricted to objects within the shared database, a single private database, or a combination of both. To improve query performance, ITASCA implements class hierarchy B-tree indexes and executes queries in parallel across multiple servers. In addition, ITASCA provides a flexible object-clustering technique allowing the user to give hints as to where to place an object (e.g., with other objects of the same type, or with other objects that reference it).

ITASCA supports both short- and long-duration transactions. Because of the distributed server architecture, the system follows a two-phase commit protocol. Object-level locking is supported, with either optimistic or pessimistic concurrency control as of Release 2.3.

Based upon "undo" logging techniques, ITASCA provides automated recovery from application failure or CPU failure. It also supports disk-mirroring to protect against media failure.

Many of the kernel-level operations in ITASCA are defined as system methods. As such, these methods may be refined for customization to a particular installation. Examples of the kernel-level methods include make-object, checkin, checkout, make-version, delete-object, and send-notification.

The ITASCA object model supports multiple inheritance and models classes as objects. Furthermore, ITASCA stores and executes methods in the database, but it additionally allows methods to reside and execute in the application as well. Both database methods and application methods can be executed on objects in the database.

Applications written in C++, C, CLOS, Lisp, and Ada may communicate directly with ITASCA through their respective application programming interfaces. ITASCA stores and manages objects in a neutral format, yet presents the objects to an application in the format of its native language. This allows applications written in various languages to share objects. For example, a C++ application may create some objects and store them in ITASCA. A CLOS application may then access those objects and modify them.

A.2.9   Objectivity/DB

Objectivity/DB [Objectivity 1993], a product of Objectivity, Inc. of Menlo Park, California, provides an integrated C++ programming interface with an emphasis on the DBMS engine for robustness and scalability. It supports a distributed client-server, rather than central-server, architecture, with all operations working transparently over a mixture of multiple databases, schemas, users, and computers, and over heterogeneous hardware, operating systems, and networks. The language interface includes a C++ class library interface, soon to be based on ODMG-93; a preprocessor that allows native pointer-based C++ programming with the same integrity advantages of the DBMS engine; a C function library; and SQL++, supporting complete ANSI SQL and many object SQL3 extensions. A large suite of administrative and GUI tools provide both an interactive and programmatic interface, and a messaging backplane allows third party tools integration at four different levels.

Objectivity/DB uses object *handles* for references to objects in an application program, thus providing a useful level of indirection. Transparent to the user, this indirection requires an extra test and pointer dereference, or a couple of cycles, which should not be measurable in most applications. However, it ensures integrity of all references, even across transaction boundaries, and it provides object level granularity for the object manager, allowing it to move, cluster, and swap objects as necessary, one of the keys required for scalability in objects and users. In addition, the use of handles allows object-level granularity for current features, such as heterogeneity and versioning, and future extensions, such as object-level security.

A higher-level Object Definition Language (ODL) is provided that allows declaration of modeling concepts such as bi-directional associations (relationships based on inverse attributes), behavior of associations between objects as they version (move, copy drop), and propagation of methods across associations. These then result in automatically generated methods and declarations for both C++ and C. ODMG ODL and most front-end design systems are also supported. The standard C++ API allows application programmers to work with any standard compilers and debuggers, with no extra pre-processors, providing object-oriented DBMS capabilities via overloading C++ operators (new, ->, etc.), and declarations via provided classes (for references, etc.). An optional C++ interface allows pure, native C++ use, including pointers, but implements them through the above-described architecture for safety and scalability.

A strong point of Objectivity/DB is its distributed client/server architecture that provides a single logical view over multiple databases on heterogeneous machines. The user sees a logical view of objects connected to objects and need not worry that one object is in a database on a Sun workstation, while another may be in a database under Windows or VMS. All operations work transparently across this environment, including atomic transactions with two-phase commit, propagating methods, and versioning. Objects may be moved between databases and platforms without affecting working applications or requiring changes to the applications. Multiple schemas may be created, without affecting other users or databases, and may be used simultaneously with shared schemas, allowing local groups to define their own models but still connect to other groups. Databases may be detached from this shared environment (federated database) and used on portable devices, reconnected or moved to a different (compatible) environment, or distributed as parts or image libraries.

Gateways to relational DBMSs are provided via third-party integration with Persistence (Section A.3.5), and more generally to any foreign data store, as long as the user installs the appropriate access methods, extending the single-logical-view to include read/write access to arbitrary foreign data stores. Autonomous work groups on separate local area networks may share in this single logical view, with automatic replication of system data and catalogues to support wider-area networks.

The on-demand object manager directly and automatically manages object access and buffering, rather than relying on system facilities such as virtual memory or manual get/put calls. Mechanisms used include multiple buffer pools locally and remotely, B-trees, hashing, scoped names, keys, and iterators, with distributed catalogues for schemas and databases. Short transactions are based on traditional (transient) locks, owned by the process, and group together an arbitrary set of operations. Long transactions are based on persistent locks, owned by the user, and provide the same arbitrary grouping. Default concurrency is two-phase locking and serialization, but extensions available include MROW, or multiple-readers concurrent with one-writer, and allow users to lock with or without wait or with timed waits, to implement more sophisticated mechanisms.

Objects may be modeled using C++ structures augmented by classes provided, including strings, dictionaries, and relationship management, as well as some particular domain libraries. A simple object is a C++ class (or C structure) with associated access methods. A complex object may include multiple **varrays**, each being a dynamically varying sized array of arbitrary structure. A composite object is any directed graph of related objects that acts as a single object, both structurally and behaviorally, via propagation of behaviors to component objects. Any number of composite objects may be contained in composite objects, and a single object may participate in any number of composites. The relationship mechanism supports uni- and bi-directional relationships, one-to-one, one-to-many, and many-to-many. Versioning is supported at object granularity, may be turned on or off at any time for each object, may be restricted to linear or allow branching with multiple writers. References to versioned objects may be to a specific version or to the default version, which may be separately specified by a method and may allow multiple defaults. Schema and object evolution are supported via versioning of the type-defining objects. Each time a type definition is changed, its defining object is versioned, allowing arbitrary changes. Objects may then be instances of the old or new type version. Object evolution or upgrading to the new type version is supported by the user writing conversion methods which are installed and invoked by the system.

Complete ANSI SQL is supported in the SQL++ product. Predicate syntax may be either C++ or SQL. The ODBC and SQL Access Group protocols are supported. Queries may be invoked programmatically or interactively, with ad hoc support. Access to object features is available via methods and traversal of relationships.

Several dozen administrative and developer tools are provided by Objectivity, each with both an interactive and programmatic interface. These include GUI object and type browsers, query browsers, report generator, tools to examine and force short and long locks, to move objects and databases, and so on. On-line incremental backup provides a consistent network-wide snapshot, including referential integrity across all databases, and runs incremental and full database backups with no need to quiesce the databases or the active applications. All tools are built around a messaging backplane, which supports four levels of integration with user and third-party tools. Integrated products include HP SoftBench (full operational level), CenterLine's Object Center (tool level), Persistence RDBMS gateway, PTech and ProtoSoft Design and Analysis (language level), and XVT and UIM/X (compatibility level).

Objectivity/DB is also resold by Digital Equipment Corporation as DEC Object/DB. Objectivity/DB platform support currently includes all Sun, all DEC, HP/9000 series, IBM RS/6000, NCR 3300, SGI, Windows 3.1, and Windows NT.

A.2.10   VERSANT

The VERSANT object-oriented DBMS is a product of Versant Object Technology of Menlo Park, California. Like GemStone, VERSANT provides database programming language interfaces to both C++ and Smalltalk. VERSANT also offers a C library interface. VERSANT is designed for multi-user applications in distributed database environments.

VERSANT is built with a logical object-based architecture, where each object is automatically assigned a surrogate OID (Section 5.2.1), which VERSANT calls a logical object identifier (LOID). Because LOIDs are independent of physical disk location, VERSANT is able to move objects internally on disk to support operations like lazy-evaluation schema evolution and dynamic reclamation of disk space.

VERSANT's distributed database capabilities stem from the fact that VERSANT LOIDs are also independent of the node on which an object is stored. Thus, VERSANT provides transparent cross-node inter-object references and transparent navigation across objects in physically distributed databases. VERSANT also supports object migration across nodes, where objects can be physically relocated from one computer to another for load balancing or for locality of reference in distributed databases. VERSANT automatically detects distributed transactions and uses the two-phase commit protocol to provide transaction integrity.

VERSANT uses an *object server* architecture; that is, the granularity of transfer in their client/server architecture is objects, as in ITASCA. Like other object-oriented DBMSs, VERSANT maintains a cache of recently used objects in the client application's virtual memory. VERSANT also maintains a page cache within its server. Unlike some competitors, VERSANT processes queries on the server using a built-in **select()** method. This reduces network traffic by filtering data prior to transmitting it over the network.

Short-term concurrency and recovery are provided with conventional transactions, implemented with object-level, two-phase locking, and both physical and logical logging. Objects may be cached across transactions.

Long-term concurrency and recovery are provided by object-level check-in, check-out, and versioning facilities. Like ITASCA, check-out operations in VERSANT physically move objects to detachable, private databases, and require no active server connection to manipulate data. This provides support for portable computers and provides some insulation from network and server failures.

In addition to its server-based **select()** method, VERSANT provides an Object SQL interface that supports the four basic SQL DML operations: select, update, insert, and delete. This interface provides either ad hoc or programmatic access, and supports more complex operations such as navigational queries.

Because VERSANT is designed for multiple programming languages, it supports its own object model which includes features of C++ such as multiple inheritance, and features of Smalltalk such as dynamic class creation. VERSANT requires neither a proprietary C++ compiler nor pre-processor because VERSANT's interface is implemented entirely in an ANSI-standard C++ class library. The VERSANT Smalltalk interface uses standard Smalltalk and thus does require use of a server-side interpreter to access data.

VERSANT also includes an interactive DBA utility (vutil) and an integrated application development toolset including a GUI builder (VERSANT Screen) and a graphical report writer (VERSANT Report).

A.2.11   POET

POET [Poet Software 1993] is a product of Poet Software of Hamburg, Germany (U.S.A. offices are in Santa Clara, California). POET is the final object-oriented DBMS we consider, and bears resemblance to the last several we have discussed. POET is based on C++. It runs on PC, Macintosh, and UNIX platforms. A client can access a database stored on any platform. A single-user version is available in addition to the client/server version.

POET allows C++ objects or structures to be made persistent by prefixing the declaration with the keyword **persistent**. POET's pre-processor produces C++ compiler input from these declarations. POET supports C++ encapsulation, object identity, inheritance, and polymorphism. It includes a library of extensions to C++, including predefined types such as dates and BLOBs, and parameterized types for sets.

Database references are automatically swizzzled into C++ pointers when objects are fetched, and vice versa when they are stored. References to deleted objects are trapped, and generate an error.

POET automatically maintains the extent of each persistent class. The extent of a class **Foo** is named **FooAllSet**. For each class **Foo**, POET also provides a **FooQuery** class used to construct queries on the class extent. The result of a query is a set. POET supports sorting and the use of indexes for query processing.

Like most of the other systems we discussed, POET supports locking and transactions, including nested transactions. POET also supports a novel alternative to conventional concurrency control: event notification. A client can call a **Watch** method on an object or set of objects to request that POET notify the client when someone performs specified operations (such as reading or writing) on the objects.

A.2.12   Other Systems

Other object-oriented DBMSs include GBase [Object Databases 1990] and STATICE [Symbolics 1987]. Like the other systems just described, these products merge object-oriented programming-language concepts of object types, methods, encapsulation, and object references with database systems concepts such as persistence, transactions, and query languages. As we have seen, some are better integrated with existing programming languages than are others.

A.2.13   Summary

Object-oriented DBMSs provide database capabilities in an existing programming language. The ones that we covered—O_2, ObjectStore, ONTOS, GemStone, ORION, ITASCA, Objectivity/DB, and VERSANT—provide a query language, object types with inheritance, caching of objects in main memory, transaction management, and remote database access. O_2, VERSANT, and GemStone provide access to the database from more than one programming language.

Object-oriented DBMSs, particularly those based on C++, have been a popular approach to object data management—the number of products using this approach attests to the fact that many people believe this is a promising direction.

A.3   EXTENDED RELATIONAL DATABASE SYSTEMS

Relational database systems are simple, are well understood, and are popular in both the research and product worlds. Therefore, a logical starting point to satisfy new database applications is through extensions to relational systems.

A.3.1   Introduction

The most important feature of extended relational systems is that they use an extension of a relational query language to fetch and manipulate data. Use of a relational query language allows well-understood techniques for query optimization to be applied to an implementation of the language. A relational query can be transformed algebraically into semantically equivalent forms relatively simply, unlike procedures in a programming language.

In extended relational systems, programming capability is generally embedded inside the query language. The query language may be extended to provide control constructs with all the capability of a programming language, and these constructs may be used in defining actions to be taken when a field is fetched or modified. Alternatively, a "trap door" may be provided in the query language to allow calls to procedures written in a conventional programming language. Note that, in either case, the query processor does not optimize across the boundary between the query language and the programming language; it operates on only the query-language portion.

We cover five extended relational DBMSs: POSTGRES, Montage, Starburst, UniSQL, and Persistence. Of these, Starburst is perhaps closest to a straight relational model. UniSQL and Persistence both include database programming language capabilities that bridge some of the gap between extended relational DBMSs and the object-oriented DBMS we covered in the previous section. At the end of this section, we examine briefly some other variations on the extended relational approach.

A.3.2   POSTGRES

The most powerful extended relational database system currently implemented is probably POSTGRES [Stonebraker et al 1986-1990], from the University of California at Berkeley. POSTGRES is named as a follow-on to the Berkeley work on INGRES a decade earlier. POSTGRES focuses on providing an extended data model and execution engine, a powerful rules system, and a novel "time travel" capability. The POSTGRES data model provides objects, OIDs, composite objects, multiple inheritance, versions, historical data, procedures, and an extended relational query language. POSTGRES capabilities are accessed through the query language, POSTQUEL, which is a substantial superset of the INGRES query language, QUEL. POSTGRES has been under construction since 1986; the following discussion is based on their Version 5.

POSTGRES provides OIDs in the form of a system-defined attribute in every relation. The OID for a tuple-valued variable **T** is referenced as **T.OID**. The OID field may be read but not updated by the user.

Attributes of relations in POSTGRES may take on all the conventional simple attribute types such as strings and integers, and may also take on values from user-defined abstract data types (ADTs). In addition, POSTGRES supports composite attributes, whose values are sets of zero or more tuples from another table. Furthermore, POSTGRES supports attributes which are arrays of base types. The following relation illustrates these kinds of attributes:

```
create EMP (name = c12, age = int4, location = point,
   salary = int4[12], manager = EMP, co_workers = EMP)
```

Here, **name** is a character string; **age** is an integer; **location** is a user-defined base type, **point**, holding the geographic position of the employee's home; **salary** is an array of 12 integers, one for each month in the year; **manager** is a tuple of type **EMP**; and **co_workers** is a set of tuples of type **EMP**. The last two fields are *composite* types, while the first three are *base* types. When a relation is constructed, POSTGRES automatically defines a composite type of the same name, which may be used as the type of an attribute in any relation. Although **manager** and **co_workers** are currently the same type the POSTGRES implementors expect to distinguish the type set-of-tuples from the type singleton-tuple at a later time.

POSTGRES supports user-defined functions (procedures) written either in the query language POSTQUEL or in C. There are four classes of functions, as follows:

1.   Functions which accept arguments of a base type and return a base type

   For example, the user could implement a function **elderly** in C, which accepts two arguments of type character string and integer, respectively and returns a boolean. After this function is **registered** with POSTGRES, the user can use the function in a POSTQUEL command, e.g., `retrieve (EMP.name) where elderly (EMP.name, EMP.age)`. During execution, the object code for `elderly` is identified from the system catalogs, dynamically loaded, and called by the execution engine. Hence, this (and other extensions) can be be performed without quiescing a running system.

2. Functions which accept an argument of type tuple and return a base type

For example, the user could implement a function, `date_of_birth` as:

```
define function date_of_birth (
 language="postquel", returntype=int4) arg is (EMP)
 as "retrieve (date_of_birth = 1993 - $.age)
 where EMP.name = $.name".
```

Here, the argument to the function is a tuple of type `EMP`, and specific fields in the argument appear in the function body (POSTQUEL statement) as parameters. The return is an integer computed from the target list of the retrieve command. There are two interpretations for this `date_of_birth` function:

a. It can be thought of as a function, or a *method*, defined for each tuple of `EMP` and referenced using function-style notation: `retrieve (date_of_birth (EMP)) where EMP.name = "Fred"`.

b. It can also be thought of as a column of *derived* data in the `EMP` table: `retrieve (EMP.date_of_birth) where EMP.name = "Fred"`.

Hence, functions defined on tuples of relations can be interchangeably thought of as functions or as columns of derived data.

3. Functions which take arguments of a base type and return a composite type

For example, consider the function

```
define function same_age (
 language="postquel", returntype=EMP) arg is (int4)
 as "retrieve (EMP.all) where EMP.age = $1".
```

Here the integer argument, `$1`, is passed to the function which returns a set of employees who have that age. Like other functions, `same_age` can be used in a query language command. However, since it returns a composite object, the attributes of this returned object can be referenced using a "nested dot" notation. Hence, the query `retrieve (same_age(EMP.age).name) where EMP.name = "Fred"` will return the names of the employees who are the same age as Fred.

4. Functions whose arguments and return type are composite objects

Another `same_age` function illustrates this case:

```
define function same_age_2 (
 language="postquel", returntype=EMP) arg is (EMP)
 as "retrieve (EMP.all) where EMP.age = $.age".
```

This function is defined for each row of **EMP** and constructs a set of employees, who are the same age as each employee.

Inheritance is also supported in POSTGRES. For example, the following **create** statement constructs a relation **student-EMP** which inherits all the fields of **EMP**:

```
create student-EMP (%time = int4) inherits EMP
```

In keeping with many object-oriented systems, POSTGRES supports multiple inheritance; hence a given relation can inherit from several different relations.

Not only does **student-EMP** inherit all the fields of **EMP** (data inheritance) but it also inherits all the methods of **EMP**, e.g., **date_of_birth** and **same_age_2**. In addition, standard function overloading is permitted, so that a user can redefine either of these functions for the **student-EMP** relation, and the POSTGRES execution routines will automatically choose the correct function to call at runtime.

POSTGRES functions, which are written in C, can either be *trusted*, in which case they are linked into the POSTGRES execution engine dynamically, or they can be *untrusted*, in which case the function is loaded into a separate address space and then accessed by a remote procedure call (RPC) protocol. Trusted functions can crash the POSTGRES engine if they behave maliciously and they can access any data, thereby creating a security loophole. On the other hand, trusted functions can be called with much lower overhead than untrusted ones.

Within a POSTQUEL function, a C or POSTQUEL function can be invoked by using the function in a command. Within a C function, POSTQUEL commands can be run, because the POSTGRES engine can allow functions to simulate POSTGRES application programs. Besides running queries, a function can directly call internal routines in the POSTGRES execution engine, a feature which the POSTGRES papers call *fast path*. For example, a function can directly execute access method calls, thereby providing very high performance by giving up many of the normal DBMS services (e.g., rules, data indepedence).

POSTGRES provides standard programming language referencing for array data types. For example, the following query retrieves Joe's salary for the month of April:

```
retrieve (EMP.salary[4]) where EMP.name = "Joe".
```

In addition to the usual collection of *base* types such as integers, floats and character strings, POSTGRES supports an abstract data type (ADT) facility whereby any user can construct arbitrary new base data types. To define a new base type, the user must specify the name of the type, an input and output function to convert instances of the type to and from the character string type, and space allocation directives for the storage manager.

Any number of *operators* can be defined for base types. Operators are unary or binary functions for which extra information is collected, so that the query optimizer and executor can use predicates containing these operators to restrict the scan of a relation. For example, consider the query:

```
retrieve (EMP.name) where EMP.location |in|
   "10, 20, 10, 20"
```

This query finds all the employees who live in a rectangle bounded by the points (10,10) and (20,20) by using the operator |in|. Since POSTGRES supports both B-tree and R-tree (multidimensional) access methods, a user can construct an R-tree index on the location field and specify that geographic searches should use the operator |in|. In this case, POSTGRES will use an indexed scan of **EMP** rather than a sequential scan if it believes the indexed scan will be cheaper.

Hence, base types can have operators written for them and can be indexed using any available POSTGRES access method. Moreover, base types are *encapsulated*, so that a user must write any *selector* functions to access pieces of the type. On the other hand, composite types automatically come with a complete collection of selector functions.

It is also possible for a more sophisticated user to define and implement new access methods in POSTGRES. Implementation of a new access method requires a user to interact with buffer management, locking, and crash recovery routines. Hence, it is an exercise which should only be attempted by sophisticated designers.

A novel feature of POSTGRES is the ability to save and query historical data. The notation **relation-name   [date]** refers to tuples that existed on the given date and allows a user to easily *time travel* to the indicated date. For example, the following query fetches the names of Joe's coworkers at the beginning of 1989:

```
retrieve (E.co_workers.name)
   from E in EMP ["Jan 1, 1989"]
   where E.name = "Joe"
```

So that POSTGRES can implement such queries, it maintains (optionally on a relation by relation basis) a history of past tuples and their deletion dates, as noted in [Stonebraker 1987].

POSTGRES also provides a version mechanism, which operates on the relation level. The command: **create MY_EMP from EMP.** creates a new version of **EMP** in a new table. In fact, **MY_EMP** is implemented as a positive and a negative delta off the **EMP** table. As a result, modifications to **EMP** get reflected in **MY_EMP**, and space is conserved by only storing difference information. Version management is performed by a novel use of the rule system, as explained in [Stonebraker, Jhingran, Goh, Potamianos 1990].

Recently, work on POSTGRES has focused on completing the type and function system to the capabilities described in this section, making the system more user friendly, and implementing large objects [Stonebraker and Olson 1993], expensive function optimization [Hellerstein and Stonebraker 1993], "chunking" of arrays [Sarawagi and Stonebraker 1994] and partial indexes.

A.3.3   Montage

In August 1992, Miro Systems, Inc., later renamed Montage Systems, Inc., of Emeryville, California, was formed to turn the POSTGRES DBMS into a commercial product and to sell, support, and service the resulting system. This section discusses the changes and additions that Montage has made to the POSTGRES code line. These modifications are organized into five main categories:

1. Conversion to SQL
2. Feature extensions
3. Feature simplification
4. Performance improvements
5. Front end toolkit

We now discuss the Montage work in each of these areas.

POSTGRES supports an extended version of the query language, QUEL, and this decision to ignore the omnipresence of SQL in the marketplace, could only be made by an academic prototype. On the other hand, a commercial system must be compatible with industry standards, and Montage has converted POSTGRES to be an SQL DBMS. To accomplish this task they have rewritten the QUEL parser. Largely, this effort was accomplished by transliterating the QUEL grammer into SQL, and then migrating the POSTGRES parser. Hence, the POSTQUEL query

```
retrieve (E.all) from E in EMP where E.dept = "shoe"
```

becomes

```
select * from E in EMP where E.dept = 'shoe'.
```

However, significant difficulties were experienced in aggregates (group by in SQL) where SQL capabilities have very different semantics from QUEL and in subqueries, which exist in SQL but not in QUEL. Montage plans to be compatible with the SQL3 standard when it unfolds.

With regard to feature extensions, Montage has rounded out several of the POSTGRES capabilities that were planned but never implemented. Specifically, POSTGRES has no mechanisms to recover from crashes when the disk is not intact, preferring to depend on either RAID-style disk redundancy or on a multiple copy system implemented by someone else [Stonebraker et al 1987]. Of course, this strategy is not commercially viable, and Montage has implemented a standard roll forward from a checkpoint capability. Furthermore, POSTGRES supports page-level locking in B-tree and R-tree indexes but class level locking on data elements. Montage has replaced this with page level locking everywhere. Furthermore, POSTGRES supports only arrays of base data types, while Montage has extended this feature to offer arrays of any data type. Lastly, Montage has made many minor extensions. For example, if **foo** is a function that returns a set of some type, then the following SQL statement is legal in the Montage system:

`select * from foo`. The corresponding statement is not supported in POSTQUEL.

There are two areas where significant feature simplification has occurred: the rule system and the type system.

POSTGRES supports a powerful rule system which allows production rules to be defined of the form: **on event do action**. This rule system allows *triggers* to be specified, such as the following rule which propagates any salary adjustment that Joe receives on to Sam:

```
on replace to EMP.salary where EMP.name = "Joe" do
replace EMP (salary = new.salary) where EMP.name =
"Sam"
```

In addition, derived data can also be supported by the rule system, for example,

```
on retrieve to EMP.salary where EMP.name = "Sam" do
instead retrieve (EMP.salary) where EMP.name = "Joe"
```

This rule returns Joe's salary whenever Sam's salary is requested. Hence, Sam's salary is a *virtual* data element, whose actual value is never considered. The full details of this rule system are described in [Stonebraker, Jhingran, Goh, Potamianos 1990].

POSTGRES has two different implementations for this rule capability. One is based on rewriting any user command into one or more commands, that automatically enforce the effects of the rule. The second implementation places markers of various kinds on database tuples, and then *fires* the appropriate rule from the executor, when the indicated event takes place. The action portion of the rule takes the appropriate action to enforce the rule.

Unfortunately, these two rule systems have slightly different semantics. Because there is no efficient way to guarantee a consistent semantics between the two implementations, users can get very confused. Also, it is a tricky performance decision which implementation to choose, when both will produce the desired effect. As a result, Montage decided to remove the marker implementation, and focus only on the rewrite code.

A second area of feature simplification concerned the type system. POSTGRES treats base types differently from composite types. Specifically, base types are encapsulated while composite types are not. Also, base types support operators while composite types do not. Lastly, base types are defined independently of the existence of any class which uses them, while composite types are automatically defined whenever a class of the same name is created. In order to make the type system more uniform, Montage has changed composite types so they are defined independent of any class definition. A composite type can then be used in any number of classes. Montage also allows the "cascaded dot" notation on base types as well as on composite types. Lastly, operators are now allowed for composite types, augmenting the capability always present for base types. At the current time, the only difference between composite types and base types is that composite types have automatic *selector* functions defined for each one of the fields in the the type. For base types, the user must provide his own selector functions to access pieces of the type.

Montage has also focused on performance enhancements to the POSTGRES engine. The company has significantly rewritten the executor to avoid redundant copies of tuples during predicate evaluation. In addition, they have recoded the sort package to speed up its execution, asserting that Montage is about twice as fast as POSTGRES on the Wisconsin benchmark and that it is about the same speed as relational engines. To go even faster, a user can, of course, implement any of the benchmark queries using the fast path feature. The judicious use of fast path could allow Montage to do well on many benchmarks.

Lastly, POSTGRES is a research project oriented toward DBMS functionality. As such it has paid little attention to user interface issues, only supplying an interface to C, based on the notion of portals [Stonebraker and Rowe 1984], and a single application subsystem, the terminal monitor, which allows a user to enter, edit, and execute POSTQUEL queries. Montage has enhanced this functionality with an application development system unlike forms-oriented fourth-generation languages. Instead it uses a *flight simulator* approach to user interaction, whereby users can *navigate* around in their data and then zoom in on areas where more detail is desired. This toolkit is similar to scientific visualization systems, from which it borrows many concepts and has points in common with SDMS [Herot 1980]. It is based on ideas for a similar interface described in [Stonebraker 1987].

A.3.4   Starburst

Another extended relational system is Starburst [Schwarz et al 1986, Lindsay and Haas 1990], developed at the IBM Almaden Research Center. In addition to providing built-in extensions to the relational model, Starburst allows the sophisticated user, such as a database administrator or advanced programmer, to make extensions to the DBMS functionality; in this sense, Starburst is similar to the database system generators we discuss later. However, the intent of the Starburst designers is to provide a single DBMS with user-defined extensions, not to provide a system to generate many database systems.

The Starburst query language extends the relational algebra, and supports user-defined extensions to query analysis, optimization, execution, access methods, and storage methods. The user may also define new literal data types with associated procedures that encapsulate type semantics. Starburst provides unique identifiers for tuples, triggers, and large values in fields.

The Starburst query language provides a number of extensions, including recursive queries and structured-result queries.

Recursive queries permit repetitive execution of a query on the results of previous queries. [Lindsay and Haas 1990] present the example of finding the names and departments for all the employees who work directly or indirectly for employee "Smith":

```
SELECT emp_name, dept_name
FROM smithorg (emp_name, dept_name, emp_eno) AS (
      /* Basis set is Smith and his department */
      SELECT e1.e_name, d1.d_name, e1.e_eno
      FROM emp e1, dept d1
      WHERE e1.e_name='Smith' AND d1.d_dno=e1.e_dno
   UNION
      /* Add emps whose mgr already selected */
      SELECT e2.e_name, d2.d_name, e2.e_eno
      FROM emp e2. dept d2, smithorg so
      WHERE so.emp_eno=d2.d_mgrno /* 'so' is dept mgr */
      AND e2.e_dno=d2.d_dno ) /* 'emp' is in his dept */
```

where employees and departments are defined as

```
emp( e_name, e_dno, ... )
dept( d_name, d_dno, d_mgrno, ... )
```

Structured result queries and *dependent cursors* in Starburst are analogous to multirelations and portals in POSTGRES: they are intended for queries that fetch composite objects that span a number of relations. A structured query consists of a conventional query to define *nodes*, equivalent to what we would call objects, plus additional queries that define joins to *child nodes,* which may be subobjects or sets of related objects. *Dependent cursors* are used to access the child nodes.

Like POSTGRES and Montage, Starburst allows user-defined literal data types stored in tuple fields. However, Starburst takes a different approach to performing operations on these data in the application program.

Recall that there are two different type systems and languages in the extended relational approach: one for the DBMS, one for the application program. In Starburst, operations on user-defined types must be performed in the query language, however, the application program is written in a language that is a combination of the programming language and the query language. A preprocessor separates the two. POSTGRES procedures, in contrast, are written in the programming language; also, POSTGRES procedures are invoked when an attribute of type procedure is accessed.

Starburst does not provide encapsulation of types with procedures in the sense of object-oriented models. However, the privilege of *unwrapping* a type— that is, accessing its internal representation—is restricted to specific users, and the database expression compiler flags violations as an error.

The Starburst features we have discussed so far are suitable for most users. A more sophisticated user can make extensions to Starburst by writing custom storage and access methods, and by modifying the query analysis and optimization phases.

Starburst permits user-defined storage and access methods by standardizing the interface to the procedures these facilities require. These generic procedures include scanning, direct access (by key or TID), insert, update, and delete of tuples in a relation. The user *attaches* these procedures to a relation and they are subsequently called whenever the corresponding operations are performed in query execution. User-defined access and storage methods provide a powerful mechanism to validate updates and to perform efficient lookups, but require a sophisticated user, since the implementation must deal with many low-level issues, including logging and recovery.

Starburst parses queries into a semantic-net representation called the Query Graph Model (QGM). The query-analysis phase is driven by rewrite rules on the QGM, traversing and translating the query graph into equivalent, more optimal, representations. The query optimizer is also rule-driven, translating the QGM representation into an execution plan using LOw LEvel Plan OPerators, or LOLEPOPs. Examples of LOLEPOPs include access methods scans, joins, and sorts. The sophisticated user can extend or modify query analysis and optimization by writing new rules, since both phases are rule-driven.

The sophisticated user can also extend the Starburst query language with *table functions*, pseudotables that are not stored in the database but are computed on the fly. Unlike relational views, which are defined in the query language, table functions are defined by arbitrary procedures in the programming language, as a Starburst storage method.

A.3.5   UniSQL

UniSQL, Inc., of Austin, Texas, has several products that deserve mention in the context of object data management:

- UniSQL/X, an extended relational DBMS with features from an object-oriented model,

- UniSQL/M, a multidatabase that can process queries that span multiple relational and extended relational DBMSs from different vendors, and

- UniSQL/4GE, a fourth-generation environment for building applications.

UniSQL was founded by Won Kim, who was also MCC's principal scientist in the development of ORION (Section A.2.7). The general approach used in UniSQL/X is to incorporate object-oriented features into SQL. UniSQL/X is like other extended relational DBMSs and SQL3 in this respect. However, UniSQL also offers a C++ binding (and a planned Smalltalk binding) that gives it some commonality with the object-oriented DBMSs we covered in Section A.2.

UniSQL/X's query language SQL/X is intended to be fully compatible with SQL, and can be used in both interactive and embedded modes. SQL/X incorporates abstract data types, procedurally-defined attributes, inheritance on tables, and BLOBs (UniSQL calls these Extended Large Objects; they can be stored in files or in the database). Many of these features you will recognize from SQL3, and from other extended relational DBMSs such as Montage.

UniSQL/X supports standard relational DBMS features including relational views, B+ trees, extendible hash indexing, and access authorization. It includes standard transaction-based concurrency control and crash recovery.

The UniSQL C++ binding provides caching of database objects as C++ objects, with swizzling of OIDs into C++ pointers; thus UniSQL provides database programming language capabilities. It differs from many of the object-oriented DBMSs on two points:

1. The UniSQL client Data Manager communicates with the UniSQL Server through SQL/X commands *or* object fetches and stores. In our Section 5.2.3 terminology [Dewitt, Maier 1990] UniSQL acts as an *object server* or a *query server*, not a *page server*.

2. The UniSQL Server is an SQL/X-driven database engine, rather than just an object server.

There are a number of advantages to UniSQL's architecture. The same asymptotic performance as the best object-oriented DBMSs is achieved for cached data. At the other end of the spectrum, where only a small amount of data is touched once (e.g., in transaction processing), or a large amount of data must be processed to produce a small amount of data used by the application (e.g., in decision support), UniSQL can theoretically achieve the performance of the best traditional relational DBMSs, by sending the query to the server for processing.

In the gray area between these extremes, UniSQL could still be expected to dominate traditional DBMS architectures, but object-oriented DBMSs might run faster since they do not require translation and reformatting of the data between the on-disk representation of pages and the in-memory representation of pages. More research is needed to understand these trade-offs.

The UniSQL/M multidatabase capability currently supports distributed queries and transactions that span Ingres, Oracle, Sybase, and UniSQL/X databases. UniSQL plans to support access to IMS as well, although they have not yet developed gateways for object-oriented DBMSs.

UniSQL/M is an interesting and unique feature in the ODMS industry that will prove very valuable in distributed databases that span relational DBMSs and ODMSs; the relational gateways provided by some object-oriented DBMS vendors are also a step in this direction, but they are currently less sophisticated than UniSQL/M.

UniSQL/4GE is a graphical environment for application development. It is aimed not just at traditional developers, but also at end-users and database administrators. It builds on SQL/X. There are three main components of UniSQL/4GE:

1. *ObjectMaster* includes a graphical user interface (GUI) design tool, a library of object "building blocks" for applications, and a tool to connect the blocks together in various ways to build applications.

2. *MediaMaster* allows end-users to create reports from a database that may include images, documents, and other data specified with a Style Editor or obtained from a Style Repository.

3. *VisualEditor* allows users to build, maintain, or browse UniSQL/X database schemas, methods, and data. It allows the user to view graphically as a tree a type hierarchy or a composite object hierarchy, and it allows the user to view object instances as a form with multimedia components.

A.3.6 Persistence

Persistence [Persistence Software 1992], a product of Persistence Software of San Mateo, California, is a commercial product which provides a tight integration between C++ and relational databases. Like UniSQL, it provides a database programming language capability on top of relational DBMS servers, but Persistence Software does not sell its own DBMS; instead it provides a front-end client for a number of popular DBMS products, including Oracle and Sybase, with plans for IMS and others in the future.

Persistence generates interfaces between C++ application objects and tables in a relational database. Each object interface communicates with a relational-object manager, which performs the work of mapping object messages into SQL commands and transforming the results of SQL commands into object instances.

The relational-object manager also performs "semantic key swizzling"— converting implicit foreign key references from the database into in-memory pointers between instances in the relational-object manager. The resulting data structure can be rapidly navigated, providing significant performance improvements for data intensive applications.

Manually interfacing C++ classes to relational tables is feasible, but becomes tedious and prone to error when many classes exist. It is also hard to ensure that the semantics of the application object model are enforced. Persistence automates this repetitive task and provides a uniform interface for each class in the model. By providing consistency checks at the model level, Persistence can also increase the confidence in the quality of the database access portion of the application.

C++ is designed to encapsulate the details of data access. Persistence performs this encapsulation by mapping classes and attributes in the application object model to tables or views in the database.

The developer has a choice of specifying the primary key attributes for each table or asking Persistence to create and maintain a unique OID for each instance. Within the class, Persistence provides creation and removal methods for instances and accessor and modifier methods for each attribute, fully encapsulating the details of data access within the methods of each class.

Persistence uses the term *association* for relationship traversal paths. Associations are based on foreign key relationships in the database. For associations, Persistence creates **get** and **set** methods in each class to access instances of the other class through the association. The cardinality of binary associations are enforced via column constraints in the database and code in the C++ classes.

For example, suppose we have two classes, **Department** and **Employee**. Each **Department** employs zero or more **Employees**, and each **Employee** works in one and only one **Department**. For this database schema, the generator would create a **getEmploys()** method in the **Department** class to get all the **Employees** associated with a particular **Department** by performing a foreign key lookup in the **Employee** table. This allows direct support of navigational queries in the developer's C++ application. Similarly, **addToEmploys()** and **rmvFromEmploys()** would add and remove instances from the set of **Employees** related to a particular **Department**.

Inheritance in the application schema maps to single inheritance in the C++ classes (Persistence currently does not support multiple inheritance). Only leaf classes are mapped to tables in the database (horizontal partitioning). Attributes and associations from parent classes are automatically propagated down to column definitions in the leaf class table.

Horizontal partitioning of tables for inheritance minimizes the total number of tables and speeds access for single instances (e.g., **fetch Employee where name = "Smith"**). It can have the disadvantage, however, of slowing access for queries across parent classes (e.g., **fetch Person where name = "Smith"**) because the query must be replicated across each subclass table.

Persistence uses client-side caching to improve performance and ensure integrity of the application data. The relational-object cache manages the conversion between relational data and application objects, and enables rapid object access and navigation by semantic key swizzling, mapping foreign key attributes into in-memory pointers. It also provides data consistency and concurrency by invoking the transaction and locking mechanisms of the underlying DBMSs.

The methods created by the Database Interface Generator never return pointers to the physical data. Instead, they return a smart pointer to the data. This smart pointer keeps a reference count and can be shared by several variables. For example, if two queries return the same tuple, both query results would point to the same smart pointer.

The smart pointer in turn contains a pointer to the data for an instance and the primary key value for an instance. To ensure consistency between the object cache and the database, it is necessary to flush the data in the cache each time a transaction is committed. When this happens, the primary key value is used to transparently re-read the data from the database.

C++ instances can refer directly to other instances through pointers. Using pointers, C++ developers can build complex in-memory structures which can be quickly navigated by following the pointer links between objects. Relational tuples, however, can only refer indirectly to other tuples through foreign key "pointers." Navigating relational structures, such as a bill of materials, requires a separate query to traverse each link of the structure in each direction.

The relational-object cache performs the task of semantic key swizzling. This has the effect of speeding performance for navigational queries once the object instances have been read in from the database.

The developer uses transactions to control the level of locking performed in the database. The types of transactions supported are: read without locks, consistent read, write immediate, and write on commit. As data is accessed or updated by the application, depending on the type of transaction, the runtime system places the appropriate locks on the corresponding tuples using the underlying DBMS's locking mechanism.

In addition to these transactions, the developer can specify either shared or exclusive locks on entire tables in the database. In cases where the application does not specify any transaction, an implicit read-write transaction is started. When the application explicitly invokes a transaction, the implicit transaction is committed and the new transaction is started.

As objects are retrieved, tuples corresponding to these objects are locked in the underlying database for the duration of the transaction. When the transaction is committed these locks are released and the data in the cache must be flushed.

When the transaction commits, only the data for the objects is flushed—the smart pointers are retained in the cache. So, the next time data corresponding to any of these objects is requested, the appropriate locks are automatically re-acquired and data is read from the database and cached.

The cache maintains a single copy of the data for the entire application. This avoids duplication of data if different parts of the application have to access data associated with a given object. Maintaining a single copy of data ensures that the data remains consistent. Different parts of the application have access to the latest version of the data and changes in one part of the application are visible throughout the application.

Once the interface code is generated for the application classes, the developer can add custom methods to the classes. The following code sample shows a simple application which logs in to the database, creates new **Department** and **Employee** instances, and sets the association between a **Department** and an **Employee**. All the methods shown in the example are generated by Persistence or provided through the Persistence Relational Object Management System (ROMS).

```
// Login to the database
PS_Roms::connect("scott", "tiger");

// Create new department in RDB
Department newDept("Sales", "Floor 1");

// Create new employee, assign to department
Employee newEmp("Smith", newDept);

// Read department by key
Department_KeyObj myKey("Eng");
Department engDept(myKey);
```

```
// Read all employees who work in department
Employee_Cltn* engineerSet = engDept->getEmploys();

// Update employee relationship
newEmp->setWorksIn(engDept);

// Delete Sales department from database
newDept->remove();
```

Persistence demonstrates an approach to bridging object-oriented programming languages to relational databases, thereby creating a database programming language. This approach allows new applications to be written in C++ using legacy relational databases. It also enables these new applications to operate concurrently with legacy applications.

This approach provides good performance by using queries to efficiently prefetch desired data from the database to take advantage of associative search and by caching the data to permit in-memory navigation. Thus, data is loaded into memory based on application needs instead of its physical organization in the database.

A.3.7   Other Systems

Other systems have been built or discussed that might be called extended relational: extensions of current products, nonrelational layers on top of relational database systems, and unnormalized relational databases. We cover these briefly here.

Some commercial relational DBMS products, such as INGRES 6.3 [Ingres 1990], have already incorporated limited object data management extensions, including user-defined literal types, rules, and programming-language procedures stored in database attributes. SYBASE [Sybase 1990] and Xidak Orion [Xidak 1990] are other examples of extended relational database system products along this line. However, systems such as these are still a long way from offering the functionality of POSTGRES, Montage, UniSQL, Starburst, and the other ODMSs we cover in this book.

PENGUIN [Wiederhold 1990] incorporates an object-oriented layer on top of a relational database system through sophisticated multirelation views. This approach is similar to Persistence and UniSQL's Data Manager, and is likely to have similar performance trade-offs.

[Dadam et al 1986], [Kemper and Walrath 1988], and [Scheck et al 1990] describe work toward database systems based on a non–first-normal-form (NF^2) data model [Scheck and Scholl 1986]. An NF^2 model offers capabilities beyond relational systems—nested relations may be used to represent composite objects and set-valued attributes. To date, such systems may not be competitive with extended relational database systems for object data management applications, but their data model is simpler. More of these ideas may be incorporated into extended relational database systems in the future.

A.3.8 Summary

Extended relational systems provide procedural capability within the query language; extend the relational model to allow user-defined types and nontabular structures, such as nested tuples, ordering, or multirelations; and incorporate new capabilities, such as inheritance, optional object identifiers, and transitive closure operations.

The extended relational database approach benefits from many years of experience and research with the relational model. It also provides a path whereby current commercial relational database systems could evolve to provide object data management capability. As yet, however, there is no agreement on how to incorporate the new functionality in the relational model, and there is limited experience with the extended relational approach. Also, because the current systems use an extended database system architecture, they have poor performance for applications that simply require persistence for programming language data, as we discussed in Section 5.2.3.

A.4 EXTENDED FUNCTIONAL AND SEMANTIC DATABASE SYSTEMS

A functional data model, as we have seen, provides a data-manipulation language based on mathematical function notation: A declarative functional query language is used to define function values. In an extended functional data model, the query language is extended to allow procedural specification of functions as well, thus becoming computationally complete. Closely related are semantic data models, also incorporating features beyond the relational model.

A.4.1 Introduction

Recall from Chapter 4 that the basis of the functional model is *objects* and *functions.* Functions map objects onto other objects, including both entities and literal values. Functions may be defined procedurally, or may be defined as *stored.* The values of a stored function are represented by the DBMS in any fashion desired—for example, by storing the values in groups with one or more of the objects that are arguments of the function.

The systems we shall discuss, IRIS and PROBE, have the extended database system architecture; that is, they define their own language environment, executed within the database system, and calls may be made from an application by embedding calls to this language within the application programming language.

Neither of these systems provides a procedural language in the DBMS; however, both allow *foreign functions,* written in the programming language, to be called from the functional query language. Foreign functions may also make calls to the query language. Since neither of these systems was written to work over a network, the issue did not arise as to where the foreign functions are actually executed; ideally the application could choose whether the workstation or the server is a more efficient location to execute the procedure.

A.4.2   IRIS and OpenODB

IRIS [Fishman et al 1984], developed at Hewlett-Packard Laboratories in Palo Alto, California, is an example of an extended functional database system. It has some similarities to extended relational systems, as the query language, OSQL, is a variation of the SQL relational language, and the original storage manager, now reimplemented, was a relational storage manager from Hewlett-Packard product development.

OpenODB [Hewlett-Packard 1993] is a productization of IRIS. Unless otherwise indicated, all of the comments on IRIS apply to OpenODB as well. OpenODB should not be confused with TI's Open OODB toolkit (Section A.5.5).

The OSQL query language provides an elegant functional notation for data access. Functions may be defined as *stored* (that is, defined by explicit values associated with objects in their domain), or in terms of compositions of other functions using OSQL. In either case, calls to OSQL are translated into an internal extended relational algebra interpreted by the storage manager. Multivalued (list or set) functions are permitted as well.

A definition of our **Document** and **Chapter** object types in OSQL would look like this:

```
CREATE TYPE Document (
   title Charstring REQUIRED,
   revision Date,
   chaps Chapter MANY );
CREATE TYPE Chapter (
   title Charstring REQUIRED,
   number Integer,
   doc Document );
```

What appear to be fields in this definition are actually stored function definitions. For example, an OSQL statement to retrieve chapter titles of documents modified after 1988 would be

```
SELECT title FOREACH Chapter c
WHERE revision(doc(c)) > 1-Jan-1988
```

Functions may also be defined explicitly. They must be defined this way if they take more than one object type as parameter:

```
CREATE FUNCTION
   checked_out(Document, Library) -> Person;
```

Although OSQL does not incorporate procedural constructs, *foreign* functions may be defined, written in a programming language such as C. These functions are automatically linked into the application program. Foreign functions provide some limited ability to perform computations that cannot be implemented in OSQL.

OSQL is used much as SQL is in conventional relational products: It is embedded in the programming language. Alternatively, IRIS provides a call-level interface. There are plans to provide a more tightly integrated implementation in OpenODB, to provide a persistent derivative of an object-oriented programming language such as C++ or CLOS, but this implementation has not begun as of the time of this writing.

Stored function (also known as property) values can be updated; other functions can be updated only where the update semantics is defined explicitly. So that we can distinguish adding an object to a multivalued function from changing the entire list of values, explicit **set** and **add** keywords are incorporated in OSQL:

```
SET  chaps(my_doc) = (chap1, chap2, chap3)
ADD  chaps(my_doc) = chap4
```

IRIS provides the equivalent of *inverse attributes* in the form of multiple automatically maintained functions representing a relationship.

Other IRIS features include the following:

- *Schema representation:* As allowed by many of the other systems we discuss, the schema may be examined as can any other data.

- *Multiple types:* Unlike any of the other systems we discuss, IRIS allows an object to have multiple types, in addition to providing a type hierarchy. A type can be associated or deassociated with an object dynamically.

- *Clustering:* IRIS provides clustering, but only for properties associated with an object. In effect, this recovers the clustering that would already be present in a straight relational or object-oriented representation of data records.

- *Versions:* A simple version mechanism is provided. An object can be made versionable, and can then be accessed only through explicit checkout and checkin commands that create new versions of the object. Locks on versions must be acquired explicitly by the user.

IRIS may be regarded as object-oriented in the sense that objects can be manipulated only through functions, and functions can be grouped with the object types on which they operate. However, no enforcement is provided for encapsulation, and the notation syntax is functional rather than object-oriented, so it is classified as such in this book.

A.4.3   PROBE

PROBE [Manola and Dayal 1986, Dayal et al 1987], developed at Computer Corporation of America (CCA) in Cambridge, Massachusetts, is a followon to earlier research on the DAPLEX system [Shipman 1981].

Using PROBE, a document in our example database might be defined as follows:

```
entity Document is ENTITY
function title(Document) -> STRING
function revision(Document) -> DATE
function chaps(Document) -> set of Chapter
```

Type **ENTITY** is the supertype of all entity objects; documents could have been defined with a supertype name after the **is** keyword, instead. Since attributes, relationships, and procedures are all represented by functions, the inheritance mechanism allows any of these properties of an object to be inherited.

All objects are identified by an OID that is generated by the system. Functions that map objects to other objects may be thought of as OID-valued; however the OIDs are not explicitly visible to the user. Functions that represent the same relationship (for example, **chaps(Document)** and **doc(Chapter)**) can be defined as inverses to maintain referential integrity.

Whereas DAPLEX supported only stored functions, PROBE allows functions to be procedurally defined in the DAPLEX query language or as arbitrary procedures in a programming language. The DAPLEX language is not computationally complete.

PROBE allows functions of multiple arguments, and each argument may be an input parameter, an output parameter, or both; for example,

```
function age(p: in out Person, years: in out integer)
```

The **age** function may be invoked with a value for either parameter, to produce a value for the other. Its value may be stored (in which case, it is much like a relation), or may be computed (say, from birthdate).

The general problem of updating functions that are defined procedurally is analogous to the problem of updating relational views. In many cases, the intent of an update can be determined automatically. In the functional model, it is perhaps more natural for the function definer to specify actions for updates explicitly, however.

A.4.4   Other Systems

VISION [Innovative Systems 1988] uses a function-based model and provides its own language rather than close integration with an existing programming language, so is classified in this book as an extended functional database system; however, the invocation syntax looks much like object-oriented Smalltalk notation.

SIM [Fritchman et al 1990] is a product based on a semantic data model. It uses the host programming language for procedural capability. GEM [Tsur and Zaniolo 1984] might be regarded as a semantic model ODMS shell built on a relational system. CACTIS [Hudson and King 1989] combines functional and semantic data modeling concepts.

A.4.5   Summary

The functional data model is mathematically simple, and provides a duality between procedurally-defined and stored data that provides logical data independence. Functional query languages have been implemented that have power equivalent to the relational algebra, and it is possible to provide computationally complete capability by allowing function definitions in a programming language.

To date, there are few commercial products based on the functional-model approach. Perhaps the functional model would have dominated the relational model in the commercial marketplace if a formal definition of the functional model had been completed in the same time frame. The functional model might also be more popular if the most common programming languages used functional notation to access data as well as procedures, so that a functional model DBMS could be integrated more naturally with application programming languages.

A.5   DATABASE SYSTEM GENERATORS

All the approaches to object data management that we have discussed so far have been designed to provide extensibility in the implementation and definition of types and operations provided by the DBMS. However, database system generators, such as EXODUS and GENESIS, go further in this regard, allowing the data model itself to be redefined and extended. In this section, we consider such systems in more detail.

A.5.1   Introduction

There is no single data model for a database system generator. The data model is defined by a special user called the *database implementor*. Both the logical data model and the physical data model must be described. The logical data model specifies the query and representation capabilities of the system, as we described in Chapter 4—for example, tables, keys, relationships, and query syntax. The physical data model specifies the access methods and the ways in which logical data schemas can be mapped to them, as we described in Chapter 5.

Recall from Chapter 3 that there are three kinds of users of other DBMSs: the *end user*, the *application programmer*, and the *database administrator*. The database implementor is a fourth kind of user, exclusive to database system generators.

A.5.2   Variations

There are two variations of database system generator, according to the architecture chosen:

- *Toolkits:* In the database toolkit approach, the database system generator provides "plug and play" customizable components for the most commonly used capabilities required in a DBMS, such as an index package, query parser and optimizer, a transaction manager, and storage manager.

- *Constructors:* In the database constructor approach, the database system generator provides a formalization of database architecture, allowing a DBMS to be generated by linking together existing modules in different ways, and using tools and high-level languages to generate DBMS modules automatically.

Most systems do not fit neatly into one of these categories—they are hybrids in the continuum between toolkits and constructors. In this section, we will describe two systems, EXODUS and Open OODB, that most closely fit the toolkit architecture, and one system, GENESIS, that most closely fits the constructor architecture.

A.5.3   EXODUS

The EXODUS database system generator [Carey et al 1988] was developed at the University of Wisconsin. It aids a database implementor in the task of generating a DBMS by providing a storage manager, a programming language, E (an extension of C++), the E compiler, a library of access-method implementations, a library of *operator methods* implementing high-level operations required by a data model, a rule-based query optimizer generator, and tools for constructing query-language optimizers. The EXODUS system is designed as a practical tool with attention to performance considerations in all aspects of the design, and it has already been used to construct DBMSs; we shall describe one such system as an example.

A DBMS generated by EXODUS consists of a parser and query optimizer, both generated automatically from a description of the target query language and operators, the E compiler, required because the output of the query optimizer is an E program, a catalog (data-schema) manager partially or wholly written by the database implementor in E, and the database engine itself. The database engine contains three layers: the operator methods (implementation of language operations), access methods, and storage manager. The database implementor may choose the operator and access methods from the libraries provided with EXODUS, or may implement his own using E. The storage manager can also be modified by the database implementor, but is normally left unchanged.

The basic representation for data in the storage manager is a variable-length byte sequence of arbitrary size, incorporating the capability to insert or delete bytes in the middle of the sequence. In the simplest case, these basic storage objects are implemented as a contiguous sequence of bytes. As the objects become large, or when they are broken into noncontiguous sequences by editing operations, they are represented using a B-tree of leaf blocks, each containing a portion of the sequence. Objects are referenced using structured OIDS; the EXODUS designers chose these over surrogate OIDs due to the efficiency considerations we discussed in Section 5.2.1.

On these basic storage objects, the storage manager performs buffer manage-ment, concurrency control, recovery, and a versioning mechanism that can be used to provide a variety of application-specific versioning schemes. Transactions are implemented using a shadowing and logging technique. Versions are imple-mented by associating a time stamp with every object identifier.

The database implementor's language E is upward-compatible with C++, providing generic classes, iterators, and support for persistent object types. References to persistent objects look much like ordinary C++ objects; the E compiler generates calls to the storage manager for buffer management. However, unlike the database programming languages we discussed in the previous section, E is not intended for the application programmer. It is used to define new operator methods and access methods, or for the catalog manager.

As a demonstration, the EXODUS system was used to develop an object-oriented DBMS. The data model for this DBMS was called EXTRA, and the query language was called EXCESS. The EXTRA data model includes support for persistent objects, object type definitions independent of extent (that is, there may be multiple collection instances for each type), type inheritance, compound objects with existence dependencies, user-defined methods for type encapsulation, de-rived attributes, automatic maintenance of inverse attributes for relationships, and complex objects including lists, sets, and arrays.

The query language EXCESS is designed to provide a uniform query interface to sets, arrays, tuples, and individual objects, all of which can be composed and nested. Also, user-defined functions, written in E or in EXCESS, appear as an integrated part of the language.

A.5.4   GENESIS

The GENESIS database system generator [Batory et al 1988, 1990] was developed at the University of Texas in Austin. It is based on high-level tools for constructing a DBMS from a library of existing modules. GENESIS does not automate all database system generation, but it is impressive that Batory's group has formalized as much of the process as they have. The GENESIS work does not yet address many needs of object data management applications; it is included in this book because of its promise for future development in the area.

The key to the success of the GENESIS work is the formalization of database architecture on which it is based. This formalization is made possible by *standard-ization* and *layering*. "Layering" refers to dividing an architecture into interacting portions that implement mappings between successive levels of data representa-tion. It must be possible to design and implement the layers independently. "Stan-dardization" refers to finding a "simplest common interface" between layers that permits many different implementations of each layer's functionality. It is usually not possible to layer and standardize the simplest common interfaces until a num-ber of alternative algorithms are well understood. [Batory et al 1988] give the ex-ample of shadowing, page logging, and db-cache alternatives for transaction re-covery; a simplest common interface can be designed that allows any of these three strategies underneath. Another example might be B-trees, hash tables, and parent–child link implementations of references discussed in this book.

The standardization and layering techniques can be applied to other domains of software engineering. Indeed the GENESIS team is now exploring new areas in which to formalize and create reusable component modules. Object-oriented database systems is one such area of future work, as the current GENESIS database generator is focused on hierarchical, network, and relational models.

The GENESIS DBMS formalism incorporates parameterized types to represent a wide variety of storage structures used by file-management systems, and a rule-based algebra to describe mappings in query optimization. GENESIS allows a mixture of record-structuring capabilities, including fixed-length and variable-length fields, scalar and set-valued attributes, nested records, and arrays. To allow this flexibility, it represents records as an unnormalized ordered tree of attributes. GENESIS also incorporates transactions and a variety of physical access methods including several variations on the indexing and parent–child link structures discussed in Chapter 3.

A particular DBMS design can be described by a set of equations. A preconstructed library of the common functions required in a DBMS is assembled by GENESIS's graphical database implementor tool known as the Database Type Editor, DaTE [Batory and Barnett 1991].

Within the limits of the predefined library and DBMS formalization, DaTE allows the database implementor to design a DBMS in minutes, performing "software layout" by graphically composing alternatives for functions such as query optimization and storage-level access methods to construct the DBMS architecture. DaTE also provides design-rule checking to ensure that only correct systems are specified. The DaTE specification is output to the GENESIS library compiler to yield the DBMS executable.

A.5.5   Open OODB

The Open OODB Toolkit [Wells, Blakeley, Thompson 1992] is being developed at Texas Instruments in Dallas, Texas, under ARPA contract. The system is architected as a framework of object services that can be incrementally improved, tailored, and configured to meet the needs of diverse applications. Configured with all of its components, the system provides a multi-user object-oriented DBMS with SQL capabilities; but the system also provides an infrastructure for experimental research and development by database, framework, environment, and system developers who want to experiment with different system architectures or components.

As such, the Open OODB Toolkit is probably best classified as a database system generator as defined in this book. The fully configured Open OODB could also be classified as an object-oriented DBMS (Section A.2). With just a few components, Open OODB could be considered an object manager (Section A.6). Incidentally, do not confuse the Open OODB Toolkit with HP's OpenODB (Section A.4.2), which has a quite different architecture.

Two main design goals have influenced the development of the Open OODB Toolkit: seamlessness and modularity. Seamlessness means that system developers should be able to add (database) functionality to host programming languages with minimal change to either the language's type system or the way in which objects are manipulated. Examples of functional extensions include persistence, concurrency control, transactions, distribution, automatic index maintainence, constraint enforcement, parallelism, replication, queries, and change management. When adding functionality to a language, a difference between the the original and the augmented language is called a "seam," or what we have called an *impedance mismatch* in this book. An example of this is when some object-oriented DBMSs require different kinds of pointers to be used to access persistent objects than to access transient objects. Some seams will always be required since the new functionality must be selectively invoked if not all data is to be affected in the same way.

Currently, Open OODB Toolkit supports C++ and Common Lisp. As an example of a seamless extension, consider the Open OODB Persistent C++ program below in which a new part replaces all occurrences of a designated part in a part assembly. Changes made to the original transient program to allow it to work on persistent data appear in uppercase. **FETCH** explicitly faults in a named component from the database; persistent subcomponents are implicitly faulted when referenced; **PERSIST** designates a new part to be separately persistent.

```
class Part {
public:
int part_number;
char* part_name;
Part* top_assy;
Part** components;
Part(int number, char* name); };

void substitute_new_part(int new_part_number,
        char* new_part_name,
        char* assy_part_name,
        int old_part_number)
{ Part* assy = (Part*)OpenOODB->FETCH(assy_part_name);
Part* new_part = new Part (new_part_number,
new_part_name);
new_part->PERSIST();
if (assy && assy->components)
{ int i = 0;
while (assy->components[i])
  {if (assy->components[i]->number == old_part_number)
  {assy->components[i] = new_part;}
  i++;}}};
```

A modular architecture should allow developers to add or modify system behavior in a straightforward, controlled fashion. The Open OODB Toolkit is architected as a collection of independent object services paralleling the Object Management Group (OMG) object services architecture (Section 6.5.3). Using object services terminology, Open OODB provides the following services: event notification (sentries), lifecycle, naming, object externalization, persistence, transactions, repository, and object query.

Unlike monolithic database systems, no functional extensions are built-in. Instead, extensions like persistence are installed as "behavioral extensions" by a mechanism called "sentries". When an operation occurs involving an object declared to have "extended" behavior, a sentry interrupts the operation and transfers control to a module called a "policy manager" responsible for ensuring that operations against extended objects behave properly. Each semantic extension is implemented by a different policy manager. Thus, there can be a policy manager for persistence and another for index maintenance. For each type of extension, there are potentially many semantic models (e.g., linear or branching versions) and a choice of ways to maintain them (e.g., local vs. remote computation, and eager vs. lazy index maintenance). Policy managers can be added independently.

This sentries strategy permits hiding the semantic extensions from applications, thus meeting the seamlessness goal. It also allows new extensions to be added, the semantics of a given extension to be changed, and implementations of a given policy to be changed or selected dynamically. For instance, a developer can configure a repository that is transient or persistent, queryable or not, versioned or not. More generally, the Open OODB Toolkit can be used to configure an object-oriented DBMS, relational database, a simple data repository, and distributed systems.

A.5.6   Summary

The development of database system generators is an indication that database systems have reached a certain level of maturity, where database development technology is reasonably well understood. They are analogous to compiler compilers in the programming-language area. Database system generators should prove useful in application areas where no existing DBMS satisfies application needs. For example, in a document-management system in a library, these systems might be used to create a relational database system that can store text and images, and that accepts a specialized variant of SQL to support text-matching operations.

On the other hand, database system generators are not practical for many applications, particularly when one of the new object data management systems that we have discussed already satisfies requirements—it takes much more effort to derive a new DBMS than to use an existing one, no matter how sophisticated the database system generator available. As a result, database system generators probably will be used in special cases, rather than as the most popular approach to object data management.

A.6   OBJECT MANAGERS

The last category of ODMS we consider is object managers. These systems generally have less functionality than do the others we have covered. They minimally provide a persistent object store with concurrent access, and they generally do not provide a query and programming language.

A.6.1   Introduction

An object manager typically provides a relatively simple data model, sometimes patterned after a programming language for which it might serve as an object store. Although some earlier programming languages, such as INTERLISP [Teitelman 1974], provide the ability to provide persistent objects over multiple sessions in the language, object managers also provide concurrency-control and disk-management capabilities.

Object managers often provide a database architecture more limited than that of the other systems we have discussed. For example, many do not provide access to data stored remotely on a network.

We shall consider three examples of object managers: Kala, Mneme, and POMS. Kala is a commercial product supplying a library of procedures for basic persistence. Mneme is a similar research prototype with somewhat fewer capabilities. POMS is a system designed to provide a persistent programming language, PS-Algol.

A.6.2   Kala

Kala is a commercial product from Penobscot Development Corporation, of Cambridge, Massachusetts. Kala is an excellent example of an object manager in the categorization defined in this book, because it is designed to be efficient for users that do not require or want all the overhead of a full DBMS. Kala also has some similarities to a database system generator such as EXODUS or Open OODB.

The Kala literature uses the term *persistent data server* to refer to what we have called an object manager. Kala is designed as a "happy medium" between a file system and a DBMS, aiming for the speed, low cost, and flexibility of files, and the reliability, shareability, and robustness of databases.

To a programmer using C or C++, Kala is simply a function library exporting a suite of facilities through an API. By linking your application's code to Kala's libraries, you obtain an executable that plays the role of a *client* in a client/server configuration against a Kala *server*.

Kala servers can communicate with other Kala servers over the network. The local server will try to fetch the requested data for you from whichever server may have it. If you do not require this capability, you can set up your application to run in a stand-alone configuration, in which application code is linked with the Kala Server code and directly accesses a Kala Store.

Kala manages both the *state* and *visibility* of persistent data:

1. Kala supports persistence of data structures, but it does not require a full data description; it only needs to know where the pointers are (as with Mneme, described in the next section). Kala has a `get/put` interface and can store any kind of data. If your application builds a linked list in memory and `puts` it in Kala, then when someone `gets` that data it will still be a linked list, topologically the same as the original even though the addresses of the nodes are all different.

2. Kala's design philosophy is that access control, security, licensing, versioning, and configurations are all facets of the same basic problem: controlling *visibility* of data. Transaction commit makes new values visible to the rest of the world by replacing the old values. Security grants make a datum visible to qualified agents until revoked. A license makes a service or a dataset visible to someone on the basis of pre-paid rights. A configuration bundles a collection of data to be always visible together.

When requested by an application call, Kala will transfer a copy of a persistent datum from the persistent store to the application memory. When a modified state needs to be made persistent, you can create a new datum in the persistent store by having Kala transfer a copy of the modified bits and pointers from the application memory back into the persistent store. You may store in a persistent datum (called a *monad* in Kala terminology) any combination of data elements, and you can decide the unit of transfer between memory and disk on a case-by-case basis.

Kala maintains a visibility environment for each client, which lets you control how much of the persistent store is accessible. The visibility environment is called a *vista*. Your current vista defines what portion of the persistent store is accessible to an application for browsing and changes. The set of data visible from your vista is known as the *horizon*. An application can only reach data which is within the horizon of the application's current vista.

A vista is a collection of *handles* for monads (persistent data units) in the persistent store. The horizon is actually larger than the set of monads for which the vista has handles: Since each monad may contain pointers into other monads, the horizon also contains all the monads pointed to by the monads for which you have handles, and transitively so. In other words, bringing a new handle into your vista potentially may add an entire connected graph of monads to the horizon. Thus, a vista in fact comprises many collections of handles. Each collection is called a *basket*. A basket is a unit of visibility and sharing.

During execution, you can change the horizon in many ways. A basket (and by implication the part of the horizon formed by its handles) can be stored persistently as a monad. A basket monad can be seen (or not seen) like any other data. You can extend the horizon by adding to your vista a basket monad, making the contents of the basket part of your vista, as opposed to just the basket monad itself. You may also dynamically modify an application's horizon by adding a basket from a different, concurrently executing application.

Kala maintains a vista for each executing application. Since these vistas can share baskets, the persistent store is partitioned into horizons that may overlap in complex and dynamic ways. You can prevent data from being accessible by an application simply by making sure that it cannot end up in that application's horizon, no matter how extended. You can also use Kala's visibility mechanism to enforce strict access rules and requirements, so that only users that satisfy authentication checks can gain access to protected data. This is the basis for access control and security.

You can allow data to be shared in a controlled way among many applications executing concurrently with Kala's visibility mechanisms. You can allow applications to act on shared pools of data, or you can make updates locally, and keep them local until they are finalized. These mechanisms are the basis for concurrency control and transaction management in Kala.

When you create a persistent datum (monad) by transferring bits and pointers from memory to the persistent store, you are taking a snapshot of a (potentially) changing datum in memory. That is, you are saving a certain state or *version* of that datum. Every time you create a new monad this way, you save a new version of the same entity. Each basket can be used to represent one group of versions, what we have called a *configuration.*

In summary, while Kala does not have some of the higher level capabilities of a full DBMS, much of the same function can be achieved by building on Kala's visibility mechanisms.

A.6.3   Mneme

Mneme [Moss and Sinofsky 1988], developed at the University of Massachusetts, is another good example of the object-manager approach. Mneme is named after the Greek word for memory, and is pronounced "nee-mee." Mneme provides object identifiers, persistence, concurrency control, and recovery. The client interface to Mneme is a set of procedures. The goal of the system is very high performance with this minimal functionality.

The Mneme data store is simply a heap of untyped objects. Mneme is not aware of the internal structure of objects, except for attributes containing OIDs. As far as Mneme is concerned, an object consists of an OID, an array of data bytes, and an array of references. As a concession to programming languages such as LISP and Smalltalk that permit nonpointer values in references—for example, to simple integer objects—Mneme maintains an "escape bit" in the reference-array elements to allow an immediate value to be stored instead.

Objects are grouped into *pools* that can have different storage-management policies. The policy—for example, for caching and clustering—is defined by the database administrator writing a *policy module*. One or more pools are stored in one operating-system *file*.

Mneme has a novel mechanism for OIDs, based on locality of reference; files are the basis for OID addressing [Moss 1989]. Mneme uses only 32 bits for OIDs, as opposed to the 64 bits used in most other systems. OIDs occur in two forms, called client IDs (CIDs) and persistent IDs (PIDs). PIDs are the form actually stored in reference arrays, and are valid only within the file where they are stored. To reference an object outside of the file, an artificial *forwarding* object is created within the file, which identifies the referenced file and remote PID in that file. Thus, local references are short and fast, but remote references require a level of indirection. CIDs are valid only for the duration of a database session, but they may reference an object in any open file. Each file has a maximum PID value, always less than 2^{20}, the maximum number of objects currently permitted in a file. Thus, through a mapping table, the space of CID values can be broken up into contiguous regions as required by the files currently open; the upper-order bits indicate the file, the lower-order bits indicate the PID within the file.

The actual OID addressing scheme is somewhat more complicated, since files are broken up into segments consisting of 1024 objects. Thus, PIDs, in turn, are structured OIDs, specifying a segment number in the upper-order bits and an object number within the segment in the low-order bits. Note the slight difference from structured OIDs in other systems. Segments are not fixed-sized pages; they are arbitrary-sized contiguous areas with an object "slot" table pointing to the 1024 objects in that segment.

A.6.4   POMS

The Persistent Object Management System, or POMS [Cockshot et al 1984], built for the persistent Algol project at the University of Edinburgh in Great Britain, is an example of an object manager motivated by a particular programming language. It provides persistent objects, object identifiers, transactions for concurrency control and recovery, translation of persistent Algol objects to and from a disk representation, and general storage management and allocation.

The kernel of the POMS system is a process for translating OIDs to memory addresses when a reference is followed to an object not in memory, and back again when an object is flushed to disk. This is achieved with a two-way hash table that allows lookups by OID or by memory address. The OIDs used are a variation on the structured OIDs, consisting of a logical page number and a physical offset on the page.

Transactions are implemented using shadow pages, using a rewrite of the logical-to-physical page map as a means for atomicity.

POMS uses a *tagged* architecture for data: Each object in memory either is self-describing or contains enough information to access a description of it. An object begins with a header word, specifying what the size of an object is, and whether it is a structure, array, or string. In the case of an array, the array bounds are stored with the object. In the case of a structure, a unique identifier is stored that has been associated with the object type by the compiler; this can be used to get the field information.

A number of special optimizations were made in the use of storage allocation on disk. An effort was made to store sequential elements of lists in the same disk page. Strings and arrays of similar sizes, or specifically, with the same $\log_2(\text{size})$, are stored in the same disk pages in order to simplify space allocation. Record types (structures) are also grouped on disk pages, according to type. Unfortunately, no performance studies were done to compare these disk-allocation strategies to other approaches, so we have no way of telling how much speedup, if any, these optimizations have provided.

A.6.5   Other Systems

Other examples of object managers are ObServer [Hornick and Zdonick 1987] at Brown University, DASDBS [Scheck et al 1990], at Technical University of Darmstadt, Germany, Emerald [Juhl et al 1988] at the University of Washington (also a persistent programming language), iMAX-432 [Pollack et al 1981] at Intel Corporation, and LOOM [Kaehler and Krasner 1983] at Xerox Palo Alto Research Center. WiSS [Chou et al 1985] from the University of Wisconsin and Camelot [Spector et al 1986] at Carnegie-Mellon University might also be categorized as object managers.

A.6.6   Summary

Kala, Mneme, and POMS are simpler than many of the other systems that we have covered—for example, they have no query language. Mneme and Kala are probably better examples of the object-manager approach, since they have a simple data model and they are designed to work with many different high-level front ends, through a call-level interface.

An object manager is useful in applications that do not require all the capability of a DBMS (and the memory and time overhead associated with this capability). Applications that might benefit include system service applications, such as a distributed mail router or file-system directory, or a real-time control program requiring a persistent, recoverable representation of system state. Object managers may also be used as the storage level of a full DBMS (for example, ENCORE on ObServer [Hornick and Zdonick 1987]), or for a persistent programming language (as is the case with POMS and Emerald).

A.7   SUMMARY

In this appendix, we covered five approaches that have been taken to ODMSs, and gave examples of prototypes and products illustrating each approach. This diversity of approaches taken to object data management is in contrast to the close consistency across implementations of the relational model.

We have made only a few general comparisons of the approaches. Comparisons can be found in the text of the book, along two dimensions:

1. *General principles:* It can be argued that a particular approach does or does not violate general principles that a database system should follow, such as data independence. These issues are covered in Chapter 7.

2. *Application-based evaluation:* It can be argued that a particular approach is or is not appropriate for the needs of a particular user application. These issues are covered in Chapter 8.

The systems we have used as examples are not likely to stand still, unless the products or projects fail altogether. The list of systems covered also is not complete; space allows coverage of only a few examples of each approach. Even if this book were revised annually, it would be difficult to maintain an up-to-date comparison of the large number of quickly evolving systems, with new releases of the products and prototypes. Until this research area stabilizes, it will be necessary to supplement this book with readings on the latest developments in the area, starting with the products and prototypes referenced here.

System
Bibliography

The following mini-bibliography is a source for the reader searching for more information about specific systems. It is alphabetized by system name, and supplies the primary bibliographic reference for each system. More information can be obtained by reading the referenced document, or by looking up the reference in the annotated bibliography to obtain comments and pointers to additional references.

A consistent terminology is used throughout the book to categorize DBMSs. The term DBMS (database management system), or more informally just "database system," is used to refer to all of the approaches, both traditional and new. An adjective is added to refer to particular kinds of DBMSs, such as relational DBMSs, extended relational DBMSs, and object-oriented DBMSs.

The term ODMS (object data management system) is used to refer to all of the new kinds of DBMSs described in the book. As a convenience, systems in this bibliography have been marked with an icon according to the category of ODMS that they fit best. These categories were defined at the beginning of Chapter 4:

Object-oriented DBMSs: These systems are based on an object-oriented model, and use a database programming language architecture, providing transparent persistence in programming languages.

Extended relational DBMSs: These systems extend relational systems with new capabilities for data modelling and procedural storage. They use an extended database system architecture, where the programming language and database language are separated.

🜒 *Functional/semantic DBMSs:* These systems incorporate ideas from functional, semantic, and object-oriented models, and use an extended database system architecture.

▣ *Object managers:* These systems generally provide less functionality than a full DBMS, but require less system resources. They generally use a procedure-call interface, and allow the user to choose which modules will be loaded.

▷⊟ *DBMS generators:* These systems allow the sophisticated user to custom-build a DBMS for a particular application or set of applications. They generally incorporate features from a number of data models.

◻ *Other systems:* This category is for systems that do not fit any of the above categories.

The system categories, names, and references are as follows:

🜒 AVANCE — A. Bjornserstadt, S. Britts, "AVANCE: An Object Management System," *Proceedings OOPSLA, ACM SIGPLAN Notices*, 23, 11, November 1988.

▣ Camelot — A. Z. Spector, J. Bloch, D. Daniels, R. Draves, D. Duchamp, J. Eppinger, S. Menees, D. Thompson, *The Camelot Project*, Technical Report CMU-CS-86-166, Computer Science Department Carnegie-Mellon University, Pittsburgh, Pennsylvania, 1986.

🜒 CACTIS — S. Hudson, R. King, "CACTIS: A Database System for Specifying Functionally-Defined Data," in [Dittrich and Day*al 1986] and [Zdo*nik and Maier 1989].

🜒 DAMOKLES — K. R. Dittrich, W. Gotthard, P. C. Lockemann, "DAMOKLES—A Database System for Software Engineering Environments," *Advanced Programming Environments: Proceedings of an International Workshop*, Springer-Verlag, June 1986.

🜒 DAPLEX — D. Shipman, "The Functional Data Model and the Data Language DAPLEX," *ACM Transactions on Database Systems*, 6, 1, March 1981.

◻ DASDBS — H. J. Scheck, H.-B. Paul, M. H. Scholl, G. Weikum, "The DASDBS Project: Objectives, Experiences, and Future Prospects," *IEEE Transactions on Knowledge and Database Engineering*, 1, 2, March 1990.

🜔 ENCORE — S. B. Zdonik, M. Hornick, "A Shared, Segmented Memory System for an Object-Oriented Database," *ACM Transactions on Office Information Systems*, 5, 1, January 1987.

▷⊟ EXODUS — M. Carey, D. DeWitt, "An Overview of the EXODUS Project," *Database Engineering*, 10, 2, June 1987. Also in [Zdonik and Maier 1989].

🜒 GBase — Object Databases Corporation, GBase Technical Summary, Object Databases Corporation, Cambridge, Massachusetts, 1990.

🜔 GemStone — R. Bretl, D. Maier, A. Otis, J. Penney, B. Schuchardt, J. Stein, H. Williams, M. Williams, "The Gemstone Data Management System," in [Kim and Lochovsky 1988].

▷⊟ GENESIS — D. Batory, J. Barnett, J. Garza, K. Smith, K. Tsukuda, B. Twichell, T. Wise, *GENESIS: A Reconfigurable Database Management System*, Technical Report TR-86-07, Department of Computer Sciences, University of Texas at Austin, Texas, March 1986. Also in [Zdonik and Maier 1989].

iMax-432   F. Pollack, K. Kahn, R. Wilkinson, "The iMAX-432 Object Filing System," in *Proceedings of the Eighth Symposium on Operating Systems Principles,* Pacific Grove, California, December 1981.

ITASCA   ITASCA Systems, Inc, *ITASCA System Overview,* Unisys, Minneapolis, Minnesota, 1993.

IRIS   D. Fishman, et al, "IRIS: An Object-Oriented Database Management System," *ACM Transactions on Office Information Systems, 5,* 1, January 1987. Also in [Zdonik and Maier 1989].

Kala   S. S., Simmel and I. Godard, *Introduction to Kala,* Penobscot Development Corporation, Cambridge, Massachusetts, 1993.

LOOM   T. Kaehler, G. Krasner, "LOOM—Large Object-Oriented Memory for Smalltalk-80 Systems," in *Smalltalk-80: Bits of History, Words of Advice,* G. Krasner, Ed., Addison-Wesley, Reading, Massachusetts, 1983.

LOGRES   S. Ceri et al, "ALGRES: An Advanced Database System for Complex Applications," *IEEE Software,* July 1990.

MATISSE   Intellitic, *MATISSE Open Semantic Database: Product Overview,* Intellitic International, Saint-Quentin-en-Yvelines, France, 1993.

Mneme   J. E. B. Moss, S. Sinofsky, "Managing Persistent Data with Mneme: Designing a Reliable Shared Object Interface," in [Dittrich 1988].

Montage   Montage Software, *Montage Users Guide,* Montage Software, Inc, Emeryville, California, 1993.

O_2 F. Bancilhon, et al, "The Design and Implementation of O_2, an Object-Oriented DBMS," in [Dittrich 1988].

Objectivity/DB   Objectivity, Inc., *Objectivity Database Reference Manual,* Objectivity, Inc., Menlo Park, California, 1993.

ObjectStore   Object Design, *ObjectStore Reference Manual,* Object Design, Inc., Burlington, Massachusetts, 1993.

ObServer   S. B. Zdonik, M. Hornick, "A Shared, Segmented Memory System for an Object-Oriented Database," *ACM Transactions on Office Information Systems, 5,* 1, January 1987.

ONTOS   Ontos, *ONTOS Reference Manual.* Ontos, Inc., Burlington, Massachusetts, 1993.

OpenODB   Hewlett Packard, *OpenODB Technical Data,* Hewlett-Packard Company, Cupertino, California, 1993.

OpenOODB   D. Wells, J. Blakeley, and C. Thompson, "Architecture of an Open Object-Oriented Database Management System," *IEEE Computer,* Vol. 25, No. 10, October 1992.

ORION   W. Kim, et al, "Features of the ORION Object-Oriented DBMS," in [Kim and Lochovsky 1988].

Orion   Xidak, *Orion System Overview,* Xidak, Inc. Palo Alto, California, 1990.

OZ+   S. P. Weiser, F. H. Lochovsky, "OZ+: An Object-Oriented Database System," in [Kim and Lochovsky 1989].

PENGUIN   G. Wiederhold, T. Barasalou, S. Chaudhuri, *Managing Objects in a Relational Framework,* Technical Report, Computer Science, Stanford University, Palo Alto, California, 1990.

⊞⌐ Persistence   Persistence Software, *Persistence Technical Overview*, Persistence, Inc, San Mateo, California, 1993.

℧⌐ POET   Poet Software, *POET Programmer's and Reference Guide*, BKS Software (now Poet Software), Hamburg, Germany, 1993.

⊞⌐ POSTGRES   M. Stonebraker, L. Rowe, "The Design of POSTGRES," in *Proceedings of SIGMOD Conference*, Washington D.C., 1986.

⅄⌐ PROBE   U. Dayal, J. Smith, "PROBE: A Knowledge-Oriented Database Management System," in *Proceedings of the Islamorada Workshop on Large Scale Knowledge Base and Reasoning Systems*, February 1985. Also in [Brodie and Mylopoulos 1986].

⅄⌐ SIM   B. L. Fritchman, R. L. Guck, D. Jagannathan, J. P. Thompson, D. M. Tolbert, "SIM: Design and Implementation of a Semantic Database System," in [Cardenas and McLeod 1990].

⊞⌐ Starburst   P. Schwarz et al, "Extensibility in the Starburst Database System," in *Proceedings of the International Workshop on Object-Oriented Database Systems*, Pacific Grove, California, September 1986.

℧⌐ STATICE   D. Weinreb, "An Object-Oriented Database System to Support an Integrated Programming Environment," *IEEE Data Engineering*, 11, 2, June 1988.

⊞⌐ UniSQL   UniSQL, *UniSQL/X Database Management System Product Description*, UniSQL, Inc, Austin, Texas, 1993.

⅄⌐ VBase   Ontologic, *VBase Functional Specification*. Ontologic, Inc., (now Ontos, Inc.), Burlington, Massachusetts, 1986.

℧⌐ VERSANT   Versant Object Technology, *Versant Reference Manual*, Versant Object Technology, Inc., Menlo Park, California, 1993.

℧⌐ VISION   M. Caruso, E. Sciore, "The VISION Object-Oriented DBMS," in F. Bancilhon, P. Buneman, Eds. *Advances in Database Programming Languages*, ACM Press, Addison-Wesley, Reading, Massachusetts, 1990.

⅄⌐ ZEITGEIST   S. Ford, et al, "ZEITGEIST: Database Support for Object-Oriented Programming," in [Dittrich 1988].

Note: Kala, GBase, GemStone, ITASCA, Matisse, Montage, O$_2$, Objectivity/DB, ObjectStore, OpenODB, Open OODB, POET, ONTOS, STATICE, VBase, VERSANT, and VISION are registered trademarks of their respective vendors. Other capitalized or all-upper-case-letter names used in this book may also be trademarks.

The Appendix contains overviews of many of these ODMSs. In addition, for readers planning to purchase an ODMS product, [Barry and Associates 1994] provides much more detailed up-to-date comparisons.

Annotated Bibliography

Icons in the margin of this bibliography indicate the type of material covered by the corresponding reference:

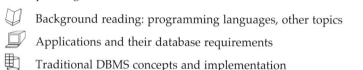

Background reading: programming languages, other topics

Applications and their database requirements

Traditional DBMS concepts and implementation

Advanced DBMS concepts

Advanced DBMS implementation techniques

Advanced DBMS prototypes and products

S. Abiteboul, R. Hall, "IFO, A Formal Semantic Database Model," *ACM Transactions on Database Systems,* 12, 4, December 1987.

> Describes a semantic data model, IFO, incorporating objects, object type inheritance, and two forms of aggregation: a "part-of" relationship (conventional aggregation), and a "set-of" relationship (where all of the aggregated objects are of the same type). This paper contributes an investigation of semantic database issues more formal than those of others.

E. Adams, M. Honda, T. Miller, "Object Management in a CASE Environment," in *Proceedings Eleventh International Conference on Software Engineering,* 1989.

> Describes NSE, a CASE environment including an object manager based on an extension of the UNIX file system. Incorporates a copy–modify–merge paradigm, rather than transaction semantics, and allows user-defined object types and associated procedures.

R. Agrawal and N. H. Gehani, "ODE (Object Database and Environment): The Language and the Data Model," in *Proceedings of the ACM SIGMOD Conference,* 1989.

> An extension of the C++ programming language to make it amenable to integration with an object-oriented database system.

M. Ahlsen, A. Bjornserstedt, S. Britts, C. Hulten, L. Soderlund, "An Architecture for Object Management in OIS," *ACM Transactions on Office Information Systems,* 2, 3, July 1984.

> Describes a prototype office-information system called OPAL, based on an object-oriented model. Later renamed and enhanced as AVANCE [Bjornserstedt and Britts 1988].

M. Ahlsen, A. Bjornserstedt, S. Britts, C. Hulten, L. Soderlund, *Making Type Changes Transparent,* SYSLAB Technical Report 22, University of Stockholm, Sweden, February 1984.

> Proposes mapping functions between versions of types, so that existing type instances do not need to be updated. Translations across multiple versions are composed as needed. The alternative to this approach is immediate update of object instances, as is done in current ODMSs.

A. Albano, L. Cardelli, R. Orsini, "Galileo: A Strongly Typed, Interactive Conceptual Language," *ACM Transactions on Database Systems,* 10, 2, 1985.

> Describes a combined query and programming language that provides procedural modularization and multiple subclass mechanisms (subsets, partitions, and restrictions), and allows both structural and encapsulated object models to coexist.

A. Albano, A. Dearle, G. Ghelli, C. Marlin, R. Morrison, R. Orsini, D. Stemple, *A Framework for Comparing Type Systems for Database Programming Languages,* Research Report CS/90/3, Department of Mathematical and Computational Sciences, University of Saint Andrews, Great Britain.

> Provides a taxonomy for comparing data models (type systems) for database programming languages, plus four papers using this framework to describe Napier88, Galileo, DBPL, and ADABTPL, respectively. These languages were presented in [Hull, Morrison, and Stemple 1989]. The framework taxonomy includes treatment of extent versus intent, orthogonality of persistence and type, static and dynamic type checking, strong and weak type checking, type constructors, type inference, types of equality, forms of subtyping, and many other database and programming aspects of the languages.

T. Anderson, A. Berre, M. Mallison, H. Porter, B. Schneider, *The Hypermodel Benchmark,* Tektronix Technical Report 89-05, Beaverton, Oregon, 1989. More recent version in [Bancilhon, Thanos, and Tsichritzis 1990].

> Presents a benchmark for comparing object-oriented database system performance with a series of 17 measurements on a hypertext document application.

T. Andrews, C. Harris, "Combining Language and Database Advances in an Object-Oriented Development Environment," in *Proceedings Conference on Object-Oriented Programming Systems, Languages, and Applications (OOPSLA),* October 1987. Also in [Zdonik and Maier 1989].

> Describes the Ontologic VBase product, an object-oriented database system. See also [Ontologic 1986], and the subsequent product in the next reference.

T. Andrews, C. Harris, K. Sinkel, J. Duhl, *The ONTOS Object Database*, Technical Report, Ontologic, Inc, Burlington, Massachusetts, 1989.

> Describes the Ontologic ONTOS product, which superceded the VBase product. ONTOS is integrated with the C++ language, and provides aggregation, generalization, transactions, versions, class extents, and remote and distributed databases.

 M. Astrahan, et al, "System R: Relational Approach to Database Management," *ACM Transactions on Database Systems*, 1, 1, 1976.

> Discusses System R, one of the first implementations of the relational model. A number of seminal papers on storage management and concurrency control came out of the System R project.

 M. Atkinson, "Programming Languages and Databases," Technical Report CSR-26-78, Computer Science, University of Edinburgh, August 1978.

> Provides probably the earliest comprehensive discussion of integration of programming languages and databases, influencing later work.

 M. Atkinson, P. Bailey, K. Chisholm, P. Cockshott, R. Morrison, "An Approach to Persistent Programming," *The Computer Journal*, 26, 4 1983.

> Describes PS-Algol, a programming language with persistent data. Based on S-Algol, an extension of Algol-W with abstract data types. PS-Algol provides persistence independent of type, transparent to executable code. Includes an implementation of transactions.

 M. Atkinson, P. Buneman, "Type and Persistence in Database Programming Languages," *ACM Computing Surveys*, 19, 2, June 1989.

> Presents a good survey of work on programming languages with persistent data. Compares different approaches with examples.

 M. Atkinson, F. Bancilhon, D. DeWitt, K. Dittrich, D. Maier, S. Zdonik, "The Object-Oriented Database System Manifesto," in [Kim, Nicolas, and Nishio 1989].

> Describes an agreement by leading researchers to define the meaning of "object-oriented" database. Classifies features as mandatory and optional. The mandatory features include object identity, user-defined types, collections, encapsulation, inheritance, late binding, persistence, large databases, concurrency control, recovery, and ad hoc query capability.

 N. Ballou, et al, "Coupling an Expert System Shell with an Object-Oriented Database System," *Journal of Object-Oriented Programming*, June 1988.

> Describes an innovative combination of two LISP-based projects at MCC, the PROTEUS expert-system development facility and the ORION object-oriented ODMS [Kim et al 1988]. PROTEUS was modified to store its knowledge base in ORION. Proteus supports knowledge representation with support and justification for knowledge data and a backward- and forward-chaining inference mechanism. The paper does not report much experience with the PROTEUS/ORION system—for example, whether adequate performance can be achieved building the expert-system shell on top of the database system—but this could be a useful direction for future ODMS work.

 R. Balzer, "A 15-Year Perspective on Automatic Programming," *IEEE Transactions on Software Engineering*, 11, 11, November 1985.

> Provides a good survey of work in automatic generation of programs from higher-level specifications, with some mention of information-management requirements.

F. Bancilhon, W. Kim, H. Korth, "A Model of CAD Transactions," in *Proceedings International Conference on Very Large Databases (VLDB),* August 1984.

> Presents one of the few discussions of transaction semantics requirements for ODMSs.

F. Bancilhon, et al, "The Design and Implementation of O $_2$, an Object-Oriented Database System," in [Dittrich 1988].

F. Bancilhon, S. Cluet, C. Delobel, "A Query Language for the O $_2$ Object-Oriented Database System," in [Hull, Morrison, & Stemple 1989].

F. Bancilhon, L. Delobel, P. Kanellakis, Eds, *Building an Object-Oriented Database System: The Story of O $_2$,* Morgan-Kaufmann, San Mateo, California, 1991.

> Describe how O $_2$ provides object identity, encapsulation, multiple inheritance, lists, sets, a global query language, and transactions. See also [Lecluse et al 1988, Cluet et al 1989, Cazalens et al 1990, Bancilhon, Delobel, Kanellakis 1991] and the O $_2$ paper in [Cattell 1991].

F. Bancilhon, D. Maier, "Multilanguage Object-Oriented Systems: New Answers to Old Database Problems?" in *Future Generation Computer,* K. Fuchi, L. Kott, Eds, North-Holland, 1988.

> Discusses the problems of database–programming language impedance mismatch, and of multiple programming languages in an object-oriented database system.

F. Bancilhon, C. Thanos, D. Tsichritzis, Eds, *Advances in Database Technology—EDBT 90,* Venice, Italy, Springer-Verlag, Berlin, Germany, March 1990.

> Contains papers on logic databases, object-oriented database systems, and extended functional-model systems.

F. Bancilhon, P. Buneman, *Advances in Database Programming Languages,* ACM Press, Addison-Wesley, Reading, Massachusetts, 1990.

> Describes database programming languages and related topics in papers collected from a September 1987 meeting of researchers. Includes both formal and practically-oriented papers, from several dozen authors.

J. Banerjee, W. Kim, H. J. Kim, H. F. Korth, "Semantics and Implementation of Schema Evolution in Object-Oriented Database Systems," in *Proceedings of the ACM SIGMOD Conference,* 1987.

J. Banerjee et al., "Queries in Object-Oriented Databases," in *Proceedings of the International Conference on Data Engineering,* Los Angeles, February 1988.

J. Banerjee et al., "Data Model Issues for Object-Oriented Applications," *ACM Transactions on Office Information Systems ,* 5, 1, January 1987.

> Discuss issues in the ORION object-oriented database system. See [Kim 1988] for an overview of ORION. The first paper discusses ORION's deferred-update approach to dealing with changes to the data schema. Objects built with the previous schema are updated when they are next fetched. The second paper discusses query-processing issues in the context of a hierarchy of types. The third paper discusses a variety of issues, including composite objects and versions.

Barry and Associates, *DBMS Needs Assessment for Objects ,* currently $1195, order phone 800-770-8407 or +1-612-953-8407; revised regularly, 1994.

> Contains over 150 tables comparing more than 600 features of current object data management products. This report covers more products than the Appendix of this book, and it does so in ten times more depth, with several

hundred pages of conveniently indexed and categorized information regularly brought up to date. While this report is obviously more expensive than a book, it is well worth its cost for readers spending a week or more evaluating which product to purchase; it is the result of substantial work (including some of my own). Sample tables and purchase information are available from the number listed.

D. S. Batory, "Modeling the Storage Architectures of Commercial Database Systems," *ACM Transactions on Database Systems,* 10, 4, December 1985.

> Gives a unifying discussion of relational database engines. The GENESIS work in the following references is partly based on this formalization.

D. S. Batory, *Concepts for a Database System Synthesizer,* Technical Report TR-88-1, Department of Computer Science, University of Texas at Austin, Texas, 1988.

D. S. Batory, J. R. Barnett, *DaTE: The GENESIS DBMS Software Layout Editor,* Technical Report, Department of Computer Science, University of Texas at Austin, Texas, 1988. Also to appear in R. Zicari, *Conceptual Modelling.*

D. S. Batory, "GENESIS: A Project to Develop an Extensible Database Management System," in *Proceedings of the International Workshop on Object-Oriented Systems,* Computer Society Press, 1986.

D. Batory, T. Leung, T. Wise, "Implementation Concepts for an Extensible Data Model and Data Language," *ACM Transactions on Database Systems,* 13, 3, September 1988.

D. Batory, J. Barnett, J. Garza, K. Smith, K. Tsukuda, B. Twichell, T. Wise, *GENESIS: a Reconfigurable Database Management System,* Technical Report 86-07, Department of Computer Sciences, University of Texas at Austin, Texas, March 1986. Also in [Zdonik and Maier 1989].

> Describe GENESIS, a database system generator similar to EXODUS [Carey et al 1986], providing a plug-together set of facilities to tailor a DBMS to engineering or other applications. The focus of GENESIS is more on auto-matic generation of DBMS modules from high-level architecture descriptions supplied by the database implementor. GENESIS is capable of generating most traditional database architectures, and is being extended for object-oriented models. See the Appendix for more information.

D. Beech, "Groundwork for an Object Database Model," in *Research Directions in Object-Oriented Programming,* B. Shriver and P. Wegner, Eds, MIT Press, Cambridge, Massachusetts 1987.

> Discusses issues related to the derivation of the IRIS data model [Fishman et al 1989]. The rationale behind the fundamental concepts of objects, types, procedures, and transactions are covered.

D. Beech, "A Foundation for Evolution from Relational to Object Databases," in *Extending Database Technology (EDBT),* J. Schmidt, S. Ceri, M. Missikoff, Eds, Computer Science Lecture Notes 303, Springer-Verlag, New York and Berlin, Germany, 1988.

> Discusses OSQL, an object-oriented extension of the SQL relational query language [Date 1987, X3H2 1984].

D. Beech, B. Mahbod, "Generalized Version Control in an Object-Oriented Database," in *IEEE Fourth International Conference on Data Engineering,* February 1988.

> Discusses more basic requirements for version control in an ODMS, includ-ing implicit and explicit creation of object versions, and semantics of refer-ences to object versions.

D. Beech, C. Ozbutun, "Object Databases as Generalizations on Relational Databases," in [OODBTG 1990].

> Proposes extensions to SQL to incorporate object identity, references, sets, and inheritance. Not fully presented or implemented, but shows promising direction.

C. Beeri, "Formal Models for Object-Oriented Databases," in [Kim, Nicolas, and Nishio 1989].

> Provides a start at a sound formal foundation for an object-oriented data model. Incorporates object identity, inheritance, classes and functions as data, methods, and encapsulation.

E. Bertino and W. Kim, "Indexing Techniques for Queries on Nested Objects," *IEEE Transactions on Knowledge and Database Engineering*, October 1989.

> Compares indexing techniques in object-oriented models. Compares indexes on hierarchies of types versus separate indexes on each type in the hierarchy. Also covers nested-attribute indexes.

J. Bezivin, J. Hullut, P. Comte, H. Liebermann, Eds, *ECOOP: European Conference on Object-Oriented Programming 1987*, Springer-Verlag, Paris, June 1987.

> Proceedings of conference on object-oriented programming-language issues. See also [Shriver & Wegner 1987] and OOPSLA proceedings.

A. Bjornserstadt, S. Britts, "AVANCE: An Object Management System," in *Proceedings OOPSLA, ACM SIGPLAN Notices*, 23, 11, November 1988.

> Describes an ODMS evolved for office applications [Ahlsen et al 1984], with a language called PAL. The ODMS supports distributed databases, nested transactions, and automatic creation of object versions on update.

J. Blakeley, W. McKenna, G. Graefe. "Experiences Building the Open OODB Query Optimizer," ACM SIGMOD International Conference on Management of Data, Washington, D.C., May 1993.

> Describes the query module for Open OODB [Wells, Blakeley, Thompson 1992], including an object query language called OQL[C++], an object query optimizer, and a code generation component that can target various Persistent C++ languages. OQL[C++] is an SQL-based language that, when combined with Persistent C++, results in a hybrid OODB/RDB. OQL[C++] uniformly supports queries over transient and persistent collections. The object query optimizer provides a fairly complete framework that includes logical algebra operators, logical transformation rules, logical to physical implementation rules, enforcement of logical and physical properties, and cost and selectivity estimation.

T. Bloom and S. B. Zdonik, "Issues in the Design of Object-Oriented Database Programming Languages", in *Proceedings Second Conference on Object-Oriented Programming Systems, Languages, and Applications (OOPSLA)*, Orlando, Florida, October 1987.

> Discusses the technical and philosophical issues in integrating a programming language into a database language. Contrasts the perspectives of extending a programming language (with persistent data, concurrency) versus extending a database system (with procedural data). Examines the problems with providing type extents and query languages. See also [Keller 1986].

D. G. Bobrow, K. Kahn, G. Kiczales, L. Masinter, M. Stefik, F. Zdybel, "Common LOOPS: Merging LISP and Object-Oriented Programming," in [Cardenas and McLeod 1990].

D. G. Bobrow, et al, "Common LISP Object System Specification," X3J13 Document 88-02R (June 1988), *SIGPLAN Notices,* 23, September 1988.

> Describes CLOS, an object-oriented version of LISP descended from INTERLISP [Teitelman 1974]. See also [Moon 1989]. STATICE [Weinreb 1988] is built on CLOS.

G. Booch, *Object-Oriented Design,* Benjamin-Cummings, Redwood City, California, 1991.

> Thoroughly studies object-oriented design, the process of encapsulating application semantics as a set of object classes. Suggestions and examples are included for Smalltalk, Object Pascal, C++, and the Common LISP Object System.

R. Bowerman, R. Fertig, *Engineering Workstations: Technology and Application Trends,* Van Nostrand Reinhold, New York, New York, 1988.

> Provides an overview of the engineering workstation revolution. It also covers CAD/CAM applications, and compares some software and hardware products in the area. Because this field has moved quickly, however, the book is already somewhat dated.

G. Bracchi, B. Pernici, "SOS: A Conceptual Model for Office Information Systems," in *Proceedings of the ACM SIGMOD Workshop on Databases for Business and Office Applications,* May 1983.

> Describes a Semantic Office System (SOS) data schema, surveys approaches to office information systems, and discusses why they are different from traditional commercial applications.

R. Bretl, D. Maier, A. Otis, J. Penney, B. Schuchardt, J. Stein, H. Williams, M. Williams, "The GemStone Data Management System," in [Kim and Lochovsky 1988].

> Describes GemStone, one of the first commercial object-oriented database systems. GemStone is a database programming language designed as an extension of Smalltalk to incorporate database capabilities. It also has a C++ interface, now [Servio 1990].

M. L. Brodie, J. Mylopoulos, J. Schmidt, Eds, *On Conceptual Modelling,* Springer-Verlag, New York, New York and Berlin, Germany, 1984.

> Discusses data models from three different perspectives: database systems, programming languages, and artificial intelligence. It is interesting to observe how similar concepts have developed, or have *not* developed, in the three fields.

M. L. Brodie, J. Mylopoulos, Eds, *On Knowledge Base Management Systems,* Springer-Verlag, New York, New York and Berlin, Germany, 1986.

> Provides a collection of articles on database and knowledge representation systems.

M. L. Brodie et al, "Next Generation Database Management Systems Technology," in [Kim, Nicolas, and Nishio 1989].

> Gives various authors' perspectives on the important future directions for database research, including revolutionary versus evolutionary perspectives, ODMS performance, integration with deductive capabilities, and multimedia.

A. L. Brown, "From Semantic Data Models to Object-Orientation in Design Data-bases," *Information and Software Technology*, January 1989.

> Considers object-oriented data models as an evolution from semantic data models, which are in turn an evolution from relational. Uses an extended version of RM/T [Codd 1979] for comparison of examples.

A. L. Brown, *Database Support for Software Engineering*, Kogan Page Ltd., London, 1989.

> Presents a comprehensive discussion of database needs and systems for CASE applications.

K. B. Bruce and P. Wegner, "An Algebraic Model of Sybtype and Inheritance," in [Bancilhon and Buneman 1990].

> Describes a formalization of inheritance semantics for object-oriented programming languages.

J. Buxton, "Requirements for APSE-STONEMAN," US Department of Defense, Washington, D.C., February 1989.

> Discusses requirements for a CASE environment for ADA. Recommends using a DBMS as the central integrating component of the support environment.

F. Cacace, S. Ceri, S. C. Reghizzi, L. Tanca, R. Zicari, *Integrating Object-Oriented Data Modelling with a Rule-based Programming Paradigm*, Technical Report 90.008, Dipartimento di Elletronica, Politecnico di Milano, Milano, Italy, November 1989.

> Describes the LOGRES project, a follow-up to ALGRES [Ceri et al 1990] designed to incorporate a rule-based language into a database system. These authors are continuing this work as part of an ESPRIT project, to allow interoperability between an object-oriented and a rule-based language by unifying their data models and allowing calls between methods in the former language and predicates in the latter.

A. F. Cardenas, D. McLeod, *Research Foundations in Object-Oriented and Semantic Database*, Prentice-Hall, Englewood Cliffs, New Jersey, 1990.

> Provides a collection of seminal papers on object data management concepts, implementations, and applications. Similar collections are [Kim and Lochovsky 1988, Zdonik and Maier 1989].

M. Carey et al, "The Architecture of the EXODUS Extensible DBMS," in [Dittrich and Dayal 1986].

M. Carey, D. DeWitt, "An Overview of the EXODUS Project," *IEEE Database Engineering*, 10, 2, June 1987. Also in [Zdonik and Maier 1989].

M. Carey, D. DeWitt, J. Richardson, E. Shekita, "Storage Management for Objects in EXODUS," in [Kim and Lochovsky 1988].

> Describe EXODUS, one of the first database system generators. EXODUS extends basic access methods into a package of plug-together capabilities. It supports OIDs, B-trees, user-defined access methods, large objects, and transactions. Other systems with similar goals are Starburst [Schwarz et al 1986] and GENESIS [Batory et al 1986].

M. Carey, E. Shekita, G. Lapis, B. Lindsay, J. McPherson, "An Incremental Join Attachment for Starburst," in *Proceedings of the Sixteenth International Conference on Very Large Databases (VLDB)*, 1990.

> Describes an implementation of parent–child links for performing joins in an extended relational ODMS, Starburst [Schwarz et al 1986]. Provides an

evaluation of the Starburst extensible architecture, based on the ease with which Starburst was extended with this new access method. See also [Shekita and Carey 1990], an evaluation of joins based on parent–child links.

M. J. Carey, D. J. DeWitt, J. F. Naughton, "The OO7 Object-Oriented Database Benchmark," in *Proceedings of the ACM SIGMOD Conference,* Washington, D.C., May 1993.

> Describes an excellent benchmark designed to be more comprehensive than its predecessor OO1 [Cattell, Skeen 1992], which produced one simple overall performance number. OO7 defines several dozen measures for comparing object-oriented DBMSs with a number of varying parameters. Work has continued on OO7 since the time of this paper.

M. Caruso, E. Sciore, "The VISION Object-Oriented Database System," in [Bancilhon and Buneman 1990].

> Describes the VISION ODMS. See also [Innovative Systems 1988].

R. G. G. Cattell, "Design and Implementation of a Relationship-Entity-Datum Data Model," Technical Report CSL-83-4, Xerox PARC, Palo Alto, California, 1983.

> Describes the data model of the Cypress DBMS, incorporating object identity, relationships of arbitrary degree and multiplicity, and a hierarchy of object types. Covers implementation issues for inheritance, client–server architecture, and general performance. Several graphical object-oriented user interfaces to the system are also described.

R. G. G. Cattell, Ed, *The Object Database Standard: ODMG-93,* Morgan Kaufmann Publishers, San Mateo, California, 1993.

> Specifies the Object Database Management Group (ODMG) standard for object-oriented DBMSs. This is the first version of the standard; ODMG is continuing with enhancements and corrections, and may join a larger standards group. The ODMG defines a programming-language independent framework for object definition and query, and a binding for various object-oriented programming languages (to form database programming languages). See Chapter 6 for an overview of the ODMG work to date.

R. G. G. Cattell, J. Skeen, "Object Operations Benchmark," *ACM Transactions on Database Systems* April 1992. Derivative paper in [Gray 1991].

> Describes the OO1 benchmark, which was designed to approximate database needs of CAD, CASE, and similar applications. OO1 focuses on characteristics (long-term checkout, reference traversal) where these applications differ from traditional business applications. It represents a simpler but less comprehensive set of measures than that given in [Anderson et al 1989].

R. G. G. Cattell, Guest Ed, Special Issue on Next-Generation Database Systems, *Communications of the ACM,* 34, 10, October 1991.

> Provides more detailed information on five of the ODMSs in the Appendix: POSTGRES, Starburst, O$_2$, ObjectStore, and GemStone. The articles follow a common framework and include benchmark results.

R. Cazalens et al, "Building User Interfaces with the LOOKS Hyper-Object System," Technical Report, Altair, Le Chesnay Cedex, France, 1990.

> Describes an innovative object-oriented graphical application-development system implemented on O$_2$ [Bancilhon et al 1988].

S. Ceri et al, "ALGRES: An Advanced Database System for Complex Applications," *IEEE Software,* July 1990.

> Describes ALGRES, a main-memory ODMS supporting an extended relational algebra, derived from an extended relational model [Abiteboul and Hall 1987]. Supports complex (nested) objects, object identity, set-valued attributes, a type hierarchy, and access from the Datalog logic language as well as a query language. Uses Informix to store the underlying relations.

CFI (CAD Framework Initiative), *CFI Storage Management Procedural Interface,* CAD Framework Initiative, Inc., Boulder, Colorado, 1990.

> Discusses part of the work of CFI, a consortium working toward standards required in the CAD industry. The Storage Management Working Group has already drafted a procedural interface proposal for basic object-oriented database functionality, with a data model incorporating objects, object types, object identifiers, relationships, and transactions.

A. Chan et al, "Storage and Access Structures to Support a Semantic Data Model," in *Proceedings Eighth International Conference on Very Large Databases,* Mexico City, 1982. Also in [Zdonik and Maier 1989].

> Discusses the implementation of ADAPLEX, accessing the DAPLEX DBMS [Shipman 1981] from ADA. Covers clustering, access methods, and mapping the user's functions to stored tables.

E. E. Chang, R. H. Katz, "Exploiting Inheritance and Structure Semantics for Effective Clustering and Buffering in an Object-oriented database system," in *Proceedings of the ACM SIGMOD Conference,* 1989.

> Examines how to use the additional semantics that object-oriented database systems provide as hints for physical clustering of data. The authors compare different approaches, reporting improvements as large as 200 percent.

E. E. Chang, *Effective Clustering and Buffering in an Object-Oriented Database System,* PhD Thesis, UCB/CSD 89/515, Department of Electrical Engineering and Computer Science, University of California at Berkeley, California, June 1989.

> Provides a thorough study of how generalization, aggregation, and other information can be used to cluster objects on data pages efficiently. The results are based on instrumented versions of CAD tools.

P. P. Chen, "The Entity–Relationship Model: Towards a Unified View of Data," *ACM Transactions on Database Systems,* 1, 1, March 1976.

> Describes the ER model. This early paper inspired considerable research in new data models to incorporate more data semantics, and also inspired many commercial products for relational database design using his formalism. Chen's basic contribution was the introduction of "entities" and "relationships," to distinguish relational tables that represent objects and those that represent associations between objects.

D. Chimenti et al, "The LDL System Prototype," *IEEE Journal on Data and Knowledge Engineering,* March 1990.

> Describes a logic database language (LDL). Although we focus on data and object management, future research in deductive languages may make it possible to combine data, object, and knowledge management in a single system. See [Zaniolo 1990].

H. Chou, D. DeWitt, R. Katz, A. Klug, "Design and Implementation of the Wisconsin Storage System," *Software Practice and Experience,* 15, 10, October 1985.

> Describes the Wisconsin Storage System (WiSS), which provides much of the

physical storage management capabilities, including large objects, for a DBMS. WiSS was superceded by the EXODUS work at Wisconsin [Carey et al 1986].

H. Chou, W. Kim, "Versions and Change Notification in an Object-Oriented Database System," in *Proceedings of the Twenty-Fifth Design Automation Conference,* June 1985.

Presents one of the better discussions of implementations for versions in database systems, focused specifically on the ORION system [Kim et al 1988].

S. Cluet, C. Delobel, C. Lecluse, P. Richard, "RELOOP: An Algebra-Based Query Language for an Object-Oriented Database System," in [Kim, Nicolas, and Nishio 1989].

Describes the RELOOP language for the O_2 DBMS [Bancilhon et al 1988]. Contrasts the approach to a functional query language for O_2 described by [Bancilhon, Cluet and Delobel 1989], and to other ODMS query languages. RELOOP is a global query language—that is, it can perform joins between types—as contrasted to the ORION or GemStone query languages.

P. Coad, E. Yourdon, *Object-Oriented Analysis,* Yourdon Press, Prentice-Hall, Englewood Cliffs, New Jersey, 1990.

Explains the process of representing an application and its databases using the object-oriented paradigm. See also [Booch 1991], which is a more extensive discussion at a less abstract level.

W. Cockshott, M. Atkinson, K. Chisholm, P. Bailey, R. Morrison, "Persistent Object Management System," *Software—Practice and Experience,* 14, 1, January 1984. Also in [Zdonik and Maier 1989].

Description of the data-storage system for PS-Algol [Atkinson et al 1983]. This basic object manager provides most of the capabilities of a database system.

E. F. Codd, "A Relational Model for Large Shared Data Banks," *Communications of the ACM,* 13, 6, June 1970.

Codd's classic discussion of the relational data model. Codd is commonly known as the father of this model. The popularity of the relational model stemmed from the model's simplicity and from the independence it afforded application programs from the physical data representation.

E. F. Codd, "Extending the Database Relational Model to Capture More Meaning," *ACM Transactions on Database Systems,* 4, 4, December 1979.

Addresses extensions to the relational model to incorporate new concepts corresponding to objects, a hierarchy of types, and many (but not all) of the other features we discuss in this book. The extended model is called RM/T. RM/T is defined more rigorously than is other work we cover, and provides a compatible evolutionary direction from relational DBMSs. This work is important reading, especially for the extended relational approach. Little progress has been made toward its implementation to date, however.

E. F. Codd, *The Relational Model for Database Management Version 2,* Addison-Wesley, Reading, Massachusetts, 1990.

Provides a detailed and understandable explanation of a subset of the features in the RM/T model that is proposed in [Codd 1979]. RM/V1 (and subsequent models RM/V2, etc.) were developed to give database system vendors successive "stepping stones" to all the functionality and semantics of RM/T, which is rather complex.

D. Comer, "The Ubiquitous B-Tree," *ACM Computing Surveys,* 11, 2, 1979.

> Surveys the variations on basic B-tree implementation. B-trees are the most important access method in nearly all database systems.

J. Conklin, "Hypertext: An Introduction and Survey," *IEEE Computer,* September 1987.

> Presents a good survey of hypertext systems, with some mention of their information representation requirements.

R. Conradi, T. Didriksen, D. Wanvik, *Advanced Programming Environments: Proceedings of an International Workshop,* Springer-Verlag, New York, New York and Berlin, Germany, June 1986.

> Comprises a good collection of papers on CASE projects for both "programming in the small" and "programming in the large." Some papers deal specifically with data management requirements.

P. Dadam et al, "A DBMS Prototype to Support Extended NF² Relations: An Integrated View on Flat Tables and Hierarchies," in *Proceedings of the ACM SIGMOD Conference,* Washington D.C., May 1986.

> Describes an extended relational ODMS based on an NF² (non–first-normal-form) data model [Scheck and Scholl 1986].

DBTG (Data Base Task Group), *CODASYL Programming Language Committee Report,* ANSI Data Base Task Group, April 1971.

> Provides the authoritative reference on the *network* data model, based on records plus parent–child (one-to-many) links between records.

O. J. Dahl, K. Nygaard, "SIMULA—An Algol-Based Simulation Language," *Communications of the ACM,* 9, 9, 1966.

> Describes Simula, the first language incorporating object-oriented data-abstraction concepts, although Smalltalk [Goldberg and Robson 1983] popularized and expanded the object-oriented programming paradigm.

C. J. Date, *A Guide to the SQL Standard,* Addison-Wesley, Reading, Massachusetts, 1987.

> Describes the SQL standard, defined by ANSI [X3H2 1984]. SQL has been very important to the success of relational DBMSs. Little progress has been made on standards in ODMSs.

C. J. Date, *Introduction to Database Systems,* Volume 1, Fifth Edition, Addison-Wesley, Reading, Massachusetts, 1990.

C. J. Date, *Introduction to Database Systems,* Volume 2, Addison-Wesley, Reading, Massachusetts, 1983.

> Provides a broad introduction to commercial database systems, particularly relational DBMSs. The second volume covers more advanced concepts. See also [Ullman 1988, Elmasri and Navathe 1989, Frank 1988].

U. Dayal, P. A. Bernstein, "On the Correct Translation of Update Operations on Relational Views," *ACM Transactions on Database Systems,* 8, 3, September 1982.

> Deals with the problem of updating virtual data (views) in the relational model. Formalizes the notion of update translation, defining conditions under which algorithms can produce correct translation of view updates. See also [Keller 1985].

 U. Dayal, J. Smith, "PROBE: A Knowledge-Oriented Database Management System," in *Proceedings of the Islamorada Workshop on Large Scale Knowledge Base and Reasoning Systems,* February 1985. Also in [Brodie and Mylopoulos 1986].

> Describes PROBE, a functional-model ODMS designed as an extension of the DAPLEX DBMS [Shipman 1981].

U. Dayal M. Hsu, R. Lochin, "Organizing Long-Running Activities with Triggers and Transactions," in *Proceedings of the ACM SIGMOD Conference*, Atlantic City, New Jersey 1990.

> Presents a paradigm for representing office and other applications through multiple cooperating agents in a workflow model based on triggers and transactions. Also includes a survey of other work on this topic, including approaches based on a fixed augmented Petri-net model of control instead of arbitrary predicate triggers.

A. Dearle, G. M. Shaw, S. B. Zdonik, Eds, *Implementing Persistent Object Bases: The Fourth International Workshop on Persistent Object Systems*, Morgan-Kaufmann, San Mateo, California, September 1990.

> Collects together a number of papers on object managers (also known as persistent object bases) and the storage level implementations of ODMSs.

T. DeMarco, *Structured Design and System Specification*, Prentice-Hall, Englewood Cliffs, New Jersey,1978.

> Describes Yourdon–DeMarco Structured Analysis, for use in CASE design and specification. See also [Yourdon and Constantine 1978].

F. DeRemer, H. Kron, "Programming-in-the-Large versus Programming-in-the-Small," *IEEE Transaction on Software Engineering*, 2, 2, June 1976.

> Distinguishes CASE tools for coordination in large projects from those dealing with the actual programming. The two have somewhat different database requirements.

D. Dewitt, D. Maier, *A Study of Distributed Architectures for Object-Oriented Databases*, Technical Report, GIP Altair, Le Chesnay, Cedex, France, 1990.

> Compares three different client–server architectures for access to data in an ODMS: file servers, using the NFS distributed file system; page servers, using a custom RPC to do page-at-a-time fetch on the network; and object servers, using a custom RPC to fetch objects from the server. Relational DBMS products represent a fourth architecture, which might be called "query servers."

K. R. Dittrich, W. Gotthard, P. C. Lockemann, "DAMOKLES—A Database System for Software Engineering Environments," *Advanced Programming Environments: Proceedings of an International Workshop*, Springer-Verlag, New York, New York and Berlin Germany, June 1986.

> Discusses database requirements for CASE environments, particularly configuration management, and a proposed object-oriented database system to support CASE and similar applications, DAMOKLES. DAMOKLES is now being developed as part of UNIBASE, a cooperative effort of German software companies and research institutions. See also [Rehn et al 1988].

K. R. Dittrich, U. Dayal, Eds, *Proceedings of the International Workshop on Object-Oriented Database Systems*, Asilomar, California, 1986.

> Provides a collection of early ODMS papers. Contains a good paper by Dittrich himself, classifying DBMSs as *structurally, operationally, or behaviorally object-oriented*, providing complex objects, operations on objects, and operational encapsulation of objects, respectively. Also see specific references in this bibliography.

K. R. Dittrich, Ed, *Advances in Object-Oriented Database Systems: Second International Workshop on Object-Oriented Database Systems,* Bad Münster, Germany, September 1988. Available as Computer Science Lecture Notes 334, Springer-Verlag, New York, New York and Berlin, Germany, 1988.

> Provides a collection of papers on ODMS concepts and implementations. Also see proceedings of first workshop in the preceding reference.

K. R. Dittrich, W. Gotthard, P. C. Lockemann, "Complex Entities for Engineering Applications," in [Cardenas and McLeod 1990].

> Describes CERM, the Complex Entity-Relationship Model, a structurally object oriented data model designed to incorporate composite objects, a type hierarchy, and versions. Designed for DAMOKLES [Dittrich, Gotthard, and Lockermann 1986]. Also presents a good description of software engineering needs, used as an example.

M. Dowson, "ISTAR—An Integrated Project Support Environment," in *Proceedings of the ACM SIGSOFT/SIGPLAN Software Engineering Symposium on Practical Software Development Environments,* January 1987.

> Describes ISTAR, which uses an entity-oriented database to track information about projects, people, documents, programs, and schedules.

J. Duhl, C. Damon, "A Performance Comparison of Object and Relational Databases using the Sun Benchmark," *ACM SIGPLAN Notices,* 23, 11, November 1988.

> Attempts to compare a relational and object-oriented database system on performance for engineering applications. The object-oriented system was generally faster, although not substantially so. See also [Cattell and Skeen 1991].

C. M. Eastman, "System Facilities for CAD Databases," in *Proceedings of the Seventeenth Design Automation Conference,* June 1980.

C. M. Eastman, "Recent Developments in Representation in the Science of Design," in *Proceedings of the Eighteenth Design Automation Conference,* October 1981.

> Gives a good overview of MCAD for architecture, and of MCAD database requirements.

R. Earnshaw, Ed, *Workstations and Publication Systems,* Springer-Verlag, New York, New York and Berlin, Germany, 1987.

> Comprises articles on computer-aided publishing (CAP), an important application area for object data management.

C. A. Ellis, M. Bernal, "Officetalk-D: An Experimental Office Information System," in *Proceedings of the Conference on Office Information Systems,* Philadelphia, Pennsylvania, June 1982.

> Describes an office workflow system based on interacting objects (such as forms) routed between distributed machines.

C. A. Ellis, S. Gibbs, G. Rein: "Groupware: The Research and Development Issues," Technical Report STP-414-88, Microelectronics and Computing Consortium (MCC), Austin, Texas, 1988.

> Presents a survey and taxonomy for work on tools for cooperative creative work. See also [Grief 1988].

M. Ellis, B. Stroustrup, *The Annotated C++ Reference Manual,* Addison-Wesley, Reading, Massachusetts,1990.

> Describes C++, an object-oriented extension of the popular C programming language remedying most of C's weak compile-time type mechanisms. The

most recent object-oriented database programming languages generally use C++ as their preferred programming language.

 R. Ellison, "Software Development Environments: Research to Practice," in [Conradi et al 1986].

Presents an overview of work in programming-in-the-large.

 R. Elmasri, S. Navathe, *Fundamentals of Database Systems*, Benjamin/Cummings, Redwood City, California, 1989.

Covers both physical and logical data modeling for network, hierarchical, relational, semantic, and object-oriented database systems. One of the first introductory database texts with some coverage of semantic and object-oriented database systems.

 J. L. Eppinger, L. B. Mummert, A. Z. Spector, *A Guide to the Camelot Distributed Transaction Processing Facility including the Avalon Language*, Technical Report, Computer Science Department, Carnegie-Mellon University, Pittsburgh, Pennsylvania, 1989.

J. L. Eppinger, L. B. Mummert, A. Z. Spector, *Camelot and Avalon*, Morgan-Kaufmann, San Mateo, California, 1991.

Describe Camelot, which could be classified as an object manager, and Avalon, a persistent C++ built on top. See also [Spector et al 1986].

 K. P. Eswaran, "Specifications, Implementations, and Interactions of a Trigger Subsystem in an Integrated Database System," Research Report RJ1820, IBM, San Jose, California, August 1986.

Discusses one of the earliest attempts to incorporate triggers, a production-rule system, into a DBMS. Triggers, which allow a user-defined procedure to be executed when a predicate is satisfied, have been slow to be incorporated into relational database porducts. With the increased importance of rule-based logic in databases, they will be found in most relational DBMSs as well as ODMSs.

 G. C. Everest, M. S. Hanna, *Survey of Object-Oriented Database Management Systems*, Technical Report, Carlson School of Management, University of Minnesota, Minneapolis, Minnesota, January 1992.

Contrasts nearly all of the ODMS products discussed in this book on a matrix of dimensions, including architecture, object model, language features, and implementation techniques. This report was prepared under a work plan from [OODBTG 1990], and was contructed from vendor answers to a survey. Although some of the information is already becoming dated, and some of the answers are incomplete, this might be a good source for readers choosing an ODMS product.

R. Fagin, J. Nievergelt, N. Pippinger, H. R. Strong, "Extensible Hashing—A Fast Access Method for Dynamic Files," *ACM Transactions on Database Systems*, 4, 3, September 1979.

Explains extensible hashing, the right way to index large numbers of records when it is desirable to find exact matches with a key. Extensible hashing improves on conventional hashing in that the size of the hash "buckets" (and therefore the number of disk accesses) to fetch a record can be kept small.

 S. Feldman, "Make—A Program for Maintaining Computer Programs", *Software Practice and Experience* 9, 4, April 1979.

Describes Make, which inspired almost all the early work in object version management for CASE environments.

M. Fernandez, *ObServer II Server Interface Specification*, Technical Report, Department of Computer Science, Brown University, Providence, Rhode Island, December 1988.
>Describes ObServer. See also [Hornick and Zdonik 1989].

P. Fischer, A. Abiteboul, H-J. Scheck, Eds, *Nested Relations and Complex Objects in Databases*, Computers Science Lecture Notes 361, Springer-Verlag, New York, New York and Berlin, Germany, 1989.
>Collects together a number of papers on supporting database objects. Covers overall architecture, data models, and database design.

D. Fishman et al, "IRIS: an Object-Oriented Database Management System," *ACM Transactions on Office Information Systems, 5*, 1, January 1987. Also in [Zdonik and Maier 1989].
D. Fishman et al, "Overview of the IRIS DBMS," in [Kim and Lochovsky 1988]. Derivative paper in [Cardenas and McLeod 1990].
>Describe IRIS, a new and reasonably elegant object manager using a functional data model. Some contributions are OSQL, an object-oriented extension of SQL, and graphical tools for examining the database. IRIS is actually built on a relational storage manager.

S. Ford et al, "ZEITGEIST: Database Support for Object-Oriented Programming," in [Dittrich 1988].
>Describes TI Labs object-oriented database system for a programming environment. The heart of this system is a persistent object store (POS) that is seamlessly integrated with CLOS object-oriented LISP [Bobrow 1988]. Good discussion of programming language integration from user interviews. This system has subsequently been integrated with C++ as well [Perez 1990].

L. Frank, *Database Theory and Practice*, Addison-Wesley, Reading, Massachusetts,1988.
>Provides well-balanced coverage of both physical (indexing, storage) and logical (data modelling, query languages) issues for conventional DBMSs.

M. J. Franklin, *Caching and Memory Management in Client-Server Database Systems*, Technical Report #1168, Computer Science, University of Wisconsin, 1993.
>Thoroughly studies techniques for caching databases on workstations, as is done in most object-oriented DBMSs; demonstrates the benefits of caching, and compares the performance of different approaches.

B. L. Fritchman, R. L. Guck, D. Jagannathan, J. P. Thompson, D. M. Tolbert, "SIM: Design and Implementation of a Semantic Database System," in [Cardenas and McLeod 1990].
>Describes SIM, an ODMS based on a semantic data model [Hammer and McLeod 1981]. SIM is available commercially from Unisys. It incorporates object identity, type hierarchies, relationships with inverse attributes, integrity constraints, transactions, and a DML. Allows multivalued literal attributes (data-valued attributes) and reference attributes (entity-valued attributes).

A. L. Furtado, K. C. Sevcik, C. S. Dos Santos, "Permitting Updates Through Views of Databases," *Information Systems, 4*, 4, 1979.
>Presents an early description of the view-update problem. See [Keller 1985] for more recent coverage.

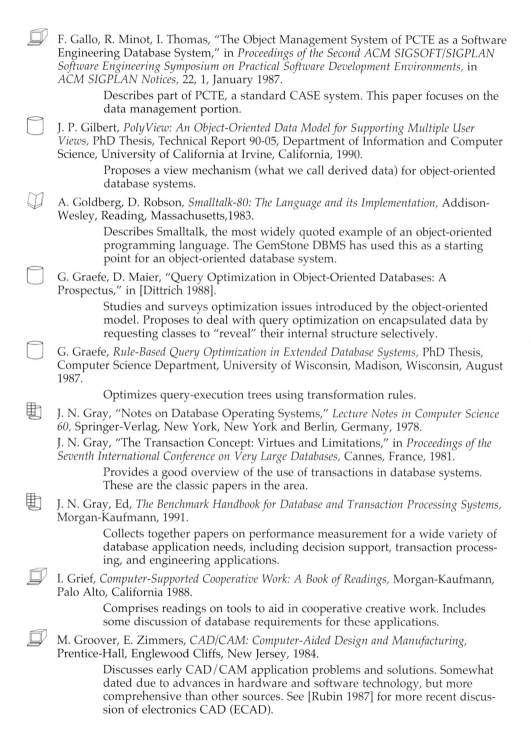

F. Gallo, R. Minot, I. Thomas, "The Object Management System of PCTE as a Software Engineering Database System," in *Proceedings of the Second ACM SIGSOFT/SIGPLAN Software Engineering Symposium on Practical Software Development Environments,* in *ACM SIGPLAN Notices,* 22, 1, January 1987.

> Describes part of PCTE, a standard CASE system. This paper focuses on the data management portion.

J. P. Gilbert, *PolyView: An Object-Oriented Data Model for Supporting Multiple User Views,* PhD Thesis, Technical Report 90-05, Department of Information and Computer Science, University of California at Irvine, California, 1990.

> Proposes a view mechanism (what we call derived data) for object-oriented database systems.

A. Goldberg, D. Robson, *Smalltalk-80: The Language and its Implementation,* Addison-Wesley, Reading, Massachusetts,1983.

> Describes Smalltalk, the most widely quoted example of an object-oriented programming language. The GemStone DBMS has used this as a starting point for an object-oriented database system.

G. Graefe, D. Maier, "Query Optimization in Object-Oriented Databases: A Prospectus," in [Dittrich 1988].

> Studies and surveys optimization issues introduced by the object-oriented model. Proposes to deal with query optimization on encapsulated data by requesting classes to "reveal" their internal structure selectively.

G. Graefe, *Rule-Based Query Optimization in Extended Database Systems,* PhD Thesis, Computer Science Department, University of Wisconsin, Madison, Wisconsin, August 1987.

> Optimizes query-execution trees using transformation rules.

J. N. Gray, "Notes on Database Operating Systems," *Lecture Notes in Computer Science* 60, Springer-Verlag, New York, New York and Berlin, Germany, 1978.

J. N. Gray, "The Transaction Concept: Virtues and Limitations," in *Proceedings of the Seventh International Conference on Very Large Databases,* Cannes, France, 1981.

> Provides a good overview of the use of transactions in database systems. These are the classic papers in the area.

J. N. Gray, Ed, *The Benchmark Handbook for Database and Transaction Processing Systems,* Morgan-Kaufmann, 1991.

> Collects together papers on performance measurement for a wide variety of database application needs, including decision support, transaction processing, and engineering applications.

I. Grief, *Computer-Supported Cooperative Work: A Book of Readings,* Morgan-Kaufmann, Palo Alto, California 1988.

> Comprises readings on tools to aid in cooperative creative work. Includes some discussion of database requirements for these applications.

M. Groover, E. Zimmers, *CAD/CAM: Computer-Aided Design and Manufacturing,* Prentice-Hall, Englewood Cliffs, New Jersey, 1984.

> Discusses early CAD/CAM application problems and solutions. Somewhat dated due to advances in hardware and software technology, but more comprehensive than other sources. See [Rubin 1987] for more recent discussion of electronics CAD (ECAD).

L. Haas et al, "Extensible Query Processing in Starburst," in *Proceedings of the ACM SIGMOD Conference,* May 1989.

> Describes query processing for Starburst [Schwarz et al 1986].

P. Hagen, T. Tonuyama, Eds, *Intelligent CAD Systems I,* Springer-Verlag, New York, New York and Berlin, Germany, 1987.

> Describes research on advances in ECAD systems.

M. Hammer, D. McLeod, "Database Description with SDM: A Semantic Database Model," *ACM Transactions on Database Systems, 6,* 3, September 1981. Also in [Zdonik and Maier 1989] and [Cardenas and McLeod 1990].

> Describes SDM, one of the more comprehensive early proposals to extend the relational data model to incorporate more semantics: objects, behavior, events, associations, and a type hierarchy.

R. Hardwick, "Why ROSE is Fast: Five Optimizations in the Design of an Experimental Database System for CAD Applications," in *Proceedings of the ACM SIGMOD Conference,* San Francisco, California, 1987.

> Discusses DBMS architectural issues to achieve good interactive performance for applications with complex interconnected objects. Important principles include fetching groups of tuples related to one object, using main memory as a cache, and creating fast OIDs.

D. S. Harrison, A. R. Newton, R. L. Spickelmier, T. J. Barnes, "Electronic CAD Frameworks," in *Proceedings of the IEEE, 78,* 2, February 1990.

> Describes the data management requirements of CAD applications, and discusses progress toward building a common *framework* for CAD tools, the underlying software to support the CAD tools, simplifying the development of CAD tools, and providing a greater degree of integration between them. See also the [CFI 1990] effort on framework standardization.

G. Harrus, F. Velez, R. Zicari, *Implementing Schema Updates in an Object-Oriented Database System: A Cost Analysis,* Technical Report, GIP Altair, Le Chesnay Cedex, France, 1990.

> Explains a preliminary cost analysis of the tradeoffs between immediate and deferred update of object instances when a database schema is modified in O_2 [Bancilhon et al 1988]. See also [Zicari 1990].

R. Haskin, "On Extending the Functions of a Relational Database System," in *Proceedings of the ACM SIGMOD Conference,* Orlando, Florida, June 1982.

> Describes an early attempt to satisfy the needs of engineering applications by adding long transactions, long data fields, and objects to the System R relational DBMS. This system is less ambitious than most of the DBMSs we discuss, including later work at IBM on Starburst [Schwarz et al 1986].

C. Hauser, P. Lucas, J. Mehl, M. Olumi, G. Wiederhold, "Software Project Databases," in *Proceedings of the ACM SIGMOD Workshop on Databases for Engineering Applications,* May 1983.

> Provides a good discussion of the use of database systems for both programming-in-the-large and programming-in-the-small, focused primarily on the latter. Includes a schema for program representation.

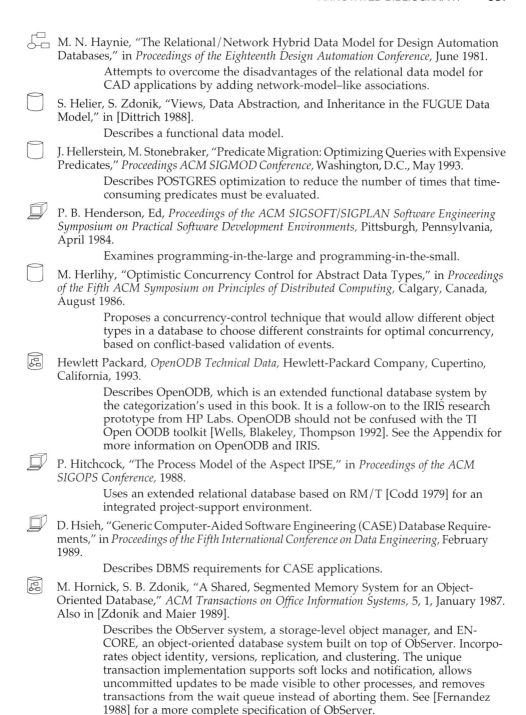 M. N. Haynie, "The Relational/Network Hybrid Data Model for Design Automation Databases," in *Proceedings of the Eighteenth Design Automation Conference*, June 1981.

> Attempts to overcome the disadvantages of the relational data model for CAD applications by adding network-model–like associations.

S. Helier, S. Zdonik, "Views, Data Abstraction, and Inheritance in the FUGUE Data Model," in [Dittrich 1988].

> Describes a functional data model.

J. Hellerstein, M. Stonebraker, "Predicate Migration: Optimizing Queries with Expensive Predicates," *Proceedings ACM SIGMOD Conference*, Washington, D.C., May 1993.

> Describes POSTGRES optimization to reduce the number of times that time-consuming predicates must be evaluated.

P. B. Henderson, Ed, *Proceedings of the ACM SIGSOFT/SIGPLAN Software Engineering Symposium on Practical Software Development Environments*, Pittsburgh, Pennsylvania, April 1984.

> Examines programming-in-the-large and programming-in-the-small.

M. Herlihy, "Optimistic Concurrency Control for Abstract Data Types," in *Proceedings of the Fifth ACM Symposium on Principles of Distributed Computing*, Calgary, Canada, August 1986.

> Proposes a concurrency-control technique that would allow different object types in a database to choose different constraints for optimal concurrency, based on conflict-based validation of events.

Hewlett Packard, *OpenODB Technical Data*, Hewlett-Packard Company, Cupertino, California, 1993.

> Describes OpenODB, which is an extended functional database system by the categorization's used in this book. It is a follow-on to the IRIS research prototype from HP Labs. OpenODB should not be confused with the TI Open OODB toolkit [Wells, Blakeley, Thompson 1992]. See the Appendix for more information on OpenODB and IRIS.

P. Hitchcock, "The Process Model of the Aspect IPSE," in *Proceedings of the ACM SIGOPS Conference*, 1988.

> Uses an extended relational database based on RM/T [Codd 1979] for an integrated project-support environment.

D. Hsieh, "Generic Computer-Aided Software Engineering (CASE) Database Requirements," in *Proceedings of the Fifth International Conference on Data Engineering*, February 1989.

> Describes DBMS requirements for CASE applications.

M. Hornick, S. B. Zdonik, "A Shared, Segmented Memory System for an Object-Oriented Database," *ACM Transactions on Office Information Systems*, 5, 1, January 1987. Also in [Zdonik and Maier 1989].

> Describes the ObServer system, a storage-level object manager, and EN-CORE, an object-oriented database system built on top of ObServer. Incorporates object identity, versions, replication, and clustering. The unique transaction implementation supports soft locks and notification, allows uncommitted updates to be made visible to other processes, and removes transactions from the wait queue instead of aborting them. See [Fernandez 1988] for a more complete specification of ObServer.

S. Hudson, R. King, "CACTIS: A Database System for Specifying Functionally-Defined Data," in [Dittrich and Dayal 1986] and [Zdonik and Maier 1989].

S. Hudson and R. King, "CACTIS: A Self-Adaptive, Concurrent Implementation of an Object-Oriented Database System," *ACM Transactions on Database Systems*, 14, 3, September 1989.

> Describe CACTIS, which evolved from semantic data models [Hammer and McLeod 1981] and functional data models. CACTIS provides object identity, relationships, derived attributes, and functional semantics. The implementation is novel in its automatic physical colocation of related objects accessed together and its lazy evaluation of derived attributes.

R. Hull, R. King, "Semantic Database Modelling: Survey, Applications, and Research Issues," *ACM Computing Surveys*, 19, 3, September 1987.

> Covers much of the work on data modeling, including the concepts of objects, compound objects, object type hierarchies, and the association of procedures with objects. Semantic data models are *structurally* object-oriented; that is, they do not generally provide procedures and encapsulation.

R. Hull, R. Morrison, D. Stemple, Eds, *Second International Workshop on Database Programming Languages*, Oregon, Morgan-Kaufmann, Palo Alto, California, June 1989.

> Bridges the gap between databases and programming languages. See specific references in this bibliography.

A. F. Hutchings, R. McGuffin, A. Elliston, B. Tranter, P. Westmacott, "CADES—Software Engineering in Practice," in *Proceedings of the Fourth International Conference on Software Engineering*, IEEE, Munich, Germany, September 1979.

> Describes a CASE system that uses a relational database for project management information.

Ingres Corporation, *INGRES 6.3 Reference Manual*, Ingres Corporation, Alameda, California, 1989.

> Describes INGRES, a popular relational database system that has been extended with elementary object data management features, including the abilities to define new literal types, to invoke programming language procedures from the query language, and to store rules in databases.

Innovative Systems, *VISION: A Technical Overview*, Innovative Systems, 1988.

> Describes the VISION DBMS, an object-oriented extended database system based on a Smalltalk-like language and a local query language. VISION incorporates object identity, multiple inheritance, independent type extension and intention, collections, and time-dependent data. See also [Caruso and Sciore 1990].

Intellitic, *MATISSE Open Semantic Database: Product Overview*, Intellitic International, Saint-Quentin-en-Yvelines, France, 1993.

> Provides an overview of the MATISSE product, which might best be categorized as an extended semantic database system. MATISSE was produced by the developers of GRAPHAEL, an earlier system.

Itasca Systems, Inc, *ITASCA System Overview*, Unisys, Minneapolis, Minnesota, 1993.

> Describes ITASCA, a commercial product version of the ORION research prototype developed at MCC [Banerjee et al 1987, Kim et al 1988]. See the Appendix for more information.

P. Jenq, D. Woelk, W. Kim, W. Lee, "Query Processing in Distributed ORION," in [Bancilhon, Thanos, Tsichritzis, 1990].

> Describes distributed query optimization and execution systems in ORION [Kim 1988].

A. Jhingran, M. Stonebraker, *A Comparison of Two Representations for Complex Objects*, Memorandum UCB/ERL M90/32, Department of Electrical Engineering and Computer Science, University of California at Berkeley, California, April 1990.

> Compares the efficiency of implementing sets in databases through a declarative specification based on attribute values versus through a list of object identifiers. However, some of the assumptions the paper makes may be questionable.

E. Juhl, H. Levy, N. Hutchinson, A. Black, "Fine-Grained Mobility in the Emerald System," *ACM Transactions on Computer Systems*, 6, 1, February 1988. Also in [Zdonik and Maier 1989].

> Presents a technique for distribution of objects on a network of computers that optimizes execution performance.

T. Kaehler, G. Krasner, "LOOM—Large Object-Oriented Memory for Smalltalk-80 Systems," in G. Krasner, Ed, *Smalltalk-80: Bits of History, Words of Advice,* Addison-Wesley, Reading, Massachusetts, 1983.

> Describes extensions to the Smalltalk programming language implementation to increase the number of objects that can be stored, with persistence (objects remain between program executions). These are first steps toward an object-oriented database system, although multiuser facilities (concurrency control, recovery) are not addressed.

R. H. Katz, Ed, Special Issue on Engineering Design Databases, *IEEE Database Engineering*, June 1984.

> Collects together papers on database issues for engineering applications, including versions and change management.

R. H. Katz, *Information Management for Engineering Design,* Springer-Verlag, New York, New York and Berlin, Germany, 1985.

> Summarizes database requirements for ECAD (computer-aided design of VLSI circuits, and also of higher-level components such as circuit boards).

R. H. Katz, T. Lehman, "Database Support for Versions and Alternatives of Large Design Files," *IEEE Transactions on Software Engineering,* 10, 2, March 1984.

> Evaluates alternatives for supporting versions in DBMSs.

R. H. Katz, E. Chang, "Managing Change in Computer-Aided Design Databases," in *Proceedings of the International Conference on Very Large Databases (VLDB),* September 1987. Also in [Cardenas and McLeod 1990]

> Proposes a framework and algorithms for change propagation in CAD databases with configurations of object versions. This is in contrast to other approaches, which simply provide change notification or invalidation of data [Chou and Kim 1985].

A. M. Keller, C. Hamon, "A C++ Binding for Penguin: A System for Data Sharing among Heterogeneous Object Models," in *Proceedings Fourth International Conference on Foundations of Data Organization and Algorithms,* Evanston, Illinois, 1993.

> Describes Penguin's "view-objects" that can be built on top of relational tables. Penguin supports both composite objects (aggregation) and inheritance (generalization). View-objects can be mapped to programming language classes in C++ in order to allow database programming language capability for relational DBMSs.

A. M. Keller, *Updating Relational Databases through Views*, PhD Thesis, Technical Report STAN-CS-85-1040, Computer Science Department, Stanford, Palo Alto, California, February 1985.

> Compares approaches to the view update-problem in the relational model. Specifies five criteria that the translations must satisfy to be updateable through the algorithms provided in the dissertation. See also [Furtado et al 1979] and [Dayal and Bernstein 1982].

A. M. Keller, "Unifying Database and Programming Language Concepts Using the Object Model," in [Dittrich and Dayal 1986].

> Clearly describes the issues in combining programming languages and databases. Examines the concepts of lifetime, extensibility, references, recovery, atomicity of operations, encapsulation, and efficiency. See also [Bloom and Zdonik 1987].

A. Kemper, G. Moerkotte, "Access Support in Object Bases," in *Proceedings of the ACM SIGMOD Conference*, Atlantic City, May 1990.

> Proposes *access support relations*, an indexing technique for ODMSs to support fast traversal of object access along reference chains—that is, nested-entity joins. Somewhat more general than GemStone and ORION approaches. Permits multivalued attributes, and subsumes replication of nested attribute values.

A. Kemper, M. Wallrath, "A Uniform Concept for Storing and Manipulating Engineering Objects," in [Dittrich 1988].

> Describes the R^2D^2 DBMS, providing long transactions, checkout to local object cache in Pascal main-memory data structures, automatic translation from NF^2 data-model representation [Scheck and Scholl 1986], behavioral encapsulation, and a query sublanguage.

J. Kent, D. Terry, W.-S. Orr, "Browsing Electronic Mail: Experiences Interfacing a Mail System to a DBMS," in *Proceedings of the ACM SIGMOD Conference*, 1986.

> Describes an electronic-mail tool, Walnut, which uses an entity-relationship database system [Cattell 1984] to store, query, and manipulate the mail. Provides feedback on important DBMS features needed to support such applications.

W. Kent, *Data and Reality*, North-Holland, New York and Amsterdam, 1978.

> Presents a good early discussion of basic data-modeling concepts, such as entities (objects), keys, and object identity.

W. Kent, "Limitations of Record-Based Information Models," *ACM Transactions on Database Systems*, 6, 4, December 1981.

> Presents one of the earliest comprehensive descriptions of drawbacks of relational and other popular data models for representing complex application data. Also appears in [Mylopoulos and Brodie 1989].

M. Ketabchi, V. Berzins, "Modelling and Merging CAD Databases," *IEEE Computer*, 20, 3, February 1987.

> Describes database needs for CAD application databases, focusing on versions of objects, composite objects and types, and design configuration management.

S. Khoshafian, D. Frank, "Implementation Techniques for Object-Oriented Databases," in [Dittrich 1988].

> Examines the problems of performing equality operations on objects and removing duplicate objects, using hashing and inference techniques.

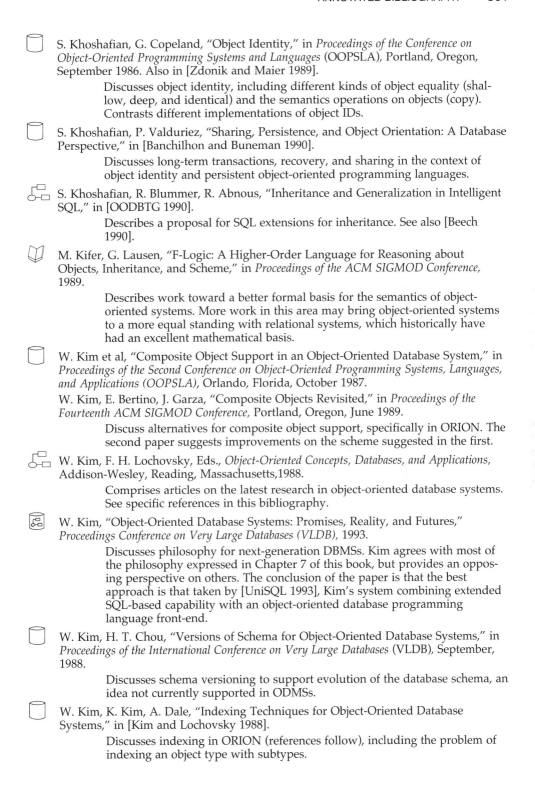

S. Khoshafian, G. Copeland, "Object Identity," in *Proceedings of the Conference on Object-Oriented Programming Systems and Languages* (OOPSLA), Portland, Oregon, September 1986. Also in [Zdonik and Maier 1989].

> Discusses object identity, including different kinds of object equality (shallow, deep, and identical) and the semantics operations on objects (copy). Contrasts different implementations of object IDs.

S. Khoshafian, P. Valduriez, "Sharing, Persistence, and Object Orientation: A Database Perspective," in [Banchilhon and Buneman 1990].

> Discusses long-term transactions, recovery, and sharing in the context of object identity and persistent object-oriented programming languages.

S. Khoshafian, R. Blummer, R. Abnous, "Inheritance and Generalization in Intelligent SQL," in [OODBTG 1990].

> Describes a proposal for SQL extensions for inheritance. See also [Beech 1990].

M. Kifer, G. Lausen, "F-Logic: A Higher-Order Language for Reasoning about Objects, Inheritance, and Scheme," in *Proceedings of the ACM SIGMOD Conference,* 1989.

> Describes work toward a better formal basis for the semantics of object-oriented systems. More work in this area may bring object-oriented systems to a more equal standing with relational systems, which historically have had an excellent mathematical basis.

W. Kim et al, "Composite Object Support in an Object-Oriented Database System," in *Proceedings of the Second Conference on Object-Oriented Programming Systems, Languages, and Applications (OOPSLA)*, Orlando, Florida, October 1987.

W. Kim, E. Bertino, J. Garza, "Composite Objects Revisited," in *Proceedings of the Fourteenth ACM SIGMOD Conference*, Portland, Oregon, June 1989.

> Discuss alternatives for composite object support, specifically in ORION. The second paper suggests improvements on the scheme suggested in the first.

W. Kim, F. H. Lochovsky, Eds., *Object-Oriented Concepts, Databases, and Applications*, Addison-Wesley, Reading, Massachusetts,1988.

> Comprises articles on the latest research in object-oriented database systems. See specific references in this bibliography.

W. Kim, "Object-Oriented Database Systems: Promises, Reality, and Futures," *Proceedings Conference on Very Large Databases (VLDB)*, 1993.

> Discusses philosophy for next-generation DBMSs. Kim agrees with most of the philosophy expressed in Chapter 7 of this book, but provides an opposing perspective on others. The conclusion of the paper is that the best approach is that taken by [UniSQL 1993], Kim's system combining extended SQL-based capability with an object-oriented database programming language front-end.

W. Kim, H. T. Chou, "Versions of Schema for Object-Oriented Database Systems," in *Proceedings of the International Conference on Very Large Databases* (VLDB), September, 1988.

> Discusses schema versioning to support evolution of the database schema, an idea not currently supported in ODMSs.

W. Kim, K. Kim, A. Dale, "Indexing Techniques for Object-Oriented Database Systems," in [Kim and Lochovsky 1988].

> Discusses indexing in ORION (references follow), including the problem of indexing an object type with subtypes.

W. Kim et al, "Features of the ORION Object-Oriented Database System," in [Kim and Lochovsky 1988].

W. Kim et al, "Integrating an Object-Oriented Programming System with a Database System," in *Proceedings of OOPSLA 1988*, September, 1988. Also in [Cardenas and McLeod 1990].

W. Kim, "A Model of Queries for Object-Oriented Database Systems," in *Proceedings of the International Conference on Very Large Databases (VLDB)*, Amsterdam, Holland, August 1989.

W. Kim, J. F. Garza, N. Ballou, D.Woelk, "Architecture of the ORION Next-Generation Database System," in [Stonebraker 1990].

> Describe how ORION was built from the ground up, with object-oriented capabilities in mind. ORION includes object identity, versions and change notification, composite objects, a query language, some kinds of schema evolution, multiple inheritance, and long transactions. It was written in LISP and supports persistent CLOS [Bobrow et al 1988] operations. See also [Banerjee et al 1987, Jenq et al 1990].

W. Kim, J-M. Nicolas, S. Nishio, Eds, *First International Conference on Deductive and Object-Oriented Databases*, Elsevier, Kyoto, Japan, 1989.

> Bridges the gap between AI and database viewpoints, covering object-oriented databases and deductive programming languages.

W. Kim, *Introduction to Object-Oriented Databases*, MIT Press, Cambridge, Massachusetts, 1990.

> Published just as this text was going to press. Focuses more narrowly than this text, but is a valuable resource for more detailed study, particularly for the ORION system on which most of the discussion is based. Kim's perspective is generally in agreement with statements made here. There is some difference of emphasis, particularly where ORION has taken an approach different from that of the competition—for example, there is more attention to automatic schema evolution and ORION's double buffering scheme, but no coverage of C++ issues, configurations, and inverse attributes.

R. King, "My Cat is Object-Oriented," in [Kim and Lochovsky 1988].

> Contrasts semantic and object-oriented data models. The title refers to the fact that "object-oriented" became a computer buzzword to sell *anything* in the late 1980s.

H. Korth, W. Kim, F. Bancillon, "On Long-Duration CAD Transactions," *Information Science,* October1988. Also in [Zdonik and Maier 1989].

> Describes concurrency control issues for engineering design applications, including extensions to current theory to allow more concurrency while keeping designs consistent, and implementation considerations.

M. Lacroix, M. Vanhoedenaghe, "Tool Integration in an Open Environment," in *Proceedings of the Second European Conference on Software Engineering,* September 1989. Available as Lecture Notes in Computer Science 387, Springer Verlag, New York, New York and Berlin, Germany, 1989.

> Contains a good review of work in configuration management for CASE.

Laguna Beach Committee, "Future Directions in DBMS Research," *ACM SIGMOD Record,* 18, 1, March 1989.

> Makes a number of predictions about the future of the area, as reported by leading members of the database research community. Object-oriented database systems was probably the most controversial topic: The majority

thought that the object-oriented approach was *not* a fruitful area for focus, that relational extensions and other alternatives had a more formal basis as well as data independence. The minority thought the object-oriented approach was important, and was misunderstood because "object-oriented" has been used to describe more than one approach. See also [Silberschatz et al 1990].

C. Lecluse, P. Richard, F. Velez, "O$_2$, an Object Oriented Data Model," *Proceedings of the ACM SIGMOD Conference,* 1988. Also in Zdonik and Maier 1989].

> Provides an unusually good definition of the formal semantics of an object-oriented data model. See also [Bancilhon 1988].

T. J. Lehman, B. G. Lindsay, "The Starburst Long Field Manager," in *Proceedings of the International Conference on Very Large Databases (VLDB),* Amsterdam, Holland, August 1989.

> Describes the implementation of large attribute values in Starburst [Schwarz et al 1986], including concurrency control and a novel disk-space allocation strategy.

B. S. Lerner, A. N. Habermann, "Beyond Schema Evolution to Database Reorganization," in *Proceedings of the ACM Conference on Object-Oriented Programming Languages, Systems, and Applications (OOPSLA), SIGPLAN Notices,* 25, 10, October 1990.

> Describes OTGen, a database tool providing automatic generation of simple database schema transformations, plus support for arbitrary schema transformations through a schema-transformation description language.

G. R. Lewis, "CASE Integration Frameworks," *SunTech Journal,* 3, 5, November 1990.

> Surveys work on frameworks for software engineering tools. These frameworks provide display, data, and control integration. ODMSs may be helpful in these frameworks, particularly for data integration facilities.

B. Lindsay, L. Haas, "Extensibility in the Starburst Experimental Database System," in *Proceedings of the International IBM Symposium on Database Systems of the 90's,* Springer-Verlag, New York, New York and Berlin, Germany, November 1990.

> Discusses Starburst query language and data-typing extensions, not all of which were implemented at the time the paper was written. See also [Schwarz et al 1986].

B. Liskov, A. Snyder, R. Atkinson, C. Schaffert, "Abstraction Mechanisms in CLU," Communications of the ACM, 20, 8, 1977.

> Describes CLU, an "object-oriented" programming language in that it provides encapsulation of types. CLU also provides parameterized types and an abstraction for iteration. It does not incorporate type generalization. See [Micallef 1988] for other object-oriented languages.

F. H. Lochovsky, Ed, Special Issue on Object-Oriented Systems, *IEEE Database Engineering,* 8, 4, December 1985.

F. H. Lochovsky, Ed, Special Issue on Object-Oriented Systems, *ACM Transactions on Office Information Systems (TOOIS),* 5, 1, January 1987.

> Cover a variety of potential database applications from object-oriented systems.

R. Lorie, W. Plouffe: "Complex Objects and their Use in Design Transactions," in *Proceedings of the ACM SIGMOD Conference Database Week,* 1983.

> Discusses the use of transactions in CAD and other design applications. Distinguish between the use of long transactions for consistency between users and of short transactions for recovery.

D. Maier, J. Stein, "Indexing in an Object-Oriented Database," in [Dittrich and Dayal 1986].

D. Maier, J. Stein, "Development and Implementation of an Object-Oriented Database System," in *Research Directions in Object-Oriented Programming*, B. Shriver, P. Wegner, Eds., MIT Press, Cambridge, Massachusetts, 1987. Derived paper in [Cardenas and McLeod 1990].

> Describe implementation issues in Serviologic GemStone, including the concept of an "identity index." See [Bretl et al 1989] for more information.

D. Maier, "Making Database Systems Fast Enough for CAD Applications," Technical Report, Oregon Graduate Center, Beaverton, Oregon, 1988. Also in [Kim and Lochovsky 1988].

> Discusses why object-oriented databases systems show promise for design-application performance requirements.

D. Maier, "Why Isn't There an Object-Oriented Data Model?" Technical Report, Oregon Graduate Center, Beaverton, Oregon, May 1989.

> Discusses variations of DBMSs called "object-oriented". Argues that it is premature to define a data model, because there is insufficient experience. Predicts that object-oriented extensions will find their way into relational systems, as well as finding new markets among engineering tool builders.

A. Makinouchi, "A Consideration of Normal Form of Not-necessarily Normalized Relations in the Relational Data Model," in *Proceedings of the International Conference on Very Large Databases (VLDB)*, 1977.

> Presents one of the earliest discussions of non–first-normal form databases. See also [Scheck and Scholl 1986, Osoyoglu 1988].

F. Manola, *An Evaluation of Object-oriented Database System Developments*, Technical Report 0066-10-89-165, GTE Laboratories, Waltham, Massachusetts, October 1989.

> Provides a good summary of the motivation for ODMSs, including a detailed analysis of the problems using relational DBMSs for CAD and CASE applications. Also compares and contrasts a number of ODMS products and prototypes available as of 1989, and covers technical issues in designing or selecting an ODMS.

F. Manola, U. Dayal, "PDM: An Object-Oriented Data Model," in [Dittrich and Dayal 1986] and [Zdonik and Maier 1989].

> Describes the data model for PROBE [Dayal and Smith 1985], an extension of DAPLEX [Shipman 1981] with a more formal definition, multiargument computed functions, and spatiotemporal semantics.

J. C. MacDonald, "CASE: Myth and Reality," in *SunTech Journal*, 3, 5, November 1990.

> Provides a good starting point to study some of the recent developments in CASE.

D. C. Mathews, "Static and Dynamic Type Checking," in [Bancilhon & Buneman 1990].

> Discusses alternatives for static and dynamic type definition, reference, and checking in programming languages.

F. Matthes, J.W. Schmidt, "The Type System of DBPL," in *Proceedings of the Second International Workshop on Database Programming Languages*, Gleneden Beach, Oregon, Morgan-Kaufmann, San Mateo, California, June 1989.

> Describes DBPL, a persistent programming language. See also [Schmidt 1977].

D. McLeod, K. Narayanaswamy, K. V. Bapa Rao, "An Approach to Information Management for CAD/VLSI Applications," in *Proceedings of the ACM SIGMOD Workshop on Engineering Design Applications,* 1983.

> Discusses the advantages of using a database system for VLSI applications. Limited discussion of the problems in using a relational database system. See also [Stonebraker and Guttman 1982].

C. McClure, *CASE Is Software Automation,* Prentice-Hall, Englewood Cliffs, New Jersey, 1989.

> Presents a survey of CASE tools, including specification, design, documentation, and all components of the development process. This book has much less technical content than some of the more academic surveys, but covers commercial applications more fully. See [MacDonald 1990, Rowe and Wensel 1989].

M. Merickel, *Stepping into CAD,* New Riders Publishing, a division of Que Corporation, Thousand Oaks, California, 1987.

> Comprises a practical guide to using one of the most popular MCAD systems, AutoCAD from Autodesk, Inc.

B. Meyer, *Object Oriented Software Construction,* Prentice-Hall, Englewood Cliffs, New Jersey, 1988.

> Covers object-oriented programming languages and concepts, primarily focussed on the Eiffel language. Also includes some object-oriented design and programming techniques.

B. Meyer, *Eiffel: A Language for Software Engineering,* Technical Report, Department of Computer Science, University of California, Santa Barbara, California, November 1985.

> Describes Eiffel, an object-oriented programming language now publicly available as a product.

J. Micallef, "Encapsulation, Reusability, and Extensibility in Object-Oriented Programming Languages," *Journal of Object-Oriented Programming Languages,* 1, 1, April/May 1988.

> Provides a good summary of the object-oriented paradigm and its implications in programming languages. Object-oriented programming languages referenced in this bibliography include C++ [Stroustrup 1986], Smalltalk [Goldberg and Robson 1983], CLOS [Bobrow 1988], CLU [Liskov et al 1977], and Simula [Dahl and Nygaard 1966].

Montage Software, *Montage Users Guide,* Montage Software, Inc, Emeryville, California, 1993.

> Describes the Montage DBMS, previously called MIRO, a follow-on to the academic POSTGRES prototype [Stonebraker 1976]. It is an extended relational DBMS. The product was initially released in 1993. See the Appendix for more information.

D. Moon, "The Common LISP Object-Oriented Programming Standard," in [Kim and Lochovsky 1988].

> Describes CLOS, which evolved from Flavors and Common Loops, as LISP extensions for object-oriented capabilities. See also [Bobrow 1988].

K. Morris et al, "YAWN! (Yet Another Window on NAIL!)," *IEEE Data Engineering,* 10, 4 December 1987.

> Describes NAIL! (Not Another Inference Language!), a logic language for knowledge management. Zaniolo [1990] cites other examples.

R. Morrison et al, *Protection* in *Persistent Object Systems,* Technical Report CS/90/7, Department of Mathematics and Computer Science, University of Saint Andrews, Great Britain, 1990.

> Presents mechanisms to preserve data integrity using the type mechanism of persistent programming languages (ADAPTBL [Stemple 1990], Napier88 [Dearle 1989]), integrity constraints, subtype inheritance, and the concept of "capabilities" from software research.

J. E. B. Moss, "Nested Transactions: An Approach to Reliable Distributed Computing," Technical Report MIT-LCS-260, PhD Thesis, Computer Science, MIT, Cambridge, Massachusetts, 1981. Also published by MIT Press, Cambridge, Massachusetts, 1985.

> Presents a good early discussion of the concept of nested transactions.

J. E. B. Moss, "Object-Orientation as Catalyst for Language-Database Integration," in [Kim and Lochovsky 1988].

> Discusses why object-oriented programming languages are well suited to the introduction of database capabilities. These arguments are the basis for the object-oriented database programming language approach.

J. E. B. Moss, S. Sinofsky "Managing Persistent Data with Mneme: Designing a Reliable Shared Object Interface," in [Dittrich 1988].

J. E. B. Moss, "Design of the Mneme Persistent Object Store," *Transactions on Office Information Systems,* 8, 2, April 1990.

> Describe Mneme, an object manager providing untyped objects with scalar and reference parts, high performance (caching, clustering, minimal translation), transactions, and large objects. The policy for concurrency, types, and other aspects of the DBMS are set by a database system implementor using Mneme.

J. E. B. Moss, "Addressing Large Distributed Collections of Persistent Objects: The Mneme Project's Approach," in *Proceedings of the Second International Workshop on Database Programming Languages,* Oregon, 1989.

> Discusses OID format and addressing in Mneme.

J. E. B. Moss, *Working with Persistent Objects: To Swizzle or Not to Swizzle,* COINS Technical Report 90-38, Department of Computer and Information Science, University of Massachusetts, Amherst, Massachusetts, May 1990. Also submitted for publication, 1991.

> Provides an excellent discussion of the alternatives for representing OIDs efficiently in a main-memory cache of objects. Presents the results of performance measurements, and an analytic model that can be used to determine how many object references are necessary to justify the overhead of swizzling OIDs into pointers.

J. Mylopoulos, M. Brodie, *Readings in Artificial Intelligence and Databases,* Morgan-Kaufmann, Palo Alto, California, 1989.

> Comprises important research articles from the last two decades on advances in database technology and in the closely related area of knowledge representation in AI.

J. R. Nestor, "Towards a Persistent Object Base," in *Proceedings ACM SIGOPS Conference* , 1986.

> Contrasts the shortcomings of current file systems and database systems for storing objects, particularly for CASE applications.

Object Databases, *GBase Reference Manual,* Object Databases Corporation, Cambridge, Massachusetts 1990.

> Describes GBase, an object-oriented extended database system written in Common LISP. GBase incorporates the logic query language G-Logis, object identity, BLOBs, type inheritance, methods written in LISP, and a federated database link to Oracle. GBase has also been marketed by Graphael, the parent corporation of Object Databases.

Objectivity, *Objectivity Database System Overview,* Objectivity, Inc., Menlo Park, California, 1990.

> Describes the Objectivity/DB ODMS, an object-oriented database programming language based on C++, much like ObjectStore and ONTOS (references follow) and VERSANT [Versant 1990].

Object Design, *An Introduction to ObjectStore,* Object Design, Inc., Burlington, Massachusetts, 1990.

> Describes ObjectStore, an object-oriented database programming language based on C++. ObjectStore is more tightly integrated with C++ than most of its competitors.

OMG, *Object Management Architecture Guide,* R. G. Soley, Ed, Object Management Group, Framingham, Massachusetts, 1993.

> Describes the architectural vision of OMG, a standards group aimed at providing an object-oriented integrated application framework. An object-oriented database special interest subgroup has been formed to focus on standards for the databases.

OMG ORBTF, *Common Object Request Broker Architecture,* Object Management Group, Framingham, Massachusetts, 1992.

> Describes the work of OMG's object request broker task force (ORBTF) toward a mechanism for definition and invocation of objects in a distributed multi-vendor environment. This specification is sometimes called CORBA, after its title. Version 2.0 of the CORBA is currently being developed. See Chapter 6 for more information on the CORBA and other OMG activities.

OMG OSTF, *Object Services Architecture,* Object Management Group, Framingham, Massachusetts, 1993.

> Provides an architecture for the object services being defined by the OMG Object Services Task Force (OSTF). This is a working document not yet publicly available; however Revision 2 of [OMG 1993] incorporates a recent version of the architecture as one chapter. Object services defines in a distributed "plug and play" fashion many capabilities (persistence, relationships, versions, transactions, and others) that would traditionally be provided by one vendor's "monolithic" DBMS. See Chapter 6 for more information on the OSTF and other OMG activities.

Ontologic, *VBase Functional Specification.* Ontologic, Inc. (now Ontos, Inc.), Burlington, Massachusetts, 1986.

> Describes VBase, an object-oriented extended database system. This first version was built around Ontologic's own language, COP. See also [Andrews and Harris 1987], and ONTOS (reference follows).

Ontos, *ONTOS Reference Manual.* Ontos, Inc., Burlington, Massachusetts, 1993.

> Describes the ONTOS ODMS, a database programming language built as an extension of C++. Except for its emphasis on C++ and performance, ONTOS is similar in approach to VBase. See also [Andrews et al 1989].

OODBTG, ANSI Object-Oriented Database Task Group, *Reference Model for Object Data Management,* Document OODB 89-01R4 ANSI/X3, DB SSG/OODBTG, August 1990.

> Presents a working draft for a report of the OODBTG for ANSI on a common object-oriented data model and recommendations for further ANSI work on object-oriented database systems. Covers both object paradigm (encapsulation, object identity) and data management paradigm (transactions, query language).

OODBTG, *Proceedings of the OODBTG Workshop,* Atlantic City, New Jersey, May 1990, and Ottawa, Ontario, October 1990.

> Comprises a collection of proposals for object-oriented database standards for data modeling, query language, transactions, object-oriented programming language extensions, and object-oriented SQL.

Z. M. Ozsoyoglu, Ed, Special Issue on Non–First Normal Form Databases, *IEEE Database Engineering,* September 1988.

> Describes relational data-model extensions to allow nested relations and other variations from strict tabular form [Makinouchi 1977].

Panel on Schema Evolution and Version Management, in Report on the Object-Oriented Database Workshop, *SIGMOD RECORD,* 18, 3, September 1989.

> Discusses some of the issues in updating a database schema and maintaining multiple versions of data and schemas. Identifies some important issues in schema evolution.

H. Penedo, E. Stuckle, "PMDB: A Project Master Database for Software Engineering Environments," in *Proceedings of the Eighth International Conference on Software Engineering,* London, England, August 1985.

> Provides a compendium of several hundred entities, attributes, and relationships required in a data schema for a software engineering database. The authors conclude that significant extensions to a simple entity-relationship data model are necessary to support such databases.

J. Penney, J. Stein, "Class Modification in the GemStone Object-Oriented Database System," in *Proceedings of the Second International Conference on Object-Oriented Programming Systems, Languages, and Applications (OOPSLA),* October 1987.

> Describes the use of immediate update of type instances to handle schema evolution.

E. Perez, *ZEITGEIST Persistent C++ User Manual,* Technical Report 90-07-02, Computer Science, TI Labs, Dallas, Texas, June 1990.

> Describes C++ interface to ZEITGEIST [Foral et al 1988].

Persistence Software, *Persistence Technical Overview,* Persistence, Inc, San Mateo, California 1993.

> Describes the only product currently available with some form of database programming language architecture built on existing relational DBMSs. See also the research background for this product [Wiederhold et al 1990], and the UniSQL system [UniSQL 1993].

Poet Software, *POET Programmer's and Reference Guide,* BKS Software (now Poet Software), Hamburg, Germany, 1993.

> Describes POET, an object-oriented DBMS for C++. See the Appendix for more information on this product.

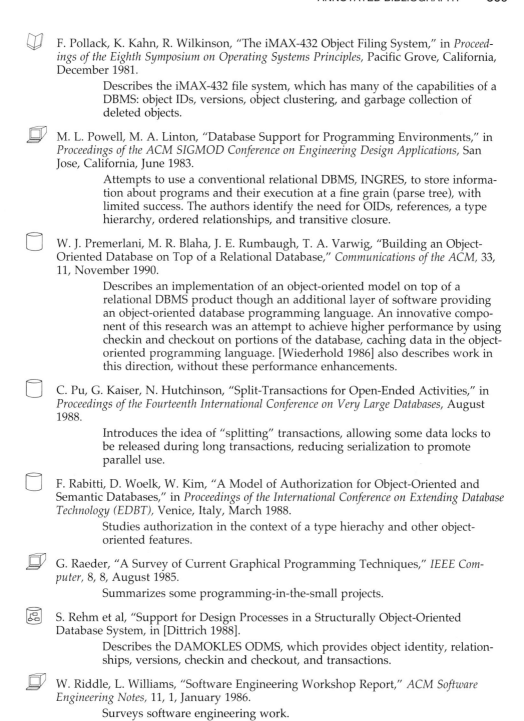

F. Pollack, K. Kahn, R. Wilkinson, "The iMAX-432 Object Filing System," in *Proceedings of the Eighth Symposium on Operating Systems Principles*, Pacific Grove, California, December 1981.

> Describes the iMAX-432 file system, which has many of the capabilities of a DBMS: object IDs, versions, object clustering, and garbage collection of deleted objects.

M. L. Powell, M. A. Linton, "Database Support for Programming Environments," in *Proceedings of the ACM SIGMOD Conference on Engineering Design Applications*, San Jose, California, June 1983.

> Attempts to use a conventional relational DBMS, INGRES, to store information about programs and their execution at a fine grain (parse tree), with limited success. The authors identify the need for OIDs, references, a type hierarchy, ordered relationships, and transitive closure.

W. J. Premerlani, M. R. Blaha, J. E. Rumbaugh, T. A. Varwig, "Building an Object-Oriented Database on Top of a Relational Database," *Communications of the ACM*, 33, 11, November 1990.

> Describes an implementation of an object-oriented model on top of a relational DBMS product though an additional layer of software providing an object-oriented database programming language. An innovative component of this research was an attempt to achieve higher performance by using checkin and checkout on portions of the database, caching data in the object-oriented programming language. [Wiederhold 1986] also describes work in this direction, without these performance enhancements.

C. Pu, G. Kaiser, N. Hutchinson, "Split-Transactions for Open-Ended Activities," in *Proceedings of the Fourteenth International Conference on Very Large Databases*, August 1988.

> Introduces the idea of "splitting" transactions, allowing some data locks to be released during long transactions, reducing serialization to promote parallel use.

F. Rabitti, D. Woelk, W. Kim, "A Model of Authorization for Object-Oriented and Semantic Databases," in *Proceedings of the International Conference on Extending Database Technology (EDBT)*, Venice, Italy, March 1988.

> Studies authorization in the context of a type hierarchy and other object-oriented features.

G. Raeder, "A Survey of Current Graphical Programming Techniques," *IEEE Computer*, 8, 8, August 1985.

> Summarizes some programming-in-the-small projects.

S. Rehm et al, "Support for Design Processes in a Structurally Object-Oriented Database System, in [Dittrich 1988].

> Describes the DAMOKLES ODMS, which provides object identity, relationships, versions, checkin and checkout, and transactions.

W. Riddle, L. Williams, "Software Engineering Workshop Report," *ACM Software Engineering Notes*, 11, 1, January 1986.

> Surveys software engineering work.

D. Ries, M. Stonebraker, "Locking Granularities Revisited," *ACM Transactions on Database Systems*, 4, 2, June 1979.

> Describes arguments for fine- and gross-grain locking in relational databases (that is, tuples versus relations). Most production implementations now lock pages. In the case of object data management, the same arguments hold; however, there is a tendency toward locks on larger grain, held for longer periods of time.

T. Risch, "Monitoring Database Objects," in *Proceedings of the International Conference on Very Large Databases*, Amsterdam, Holland, August 1989.

> Describes a method for actively interfacing IRIS [Fishman et al 1987] to application programs, asynchronously invoking specified procedures when preconditions become satisfied.

J. B. Rosenberg, "Geographical Data Structures Compared: A Study of Data Structures Supporting Region Queries," *IEEE Transactions on Computer-Aided Design*, 4, 1, January 1985.

> Studies multidimensional index implementations. See also [Samet 1990], an entire book on the subject.

L. A. Rowe, S. Wensel, Eds, *Proceedings of 1989 ACM SIGMOD Workshop on Software CAD Databases*, Napa, California, February 1989.

> Comprises a collection of short papers on CASE (not CAD) work and related object-oriented databases. System details will not be found here, but the papers provide overviews and references.

L. A. Rowe, private communication, 1990.

> Unpublished work provided a persistent object-oriented LISP language by storing objects in POSTGRES. This is the closest possible thing to an extended relational database programming language, a difficult system to build because of the mismatch of data models between programming language and database language. See also [Persistence 1993].

S. Rubin, *Computer Aids for VLSI Design*, Addison-Wesley, Reading, Massachusetts, 1987.

> Provides good coverage of CAD tool technology for VLSI.

J. Rumbaugh, "Relations as Semantic Constructs in an Object-Oriented Language," in *Proceedings of the ACM Conference on Object-Oriented Programming Systems, Languages, and Applications (OOPSLA)*, Orlando, Florida, October 1987.

> Discusses the problem of representing relationships in object-oriented models based on attributes, including most of the concepts covered in Section 4.3 of this book (multiplicity, degree, access syntax).

J. Rumbaugh, "Controlling Propagation of Operations using Attributes on Relations," in *Proceedings of the ACM Conference on Object-Oriented Programming Systems, Languages, and Applications (OOPSLA)*, San Diego, California, September 1988.

> Suggests tagging relationships between object types to indicate whether operations such as deletion and copying should be propagated to related objects when connected by the given type of relationship. This allows custom-tailored composite objects.

K. Salem, H. Garcia-Molina, "System M: A Transaction Processing Testbed for Memory Resident Data," in [Stonebraker 1990].

> Describes System M, a simple object manager designed for transaction processing in main memory. The system's biggest contribution is probably in showing the gains to be had in performance by utilizing main-memory databases.

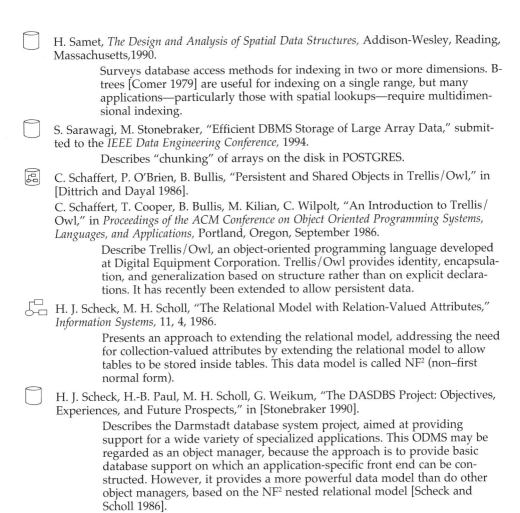

H. Samet, *The Design and Analysis of Spatial Data Structures,* Addison-Wesley, Reading, Massachusetts,1990.

> Surveys database access methods for indexing in two or more dimensions. B-trees [Comer 1979] are useful for indexing on a single range, but many applications—particularly those with spatial lookups—require multidimensional indexing.

S. Sarawagi, M. Stonebraker, "Efficient DBMS Storage of Large Array Data," submitted to the *IEEE Data Engineering Conference,* 1994.

> Describes "chunking" of arrays on the disk in POSTGRES.

C. Schaffert, P. O'Brien, B. Bullis, "Persistent and Shared Objects in Trellis/Owl," in [Dittrich and Dayal 1986].

C. Schaffert, T. Cooper, B. Bullis, M. Kilian, C. Wilpolt, "An Introduction to Trellis/Owl," in *Proceedings of the ACM Conference on Object Oriented Programming Systems, Languages, and Applications,* Portland, Oregon, September 1986.

> Describe Trellis/Owl, an object-oriented programming language developed at Digital Equipment Corporation. Trellis/Owl provides identity, encapsulation, and generalization based on structure rather than on explicit declarations. It has recently been extended to allow persistent data.

H. J. Scheck, M. H. Scholl, "The Relational Model with Relation-Valued Attributes," *Information Systems,* 11, 4, 1986.

> Presents an approach to extending the relational model, addressing the need for collection-valued attributes by extending the relational model to allow tables to be stored inside tables. This data model is called NF^2 (non–first normal form).

H. J. Scheck, H.-B. Paul, M. H. Scholl, G. Weikum, "The DASDBS Project: Objectives, Experiences, and Future Prospects," in [Stonebraker 1990].

> Describes the Darmstadt database system project, aimed at providing support for a wide variety of specialized applications. This ODMS may be regarded as an object manager, because the approach is to provide basic database support on which an application-specific front end can be constructed. However, it provides a more powerful data model than do other object managers, based on the NF^2 nested relational model [Scheck and Scholl 1986].

J. W. Schmidt, "Some High Level Language Constructs for Data of Type Relation," *ACM Transactions on Database Systems,* 2, 3, September 1977.

> Describes Pascal/R, an extension of Pascal to permit relations as a data type in the programming language. See also [Rowe and Schoens 1979].

P. Schwarz et al, "Extensibility in the Starburst Database System," in [Dittrich and Dayal 1986].

> Describes Starburst, an extended relational database system. It has goals similar to EXODUS [Carey et al 1986] and POSTGRES [Stonebraker and Rowe 1986], but with less emphasis on tailorability than the former, and more emphasis than the latter. See also [Lehman and Lindsay 1989, Haas et al 1988, Lindsay and Haas 1990, Carey et al 1990].

Servio Corporation, *GemStone Reference Manual,* Servio Corporation, Beaverton, Oregon, 1993.

> Describes GemStone, one of the world's first object-oriented database system products [Bretl et al 1988], marketed by Servio Corporation, formerly Serviologic.

E. J. Shekita, M. J. Carey, "Performance Enhancement Through Replication in an Object-Oriented Database System," in *Proceedings of the ACM SIGMOD Conference, 1989.*

> Explores performance improvements to object-oriented database systems by replicating fields of objects in other objects from which they are frequently referenced. Since relational databases use primary key data values to reference objects in other relations, they start out with some performance advantage on this point.

E. J. Shekita, M. J. Carey, *A Performance Evaluation of Pointer-Based Joins,* Technical Report 916, Department of Computer Science, University of Wisconsin, Madison, Wisconsin, March 1990.

> Studies various forms of joins based on B-trees and parent–child links in a relational database system. The conclusion is that certain forms of pointer-based joins outperform their index-based counterparts.

D. Shipman, "The Functional Data Model and the Data Language DAPLEX," *ACM Transactions on Database Systems,* 6, 1, March 1981.

> Describes DAPLEX, which is not an object-oriented database system, but which does provide a more object-centric replacement for the relational data model, using functions mapping entities to other entities and values. See [Manola and Dayal 1986, Dayal and Smith 1985, Chan et al 1982] for followons to this work.

B. Shriver, P. Wegner, Eds, *Research Directions in Object-Oriented Programming,* MIT Press, Cambridge, Massachusetts, 1988.

> Comprises a collection of articles, primarily on object-oriented programming language issues such as inheritance and encapsulation. Also includes a few articles on object-oriented databases.

A. Silberschatz, M. Stonebraker, J. D. Ullman, Eds, *Database Systems: Achievements and Opportunities,* Report of NSF Workshop in Palo Alto, published as Technical Report TR-90-22, Computer Science Department, University of Texas, Austin, Texas, February 1990.

> Summarizes the consensus of 20 leading researchers in database systems who meet to discuss future areas for research. Called the Lagunita report. Research on next-generation database applications and on heterogeneous distributed databases were identified as most important. Unlike the earlier Laguna report [Laguna Beach Committee 1989], which has been criticized as an attack on object-oriented database research by relational database researchers, the Lagunita report forwards needs for next-generation databases with which it would be hard to argue: multimedia data, rules, versions, long-duration transactions, and scaling up to very large databases on tertiary storage.

S. S. Simmel, I. Godard, *Introduction to Kala,* Penobscot Development Corporation, Cambridge, Massachusetts, 1993.

S. S. Simmel, I. Godard, "The Kala Basket, A Semantic Primitive Unifying Object Transactions, Access Control, Versions, and Configurations," *Proceedings of the OOPSLA Conference,* ACM Press, 1991.

> Describes Kala, which is best categorized as an object manager in the architecture framework defined in this book. Kala also has some of the properties of a DBMS generator, in that it can be tailored in some ways. See the Appendix for more information on Kala.

A. H. Skarra, S. B. Zdonik, "Type Evolution in an Object-Oriented Database," in *Research Directions in Object-Oriented Systems,* MIT Press, Cambridge, Massachusetts, 1990. Also in [Cardenas and McLeod 1990]

> Proposes a solution for schema evolution in ODMSs based on multiple versions of types. Uses error handling and version control mechanisms to make many kinds of type changes invisible to programs.

A. H. Skarra, S. B. Zdonik, "Concurrency Control for Object-Oriented Databases," in [Kim and Lochovsky 1988].

> Discusses concurrency control based on object-specific semantics.

J. B. Smith and S. F. Weiss, Eds, *Hypertext: CACM Special Issue,* 1988.

> Comprises a collection of articles and a survey on hypertext. See also [Conklin 1987].

J. M. Smith, D. C. P. Smith, "Database Abstractions: Aggregation and Generalization," *ACM Transactions on Database Systems,* 2, 2, June 1977.

> Presents the most widely-referenced discussion of two data-modeling extensions essential for object data management. Aggregation is grouping of objects together into composite objects. Generalization is a hierarchy of types of objects.

J. M. Smith, et al, "ADAPLEX Rationale and Reference Manual," Technical Report CCA-83-8, Computer Corporation of America, Cambridge, Massachusetts, May 1983.

> Describes ADAPLEX, the functional model DAPLEX embedded in the programming language Ada.

K. E. Smith, S. B. Zdonik, "Intermedia: A Case Study of the Differences between Relational and Object-Oriented Database Systems," in *Proceedings of the ACM SIGMOD Conference,* 1987.

> Discusses the use of databases for a hypertext application. Interesting because the application was implemented in both a relational and an object-oriented system, for comparison.

A. Snyder, "Encapsulation and Inheritance in Object-Oriented Programming Languages," in *Proceedings of the ACM Conference on Object-Oriented Programming Systems, Languages, and Applications,* Portland, Oregon, September 1986.

> Discusses semantics of inheritance, including the distinction between subtypes for specification and implementation.

A. Z. Spector, J. Bloch, D. Daniels, R. Draves, D. Duchamp, J. Eppinger, S. Menees, D. Thompson, *The Camelot Project,* Technical Report CMU-CS-86-166, Computer Science, Carnegie-Mellon University, Pittsburgh, Pennsylvania, 1986.

> Describes Camelot, an object manager that is a cross between a distributed virtual memory manager and a database system. Camelot provides access to persistent objects under transactions. See also [Eppinger 1989].

M. Stefik, D. Bobrow, "Object-Oriented Programming: Themes and Variations," *Artificial Intelligence Magazine,* January 1986.

> Discusses history of object-oriented programming languages and databases, with particular focus on use in AI applications.

M. Stefik, G. Foster, D. Bobrow, K. Kahn, S. Lanning, L. Suchman: "Beyond the Chalkboard: Computer Support for Collaboration and Problem-Solving in Meetings," *Communications of the ACM,* 30, 1, 1987.

> Discusses the use of computers in a new kind of application: An on-line multimedia communication facilitator between collaborators on a project. This is a likely candidate for object data management.

J. Stein, T. L. Anderson, D. Maier, "Mistaking Identity," in [Hull, Morrison, and Stemple 1989].

> Presents a theoretical discussion of different ways to identify objects. Argues to reintroduce the advantages of value-based identity (as in relational systems) alongside unique-ID–based identity in object-oriented database systems.

M. Stonebraker, "The Design and Implementation of INGRES," *ACM Transactions on Database Systems,* September 1976.

> Describes INGRES, which, like System R [Astrahan et al 1976], was one of the first major implementations of the relational data model. POSTGRES [Stonebraker 1987] is a more recent project at UC Berkeley to incorporate object semantics in a relational DBMS.

M. Stonebraker, A. Guttman, "Using a Relational Database Managment System for CAD Data," *IEEE Database Engineering Bulletin,* 1982.

> Discusses opportunities and problems in using relational databases for CAD.

M. Stonebraker, H. Stettner, N. Lynn, J. Kalash, A. Guttman, "Document Processing in a Relational Database System," *ACM Transaction on Office Information Systems,* 1, 2, April 1983.

> Attempts to use a relational DBMS to store documents. This may work for storing information about whole documents, but is inefficient when individual sections, paragraphs, or lines of a document are decomposed in the DBMS.

M. Stonebraker, "Inclusion of New Types in Relational Database Systems," in *Proceedings of the Second Conference on Data Engineering,* Los Angeles, California, 1986.

> Discusses techniques to introduce new literal data types (as opposed to entity types) in a relational data model, by defining all of the operations that a DBMS requires in order to use them (ordering, space allocations, and so on).

M. Stonebraker, L. A. Rowe, "The Design of POSTGRES," in *Proceedings of the ACM SIGMOD Conference,* Washington D.C., 1986.

M. Stonebraker, "The POSTGRES Storage Manager," in *Proceedings of the 13th International Conference on Very Large Databases,* Brighton, England, 1987. Also in [Zdonik and Maier 1989].

M. Stonebraker, L. A. Rowe, "The POSTGRES Data Model," in *Proceedings of the International Conference on Very Large Databases (VLDB),* September 1987. Also in [Cardenas and McLeod 1990].

M. Stonebraker, L. A. Rowe, M. Hirohama, "The Implementation of POSTGRES," in [Stonebraker 1990].

> Describe POSTGRES, an approach to extending the relational model to incorporate engineering and object-oriented applications. POSTGRES provides an extended POSTQUEL query language, including a transitive closure operation, OIDs, POSTQUEL-defined attributes, user-defined primitive types and access methods, triggers, inferencing, a *portal* mechanism to refer to records from multiple relations, and a relation type hierarchy.

M. Stonebraker, L. A. Rowe, "Portals: A New Application Program Interface," in *Proceedings of the International Conference on Very Large Databases (VLDB),* Singapore, September 1984.
> Describes portals, which provide a way to fetch tuples more flexible than conventional embedded queries in relational DBMSs, allowing groups of related tuples to be fetched at a time.

M. Stonebraker, Special Issue on Database Prototype Systems, *IEEE Transactions on Knowledge and Data Engineering,* 2, 1, March 1990.
> Includes articles on the ODMSs POSTGRES, Starburst, ORION, IRIS, and O_2 used as examples in this book, as well as the logic database language LDL and object managers DASDB, System M, Bubba, and Gamma.

M. Stonebraker, M. Olson, "Large Object Support in POSTGRES," *Proceedings IEEE Data Engineering Conference,* Vienna, Austria, April 1993.
> Describes BLOB implementation in POSTGRES.

M. Stonebraker, A. Jhingran, J. Goh, S. Potamianos, "On Rules Procedures, Caching and Views in Data Base Systems," *Proceedings ACM SIGMOD Conference,* Atlantic City, New Jersey, June 1990.
> Describes rules in POSTGRES, and their use for version management.

M. Stonebraker, et al,, "Third-Generation Database System Manifesto," ACM SIGMOD Record 19, 3, September 1990.
> Argues for extending relational database systems rather than building new object-oriented database systems. This paper has provoked much controversy in the field. Many of the tenets in Chapter 6 are derived from this paper, however, there are important differences and we come to different conclusions.

B. Stroustrup, *The C++ Programming Language,* Addison-Wesley, Reading, Massachusetts,1986.
> Presents the AT&T C++ variation of object-oriented C, which has become the most popular basis for recent object-oriented database programming languages. See [Ellis and Stroustrup 1990] for most recent specification of the language.

B. Stroustrup, "What is Object-Oriented Programming?," *IEEE Software,* 5, 3, May 1988.
> Describes issues and definition of the object-oriented programming paradigm.

Sybase, *SYBASE Reference Manual,* Sybase Corporation, Emeryville, California, 1989.
> Describes SYBASE, a popular relational database product. Sybase Corporation was a pioneer in the relational marketplace in that they added procedural constructs to their implementation of SQL, one step towards object data management.

W. Teitelman, *INTERLISP Reference Manual,* Xerox Palo Alto Research Center, Palo Alto, California, 1974.
> Covers INTERLISP, which was actually one of first popular implementations of a persistent object manager. INTERLISP permitted users to save all of their data and procedures over many sessions, simply by writing out memory to disk. However, it was a not an ODMS, as it did not allow shared data, and the data had to be loaded in the same memory addresses. See [Cockshot et al 1983] for an example of a more powerful persistent programming language.

W. Tichy, "Revision Control System," in *Proceedings of the IEEE Sixth International Conference on Software Engineering*, September 1982.

> Describes RCS, a system to keep track of versions of configurations of objects in a CASE environment. RCS has some of the capabilities of more general object data management systems.

 D. Tsichritzis and F. Lochovsky, "Hierarchical Database Management: A Survey," *ACM Computing Surveys*, 8, 1, March 1976.

> Presents a tutorial overview of the most commonly used DBMSs with hierarchical data models—IMS and System 2000. Hierarchical systems represent relationships between records using parent–child links as in the network model [DBTG 1971], but they do not give equal weight to all relationships: one link must be chosen to define the hierarchy at each level (that is, each record type).

 D. Tsichritzis, A. Klug, Eds, "The ANSI/X3/SPARC DBMS Framework: Report of the Study Group on Database Management Systems," *Information Systems*, 3, 1978.

> Presents the final report of an ANSI study group on standardization of DBMSs. The three-level database architecture (called the internal, conceptual, and external levels in Chapter 3) is forwarded by this report, along with descriptions of dozens of interfaces that arise in the overall database architecture.

 D. Tsichritzis, F. H. Lochovsky, *Data Models*, Prentice-Hall, Englewood Cliffs, New Jersey, 1982.

> Summarizes basic data models. Probably the best book on this topic; [Kent 1981] covers more abstract and advanced issues.

 D. Tsichritzis, Ed, *Office Automation*, Springer-Verlag, New York, New York and Berlin, Germany, 1985.

> Comprises a collection of papers on office applications and their use of advanced database systems and expert systems technology.

 S. Tsur, C. Zaniolo, "Implementation of GEM—Supporting a Semantic Data Model on a Relational Back End," in *Proceedings of the ACM SIGMOD Conference*, May 1984.

> Describes implementation issues in GEM [Zaniolo 1983].

 J. Ullman, *Principles of Database and Knowledge-Based Systems*, Volumes 1 and 2, Computer Science Press, Rockville, Maryland, 1989.

> Provides good coverage of relational normal forms, query languages and optimization. This newest version of this classic text on database systems (formerly *Principles of Database Systems*) includes some discussion of object-oriented databases.

 Unify, *UNIFY Reference Manual*, Unify Corporation, Sacramento, California, 1988.

> Describes UNIFY, a relational DBMS that incorporates parent–child links.

 UniSQL, *UniSQL/X Database Management System Product Description*, UniSQL, Inc, Austin, Texas, 1993.

> Provides an overview of the UniSQL/X DBMS. Product descriptions are also available for UniSQL/M, a multi-database allowing SQL/X queries to be processed over a distributed, multi-vendor DBMS environment with multiple data models, and UniSQL/4GE, a 4th-generation development environment for building DBMS applications. UniSQL's products might best be described as extended relational. However, a C++ binding is provided similar to database programming languages. See the Appendix for more information.

Versant, *VERSANT Technical Overview,* Versant Object Technologies, Inc., Menlo Park, California, 1990.

> Describes VERSANT, which is similar to [Objectivity 1990] and other C++ based database programming languages. A novel feature of VERSANT is a built-in public and private database mechanism.

 A. I. Wassermann, *Software Development Environments,* IEEE Computer Society Press, Los Alamitos, California, 1981.

> Presents an early survey of CASE tools.

 W. Weihl, "Data Dependent Concurrency Control and Recovery," in *Proceedings of the Second Annual ACM Symposium on Principles of Distributed Computing,* Toronto, Canada, August 1988.

> Takes advantage of object-oriented semantics to provide more concurrency than traditional semantics based on read–write semantics [Gray 1981]. For example, to increment a count, you do not have to lock the count value for an entire transaction.

 D. Weinreb, "An Object-Oriented Database System to Support an Integrated Programming Environment," *IEEE Data Engineering,* 11, 2, June 1988.

> Describes STATICE, a database programming language for Symbolics LISP workstations. Provides object identity, inverse attributes, multiple inheritance, user-defined literal types, and a query language. Implements optimistic transactions with local caching, B-trees, and parent–child links. Closely integrated with Common LISP. Might be regarded as an object-oriented data model, or as a functional data model descended from DAPLEX [Shipman 1981].

 S. P. Weiser, F. H. Lochovsky, "OZ+: An Object-Oriented Database System," in [Kim and Lochovsky 1989].

> Describes OZ+, an object-oriented ODMS developed at the University of Toronto and used in an office information system. A major contribution of OZ+ is a rule-based control mechanism, allowing self-triggering procedures to be executed on objects, with multiple objects executing concurrently. OZ+ was built on top of the storage manager of an existing relational DBMS, Empress.

 D. Wells, J. Blakeley, and C. Thompson, "Architecture of an Open Object-Oriented Database Management System," *IEEE Computer,* 25, 10, October 1992.

> Describes OpenOODB, an object-oriented DBMS research prototype. It provides a better integrated database programming language than many of the commercial products. It also provides some of the functionality of a DBMS generator, because the system is implemented as OMG Object Services (Section 6.5.3), making it possible to mix, match, and separately improve or tailor individual object services (events, naming, persistence, transactions, distribution, query, change management, indexing, replication). Seamlessness allows addition of these "behavioral extensions" to host programming languages, currently C++ and Common Lisp. See also [Blakeley, McKenna, Graefe 1993]. This system should not be confused with HP's OpenODB product [HP 1993].

 G. Wiederhold, *Database Design,* McGraw-Hill, New York, New York, 1977.

> Provides an excellent survey of physical database technology and design of databases for optimal performance. Covers storage organization, B-tree and hash indexing, data encoding, reliability, and protection.

G. Wiederhold, "Views, Objects, and Databases," *IEEE Computer,* 19, 2, December 1986.

> Presents an argument that relational databases can support objects through a new kind of multirelational view, called *view-objects.* Takes that position that it is better to store objects in a normalized form, since one user's object may differ from another's. Mappings must then be defined to and from the normalized representation. There is merit to this argument; the main disadvantage is one of performance, as discussed in Chapter 5.

G. Wiederhold, T. Barasalou, S. Chaudhuri, *Managing Objects in a Relational Framework,* Technical Report, Computer Science Department, Stanford University, Palo Alto, California, 1990.

> Describes PENGUIN, a system to provide object-oriented database semantics on top of a relational DBMS. Supports view-object *generators* and *decomposers* to transfer data from the relational representation to an in-memory object representation and back again. This report contains an updated version of [Weiderhold 1986] as motivation for this approach.

M. Winslett, S. Chu, *Using a Relational DBMS for CAD Data,* Technical Report UIUCDCS-R-90-1649, Department of Computer Science, University of Illinois, Urbana, Illinois, 1990.

> Describes an experiment in using a relational database system, UNIFY [Unify 1988], to store data for a CAD tool, Magic. This study shows that a relational DBMS can be competitive with custom-built representation of data in a CAD tool if (1) the RDBMS is bound directly into the user process, rather than interprocess calls being used, as they are in nearly all current RDBMS products; (2) the RDBMS provides parent–child links to represent relationships, also not present in most current products; and (3) the application loads all data at the beginning of a session and dumps them at the end.

X3H2, *Database Language SQL,* ANSI X3.135-1986, American National Standards Institute, New York, New York, 1986.

X3H2, *Database Language SQL,* ANSI X3.135-1989, American National Standards Institute, New York, New York, 1989.

X3H2, *Database Language SQL,* ANSI X3.135-1992, American National Standards Institute, New York, New York, 1992.

> These specifications describe successive revisions of the SQL standard: SQL-86 (SQL1), SQL-89, and SQL-92 (SQL2). SQL is now a universal standard for database access, although few if any systems conform to the complete specification. Work is now underway on what is known as SQL3, which includes procedural statements and some object-oriented features. See the Appendix for more information.

Xidak, *Orion System Overview,* Xidak, Inc., Palo Alto, California, 1990.

> Describes Orion, an extended relational-database system specialized for engineering applications, with particular emphasis on performance and query-language extensions. Not to be confused with the ORION object-oriented database research prototype from MCC [Kim et al 1989].

E. Yourdon, L. Constantine, *Structured Design,* Yourdon Press, Englewood Cliffs, New Jersey, 1978.

> Describes Yourdon's software-development methodology and diagramming techniques, which have been among the most popular for CASE. Such structured methodologies are well adapted for providing computer assistance in the process, and for storing software project information in databases. See also [Coad and Yourdon 1990].

C. Zaniolo, H. Ait-Kaci, D. Beech, S. Cammarata, L. Kerschberg, D. Maier, "Object-Oriented Database Systems and Knowledge Systems," in *Expert Database Systems, Proceedings from the First International Workshop,* L. Kerschberg, Ed, Benjamin/Cummings, 1986.

> Provides a good overview of the object-oriented database area: present and future directions for research, and the advantages of the approach.

C. Zaniolo, "The Database Language GEM," in *Proceedings of the ACM SIGMOD Conference,* San Jose, California, 1983. Also in [Zdonik and Maier 1989].

> Describes an extension of the INGRES QUEL language [Stonebraker 1976] to incorporate object identity, aggregation, generalization, nulls, and set-valued attributes. See also [Tsur and Zaniolo 1985].

C. Zaniolo, "Deductive Databases—Theory Meets Practice," in [Bancilhon, Thanos, and Tsichritzis 1990].

> Presents arguments for the viability of deductive databases in practice. Includes a variety of examples from the author's experience with LDL, a logic database language [Chimenti et al 1989]. Another system for knowledge management is NAIL!, described in [Morris et al 1987].

S. B. Zdonik, D. Maier, Eds, *Readings in Object-Oriented Database Systems,* Morgan-Kaufmann, San Mateo, California, 1989.

> Comprises the largest single collection of important papers in the area of advanced database systems in the 1980s. The editors provide good summaries of the important issues for each group of papers. All the papers appear elsewhere at earlier dates, but we frequently reference this collection in the bibliography as a convenience to the reader.

R. Zicari, "A Framework for Schema Updates in an Object-Oriented Database System," Technical Report 39-89, GIP Altair, Le Chesnay Cedex, France, October 1989. Also in [Bancilhon, Delobel, Kanellakis 1991].

> Describes schema modification in O_2 [Bancilhon et al 1988] with the integrity consistency checker ICC. Currently performs immediate rather than "lazy" update of object instances. Expands on earlier work identifying schema invariants and integrity assertions [Kim and Chou 1988]. See also [Harrus, Velez, Zicari 1990].

INDEX